2006

North Korea

North Korea

The Struggle Against American Power

Tim Beal

Pluto Press
LONDON • ANN ARBOR, MI

First published 2005 by Pluto Press
345 Archway Road, London N6 5AA
and 839 Greene Street, Ann Arbor, MI 48106

www.plutobooks.com

British Library Cataloguing in Publication Data
A catalogue record for this book is available from the British Library

ISBN   0 7453 2014 7 hardback
ISBN   0 7453 2013 9 paperback

Library of Congress Cataloging-in-Publication Data
Beal, Tim.
  North Korea : the struggle against American power / Tim Beal.
    p. cm.
  Includes bibliographical references.
  ISBN 0–7453–2014–7 (hardback) — ISBN 0–7453–2013–9 (pbk.)
  1. Korea (North)—Politics and government. 2. Korea (North)—Military
policy. 3. Nuclear weapons—Korea (North) 4. Korea (North)—Foreign
relations—United States. 5. United States—Foreign relations—Korea
(North) 6. World politics—21st century. I. Title.
  DS935.5.B43 2005
  951.9304'3—dc22
                                                        2005008411

10 9 8 7 6 5 4 3 2 1

Designed and produced for Pluto Press by
Chase Publishing Services Ltd, Fortescue, Sidmouth, EX10 9QG, England
Typeset from disk by Stanford DTP Services, Northampton, England
Printed and bound in the European Union by
Gutenberg Press, Malta

Contents

List of Maps, Figures and Tables

MAPS

FIGURES

TABLES

Timelines

Acknowledgements

So many people have contributed in manifold ways to producing this book that singling out individuals is a frightening, if gratifying, task. I am grateful to innumerable Koreans, North and South, and in the United States, New Zealand and elsewhere, who personally or by email have encouraged me to engage the issue of what may broadly be called, in Roh Moo-hyun's phrase, 'peace and prosperity' for the Korean people and I hope this book makes some contribution to that cause. My intellectual debts are best calculated by looking at the bibliography, but if anyone should attempt to categorise this book as 'anti-American', as no doubt some will on the spurious confusion between opposing particular political policies and being hostile to a people, then it should be noted that the authorities most frequently drawn upon, such as Bruce Cumings, Sig Harrison, Dan Oberdorfer and Leon Sigal, are American.

On a personal level I am particularly grateful to Gill Goddard, East Asian Studies Librarian at the University of Sheffield, and James Grayson, Director of the Centre for Korean Studies there, for helping me mine their Korean collection. My stays in London were made possible, and always pleasant, by the hospitality of Pat and Bärbel Daly and Lesley Sheringham, of Arthur Probsthain's famous Asian bookshop, whose smile was always welcoming. Hazel Smith who first encouraged me to move from articles and papers on Korea to the more daunting challenge of a book. Karin Lee, and John Feffer, who provided hospitality, and sanity, in Washington. On the home front, Kala S. Retna and John Beal were forbearing of my frequent absences, both of body and of mind. Christine Dann gave soothing and wise advice and was largely instrumental in the establishment of the New Zealand Korean Peace Committee. Still in New Zealand I have no greater long-term debt than to Don Borrie who, decades ago, founded the NZ-DPRK Society with Wolf Rosenberg and has laboured over the years to foster better understanding of the DPRK in New Zealand and to improve relations between our two countries.

Peter Thirkell, Val Lindsay, and my colleagues at the School of Marketing and International Business at Victoria University of Wellington have been tolerant of my attention to Korean issues in the best tradition of accepting that scholarship leads beyond the narrow confines of academic departments. In this respect, Stephen Epstein, my colleague at Victoria who straddles European Classics and Korean Studies, was a supporting encouragement. Gordon Anderson and Sally Davenport, of the Research Committee of the Faculty of Commerce and Administration, provided some much appreciated research funding. Hugh Blackstock in Earth Sciences produced the maps very speedily and efficiently.

Julie Stoll, Sejal Chad and Roger van Zwanenberg of Pluto Press patiently and professionally kept me focussed on producing the best possible manuscript pretty much on time, but not at the expense of thorough research and careful writing.

I owe special thanks to Yang Wen, who brought her librarian skills to bear on bibliographic matters, both helping me locate books in Sheffield, London and Washington, and keeping citations in proper, professional order.

My greatest personal debt in bringing this project to fruition is to Ankie Hoogvelt. Although she should have known better, having put up with my vagaries for many years, she was so generous with her hospitality in Sheffield and unstinting with her time in reading and meticulously commenting on draft chapters.

Introduction

Born out of the division of Korea following the surrender of the Japanese empire in 1945, North Korea had been one of the star performers of the developing world, vigorously industrialising on the basis of a proclaimed programme of 'self-reliance'. However, in the 1990s, following the collapse of the Soviet Union, it was plunged into a dreadful economic crisis which caused widespread death and malnutrition. Even today, according to the World Food Programme, about a quarter of the population are in need of international aid.[1] The economic crisis was compounded by bad weather but it had its roots in the long-standing hostility of the United States, which had long imposed sanctions and threatened military action, including nuclear strikes, and the geopolitical environment that engendered. The crisis of the 1990s was exacerbated by a escalating confrontation with the United States over nuclear issues. This period of crisis and privation came to be called the 'Arduous March'.

In 1994 the DPRK – Democratic People's Republic of Korea to give it its formal name – had signed an agreement with the United States called the Agreed Framework. Under this, the Koreans mothballed their graphite-moderated nuclear reactors which the Americans suspected had produced plutonium that could be used in weapons, in exchange for a package which included two light-water reactors, heavy fuel oil as interim compensation for the electricity forgone, formal guarantees against nuclear attack and movement towards lifting of sanctions and the normalisation of relations. Although the North Koreans were generally punctilious about complying with the Agreed Framework, the United States was dilatory in keeping its promises, partly because Clinton had lost control of Congress to the Republicans.

In 1997 Kim Dae-jung, a long-time opposition leader, was elected president of South Korea (Republic of Korea or ROK). He soon enunciated a policy on engagement with the North which came to be labelled the 'Sunshine Policy'. North Korea was initially sceptical, because peace accords between North and South had fallen apart in the past, but after secret negotiations a summit took place in Pyongyang in June 2000 between Kim Dae-jung and DPRK leader Kim Jong Il.

The easing of North–South relations warmed up that between the DPRK and the US. North Korea's third-ranking leader, Jo Myong Rok, visited Washington in early October 2000, had a meeting with Bill Clinton and invited Secretary of State Madeleine Albright to the DPRK. On 10 October 2000, on the eve of her visit, and on the occasion of the 55th anniversary of the founding of the Korean Workers' Party, North Korea proclaimed that the 'Arduous March' was over.[2] She returned to Washington with an invitation to President Bill Clinton to visit Pyongyang and to consign to history the enmities of the past.

Pyongyang's elation was premature and North Korea was forced to continue the Arduous March. George W. Bush won the election and there was an abrupt change of Korean policy. This shift was not confined to Korea, and it was soon labelled as the ABC – Anything But Clinton – policy. Influenced by 'neoconservatives', the Bush administration was to withdraw from international treaties and embark upon a programme of confrontation with countries and peoples it regarded as an impediment to American interests. This more aggressive stance, which was to lead to the invasion of Iraq, predated 11 September 2001 and was built into administration policy from the beginning. The attacks of 9/11 were used by President Bush and his advisors to legitimise plans and policies already in place. Whilst it is important not to overlook the continuities between Clinton and Bush, and the underlying drivers of American imperialism, there were definite fissures in policy, and in few places would they be more significant than in Korea. Clinton, under pressure from Kim Dae-jung, had been moving to a less hostile position and Gore, had he become president, might have continued the process towards normalisation of relations and the implementation of the Agreed Framework. It is an open secret in Washington that the new Bush administration did not want coexistence, however frosty, with the DPRK, but its destruction; what is euphemistically called 'regime change'.[3] Worried by this, President Kim Dae-jung flew to Washington in March 2001 to try and salvage things, but was rebuffed.

Relations between Washington and Pyongyang became increasingly acrimonious. North Korea was labelled as part of an Axis of Evil and mentioned as a possible target in the Nuclear Posture Review. However, although the Agreed Framework was much disliked by the administration as a relic of the Clinton era, it limped on. Then, in October 2002, a crisis erupted.

This is how the US State Department tells the story:

Following the inauguration of President George W. Bush in January 2001, the new Administration began a review of North Korea policy. At the conclusion of that review, the Administration announced on June 6, 2001, that it had decided to pursue continued dialogue with North Korea on the full range of issues of concern to the Administration, including North Korea's conventional force posture, missile development and export programs, human rights practices, and humanitarian issues. In 2002, the Administration also became aware that North Korea was developing a uranium enrichment program for nuclear weapons purposes.

When U.S.–D.P.R.K. direct dialogue resumed in October 2002, this uranium enrichment program was high on the U.S. agenda. North Korean officials acknowledged to a U.S. delegation, headed by Assistant Secretary of State for East Asian and Pacific Affairs James A. Kelly, the existence of the uranium enrichment program. Such a program violated North Korea's obligations under the NPT and its commitments in the 1992 North–South Denuclearisation Declaration and the 1994 Agreed Framework. The U.S. side stated that North Korea would have to terminate the program before any further progress could be made in U.S.–D.P.R.K. relations. The U.S. side also made clear that if this program were verifiably eliminated, the U.S. would be prepared to work with North Korea on the development of a fundamentally new relationship. In November 2002, the member countries of KEDO's Executive Board agreed to suspend heavy fuel oil shipments to North Korea pending a resolution of the nuclear dispute.[4]

Since these are the people who brought us stories about Iraq's weapons of mass destruction, we might just be sceptical. And we would be right.

Here is an alternative version of events, as described, and documented, in this book. Some of it is necessarily speculative but I do take care to distinguish between what is known, what is uncertain, and what is contested.

The Bush administration made no secret of its antipathy towards North Korea and its dislike of the Agreed Framework. Richard Armitage has headed a team (which included Paul Wolfowitz) which had savaged Clinton's Korea policy in 1999. However, North Korea was complying with the agreement which could not legally be terminated unless an infringement could be found. That's where enriched uranium comes in.

The State Department claims that it was in 2002 that the administration became aware that North Korea had an enriched uranium programme. However, in 1999 a prominent Republican

Congressman, Benjamin Gilman, had issued a report which claimed that North Korea had such a programme but complained that it did not contravene the Agreed Framework:

That is because the Clinton Administration did not succeed in negotiating a deal with North Korea that would ban such efforts. It is inexplicable and inexcusable.[5]

In fact, an enriched uranium programme would not directly infringe the Agreed Framework, but it would violate the North–South Denuclearisation Agreement, which the Agreed Framework pledged to uphold.

So two sets of questions arise. Did North Korea have a highly enriched uranium (HEU) programme and did they admit to it, as the State Department claims? Secondly, why was this suddenly brought up in October 2002?

Let's start with the admission. This is contested ground but the best bet is that the Koreans said they were entitled to have nuclear weapons and the Americans heard what they wanted to hear. In any case North Korea soon made it clear that it did not have a programme to enrich uranium for weapons, had not admitted such a programme, and accused Kelly of lying.[6]

What about the programme itself? The most recent and authoritative take on that is by Selig Harrison, the veteran American journalist and author. Writing in the prestigious mainstream journal *Foreign Affairs* he comes to the conclusion that the DPRK probably had a low-enriched uranium (LEU) programme designed to provide fuel for the reactors promised under the Agreed Framework.[7] He notes that the US has not published any evidence on the alleged HEU programme, and has not supplied any to the other parties in the Six-Party talks – China, South Korea, Japan and Russia. He also points out that China has publicly said that it does not know if North Korea has such a programme and that the US has not provided any convincing evidence. There are press reports that South Korea, for one, does not believe the US allegations.

One of the reasons that South Korea has not been making too many waves about the alleged North Korean programme is that it has been revealed that it had itself produced highly enriched uranium in experiments. So while there is no evidence that North Korea has contravened the North–South Denuclearisation Agreement, we do know that South Korea has.

Why did the Bush administration suddenly bring up the HEU allegation in October 2002? Jonathan Pollack, writing in the US *Naval War College Review*, suggested that the 'intelligence community' had come to the conclusion that North Korea had a HEU programme which could produce a nuclear weapon in some years' time, but it was the summit between Kim Jong Il and Japanese Prime Minister Koizumi in September 2002 that 'triggered' the Kelly mission. The Japanese had kept preparations secret from the Americans who, when they were told, feared that it would lead to a rapprochement between Tokyo and Pyongyang with serious repercussions for their strategy in East Asia.[8]

Harrison agrees with this but brings in South Korea, noting that despite US objections, North–South relations were improving and that they were in the process of reconnecting the railway system, separated in the 1940s. He writes,

> Kelly's confrontation with [North Korean First Deputy Foreign Minister] Kang seems to have been inspired by the growing alarm felt in Washington in the preceding five months over the ever more conciliatory approach that Seoul and Tokyo had been taking toward Pyongyang; by raising the uranium issue, the Bush administration hoped to scare Japan and South Korea into reversing their policies.[9]

There was another reason for the Americans to be worried about South Korea. There was rising anti-Americanism and a presidential election looming in which they were concerned that human-rights lawyer Roh Moo-hyun might defeat their preferred candidate, conservative Lee Hoi-chang. They were right to be concerned. Roh won the election and has been a bit of a thorn ever since. Most recently, after Bush's re-election, he made a whirlwind tour of Asian and European capitals in December 2004 trying to garner support to force Washington to negotiate seriously with Pyongyang.

Détente in Northeast Asia would seriously impact on US strategy, which is based on keeping Japan and (South) Korea away from China. It would also remove one of the underpinnings for Missile Defense, and for the profits of the military-industrial complex, struggling to find appropriate enemies with the end of the Cold War.

So that's what this book is about. Penetrating beneath the official line to unearth what is happening.

There is an obvious parallel with Iraq in the nuclear confrontation between the United States and North Korea. Bush and Blair argued that they were forced to act because of what Iraq had done. Iraq, they said, had weapons of mass destruction and was threatening the region, and the coalition countries. There were other similarities as well; human rights, multilateralism, the United Nations and 'the international community', and many of the main supporting actors appear in both stories; Hans Blix and Mohamed ElBaradei for instance. The essential argument was that the United States, and its allies, were reacting to Iraq's infringements of international norms and its threatening behaviour. Few informed and dispassionate observers would see it that way now. Rather it is clear that Bush, Blair and team fabricated or 'sexed-up' evidence in order to invade Iraq for reasons connected with its strategic position in respect of Middle East and Central Asian oil, and Israel. There was little that Iraq could do, bar surrender, to avoid the invasion.

Somewhat the same process has been happening in respect of Korea. Most books on the issue assume that it is North Korea that is creating the problem and the United States that is searching for the solution. This book, on the contrary, approaches it from a different angle. As with Iraq, the confrontation is primarily driven by the United States for a variety of reasons including imperial strategy, the needs of the military industrial complex, political jousting in Washington, all built on a 50-year-old grudge against the first country it did not defeat. The Korean War ended in a military stalemate and an armistice.

Most of the documentation used in this book comes from mainstream, sometimes conservative, American and South Korean sources. Much of what is here will come as a surprise to anyone whose knowledge of Korean affairs is limited to the US and European media, although surprising things can be discovered there if you go digging.

The picture we get of North Korea from the media is of unremitting gloom and oppression, of a bizarre, capricious and unpredictable leadership, deeply hostile to the world which it wants to keep at bay by threatening it with nuclear weapons. It is seen as a land stuck in a time-warp, a Stalinist gulag. The reality, as I hope this book will show, is far more complex. Let me bring in a few snippets here, just to illustrate.

New Zealander Major Seth Le Leu of the Salvation Army, writing of his visit to their yogurt-packaging project in the DPRK in late 2004, gives a picture of a government trying in diverse ways to improve and diversify the food supply, and being willing to accept the Salvation

Army logo on the yogurt packaging.[10] I have visited a World Food Programme-assisted biscuit factory near Wonsan, on the east coast and there was no attempt to hide the provenance of the bags of donated ingredients – many of which were US aid, and bore the stars and stripes.

British mining engineer Robert Willoughby, working on a project in North Korea in 1999 describes drinking after work with his Korean counterpart, talking 'freely about mining, work, bosses, families, life, football, the state of the world and his own country. "See what happens when five decades of sanctions actually work?" he asked. "Do you really think we want war with the US?"'[11]

Many visitors note that there is an official differentiation between foreigners, such as Americans, and their government. The US government is seen as responsible for the sanctions which are blamed for the privations suffered, but foreigners themselves can, and do, receive a warm welcome when the initial inhibitions are overcome. This is especially true of aid workers who make extended, or frequent, visits to North Korea.[12]

However, even first-time visitors, if they are not burdened with obvious antagonism, encounter a 'normal' response from the people they encounter. American Jim Worthington, who visited the Rajin special economic zone from China, recounts that,

> Going through NK customs seemed routine and uneventful; most of the guys in the brown uniforms were courteous and friendly, one even struck me as a bit fatherly. ... Seeing I was from the U.S., one of the younger customs men smiled and said, 'I'm going to visit your country next year!'[13]

American scientist Siegfried S. Hecker, who visited the Yongbyon nuclear reactor in January 2004 in an attempt to verify North Korean claims that they had a nuclear deterrent, finished his testimony to the US Senate Committee of Foreign Relations by saying, 'Finally, Mr Chairman, I found the trip to be remarkable. Our DPRK hosts were most courteous and cooperative.'[14]

The reality, as we shall see, is that North Korea is eager to achieve normal diplomatic and economic links with the United States and the world in general. It is especially keen to develop good relations with the South, and that desire is shared by the government in Seoul. North Korea's strategy to bring this about may, at times, be inept and counterproductive, but it does need to cope with a policy of undisguised hostility from Washington. Walking out of the Six-Party talks, as Pyongyang did in February 2005, was a foolish tactic but it was not an indication, as was often portrayed in the media, that it was hell-bent on acquiring nuclear weapons. On the contrary, as American Leon Sigal points out, it was part of a tit-for-tat strategy to force Washington to engage in meaningful negotiations, negotiations that in all likelihood would lead to its abandonment of a nuclear deterrent:

> Pyongyang isn't asking for much. It wants to exchange 'words for words' and 'action for action'. It wants Washington to commit now to normalize relations and give it written assurances not to attack it, impede its economic development, or overthrow its government. It also wants the United States to join Japan and South Korea in resuming shipments of heavy fuel oil promised under the 1994 Agreed Framework, take it off the list of state sponsors of terrorism, and relax related sanctions.[15]

The flow of refuges from North Korea is often produced as clear evidence of the horrors of life there under an oppressive and hated regime. The reality is somewhat less clear-cut. Undoubtedly the economic situation is bad and many people suffer great deprivation. Moreover, as aid workers point out but the mainstream press tends to skirt over, the increasing role of the market economy since the reforms of July 2002 has, not surprisingly, greatly increased social inequalities. Some people are better off but many are worse off. Added to these push factors there is also the lure of the resettlement allowance that Seoul provides to those who reach the South. This is a heritage of the past when refugees were few and made good propaganda, and the South Korean government is planning a cutback. In Korean affairs, what happens on one side the of border usually happens in some fashion on the other; North Korea also gives a golden welcome to those who publicly defect from the South.[16]

The refugee issue is very much a live issue in the United States where it gets a lot of Congressional and media attention, but this seldom penetrates beneath the surface. For instance, a poll of 100 North Korean refugees in the South conducted by a South Korean paper in September 2004 showed that a third would return to the North if they could.[17] A major survey in December 2004 by the South Korean Ministry of Unification found that only 9 per cent of refugees gave 'political dissatisfaction' as their reason for fleeing.[18] About the same time a South Korean paper revealed that helping refugees in getting from North Korea to the South via China had become a very profitable business, with brokers getting a good cut of the resettlement allowance.[19]

The situation in North Korea, and the causes thereof, are much more complex and multi-faceted than the picture we are usually given. There is also a huge amount that we don't know, or can only see though a glass darkly, a glass moreover often provided by those with a vested interest in promoting a particular perception. There is a great need to demystify North Korea and to deconstruct the stories we are told. We must also avoid, unless in inverted commas or with due elucidation, words and phrases that have long since lost their original meaning or are used in ways quite contrary to it – socialism, democracy, pre-emptive and the like.

THE STRUCTURE OF THE BOOK

The book falls into two main parts, with a concluding chapter.

Part I gives a chronological survey from the earliest days up to the end of the first Bush administration in 2004. The first chapter takes the story from the mythical founder of Korea, Tangun through to the liberation form the Japanese in 1945. Chapter 2 covers the period up to the first nuclear crisis in the early 1990s. The rest of that decade, up to the end of the Clinton administration and Pyongyang's premature declaration of the end of the Arduous March, occupies the third chapter and Chapter 4 takes us through the reigniting of the crisis up to the final days of 2004.

Part II focusses on some key themes and topics. Some issues which I would dearly liked to have included, such as economic, social and technological change in North Korea, will have to wait for the next book. Chapter 5 looks at issues which are primarily internal. We look firstly at human rights and particularly concerns about public executions, experiments on prisoners, prison camps, religion, the use of concern over human rights as a propaganda weapon and economic deprivation. Then we turn to international aid discussing whether it props up a regime which it would be better to change as quickly as possible, whether aid is diverted to the military and finally the role of internal aid agencies in building bridges and facilitating reform. The penultimate section of this chapter looks at refugees and the chapter concludes with a discussion on the way forward and how we might best promote human rights and economic rehabilitation.

Chapter 6 takes us into the world of narcotics, and the charge that production and export of illegal drugs is sponsored by the

North Korean state. Then we turn to terrorism firstly looking at assassination, such as the Rangoon bombing of 1983, then coming to indiscriminate, terror attacks, such as the bombing of KAL flight 858 in 1987. The next section looks at military affairs, focussing on weapons of mass destruction, chemical and biological weapons, the export of missiles, missile development and capability and the size and capability of North Korea's conventional armed forces. The final section examines the military balance between North Korea and her adversaries.

Chapter 7 focusses on the nuclear confrontation between the DPRK and the United States, bringing together the key issues and events described in Part I. It is accompanied by a detailed chronology, in Appendix IV, which not only gives dates for the main incidents in North Korea's nuclear development, but also situates them within the wider context of the global nuclear threat.

The concluding chapter, 'On the Precipice', looks at the situation at the end of 2004 and the options for the Bush administration and the newly nominated Secretary of State, Condoleezza Rice. There are basically three options. The first is to continue the Powell/Armitage strategy of talks without negotiations. This will continue the stalemate because Pyongyang will negotiate, but not surrender, and neither Seoul nor Beijing will exert sufficient pressure to force a change on North Korea. The second option, advocated by the neocons, is to engineer a change of government in Seoul so that it will comply with Washington's wishes to bring about 'regime change' in Pyongyang by whatever means possible.

The third strategy is to engage in real negotiations with a commitment to a positive outcomes. I disagree with the usual opinion that such negotiations would be inordinately difficult. On the contrary, I think that if the US does want a peaceful and secure resolution it can achieve that relatively easily.

There are three reasons for this:

1　The US is so much more powerful than the DPRK. It threatens North Korea but in truth is not threatened itself. It has so many of the cards. Nothing in an agreement can really imperil it. No amount of North Korean 'cheating', if that were to happen, would seriously endanger the United States
2　The other main actors, except perhaps Japan, want a peaceful resolution that preserves the DPRK

3 Peace with the United States and normalisation of relations is the main foreign policy objective of the DPRK.

At this stage it is unclear which option the second Bush administration will choose. The role of neocons and hawks may have been strengthened but they face the same constraints as before, from the resistance in Iraq to resistance in Northeast Asia – the refusal of China, South Korea, Russia and, to some extent Japan, to force North Korea to yield without adequate security guarantees and compensation. Whatever happens, I hope this book will contribute to a better understanding of North Korea's Arduous March, and help in some way to bring it to an end, so that all Koreans may live in a peninsula free from external threat and interference, enjoying peace and prosperity.

NOTE ON SPELLING AND NAMES

The spelling of Korean words in the Latin alphabet is a troublesome matter. I have not attempted to use the scholarly McCune-Reischauer transliteration as such for Korean words but have used the forms most common to the English-speaking reader. In most cases this causes no great problem or confusion, and is the approach taken by virtually all books not aimed at Korean specialists. However, there are two areas where problems arise. Firstly the Republic of Korea introduced a spelling reform in 2000, bringing in new forms for some very common words: Pyongyang became *Pyeongyang*. Kumgang, *Geumgang*, Kaesong, *Gaesong*, and Pusan was transmogrified into *Busan*. Whilst government agencies and some newspapers (e.g. *JoongAng Ilbo* and *Korea Herald*) have moved to the new spelling, other South Korean newspapers (e.g. *Korea Times*), the North Korean press and the international media generally have stayed with the old spellings, and I have stayed with them, except when the words are in quotations.

The spelling of personal names is often idiosyncratic and again I have stuck with familiar forms, such as Syngman Rhee (rather than Yi Sung-man) or that used by the persons themselves. Most Korean names are given in Korean order, with the family name first. For given names I have followed the respective styles of North and South. Thus Kim Jong Il but Kim Dae-jung. However some names are given in a different form or order if they are already established in common usage (e.g. Syngman Rhee). The same applies to Chinese and Japanese names, though the Japanese are more likely to invert the name order (e.g. Koizumi Junichiro is usually written Junichiro Koizumi). I have used the Korean nomenclature for the seas on either side of the peninsula; thus East Sea, rather than the more familiar Sea of Japan and West Sea instead of Yellow Sea.

For the few Chinese words I use the *pinyin* transliteration. This is the standard on the Mainland and is now widely adopted in Taiwan as well; thus Mao Zedong rather than Mao Tse-tung.

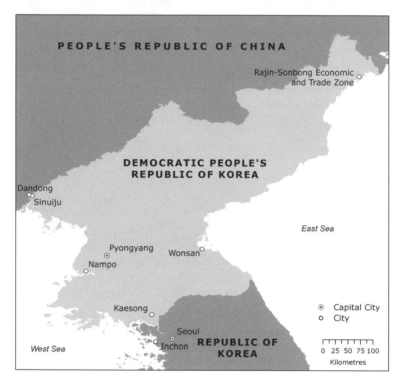

Map 1   Korea: the divided peninsula

Map 2   The Korean peninsula: strategic hub of Northeast Asia

Part I

Fulcrum of Geography, Anvil of History: DPRK in Historical Perspective

Introduction to Part I:
Time and Place, from Past to Present

Geography and history are intertwined. The Middle East, for example, has long attracted the interest of outsiders, and continues to do so today. They came, or so they said, to bring the blessings of religion, civilisation, commerce, law and democracy. In doing so they transformed the land and its people, not always to their liking or expectation. Thus geography, in its turn, is affected by man's affairs. We cannot imagine a Middle East that would not be a place of creativity, of conflict and historical importance. Place matters. Korea, like the Middle East, has been both blessed, and cursed, by its location.

The Korean peninsula is not rich in oil, or other natural resources, but it does have a strategic position. It is where Russia, China and Japan connect. It was the route by which religion and much culture passed from the Asian mainland to Japan. Korea was the springboard for the Mongols' attempted invasion of Japan and the route Japan took for its attempted invasion of China and mainland Asia. In 1904 the United States signed away an interest in Korea, allowing it to pass into Japanese dominance in exchange for Japanese connivance in American occupation of the Philippines. By the end of the Pacific War, in 1945, the US was back into Korean affairs, and has been a dominant force ever since making America, in effect, part of the strategic circle around the Korean peninsula, joining Russia, China and Japan. Moreover, Korea has become a vital part of US strategy in East Asia. It is important for the US that the countries in the region do not coalesce around a central, competing power. In the 1930s that was Japan, today it is China. A divided Korea, with a northern part that is seen as threatening, keeps South Korea and Japan tied to America. There are countervailing forces, as we shall see. In particular, a peacefully and consensually united Korean peninsula providing not merely a large market but a land bridge from easternmost Asia to westernmost Europe, would offer considerable economic benefits to the region, especially to Japan, as well as to Korea itself. Geography exerts a strong and continuing influence on Korean affairs.

However, the main determinant of history is history itself. Russia retains Chechnya, China holds on to Xinjiang, and the United States invades Iraq not merely because of the inherent value of these lands, but for complex historical reasons, both macro and micro. Macro-history has given the United States – or perhaps we should say the American people have wrested from history – a demand for oil and the military power to seize it. Micro-history has contributed its own influences. The legacy of George H. Bush's Gulf War to his son, neoconservatives and the Israel lobby, 9/11 and the struggle against Islamic nationalism, and the exigencies of the American political landscape and electoral cycle, the collapse of Soviet countervailing power, the weakening of Saddam Hussein and the destabilisation of his power by ten years of sanctions are just some of the major factors. This is not a book about Iraq so I don't need to attempt to go into that, but reference to familiar things centre stage, in the limelight, may help us to understand the less familiar off to the side. It is clear that to understand an event such as the invasion of Iraq, we need to be cognisant of the geographical and historical forces at play. So, too, with Korea.

Part I presents a broad sweep of Korean history up to the present day. That is a daunting task and specialists will inevitably find fault in details. However, an overview is necessary to lay a foundation on which the arguments of the book may rest. Few people are familiar with Korean history, and even fairly recent events are soon encrusted with layers of bias, and frequently propaganda. I do not pretend to be impartial and my opinions and judgements may sometimes raise eyebrows. Emphasis may be found to have been placed on incidents or connections that are not usually stressed in mainstream accounts, but virtually all the sources used are 'Western', mainly US or South Korean. I have referenced where necessary but have tried to keep that to a minimum in this part of the book in order not to impede the flow of the story; referencing, statistics and data are more detailed in Part II. However, much of the material is contentious, or at variance with the mainstream media perspective with which most readers will be more familiar, so there is no escaping a lot of endnotes.

The treatment is roughly chronological, although I jump over the years when links to later, and especially current, events suggest themselves. It is important to connect the past with the present, so that history informs our understanding of the world around us. Chronological tables, or timelines, are interspaced though this part to enable the reader to see what happened when. The listed events are obviously only a tiny fraction of what I would have liked to have included. I have tried to avoid testing the reader's patience with too much detail while providing a meaningful chronological skeleton.

The focus in this part is on international relations, rather than on domestic developments, which are treated in more detail in Part II. However, nowhere are domestic affairs discussed in isolation from the international context, it is merely a matter of emphasis. Because of its strategic location, and because it is so small compared to the four countries that impinge on it, events on the Korean peninsula can only be understood within the international context that does so much to influence them. The construction of North Korea's *Juche* policy, for instance, or its programme to develop a nuclear deterrent, are by no means irrational, bizarre or inexplicable. The explanations lie within the course of historical events. These, in turn, are largely driven by the major players, rather than the Koreans themselves. This interplay of intrinsic and exogenous forces, within a historical perspective, is the subject of this part of the book.

1
The Roots of Modern Korea: From Tangun to Liberation

TANGUN AND THE CONSTRUCTION OF KOREA

Where shall we begin this story of North Korea's arduous march? Perhaps the best starting point is with King Tangun the mythical king who founded the kingdom of Chosun – Morning Calm – in 2333 BC. That is not merely because this is where Koreans usually start their national history (though some like to push it back further) but because his capital is close to modern Pyongyang. Tangun has been appropriated by the DPRK which sees itself as the inheritor and protector of the tradition and the embodiment of Korean nationalism. It may be no coincidence that a ceremony to dedicate Tangun's reconstructed mausoleum near Pyongyang was held in October 1994, just three months after the funeral of Kim Il Sung. The Korean word-processor programme of the Pyongyang Informatics Center is named after the legendary king and when, in 2001, Christian groups in South Korea destroyed statues of Tangun this was condemned in Pyongyang as '… a negation of the Korean nation and an unpardonable challenge and crime against all the Koreans who have valued its history and traditions'.[1]

Written history does not appear for a long time after the Tangun period, a few centuries before Christ, but the oral tradition survived and is still powerful. Sometime in the first millennium BC Chinese culture spread into the peninsula, and from there into Japan. The emergence of an iron culture, with its huge impact on agricultural and military technologies, and the expansion of rice cultivation led to the establishment of an agrarian economy and substantial population growth. Around the beginning of the 'Christian era' we see the establishment of the three contesting kingdoms of Paekche, Koguryo and Silla which came to dominate the Korean peninsula and part of what is now the Chinese Northeast (Manchuria).

Paekche in the southwest was the route by which Buddhism was introduced to Japan in 552. Paekche had established Buddhism as the state religion in 384, but prior to that it had instituted the

---

The mausoleum of King Tangun

'Tangun, the father of our nation, founded Korea or ancient Korea (Josun [Chosun]), the first state in the East, with Pyongyang as it capital, 5,000 years ago. This marked the end of the primitive age in our country, which had lasted for over a million years, and then entry of our nation into the age of statehood, an age of civilization.' So starts the book *Tangun, Founder-King of Korea*, published in Pyongyang in 1994. That certainly puts Chinese history in its place. I bought the book when I visited the mausoleum in April 2004. It cost 2 euros. Admission to the mausoleum costs 10 euros and for 100, we were told, we could view the bones. We declined.

In 1936 an Association for the Repair of the Tomb of Tangun was set up with funds from supporters, but it seems to have run foul of the Japanese and its memorial was removed from the site. In the early 1990s, as economic difficulties mounted with the collapse of the Soviet Union, the regime turned increasingly to Korean history, and nationalism, for re-legitimisation. The tomb was excavated and the mausoleum built. The association's memorial was restored at the same time, linking the Tangun heritage to the anti-Japanese struggle.

---

custom of father-to-son royal succession, a tradition which lives on in North Korea today, quite overwhelming both Marxist and general republican/modernist influences. Family succession within an ostensibly non-hereditary political system is by no means confined to North Korea; we have the Nehru dynasty in India, Bhutto in Pakistan, Bandaranaike in Sri Lanka, Sukarno in Indonesia, Lee in Singapore and the Bush family in the United States. It is one of the ironies of our time that both Kim Jong Il and George W. Bush have inherited their father's positions, by different mechanisms but with the same result, despite it being quite at odds with the declared political culture. South Korea has not yet had a family succession but that may not be far off. Park Geun-hye, daughter of military dictator Park Chung-hee who ruled South Korea from his coup in 1961 to his assassination in 1979, won the leadership of the main opposition Grand National Party (GNP) in March 2004 following the resignation, in yet another corruption scandal, of Choe Byung-yul.[2]

KOREA: SHADOWS OF THE PAST

Koguryo occupied the north of the peninsula and part of Manchuria, and it is this legacy which the DPRK sees as the mainstream of Korean history. In 427 the capital moved to Pyongyang. History reasserted its power to complicate the present in 2003 when it is alleged that China blocked North Korea's claims to have the Koguryo tombs declared a UNESCO world heritage site.[3] One of the reasons that China is

Map 3   Shadows of the past: the ancient kingdom of Koguryo straddles modern boundaries

concerned about a possible traumatic collapse of the DPRK is that it would send a further, and larger, flood of refugees into its Northeast provinces (Manchuria), swelling the ethnic Korean population there which, according to South Korean data, is already over 2 million.[4] It is not difficult to see the possibility of irredentist claims to former Koguryo territory arising in a future unified Korea.

It was the third kingdom, Silla, centred at Kyongju in the southeast, that unified Korea in 668. Although the peninsula was to be fragmented again over the course of time, and although it is divided today, from that period on unification became the norm. Again, although there were invasions and occupations – by the Chinese, the Mongols and the Japanese, with perhaps the Americans counted as well, there were never the waves of migration that frequently re-fashioned the ethnic and political map of Europe. Despite significant regional differences (in South Korea elections have often revolved around region rather than party platforms) a unified Korean peninsula has become the default, the natural state of things to which the country will revert.

Perhaps the greatest unifying factor for nation building, and one which tends to differentiate one nation from another is language. The origins of the Korean spoken language are uncertain but we have some significant milestones when it comes to the written language. The Chinese writing system was introduced into Korea during the Three Kingdoms, and from there to Japan. Whereas the Japanese adapted Chinese characters to construct a supplementary system (*kana*) that would allow them to cope with the grammatical differences between the Japanese and Chinese spoken languages, the Koreans went further and developed an artificial system called *Hangul* to represent Korean. Japanese is written in a combination of Chinese characters (*kanji*) and kana; Korean can be written exclusively in Hangul, and in North Korea virtually always is. In South Korea most of the writing is done in Hangul, but Chinese characters (*Hanja*) are still common. For some years teaching of Hanja was dropped from the education system but has now returned. Again an irony; although the DPRK owed its survival during the Korean War (and perhaps today) to China, it has most steadfastly turned its back on Hanja in favour of Hangul, officially ceasing use of Hanja in 1949.

It is said that *idu*, a phonetic writing system similar to kana (and which might have served as a model for the Japanese) was created in 692 but the major step was the invention of Hangul in 1444, and its promulgation in 1446, during the reign of King Sejong. Originally called 'the correct sounds for the instruction of the people' it was only in the nineteenth century that its use became widespread.[5] Nowadays Hangul gives Koreans, and Korean visual space, an identity which clearly distinguishes Korea from its neighbours. Whereas most people cannot distinguish between Chinese and Japanese script, Hangul gives a Korean newspaper, or a Korean cityscape with its signs and notices a distinctiveness. Korea also boasts developments in printing, with block printing of the Buddhist classics in 1001 and the first use of metallic type in 1234.

Silla eventually declined and the next dynasty to rule over all of Korea was the Koryo (918–1392). The founder of the dynasty, Wang Kon, saw himself as the legitimate successor to Koguryo, and he chose a shortened version to name his dynasty ('high mountains and sparkling waters'). The main Koryo capital was Kaesong, now in North Korea close to the border with the South. Kaesong became the site for initial armistice negotiations during the Korean War (before they moved to Panmunjom) and it is today the location where the Hyundai corporation is constructing an industrial park for small and medium enterprises from South Korea.[6]

These historical names live on today. It is from Koryo that we get the English word 'Korea', although there is some dispute about the spelling of the word. Some nationalists, north and south, want the English name to be changed to, or more precisely, revert to 'Corea'. They claim that the current spelling was a machination by the Japanese to put Japan further ahead in the alphabet and that 'Corea' was the normal way of spelling the word before then.[7] Air Koryo is the name of the DPRK airline, and Koryo is in the Korean version of one of South Korea's leading universities, Korea University. One of the most expensive hotels in Seoul is called the Silla and one of Pyongyang's is the Koryo.

Geography made Korea the natural conduit for anyone from the Asian mainland wanting to invade Japan. The Chinese showed no desire to do that, but the Mongols, who were rather partial to invasions, did. During the thirteenth century they occupied Korea and attempted to use it as a springboard from which to invade Japan. In this they were foiled by the *kamikaze*, the 'divine wind' which scattered their fleet. The Mongol empire soon ebbed but at the turn of the sixteenth century the Japanese shogun Hideyoshi made two attempts to invade Korea, as part of a plan to extend Japanese power deep into the Asian mainland, a plan revived by imperial Japan in the twentieth century. Hideyoshi was thwarted by the 'turtle boats' of Admiral Yi Sun-shin, the world's first armour-clad warships. There are interesting parallels between Hideyoshi's invasion and the Korean War. The Chinese (at that time under the Ming dynasty) sent an expeditionary force to help the Koreans, just as China despatched troops to aid North Korea in repelling the Americans in 1950. The Japanese retreated to an enclave around Pusan, just as the South Korean forces did in 1950 (the Pusan Perimeter). Admiral Yi demonstrated the crucial importance of sea power to a conflict on the Korean peninsula, a demonstration repeated by MacArthur's Inchon landing in 1950 which turned the flank of the North Korean army and forced a rapid retreat. These are lessons unlikely to be forgotten by military planners in Pyongyang and they undermine the credibility of the frequent accusation that North Korea might again invade the South.

CHOSUN DYNASTY

The Japanese invasions happened during the period of the Yi, or Chosun, Korea's longest ruling, and last, dynasty (1392–1910). It was originally established in Kaesong but the capital was moved to Hanyang, part of modern Seoul, in 1396. Seoul continued to be the capital during the Japanese colonial period (1910–45) and has been the seat of the Republic of Korea, except for a period during the Korean War when the government moved to Pusan.

In 1636 Korea was invaded and defeated by the Manchu, who were in the process of overthrowing the Ming to establish the Qing dynasty in China (1644–1911). The Manchu, being from the steppes north of China proper, were more expansionist than 'Chinese' (i.e. Han ethnicity) dynasties such as the Ming. Tibet was another acquisition of the Manchus and it, too, became a tributary state of the Qing. The present claim of the People's Republic of China (and of the Republic of China on Taiwan) to Tibet and Xinjiang originates from this tributary status. It is not inconceivable, though unlikely, that had not a period of Japanese colonialism intervened, Korea might have passed into the modern Chinese state as Tibet and Xinjiang have done. Alternatively it might have declared independence with foreign help, as Mongolia did.

The Chinese tributary system was very different from Western empires such as the British or French and it entailed little more than a periodic tribute mission to Beijing. Missions from Burma and Laos came every ten years, but the Koreans came annually. According to historians, these missions and the tributary relationship were usually to the financial advantage of the tributary state, with the emperor's gifts, and trade, more than compensating for the tribute.[8] Media people add a bit more spice to things. 'We used to ship them tens of thousands of virgins every year', claimed one South Korean recently.[9] Be that as it may, the relationship with China did not prevent Chosun Korea retreating into itself, becoming known as the 'Hermit Kingdom', a seclusion that was not formally and finally breached until the Japanese imposed a treaty opening the ports Pusan, Wonsan and Inchon in 1876.

Looking ahead for a moment, there is widespread speculation that a modern form of the tributary relationship is being formed as fast-growing China displaces the United States as South Korea's major economic partner.[10] Moreover, military and diplomatic power (as evidenced by the hosting of the Six-Party talks 2003–04) follows economic power. The same thing is happening with Japan, although to a lesser extent. It can be argued that the key thrust of US policy in respect of East Asia is to block the development of the relationship between its 'allies', South Korea and Japan, on one hand, and China, on the other. To achieve this, a permanent crisis on the Korean peninsula, and a demonic and demonised North Korea are necessary. This is a theme we will return to later.

THE ARRIVAL OF THE EUROPEANS AND CHRISTIANITY

The Japanese were not the only strangers on the horizon, or the only threats to Korean seclusion during the Chosun period. A Dutch ship was wrecked off Cheju island in 1653, a harbinger of things to come. In many ways it was not people and guns that had the most impact, but ideas. Christianity was introduced in 1777 and although persecution (of Catholics) began in 1791 the influx was eventually ineluctable. Today South Korea, along with the Philippines, are the only countries in Asia with a substantial Christian presence, some 20 per cent of the South Korean population describing themselves as Protestant and a further 6 per cent as Catholics. Together these Christian adherents are roughly equal to the percentage of Buddhists.[11] Even more significant, is that the percentage of Christians is rising and is linked with urbanisation and affluence:

> [South] Korean city-dwellers, particularly those in the more modern and affluent sections of Seoul, are not only more likely than other Koreans to be religious, but they are more likely, when they are religious, to be Christian rather than Buddhist.[12]

Christianity is far less strong in the North, but even there Christianity continues, with the main Presbyterian church at Pongsu being packed for Sunday service, admittedly with a rather ageing congregation.[13] Following Kim Jong Il's visit to Russia in July/August 2001, a Russian Orthodox church is under construction in Pyongyang.[14] We return to this issue in Chapter 5.

Christianity did not have an easy ride in Chosun Korea and persecution is said to have commenced in 1791. Korea was particularly prolific, but not unique, in generating syncretic religions, with Christianity part of the cocktail. Choe Jae-woo's *Donghak* (Eastern Learning), established in 1860, was a mixture of Taoism, Buddhism, Neo-Confucianism, Catholicism, and indigenous shamanism (a form of animism in which shamans are intermediaries between men and the spirit world). Donghak had egalitarian overtones and contributed to peasant revolts, in some ways paralleling the Taipings in China. Choe himself was executed in 1864 but his teachings spread and re-emerged in the *Chondokyo* (Heavenly Way) religious movement which did much to inspire Korean nationalism and which continues to this day, North and South. Kim Il Sung regarded Chondokyo as a 'national religion' and the Chondoist Chongu Party, founded in 1946 is one of the small pantheon of non-Communist parties allowed to coexist with the Korean Workers' party (KWP), without, it may be presumed, much in the way of power. When Kim Dae-jung made his historic visit to Pyongyang in June 2000, and gave a banquet for Kim Jong Il, Ryu Mi Yong, Chairwoman of the Central Committee of the Chondoist Chongu Party was, along with the Chairman of the Korean Social Democratic Party, among the ten named North Korean participants.[15]

Another syncretic Korean religion that should be mentioned is the Reverend Sun Myung Moon's Unification Church, though this was a much later invention, stemming, according to the Unification Church website, from a private meeting he had with Jesus on a Korean hillside in 1935. Although 'the Moonies' are mainly known for mass weddings and allegations of brainwashing, their Church has had a very interesting political career, including deep involvement in bribing members of Congress in Washington in the 1970s.[16] It still has a formidable footprint in Washington, owning both the *Washington Times* (not to be confused with the rather more prestigious *Washington Post*) and *United Press International* and reportedly has a strong influence on the Bush administration.[17] Recently, despite Moon's anti-Communism, it has been involved in the construction of a car factory in North Korea.[18]

The influence of Christianity in generating syncretic 'Koreanised' religion does not stop there. Some have argued that the cult of Kim Il Sung and Kim Jong Il, as manifested in the concept of *Juche* (self-reliance), also owes much to Christianity which it draws on and distorts.[19]

That Dutch ship wrecked in 1653 was a harbinger not merely of Christianity, and a whole host of other ideas to challenge the status quo, including liberalism and Marxism, but also of the thrust of the capitalist world system to 'open up' recalcitrant countries. This happened to Korea, China and Japan, who all had 'unequal treaties' imposed upon them, but it was only the Japanese who were able to recover quite quickly and, with the success of the Meiji Restoration, starting in 1868, were able to transform themselves from prey to predator, with disastrous results for their neighbours, and ultimately in 1945 for themselves. The 'opening up' was done by what was subsequently called 'gunboat diplomacy', a combination of law and violence by those above the law, which remains a characteristic of the system today. The term 'gunboat diplomacy' has fallen out of favour, partly perhaps because only rogue regimes have gunboats, while respectable countries have naval assets, and 'naval assets diplomacy' hasn't quite the right ring to it. The modern term is 'coercive diplomacy' used, if not invented, by President Clinton's North Korea Advisor and former Defense Secretary, William J. Perry. A recent book published by the Orwellian-named United States Institute of Peace – a Congressional think tank for whom 'peace' seems to be synonymous with 'pacification' – notes that

> With increasing frequency, U.S. leaders look to achieve their foreign policy goals by marrying diplomacy to military muscle. Since the end of the Cold War, 'coercive diplomacy' – the effort to change the behavior of a target state or group through the threat or limited use of military force – has been used in no fewer than eight cases.[20]

One of those eight cases was Iraq. Another was North Korea.

A SHARED VISION OF EMPIRES

History is not only a matter of recording change, but also of noting continuity, especially that which is obscured by change. Much of what happens today in international affairs resounds with echoes of the past, so much so that the word 'imperialism' is enjoying a restoration which would have gladdened the hearts of earlier architects of empire.

Back at end of the nineteenth century, Europeans, Americans and increasingly Japanese, talked unashamedly of empire, and if that was unattainable because of competing claims from other powers, then 'spheres of influence'. Failing that, the fallback position was 'most favoured nation' status, whereby concessions given to one power were extended to the others in the club. The club in East Asia at that time mainly comprised the British, the Americans, the Russians, the French, and last but for a while foremost, the Japanese. Korean histories (North and South) punctuate their accounts of the treaties of this period with stories of popular resistance. Thus, in 1886 a French fleet was attacked on the Han river, on which lies Seoul, and the American ship *Sherman* was destroyed on the Taedong, which flows through Pyongyang. The Americans were again fired upon in 1871 and the Japanese in 1875. But the thrust to open the hermit kingdom was unstoppable. The Japanese imposed a treaty in 1876 which opened Pusan, Wonsan and Inchon (close to Seoul) to Japanese trade. This was followed in 1883 by a Korean–American treaty of 'Friendship and Commerce'. Treaties with major European powers came in the wake.

Pressure from outside was mirrored by domestic developments. 1884 saw two manifestations of modernism, although the first carried heavy historical baggage. The *Taeguk* flag – the current Republic of Korea flag – was designed around the ancient Chinese symbols of yin and yang, and trigrams derived from the ancient Chinese classic *Yi Jing (I Ching)*, the *Book of Changes*. The same year saw the founding of the first modern newspaper in Korea.

Timeline 1   From Tangun to Japanese annexation

Date	Event
2333 BC	Tangun founds kingdom of Chosun (Morning Calm) near modern Pyongyang
427 AD	Koguryo capital moved to Pyongyang
668	Silla unifies Korea – this is disputed by northern historians who claim Koyo was first
918	Koryo founded
1231	First invasion by Mongols
1392	Yi dynasty founded in Kaesong
1393	Yi kingdom named Chosun (Morning Calm)
1396	Capital moved to Hanyang (Seoul)
1446	Hangul phonetic writing system invented (King Sejong)
1592	Japanese shogun Hideyoshi invades Korea, repulsed by Yi Soon-shin's ironclad 'turtle boats'

1866	French fleet in Han river (Seoul) repulsed; American ship *Sherman* destroyed on Taedong (Pyongyang)
1883	Korean–American treaty of 'Friendship and Commerce'; treaties with European powers follow
1895	Treaty of Shimonoseki: China cedes Formosa (Taiwan) to Japan, recognises 'independence of Korea'; Queen Min murdered
1905	Taft–Katsura agreement by which US accepts Japanese colonisation of Korea in exchange for Japanese acceptance of US control of Philippines
1910	
22 August	Annexation of Korea by Japan

A decade later, in 1894, the Donghak rebellion and the Sino–Japanese war marked the beginning of a period of bloody turmoil that would wreak havoc on East Asia for close on a century. Fighting came to a pause with the Korea Armistice in 1953 and, after a renewed flare up in Indochina, where the 'American War' succeeded the 'French War' (to use Vietnamese parlance), to be followed by the Khmer Rouge rise and fall in Cambodia, the region came to relative peace in the early 1990s. The Donghak rebellion symbolised the internal failure of the Chosun dynasty, at the very time when Japanese designs on China provided much of the motivation for their subjugation of Korea. For the Japanese imperial thinkers of the time, as for Hideyoshi before them, Korea was valuable in itself but was, more importantly, the bridgehead to China and the Asian mainland. Again, there are parallels with modern US policy.

THE COMING OF THE JAPANESE

The Chosun court requested Chinese assistance to suppress the Donghak rebellion, and this brought in the Japanese, and precipitated war. This first Sino–Japanese war did not take long and at the Treaty of Shimonoseki in 1895 China ceded Taiwan, known internationally then, and until fairly recently, by its Portuguese name of Formosa (from *ilha formosa*, 'beautiful island'). Taiwan became Japan's first colony (if we exclude the Ryukyu Islands, or Okinawa, which was incorporated as a province) and so Japan joined the club of imperialists. The distinguished American scholars Reischauer, Fairbank and Craig succinctly described Japan's enthusiastic participation in club activities:

... the [Japanese] government's subsequent efforts to dominate Korea showed clearly that it was adopting the imperialistic strategy of the contemporary West. In the resulting Sino–Japanese and Russo–Japanese wars, Japan obtained Taiwan, the Pescadores, southern Sakhalin, and Liaotung, and control over South Manchuria and Korea. The latter it annexed outright in 1910, without protest by any Western nation. Entering World War I as Britain's ally by treaty, Japan picked up the German colonial possessions in East Asia and the North Pacific and sat at Versailles as one of the Five Great Powers – the only non-Western nation to have been accepted as a full equal by the great nations of the West.[21]

In the Treaty of Shimonoseki, China also recognised 'the independence of Korea' which meant that she acknowledged that she was in no position to resist Japan's seizure of that independence. The formidable Queen Min, who was pro-Chinese, was murdered in a horrible fashion – raped, by some accounts, stabbed and doused in kerosene and burnt – by a mixed gang of Japanese and Korean troops. The Japanese strengthened their de facto control over Korea. The Japanese ushered in many modernising reforms and were to have a huge transformative effect on Korea over the next 50 years. Japanese colonialism also had a major, though lesser, impact on Taiwan. It did much to lay the economic foundations that, from the 1950s, enabled Taiwan to utilise the capital and manpower resources that had fled the Mainland during the Chinese civil war. Owing to this, and to substantial US aid, Taiwan swiftly became one of the East Asian 'Tigers'. It also nurtured a sense of separation and difference from the Mainland that is manifested today in aspirations for Taiwan independence.

The turn of the century saw Korea enter the railway age, with the construction of a line from the port of Inchon to Seoul. The Japanese then, as now, were committed to railway development and as they extended their control over the Korean peninsula and into Manchuria, railway building was a key element in their strategy. Railways for many years had huge military significance as well as economic importance. The Japanese pushed the railway up to the Manchurian border to prosecute the Russo–Japanese war in 1904, bringing in troops from Japan to build and guard the line. However, what the military started, the civilian sector inherited and railways became a vital artery for economic development. Railways, like the Internet, gain value exponentially with growth and linkages, and the Korean railway network was in the fortunate position (unlike the

Japanese) of being able in time to connect to the Eurasian network, and specifically to the Trans-Siberian Railway. However, because of political barriers this has been more a matter of potential rather than practice. By the 1930s it was possible to go by train from Pusan to Paris, but the number of people who did so must have been very few. War, and separation of the two Koreas, broke the links but nowadays, with the north and south railway networks being reconnected, the dream of an 'iron silkroad', to use Kim Dae-jung's phrase, is on the horizon again.[22]

The Russo–Japanese War of 1904–05 was as brief as the war against China and led to a further erosion of Korean sovereignty. A surprise Japanese attack on the Russian naval base at Port Arthur (Lushun, south of Dalian on the Liaodong Peninsula) in February 1904 immobilised the Russian far eastern fleet. Port Arthur, which had been Russia's booty from the Sino–Japanese War, surrendered in January the following year. The Japanese won a further major victory at Mukden (modern Shenyang) in March 1905 and two months later destroyed a Russian fleet which had been sent from the Baltic in a battle in the Tsushima Straits, between Korea and Japan. Defeated at land and on sea the Russians sued for peace, which was signed at the Treaty of Portsmouth (in New Hampshire) on 5 September 1905. In the treaty the Russians acknowledged that Korea was a Japanese protectorate. The Anglo–Japan Treaty of Alliance, originally signed in 1902, was revised in 1905 and the British, too, recognised the Japanese protectorate. In the same year there was a secret agreement between the United States and Japan, the Taft–Katsura agreement, by which the US agreed to Japanese control of Korea in exchange for Japanese acceptance of American dominance in the Philippines.

Japan's tightening grip on Korea did not go unresisted and in 1909 Ito Hirobumi, the former Japanese Resident-General in Korea – the Paul Bremer of his day – was assassinated by a Korean patriot, Ahn Chong-keun. Nevertheless, the Japanese were unstoppable and on 22 August 1910 Korea was formally annexed. It was done, as such things are, up to and including the invasion of Iraq, ostensibly for the benefit of the natives, and in their best interests, as the proclamation made clear:

> Notwithstanding the earnest and laborious work of reforms in the administration of Korea in which the Governments of Japan and Korea have been engaged for more than four years since the conclusion of the Agreement of 1905, the existing system of government in that country

has not proved entirely equal to the duty of preserving public order and tranquillity; and in addition, the spirit of suspicion and misgiving dominates the whole peninsula.

In order to maintain peace and stability in Korea, to promote the prosperity and welfare of Koreans, and at the same time to ensure the safety and repose of foreign residents, it has been made abundantly clear that fundamental changes in the actual regime of government are absolutely essential. The Governments of Japan and Korea, being convinced of the urgent necessity of introducing reforms responsive to the requirements of the situation and of furnishing sufficient guarantee for the future, have, with the approval of His Majesty the Emperor of Japan and His Majesty the Emperor of Korea, concluded, through their plenipotentiaries, a treaty providing for complete annexation of Korea to the Empire of Japan.[23]

RESISTANCE AND FACTIONALISM

Thus commenced the formal Japanese colonialisation of Korea, which was to last 35 years, until it was brought to an end by Japan's surrender in 1945. It brought considerable economic and social development to Korea, but a development fashioned for Japanese interests and so distorted. It was also development at terrible cost, not merely in terms of human suffering, but also national pride, and that reverberates to this day. There are innumerable instances of this heritage, many of which will come up in the course of this book, but perhaps one set will suffice at this point.

Arguably the most horrendous crime of the Japanese colonial period was the forcible drafting of colonial women to serve as prostitutes for the army. According to South Korean sources, some 200,000 women, 80 per cent of whom were Korean, were 'victims of the Japanese sexual slavery in the Asia-Pacific area before and during World War II'.[24] Described by KCNA as 'the immoral state crime of the blackest dye in the 20th century committed in Korea and other countries', what particularly offends Koreans, North and South (and many Japanese), is the failure of the Japanese government to acknowledge let alone apologise for the crime and recompense the victims.[25] The issue was kept under wraps for many years, no doubt helped by a sense of shame amongst the surviving women, but it surfaced in the early 1990s. Since 8 January 1992 there has been a weekly demonstration in front of the Japanese embassy in Seoul. On 17 March 2004 rallies were held in seven countries (including

Japan) to commemorate the 600th weekly rally in Seoul, which was attended by protesters from Okinawa.[26]

While this was happening on the streets of Seoul a connected drama was unfolding in the National Assembly, already in turmoil in the buildup to the impeachment of President Roh Moo-hyun on 12 March. On 2 March the National Assembly passed a bill introduced by Kim Hee-sun of the pro-Roh Uri Party to set up a special committee that 'will inquire into pro-Japanese collaborators during Japan's colonial rule from 1910 to 1945'.[27] Subsequently Ms Kim alleged that the Speaker of the National Assembly, Park Kwan-yong had tried to cut a deal by which he would support the bill in exchange for help in stopping an investigation into his father, who had served the Japanese as a policeman.[28] According to Lee Wha Rang, who describes himself as 'a Korean Nationalist Exile in America', and who writes frequently for the US-based Kimsoft website, there was a fracas in the assembly and Kim Hee-sun was manhandled while 'a group of assembly men and women watch[ed] her with contemptuous sneers'. In the article, robustly entitled 'War of liberation continues: South Korea is still a Japanese colony. The sons and daughters of pro-Japanese traitors rule South Korea', Lee argued that this was symbolic of a deep split among the people of South Korea. The main person Lee singles out was Park Geun-hye, who was shortly to be elected leader of the main opposition party, the Grand National Party (23 March). Park is the daughter of Park Chung-hee, South Korea's dictator-cum-President during the 1960s, widely seen as the architect of the country's economic success. Park Chung-hee, as we shall discuss later in more detail, served in the Japanese Army, mainly in Manchuria, and was involved in the suppression of Chinese and Korean resistance to the Japanese empire. Lee argues that Park Chung-hee was by no means alone in supporting the Japanese, but that

> Japan's annexation of Korea in 1910 was welcomed by a sizeable majority of the Korean elite and people. These pro-Japanese traitors believed that the Korean people would be better off by becoming Japanese, and they stopped speaking Korean, wearing Korean clothes, eating Korean foods, and so on. They competed with each other to become more Japanese than the Japanese themselves.[29]

While the issue of the Japanese past, both crimes and collaboration, was being argued out in Seoul in 2004, Japanese Prime Minister Koizumi had started the year by making yet another visit to the

Yasukuni Shrine, a controversial cemetery in Tokyo in which some convicted Japanese war criminals are interred. An official visit by a Japanese politician is a hugely symbolic event which always draws protests from China and both Koreas.[30]

However, it would be misleading to over-emphasise the effect of the trauma of the Japanese period. There is also a strong element of pragmatism in Korean political culture, perhaps due to the influence of Confucianism combined with the necessities faced by small nations surrounded by more powerful neighbours. South Korea has managed to develop reasonably good relations with Japan over the years. Relations between Japan and DPRK have been much more difficult but the Kim–Koizumi summit of September 2002, although it came unstuck for reasons which we will go into later, did indicate that a rapprochement was possible. And, as for Park Geun-hye, the fact that she is her father's daughter (and draws much of her standing from that) has not automatically made her persona non grata in Pyongyang. On the contrary, she was feted on a trip to Pyongyang in May 2002. Kim Jong Il sent a plane to Beijing for her and when she suggested an inter-Korean football match this was arranged immediately.[31] The DPRK made no adverse comment on her election as leader of the Grand National Party (GNP), which was an unusual departure, and it is quite likely that if the conservative GNP were to come back to power then relations with the North would improve more than under a leftist government, for somewhat the same reasons that Nixon was able to build bridges with China.[32]

KIM IL SUNG AND HIS CONTEMPORARIES

On 15 April 1912 the man who was to pass into history as Kim Il Sung was born at Mangyongdae outside Pyongyang. The place is now, not surprisingly, a shrine and since Kim's early life has been much mythologised (as well as demonised) this makes it often difficult to pin down the facts. According to his autobiography he was originally named Kim Song-ju but this was changed to Kim Il Sung on the insistence of his comrades. Names would, in fact, be a major issue of cultural subjugation during the Japanese period, when Koreans were pressured to adopt Japanese names.

Although Kim Il Sung would turn out to be the most famous Korean nationalist of the twentieth century he was not, of course, alone. Indeed much of his importance stems from his later eminence, and the founding of a virtual dynasty, under his son Kim Jong Il.

Timeline 2   The struggle for independence and buildup to war

1912
15 April   Birth of Kim Il Sung (1912–1994) near Pyongyang
1919
1 March   Declaration of Independence
1920
February   Korean Independence Army founded in Manchuria
1937
4 June   Battle of Ponchobo – Kim Il Sung's guerrillas briefly liberate Japanese-held town in the major success of armed anti-Japanese struggle
1941
16 February   Birth of Kim Jong Il, son of North Korean guerrilla leader Kim Il Sung
1943
1 December   Cairo Declaration; China, US, UK agree that 'that in due course Korea shall become free and independent'
1945
15 August   Liberation of Korea; US proposes to Soviet Union the division of Korea along the 38th parallel. USSR agrees on 16 August
22 August   Arrival of Soviet forces in Pyongyang
8 September   Arrival in Korea of US forces under General John R. Hodge
1946
12 December   South Korean Interim National Assembly established in Seoul
1947
20 February   NK Provisional People's Committee becomes People's Committee, Kim Il Sung elected chairman
17 September   US refers 'Korean problem' to UN General Assembly
1948
3 April   Beginning of rebellion on Cheju island in South Korea
15 August   Establishment of the Republic of Korea with Syngman Rhee as president
25 August   Establishment of Democratic People's Republic of Korea with Kim Il Sung as premier
19 October   Mutiny of South Korean 14th regiment at Yosu
12 December   UN General Assembly declares the Republic of Korea to be the legitimate government in Korea
31 December   Withdrawal of Soviet troops from North Korea

1949

29 June	Withdrawal of US troops except for 500 Korean Military Advisory Group (KMAG)
1 October	Establishment of the People's Republic of China
29 October	Communist Party and affiliated organisations outlawed in South Korea

1950

12 January	US Secretary Of State Dean Acheson says 'the [US] defensive perimeter runs along the Aleutians to Japan and then goes to the Ryukyu [Okinawa] and the Philippines'
26 January	Signing of US–ROK Defense Support Agreement

That along with longevity and the accidents of history give him an historical prominence that tends to overshadow people who were, at the time, of greater consequence. Having said that, it should also be noted that there has been a tendency in Western historiography to understate the less-visible anti-Japanese struggle of 'Communists' such as Kim Il Sung, and those fighting with the Chinese Communist Party, in favour of the more accessible figures such as Syngman Rhee and Kim Ku. And, until the last few years, any portrayal of the role of Kim Il Sung, or the left generally in Korean nationalism, was prohibited in South Korea.

The resistance to the Japanese took a variety of forms from the passive (such as choosing a Japanese name that had a double meaning) to the violent, such as the assassination of Ito Hirobumi or the guerrilla warfare waged by Kim Il Sung in the Manchurian border region. On 1 March 1919 (*Samil*, or '3-1' in Korean), a nationwide unarmed demonstration for Korean independence was launched, and became known as the Samil Movement. It thus preceded the 4 May Movement in China (the '5-4', *Wusi*, movement in Chinese) and flowed from the same sources – a desire for freedom from the Japanese inspired by the Wilsonian rhetoric of self-determination that dominated discourse at the Versailles Peace Conference being held at that time. Not for the last time did Koreans, and Chinese, find that the rhetoric did not apply to them any more than it did to those in European colonies. The Japanese brutally repressed the demonstrations, with 2,000 causalities and 19,000 imprisoned according to official figures.

In April, meetings in Shanghai and in Seoul set up a provisional government of the Korean Republic. But the world's leaders, including Wilson, trying to organise the postwar world in cooperation with Japan, made no response.[33]

The Korean Nationalist movement in the interwar period was as fractious as is current South Korean politics and the provisional government in Shanghai, though it lasted into the 1940s, moving to Chungking (Chongqing) with the Chinese Nationalist government under Chiang Kai-shek, was never unified, and never effective. Syngman Rhee, who was later to become the first President of the Republic of Korea (15 August 1948) was nominal president of the provisional government but quarrelled with other leaders such as Yi Tong-hwi (a former royalist army commander) and Kim Ku, who became allied to the Chinese nationalists. Rhee stayed in the United States, lobbying Washington. This proved valuable to him and when, after 1945, the Americans were looking for a Korea leader, he was their natural choice.

THE BOLSHEVIKS AND THE ANTI-COLONIAL STRUGGLE

Abandoned by the 'world's leaders', who were in fact no more than the victors of the First World War, many Asian nationalists turned to the only force that did offer support against colonialists, whether it be Japanese, European, or, in the Philippines, the United States – the new Soviet regime. The Bolshevik government had turned its back on Tsarist imperialism and aligned itself with the anti-colonial struggle. This went beyond disinterested 'proletarian solidarity' because the Soviet Union was itself threatened by those imperialist powers so it was partly a matter of a united front against a common enemy. This was later to be a main issue between Trotsky and Stalin. The former wanted to press ahead with world revolution, arguing that was the only way to safeguard the revolutionary regime in Russia, while Stalin came out in favour of 'socialism in one country' and went on, over the course of the next two decades, to sign treaties and enter into alliances, to play the 'balance of power game', with the world powers – Nazi Germany, Britain, US and Japan. However back in the 1920s the battle lines were clearer and 'Communism (became) the chief vehicle for Korea's anti-Japanese patriots'.[34]

Not all patriots became Communists, but the Soviet Union became the main supporter of a wide range of nationalist, anti-Japanese, movements, including Sun Yat-sen's Nationalist party in China. A delegation from the provisional Korean government in Shanghai visited Moscow in January 1920 and received a donation of one million roubles. The following month a 'Korean Independence Army' was founded in Manchuria, then still under Chinese control.

It was not all a matter of politics in exile and armed struggle. But there was a third course. Back in Korea the transformation of social life under the Japanese produced its own dynamic. The year 1920, for instance, saw the establishment of two newspapers in Seoul that are prominent to this day – the *Chosun Ilbo* (*'Korea Daily'*) and the *Donga Ilbo* (*'East Asia Daily'*). Within the constraints of Japanese hegemony, these papers nurtured a sense of Korean identity. The distinction between coexistence and collaboration is a blurred one. It is perhaps no coincidence that both are now considered pro-American and rightwing – especially the Chosun Ilbo.[35] In another twist, the owners of Donga Ilbo bought what was later renamed Korea University, which ranks with Yonsei (founded in 1885 by the American Presbyterian missionary Horace G. Underwood) as South Korea's most prestigious private universities. Whatever compromises may have been made, given the 'developmental mission' of Japanese colonialism this process of cultural modernisation was both inevitable, and would eventually have brought about its own end.

Political parties and groups also sprang up in Korea during the 1920s – the Korean Labour party in 1924, the Korean Communist party and the Korean Communist Youth Association both in 1925. The following year saw the Japanese government-general moving into the Capitol building in Seoul, an interesting architectural edifice in European style, signifying modernity, which came so much to symbolise Japanese rule that it was pulled down by President Kim Young-sam in 1995.

JAPAN'S ATTEMPT AT ASIAN EMPIRE

However Korean domestic politics were overshadowed by other events, especially the expansion and development of the Japanese empire. Korea was, for Japan, a beachhead on the Asian mainland and the starting point of the journey, not the destination. The next stop was Manchuria, called by the Chinese Dongbei, the Northeast, and coincidentally an area of which the western part had been under the sway of the ancient kingdom of Koguryo. In 1931 the Japanese army engineered the 'Manchurian Incident', in which they attacked Chinese forces in Mukden (Shenyang) in 'retaliation' for planting of a bomb on the Japanese railway north of the city. The following year the puppet state of Manchukuo (*manzhuguo*) was established under the nominal control of Pu Yi, the 'last emperor' of the Qing dynasty.[36]

The Japanese attempted to extend the empire northeast into Mongolia and Siberia; their participation in the Siberian Intervention of 1917–23, in which the Allies had attacked the Soviet Union from the east, had given them a taste for the area and its rich resources. However vigorous Soviet resistance, especially in the battles at Nomonhan and Khalkhyn Gol in 1936 in which the Japanese got a severe drubbing put paid to this and they turned their attention south, to China and Greater East Asia.[37]

In July 1937 the Lugouqiao (Marco Polo Bridge) incident near Beijing ignited the second Sino–Japanese war and the following month they were attacking Shanghai, China's commercial capital. The political capital had in fact been moved from Beijing to Nanking (Nanjing) by Chiang Kai-shek in 1927 (he was later to move to Chongqing in retreat from the Japanese and then, in 1949, to Taipei to escape the Communists) and it was here that various Korean politicians, most prominently Kim Ku, had come together to form the Korean National party in July 1935. Despite Kim Ku's affinity with Chiang Kai-shek, neither his party nor the Korean provisional government was given much freedom of action and they had little effect on the Japanese. Kim Ku did achieve some personal fame with a terrorist attack on the Japanese in Shanghai in 1932 in which he lost a leg but gained the nickname 'the Assassin'.

However, it was up in Manchuria, which by then had a substantial Korean population, that the resistance to Japan was fiercest and most effective. In the midst of this was Kim Il Sung who, by the mid 1930s was a significant guerrilla leader. The Japanese considered him one of the most 'effective and dangerous' guerrilla leaders and set up a special counter-insurgency unit to track him down.[38] Relatively effective and dangerous he might have been but neither he nor the Korean armed resistance in general came anywhere near dislodging the Japanese. Nor, for that matter, did the Chinese, despite the exploits of the Communist Eighth Route Army. Liberation from the Japanese was to come from elsewhere, principally the United States but also, in August 1945, from the Soviet Union.

Nevertheless, the importance of Kim Il Sung's guerrilla warfare cannot be measured in military terms alone. More important was the legitimacy it gave him personally and the state he founded, the DPRK, as a standard bearer of Korean nationalism. It has helped to give the DPRK a resilience which has astounded its enemies. This has not come about without considerable attention to myth making and nurturing, which has been extended to his son, Kim Jong Il. This first son (a position especially important in Korean culture) was born in 1941 or 1942, according to the source, probably somewhere south of Khabarovsk, either in the Soviet Union or China. However, according to North Korea historians he was born on the slopes of Mt Paektu, the Korean sacred mountain on the Korean-Chinese border. Thus we get the 'Three Generals of Mt Paektu' – Kim Il Sung, Kim Jong-suk, Kim Jong Il – the father, mother and son, linking the Kim family into Korean mythology. Kim Il Sung is portrayed as having led Korea to defeat the Japanese before going on, in 1953, to defeat the Americans. Neither of these assertions is factually true. The Japanese were defeated by the Americans and their allies (including the Soviet Union) and the Americans were fought to a draw by the Chinese. Size does matter. Nevertheless the assertions have a mythic validity that transcends the strictly factual.

PRELUDE TO LIBERATION

The final two years of the Second World War saw a number of meetings at which the Allies gathered to dispose of the postwar world. At the Cairo Conference in November/December 1943 the United States, the United Kingdom and the Republic of China (i.e. Chiang Kai-shek) agreed that 'in due course Korea shall become free and independent'. Koreans were angry and disappointed, seeing no reason for the qualifying phrase 'in due course'. The British, who still had a large if precarious empire, were nervous at any mention of 'independence'. Roosevelt thought in terms of a period of tutelage which would prepare people with no (recent) experience of self-government, such as the Koreans, with training in governance that would fit them for a US-dominated postwar order, 'and provide an entry for American interests in China'[39] Elsewhere Stalin had advocated immediate Korean independence. This was consistent with Soviet policy in East Asia and presumably reflected a confidence that an independent Korea, while not being a client state like the Mongolian People's Republic, would be pro-Soviet.

At the Yalta Conference in February 1945 the Soviet Union accepted a US and British request and agreed to enter the war against Japan, with whom it had prudently signed a treaty of neutrality in 1941, within three months of the end of the war in Europe. This it did, to the day, declaring war against Japan on 8 August 1945. The Anglo-

US desire to have the Soviet Union enter the Pacific War presumably indicated that they were not confident that the atomic bomb would bring the Japanese to surrender so quickly. The Soviet declaration of war was perhaps triggered by the bombing of Hiroshima on 6 August. Meanwhile, at the Potsdam Conference in Berlin, 16 July–2 August, the Allies met to discuss postwar Europe and the final stages of the war against Japan. In the Potsdam Declaration of 26 July, the US, UK and China, declared: 'The terms of the Cairo Declaration shall be carried out and Japanese sovereignty shall be limited to the islands of Honshu, Hokkaido, Kyushu, Shikoku and such minor islands as we determine', reiterating that Japan's colonisation of Korea was at an end. The Soviet Union did not sign this declaration because it was not then at war with Japan, but presumably Stalin concurred.

COLLAPSE OF THE JAPANESE EMPIRE

After this things moved very quickly. On 9 August Nagasaki was destroyed by the second atomic bomb and the following day the Soviet Union acquiesced to a US suggestion that Korea be divided, and at the 38th parallel. This surprised the Americans. The decision, which was to have disastrous consequences, had been arrived at in a hurried, and harried, manner:

> ... two young colonels, Dean Rusk and Charles H. Bonesteel, [were directed] to withdraw to an adjoining room and find a place to divide Korea. It was around midnight on August 10–11, the atomic bombs had been dropped, the Soviet Red Army had entered the Pacific War, and American planners were rushing to arrange the Japanese surrender throughout the region. Given thirty minutes to do so, Rusk and Bonesteel looked at a map and chose the thirty-eight parallel because 'it would place the capital city in the American zone'; although the line was 'further north than could be realistically reached ... in the event of Soviet disagreement', the Soviets made no objection – which 'somewhat surprised' Rusk.[40]

In fact Stalin seems to have been very cautious in East Asia giving, for instance, very little assistance to the Chinese Communists in their struggle against Chiang Kai-shek. Therefore, allegations that he was a driving force behind the Korean War would appear rather suspect.

The Japanese emperor surrendered on 15 August 1945 in a speech famous for it being the first time his subjects had heard his voice on the radio, and for his use of splendid euphemisms that yielded nothing in vacuity to the best a modern spin doctor can offer:

> ... we declared war on America and Britain out of our sincere desire to insure Japan's self-preservation and the stabilization of East Asia, it being far from our thought either to infringe upon the sovereignty of other nations or to embark upon territorial aggrandizement.
>
> But now the war has lasted for nearly four years. Despite the best that has been done by everyone – the gallant fighting of our military and naval forces, the diligence and assiduity of our servants of the State and the devoted service of our 100,000,000 people – the war situation has developed not necessarily to Japan's advantage.[41]

Although the war had turned out 'not necessarily to Japan's advantage', the surrender was not entirely to Hirohito's disadvantage, because the Americans had changed their original intention of hanging him, to preserving the emperor system in order better to control Japan, and to scoop up the Japanese empire. This was to have serious consequences in South Korea, where the US military occupation inherited and continued in many respects the Japanese system and power structure.

Things were different in the North. The Soviets had much more contact with the anti-Japanese resistance, in which Kim Il Sung was a leading, but not the only figure, and they could draw on many Koreans who had lived in the Soviet Union. Not as many as they should have had because in 1937 Stalin, fearful of Korean collaboration with the Japanese, had exiled most of the Koreans residing in the Soviet Far East to Central Asia.

The Soviet forces landed at the eastern port of Wonsan on 20 August and that day issued the first General Order, urging the establishment of People's Committees. Two days later Soviet forces arrived in Pyongyang but it was not until 9 September that Kim Il Sung returned to Korea. Meanwhile, down in Seoul, a Korean People's Republic had been proclaimed on 6 September, but was ignored when US forces arrived two days later under General John R. Hodge.

FATEFUL DIVISION

Thus Korea was liberated, but divided, and this division had a profound effect on what was to follow. Without division the Korean peninsula would not have attracted the massive aid from the US,

USSR and China which was to stimulate such astounding economic growth and social transformation. An undivided, perhaps neutral, Korea would not have excited so much foreign interest and growth would have been less. However, this has come at a terrible cost, which is still being paid. The division of the peninsula, once made, soon began to harden. Problems which might have been manageable, albeit with some violence, on the national scale became more intractable because of the creation of two states which by taking very different approaches exacerbated the conflict within Korean society. As Cummings observes,

> With fifty years of hindsight – or even five, in 1950 – we can imagine a cauterising fire that would have settled Korea's multitude of social and political problems caused by the pressure cooker of colonial rule and instant 'liberation', a purifying upheaval that might have been pretty awful, but nothing like the millions of lives lost in 1950–53, or the thousands in the April Revolution of 1960 [which overthrew Syngman Rhee] or the Kwangju Rebellion of 1980 [against Chun Doo-hwan].
>
> Had the Americans and Russians quit Korea, a leftist regime would have taken over quickly, and it would have been a revolutionary nationalist government that, over time, would have moderated and rejoined the world community – as did China, as Vietnam is doing today.[42]

In addition, the division was to give the United States a dominant role in Korean affairs, and a divided Korea, in turn, became a central pivot of US strategy in East Asia.

2

Years of Struggle, Years of Hope: Korean War to First Nuclear Crisis

1945–50: THE ESTABLISHMENT OF TWO REGIMES

Within a few years after 1945 two regimes came to be established in Korea, each becoming formalised into a state and each claiming sovereignty over the whole peninsula. In theory there was a US–Soviet trusteeship, just as in theory the United Nations was a neutral body which was to oversee the establishment of a popular, representative government for Korea. In practice, the Soviet Union and the United States could not agree and neither would abandon its client to the vagaries of popular politics. In addition the United Nations, then as now, was dominated by the US which seldom did not get its way, as the only constraint was the Soviet veto. For the Chinese seat on the Security Council was held by Chiang Kai-shek's rump government in Taiwan until the 1970s. Had Korea not been divided and had there not been foreign intervention then it is likely that there would have been a leftist government, and some chaos and social dislocation, but things would have settled down as the government adjusted to the realities of the international order. As it was, the division led to social upheaval in the North, a migration of the politically dispossessed (landlords, collaborators and Christians) to the South, and in the South fierce repression as the unpopular Syngman Rhee established his power. The division also led to the Korean War, with some 3 million casualties and immense destruction, followed by a half century of contested legitimacy.

On 10 October 1945 the North Korean chapter of the Korean Communist Party was formed; this was to become the Korean Workers' Party (KWP) on 28 August 1946. In December 1945 there was a meeting in Moscow at which the USSR, Britain and the US agreed to 'the establishment of Korea as an independent state' and proposed a period of trusteeship.[1]

In February the following year a Provisional People's Committee (PPC) – the forerunner of the DPRK government – was established in Pyongyang with Kim Il Sung as chairman. The following month

46

the PPC promulgated land reform, cementing its popularity with the majority who benefitted and arousing the hatred of those who lost their privileges. As in China, land reform was a trump card for the Communists, and the failure to carry out similar reforms in the South was criticised by the more astute American observers. The Yale anthropologist Cornelius Osgood, for instance, pointed out 'the similarity between stated American objectives and Soviet reforms of land and labor conditions in the North'.[2] Ironically, land reform was carried out very successfully in Taiwan in the 1950s under American tutelage, but that was possible because the ruling Nationalist government there consisted mostly of people from Mainland China who had no particular ties to Taiwanese landlords.

Syngman Rhee did not have the 'Taiwan option' because the landlord class, and the state apparatus inherited from the Japanese, were an essential part of his limited domestic support. If popular measures were ruled out , both by personal inclination and the logic of domestic politics, then repression became the only recourse. In April 1948, for instance, insurgency broke out on Cheju island and this was not crushed until the eve of the Korea War. Up to 20 per cent of the population were killed or fled to Japan and more than half the villages on the island were destroyed.[3] Even the army was not immune to rebellion, and the 14th regiment, bound for Cheju, mutinied in the port city of Yosu in October 1948. The Yosu rebellion was soon crushed but resistance continued, and was reignited by the Korean War, when the Northern troops swept through most of the country, apart from that beyond the 'Pusan perimeter'. This continued for a decade after the armistice. The last guerrilla, a peasant woman called Chung Soon-duk, was not captured until 1963, and then she languished in jail for 23 years. According to Associated Press, she and her husband

> ... were among thousands of leftist farmers who believed in North Korea's promised 'liberation' from landlords and took up arms in Chiri's thick forests and jagged ravines. They kept fighting, long after North Korean troops retreated and even after the Korean War ended in 1953 with an uneasy truce.
>
> Her husband died in battle in 1952. By 1955, most of the Chiri Mountain guerrillas had been killed or surrendered, but Chung and others continued raiding police stations and villages, even though they had no communication with North Korea.
>
> Chung's life on the run ended in a shootout with police on Nov. 12, 1963.[4]

Chung was released on parole in 1985 but her request to be allowed to go to the North, where she would have been fêted as a heroine, was refused and she died in Seoul, aged 71, in 2004. Guerrilla activity and other resistance against the Kim Il Sung regime in the North seems to have to have been less widespread and less successful, partly due to the option of fleeing South, which according to one estimate, some 500,000 people did.[5]

These refugees in the South provided a rationale, and a constituency, for 'liberating the North' and in the buildup to the outbreak of the Korean War in 1950 there was much talk, and some action. Incursions from the South on occasions outnumbered those from the North as both sides tested the waters. The division of Korea had been imposed from outside and few, if any, Koreans agreed with that. 1948 had seen the establishment of two governments – the Republic of Korea (15 August) and the Democratic People's Republic of Korea (9 September) – both of which claimed sovereignty over the whole peninsula. The United Nations, then as now, found it difficult to stray too far from US policy and in December of that year recognised the ROK as the legitimate government of Korea. In February 1949 a DPRK application to join the UN was rejected. The Soviet Union vetoed the ROK's application in this, and subsequent years and thus, it was not until 17 September 1991 that both Koreas simultaneously entered the United Nations.[6]

Meanwhile the Cold War was intensifying, and in much of Asia, Vietnam being the prime example, this was intertwined with the anti-colonial movement. By 1949 the Communists were victorious in the Chinese civil war, having taken the Mainland and ready to finish off the remnant Guomindang (Kuomintang) who had fled to Taiwan. Apart from the inspiration this must have given Kim Il Sung, the ending of hostilities on the Chinese Mainland resulted in many battle-hardened Koreans, who had been fighting with the Communists, returning home. This was mirrored by a degree of disengagement by the USSR and the US from the Korean peninsula; Soviet troops left in December 1948 and the bulk of the US forces were withdrawn in June the following year, leaving a 500-man Korea Military Advisory Group (KMAG).

Symbols and signs played a large, but uncertain, part. On 12 January 1950 Secretary of State Dean Acheson, in a speech stated that the US 'defensive perimeter runs along the Aleutians to Japan and then goes to the Ryukyu [Okinawa] and the Philippines'. This was subsequently criticised as having 'given the green light to the

Communists' to invade South Korea, a charge denied, with some justification, by Acheson.[7]

1950–53: THE KOREAN WAR

There has been a lot written on the Korean War, especially its immediate origins, the course of military events and the protracted negotiations that led to an armistice after three years of bitter fighting. The American historian Bruce Cumings offers the most authoritative and varied survey of these events, but there are many others, quite a few of whom disagree with him on a number of points. It is not surprising that the Korean War attracted so much attention, and a certain amount of controversy even within the United States. The war was the first that the United States did not win – it ended in a military stalemate – and although it was overshadowed a decade later by the war in Vietnam, it did much to fashion US policy in East Asia that continues to today. It also reversed the demobilisation and civilianisation of the US economy that followed the end of the Second World War and established the military-industrial complex at the centre of things where it has remained to this day, even increasing in importance in recent years despite the end of the Cold War.[8] A presence in Korea had been a part of US planning since at least 1942 and there is no reason to suppose that, once there, they would willingly leave.[9] The US retains bases in many places 60 years after the war where there is no apparent justification; Germany is an obvious case. However, the war in Korea did much to anchor the US military into the Korean peninsula, and Japan, to an extent that would not have been sustainable without it. The war also allowed the South Korean military to recast itself from being primarily a vehicle of internal suppression to being one which was defending the country against an external enemy, and the continued domestic suppression could be presented as a necessary containment of fifth columnists. It enabled opponents of the regime, and Koreans in the north, to be externalised; 'North Korea' became as much a foreign country as China or Japan. So effective was the Korean War in legitimising the US military presence, and the role of the South Korean military, which was to dominate society for close on four decades after the war, that one of the functions of the annual US-ROK military exercises is to refresh memories of the war (see Chapter 6).

The Korean War left scarcely any family in the peninsula untouched, and led to a deep polarisation which lasts to today.

Although young people especially are moving on, the war still scars the older generation. One of the big differences between German reunification and that in Korea is that Germany did not have to face the heritage of a civil war.

The Korean War also had profound effects on the region. Although early US plans to de-industrialise postwar Japan had been abandoned because of developments on the Asian mainland, particularly the success of the Communists in the Chinese civil war, the Japanese economy of the late 1940s was in the doldrums and many considered that it would never again be a major economic power. The Korean War changed all that and it provided the 'elixir' which revitalised the Japanese economy.[10] It also rehabilitated Japan in the eyes of Washington. The United States restored Japan's independence and allowed, even encouraged, the process of remilitarisation which is such a potent force today in fuelling the crisis in Japan–DPRK relations. The United States also moved to protect the rump Nationalist government on Taiwan from Communist invasion, thus preserving the de facto independence of Taiwan, with profound consequences. The Korean War also led the United States to the Vietnam War and did much to fashion US policy, and attitudes, towards the East for the rest of the century, and beyond.

The origins of the war itself, and the role of Stalin, remain a contentious issue, despite US access to Soviet archives which give a detailed account accepted by most historians.[11] Full-scale fighting erupted on 25 June 1950 with a Northern offensive that took Seoul within three days. The DPRK described this as a 'counter-attack' although few outside observers accept this claim if for no other reason than its astonishing military success. However, Syngman Rhee had been boasting that his army was going to march North and unify the country and there had been frequent skirmishes between the two sides. Despite the boasts of Syngman Rhee and his generals, it was apparent after the event that they were no match for the North, and presumably they were aware of this beforehand. And therefore, some have suggested that it was precisely because they were weak and wanted to embroil the United States in their war that they provoked an attack from the North.[12] Perhaps the most balanced assessment, though one attacked by many conservatives, is that by Bruce Cumings.[13] He notes:

> The point is not that North Korea was an innocent party to this fighting [mutual incursion prior to 25 June] but that both sides were at fault – and

according to several statements by General Roberts, the KMAG commander, the South started more of the battles than did the North.[14]

The outbreak of the Korean War may best be viewed as primarily a Korean matter, analogous to the civil wars in seventeenth-century England, nineteenth-century America or twentieth-century China. However, in the Korean case, the intervention of outsiders made the crucial difference. It was the intervention of the Chinese in late 1950 that saved the DPRK from extinction. They drove the United Nations forces down past Seoul but were subsequently pushed back to what became the DMZ and fierce fighting for two years did little to move the line of control. What was ostensibly the United Nations Command (UNC) was essentially the US by another name. Americans made up the bulk of the forces, and were even more dominant in terms of firepower, logistics and materiel. But it was in terms of command and control that the American role was most pronounced. As in Iraq a half-century later, whatever the title, be it UNC or Coalition, there was no doubt who was in charge. When the armistice finally came to be signed in 1953 there were two signatories – General Nam Il of the Korea People's Army for the DPRK and the PRC, and US Lt Gen. William K. Harrison for the United Nations. The Republic of Korea was not a signatory, an absence that was to bedevil Seoul's attempt to insert itself into the confrontation between Pyongyang and Washington in later years, especially from Kim Dae-jung onwards.

By comparison with the American involvement, the Chinese intervention was relatively short-lived – the last Chinese troops withdrew in 1958. The Soviet Union had no direct role in the conflict, although it supplied much materiel and some advisors. Both China and Russia after a time established diplomatic and economic links with the Republic of Korea. By 2003 it had become China's fourth largest export market (4.8 per cent) and third largest source of imports (9.7 per cent). China is now the ROK's largest trading partner and destination for FDI. The United States is different. Not only did the US rescue the ROK, it nearly destroyed the DPRK (coming close to precipitating a nuclear war against China in the process) and it has continued to dominate the South ever since; the commander of the Korean–US combined forces command is an American, his deputy a South Korean.[15] It still has some 37,000 troops in Korea, as well as bases in the region, especially Okinawa. It nuclearised the Korean peninsula. It threatened to use nuclear weapons several times during the Korean War and since, and deployed them in the South from 1958, contrary to the Armistice Agreement. The number of nuclear warheads reached a peak of 950 warheads in 1967. With the passage of time local deployment became unnecessary and in 1992 President George H. Bush in theory removed the remaining weapons, although this is disputed by the DPRK.[16] The North Korean claim was usually dismissed by most observers but, according to South Korean press reports, de-classified documents obtained by the Japanese Kyodo agency in 2004 told a different story:

> The newly declassified documents also showed the U.S. kept nuclear weaponry in South Korea until at least 1998, despite officially claiming it had withdrawn all nuclear warheads in 1991, Kyodo reported.[17]

Moreover, The US continues today openly to discuss developing new-generation nuclear weapons for use in Korea even while demanding that the DPRK abandon nuclear weapons.[18]

The lessons of Inchon

Korea, being a long, thin peninsula, invites outflanking amphibious landings if the defence is stretched and can offer only light resistance at the beachhead. This was the case at Inchon where the US marshalled 80,000 troops against a few thousand defenders on the shore. This could not be replicated after the Chinese intervened in force but it probably put any postwar Northern attempt at replicating the June 25 offensive off the agenda, despite the frequent claim that the United States needs to keep a military presence in Korea to deter an invasion from the North. Moreover, an amphibious landing, bypassing the heavily defended DMZ, would probably be the best way for US/ROK forces to invade the DPRK. Joint amphibious exercises are a feature of US preparedness, and are also used as part of the coercive part of coercive diplomacy when it wants to put pressure on Pyongyang, such as, for instance, during the 2004 Six-Party Talks.[19] For its part, Pyongyang tested shore-to-ship missiles about the time Roh Moo-hyun was being inaugurated in February 2003, presumably as a (rather ham-fisted) statement of its defensive capabilities.[20]

This continued, deep-level involvement by the United States in Korean affairs requires explanation, and this will be offered in the course of this book. In recent years the DPRK has become the main ostensible justification for the US Strategic Missile Defense Initiative, although it is widely acknowledged that the real target is, in fact, China.[21] Tension with the DPRK, and the portrayal of a 'North Korean threat' which is widely believed, though it is mainly hype rather than reality, has served in the past to keep South Korea and Japan in line, and estranged from China. The DPRK maintains very substantial armed forces and although it will be argued that the reason for this is mainly defensive and primarily a response to a perceived threat from the US and the ROK, their existence can be plausibly advanced as justification for a US military presence – the 'tripwire' to deter aggression. However, beyond all these specific causes there is an underlying animus against the DPRK which prevents them being solved. This forms a bedrock on which the more tangible reasons sit. The Korean War was the first war that the United States did not win. Coming just a few years after it had defeated the formidable axis powers led by Germany and Japan it was fought to a standstill by an Asian peasant army, 'ragged and ill-equipped' in Acheson's words.

Timeline 3   The Korean War

1950

25 June	Outbreak of Korean War; US as UN Secretary General to convene Security Council
28 June	Seoul falls to North Korean forces
30 June	Truman orders US ground forces to Korea
7 July	MacArthur appointed UN commander in Korea
15 September	UN forces make amphibious landing at Inchon
1 October	Third ROK Division crosses 38th parallel
2 October	Chinese premier Zhou Enlai issues warning, via Indian ambassador in Beijing that if US forces cross the 38th parallel China will enter the war
26 October	UN forces reach Chinese border
27–31 October	Chinese launch first offensive
30 November	President Truman refers to possible use of atomic bombs in Korea
4 January	Fall of Seoul to Communist forces
1951	
1 March	UN forces recapture Seoul
11 April	Truman dismisses MacArthur; Matthew Ridgeway named new Supreme Commander
10 July	Armistice talks begin in Kaesong (DPRK, PRC, UNC)
12 November	Operation Ratkiller begins against suspected guerrilla groups in South Korea
1952	
18 February	USSR claims that UN Command is using biological warfare in Korea

| 25 May | President Syngman Rhee declares martial law in Pusan |
| December | Dwight Eisenhower, President-elect, inspects Korean military situation |

1953

5 March	Death of Joseph Stalin
10 July	Syngman Rhee refuses to sign, but agrees not to disrupt, the Armistice Agreement
27 July	Armistice Agreement signed at 10.00. Lt Gen. William K. Harrison signs for UN, Gen Nam Il for NK and China

Martin Woollacott, writing of the United States' reluctance to come to terms with the limits of its power in respect of Iraq, notes:

> All three countries [of the 'Axis of Evil'] had imposed notable defeats on the United States. North Korea, with the help of China, sent American forces reeling back from the Yalu half a century ago. ..//..These things rankled with many powerful Americans. Others, by contrast, took them as evidence of the limits of the possible, as the result of mistaken American policies, or even as indications that these 'enemy' countries might be to some extent in the right. ..//.. The American instinct for revenge, evident also in the treatment of Vietnam, Cuba, Nicaragua and, for many years, China, is more marked than that of other powers. Perhaps America's lack of the experience of defeat on its own continent made reverses in the wider world especially difficult to swallow when they inevitably came.[22]

This 'grudge' has informed much of American thinking and has hindered, perhaps prevented, the resolution of the problems unleashed by the Korean War.

1954–72: POSTWAR RECONSTRUCTION AND CONTESTATION

The Armistice was precisely that, merely a cessation of actual fighting, and did not lead to a peace treaty though there have been a number of attempts over the years to bring this about. Tension on the Korean peninsula has gone up and down, often as a result of events far away. That was inevitable given the relationship of the two Korean states to their patrons, but it was mainly due to the continued involvement of the United States. In America the Korean conflict became 'the forgotten war', as often attention was focussed elsewhere, first in Europe, where lay the main confrontation with the Soviet Union, and a less visible one with Western Europe, and next in the Middle

East, with conflicts over oil and Israel, and third elsewhere in Asia, especially Vietnam and China. Nevertheless, the US continued to play a dominant role in the affairs of the peninsula. It nurtured the ROK with massive civilian and military aid, to which should be added the local expenditure on US forces in Korea. It provided a market for the South's export-led growth, and access to technology. The 'Miracle on the River Han', as the South Korean economic success came to be called, after the river running through Seoul, was based on the US relationship. Success was by no means automatic and in many ways it was due to the ability of Park Chung-hee and his successors, and the South Korean elite generally, to stand up to the Americans, and even to manipulate them; Sun Myung Moon's Unification Church was particularly adept at this.

Timeline 4   From Armistice to 1972 joint communiqué

1953
16 August	ROK and US sign Mutual Defense Treaty
19 September	DPRK–USSR agreement on economic cooperation
23 November	DPRK and PRC conclude agreement on cultural and economic cooperation

1954
15 June	Announcement of the failure of the Geneva Conference to solve the Korea problem

1955
15 February	DPRK proposes diplomatic relations to Japan
15 December	Foreign Minister Pak Hon-yong, leader of southern Communists, is sentenced to death in Pyongyang on charges of espionage for ROK

1956
23 April	Third Congress of KWP; Kim Il Sung elected chairman

1957
1 January	Five-Year Plan (1957–61). Emphasis on heavy industry; completed one year early in 1960
18 October	Plenary session of KWP CC adopts principle of political self-reliance
November	Kim Il Sung visits USSR for 40th anniversary of October Revolution

1958
January	US deploys nuclear weapons in SK
26 October	Chinese forces complete their withdrawal from DPRK

1960

27 April	Syngman Rhee resigns as president and goes into exile
June	Sino–Soviet split becomes public

1961

11 July	PRC-DPRK Treaty of Friendship, Cooperation and Mutual Assistance
16 May	Military coup in South Korea led by Major General Park Chung-hee overthrows Chang Myon government
10 July	Treaty of Friendship, Cooperation and Mutual Assistance between DPRK and USSR signed

1962

5 June	DPRK joins International Olympic Committee

1967

13 December	Conviction in Seoul of 34 alleged North Korean spies, kidnapped from West Germany
1967	US nuclear arsenal in SK peaks at an estimated 950 warheads in eight types of weapons. By the mid 1980s the number will drop to about 150 warheads

1968

21 January	DPRK guerrillas infiltrate Seoul and attack Chong Wa Dae (presidential palace)
23 January	US intelligence ship USS Pueblo seized by North Korean naval vessels
1 July	Sixty-two nations (including the US and USSR, but not NK) sign the Nuclear Non-Proliferation Treaty (NPT)

1969

9 October	DPRK signs trade agreement with Finland

1970

31 March	Japanese Red Army terrorist group hijacks Japan Airlines 'Yodo' airliner to North Korea

1971

1 January	Six-Year Economic Development Plan (1971–76) launched
23 August	Unit 684 rebels, tries to kill Park Chung-hee

1972

1 January	Kim Il Sung proposes inter-Korean peace treaty
21 February	Nixon's surprise visit to China; Sino–US rapprochement and the 'China card'
4 July	Joint North–South Communiqué which stipulates that unification should be based on three principles: Jaju (self-determination), peaceful means and grand national unity
27 December	New North Korean state constitution; Kim Il Sung becomes president

Syngman Rhee became increasingly unpopular and autocratic after the war, and economic growth was slow. He was ousted in a student-led protest in 1960, flown by the US to exile in Hawaii (where he had spent much of his earlier life) and died, not much lamented either in Korea or Washington, in 1965. There was a brief period of democratic rule before the coup led by Park Chung-hee, which established a series of military governments that lasted until 1992. Park Chung-hee is credited with establishing the framework for rapid economic growth, and a state which while being repressive and violent, was effective both domestically and internationally. Domestically it was able to contain dissent without recourse to US intervention, and in time gain legitimacy, not unchallenged but widely accepted. Corruption was, and remains, endemic but it took place within in the context of a 'strong state' and therefore unlike, say, Indonesia (a 'weak state') it did not de-rail economic growth. Internationally, the ROK whilst utilising US patronage was able to create a certain degree of space for itself, establishing diplomatic and economic relations with an increasing number of states, so much so that for much of the world it came to be seen and described simply as 'Korea', in contradistinction to the DPRK which remained 'North Korea'. One place, outside the Socialist bloc, where the DPRK did in a sense hold its own was, ironically, Japan. Koreans in Japan, many of whom had been forcibly conscripted in the prewar period, and harshly treated, tended to look towards the DPRK rather than the ROK, presumably because it was seen as a stronger symbol of Korean nationalism and culture. More than 90,000 chose to emigrate to the DPRK between 1959 and 1984 even though the majority had originally come from the South. For the Japanese government it was a form of 'ethnic cleansing', helping rid Japan of an unwelcome minority who were prone to crime and needing social assistance.[23]

Much the same process of pursuing economic growth and modernisation on one hand, while seeking domestic and international legitimacy on the other, went on in the North. The differences were considerable but so were the similarities. There has been a tendency from all quarters to emphasise the former, often taking rhetoric at face value without analysis, and neglect the latter. For example, a concerted programme of propaganda and conscious indoctrination, which the North is always accused of, actually was a vital component of both states. Significantly, when that programme eased off in the South under the impact of democratisation in the 1990s, there developed a quite distinct generational split in attitudes towards

Political dynasties: Park – father and daughter

Park Chung-hee was born in 1917 and, like many others, saw service to the empire not only as the route to personal success but perhaps also as the natural thing to do. He did well in the Japanese military and served as a lieutenant in the imperial army in Manchuria, taking the Japanese name Masao Tagaki. Did Park/Takagi see himself as unpatriotic, as a collaborator? Probably no more so than those who served the British Raj and then went on to command the armies of India and Pakistan.

In 1945 he joined the (South) Korean military academy but was arrested in 1948, during the Yosu mutiny, as a Communist. He was sentenced to death, but this was commuted by President Syngman Rhee, on advice from his American military advisor, James Hausman. Park turned over a list of supposed Communists in the armed forces and joined military intelligence where his job was to hunt down, yes, Communists. He led a coup in 1961 against the short-lived democratic government that took over after the fall of Syngman Rhee. His past at first alarmed the Americans but the US embassy in Seoul pointed out that he was no danger 'mainly because his defection from communists and turnover apparatus (sic) would make him victim no. 1 if communists ever took power'.[24] The embassy wasn't quite right because Park was no puppet; he wrested a considerable amount of independence from the Americans whilst yet again doing his duty to the empire; for instance a large contingent of troops were sent to Vietnam. However, he counterbalanced US influence by establishing diplomatic relations with her allies. Most important, he disregarded US economic advice and followed the Japanese model to establish a corporatist, export-led but relatively self-sufficient economy, with echoes of the North's *Juche*. His style was dictatorial and repressive, but effective and he is widely seen as the father of South Korean economic success. There is today nostalgia amongst substantial segments of the South Korean electorate for the certainties of his reign, and this has worked to the benefit of his daughter, Park Geun-hye.

Park Chung-hee was assassinated by the head of the Korean Central Intelligence Agency, Kim Jae-kyu, on 26 October 1979, during a whisky-fuelled dinner discussing how to cope with popular discontent.[25] After a short interregnum, Park was succeeded by two other generals, Chun Doo-hwan (who perpetrated the Kwangju massacre in 1980 in which hundreds died[26]) and Roh Tae-woo, until civilian rule was established with the election of Kim Young-sam in 1992.

The Park family did not bow out of Korean history with the assassination. Park Geun-hye, a computer science graduate from the Jesuits' Sogang University and already a member of the National Assembly, rose to prominence in 2002, partly by undertaking a well-publicised visit to North Korea, where she met Kim Jong Il.

In March 2004 she was elected leader of the opposition Grand National Party and immediately set about distancing herself from the previous conservative leadership and its role in the botched impeachment of President Roh Moo-hyun. She started to reposition the GNP, questioning the National Security Law, announcing a visit to the Kwangju cemetery that commemorates the victims of Chun Doo-hwan's massacre, and declaring herself ready to be special envoy to North Korea, and mediator between Pyongyang and Washington.[27]

the North.[28] State building, in the Confucian tradition, was achieved not so much by force but by incessant persuasion and an emphasis on the moral qualities of the leader.

Moral qualities were not sufficient in themselves, and leaders had to deliver economic benefits. In this the North was more successful than the South during this early period, but that superiority was not to last, because it was built on shaky foundations, which finally crumbled in 1990 with the collapse of the Soviet Union. Significant economic growth was achieved but it was based ultimately on a particular trade/aid relationship with the Soviet Union. This allowed industry to be rapidly developed and this, in turn, fed into higher agricultural yields based on industrial inputs in four categories – chemical fertilisers, mechanisation, irrigation and electrification.

By the end of 1953 the DPRK had established aid, trade and support agreements with both the Soviet Union and China. This balancing of the two patrons was to become an inevitable characteristic of foreign policy, and became more marked after the Sino–Soviet split, which became public in 1960. Seoul had but one sun in the sky, Washington, but Pyongyang had two and this basic fact dominated the international strategies of both Koreas. However, neither of them neglected other heavenly bodies, despite the familiar journalistic cliches about North Korea being a new 'hermit kingdom'. As early as February 1959 the DPRK was proposing diplomatic relations with Japan, a goal that has still not been achieved. In 1962 it joined the International Olympic Committee and in 1969 signed a trade agreement with Finland. The 1960s also saw overtures being made to the United States although these were overshadowed by incidents such as the capture of the US spy ship Pueblo in 1961 (a year after the Soviet Union shot down the American U2, capturing Gary Powers).

Kim Il Sung survived the aftermath of the Korean War, when he was susceptible to internal criticism and vulnerable to a Chinese-sponsored 'regime change' had they so desired, and consolidated his position. There were basically three contending groups – those who had worked with the Chinese Communists, Southern Communists (the Communist party had, after all, been founded in Seoul, and was centred there), and his own group, tied together by experience in Manchuria and the Soviet Union. Kim outmanoeuvred his rivals, and in December 1995, Pak Hon-yong, Foreign Minister and leader of the Southern Communists, was sentenced to death on charges of espionage for the ROK.

Political dynasties: Kim – father and son

Kim Il Sung was born on 15 April 1912 at Manyongdae, outside Pyongyang and died 8 July 1994, aged 82. His reconstructed birthplace is now a national shrine, as is his mausoleum, the Kumsusan Memorial Palace where his embalmed body lies in state, to be viewed by foreigners and Koreans. Curiously it appears that schoolchildren are not taken to the mausoleum. His birthday is celebrated as a national holiday (Day of the Sun) and the DPRK uses a Juche dating system much as was done in the French Revolution. The Juche era starts with Kim's birth and years are numbered from that, so that 2004 is Juche 93. It is used in addition to the international one.

His eldest son, Kim Jong Il, was born 16 February 1941, or 1942, near Khabarovsk or on the slopes of the sacred Mt Paektu, depending on source. In 1974 he was formally designated as successor to his father, something which was unique in an avowedly Socialist country. The succession seems to have proceeded smoothly, and surprisingly slowly, after Kim Il Sung's death. The only public expression of protest in North Korea was the defection of Hwang Jang Yop in 1997; he apparently told the Americans on a visit to Washington in 2003 that he still admired Kim Il Sung, but loathed the son.[29] The designation of President has been reserved, in perpetuity, for Kim Il Sung, as has the title of *Suryong* (Great Leader). Kim Jong Il is referred to as *Yongdoja* (Dear Leader) and has the positions of Secretary-General of the Korean Workers' Party and Chairman of the National Defence Commission. Lacking the charisma of his father he was portrayed abroad as a playboy. His reception of Kim Dae-jung during the Pyongyang Summit of June 2000, with a Confucian deference to the older man, was a shock to South Koreans brought up on many years of hostile propaganda. As a result he became, for a while, a bit of a cult figure. Very little reliable information is available on him, and balanced appraisals are uncommon, but he is seen as intelligent, well-informed with a special interest in information technology which he regards as a key to his country's economic rehabilitation.

He is often referred to as 'General' and is credited with the *Songun*, or 'army-first' policy, but he has no military training or background (on the contrary his early love was film) and it is likely that this is to keep the military onside as he tries to move ahead cautiously with economic reform, opening to the outside world, and technological modernisation, while keeping the US at bay. No easy task.

Domestic opposition was only part of the story. Both North and South were active in trying to destabilise each other. By some reports up to 10,000 agents were sent by Seoul to the North between 1953 and 1972 to 'destroy strategic facilities or collect information'.[30] It would be surprising if assassination had not also been on the agenda.

That was certainly the charge in the other direction where it was claimed that 'North Korean guerrillas' attacked the presidential palace (Chong Wa Dae, or the Blue House) on 21 January 1968 in an attempt to assassinate Park Chung-hee. They were unsuccessful and Park set up Unit 684 to train to assassinate Kim Il Sung. The strange story of this hit team was hidden for many years and only really surfaced when it became the subject of a blockbuster South Korean film, *Silmido* in 2003. The film claims that the 31 members of the unit were recruited from ex-criminals who were given little choice and certainly their fate was dreadful. They were trained on the offshore island of Silmido, but by the time their training was finished, in 1969, relations between Seoul and Pyongyang had thawed and the raid was put off. The men were kept on Silmido and it was said that the authorities considering that disbanding the unit was too dangerous decided to machine-gun them. However, before that could happen Unit 684 rebelled in August 1971, killed their trainer/guards and made their way to Seoul. There they were surrounded by loyal troops; most committed suicide but four were arrested and subsequently executed.[31]

The following January, Kim Il Sung in his annual New Year speech proposed an inter-Korean peace treaty. Talks were held by mid year and on 4 July 1972 the historic Joint North–South Communique was signed. The first of seven clauses stated that:

The two sides reached an agreement on the following principles of the reunification of the country:

- Firstly, reunification should be achieved independently, without reliance upon outside force or its interference;
- Secondly, reunification should be achieved by peaceful means, without recourse to the use of arms against the other side;
- Thirdly, great national unity should be promoted first of all as one nation, transcending the differences of ideology, ideal and system.[32]

The communiqué did not bear fruit (see below), at least not until the Pyongyang Summit of June 2000, but it did set the format for detente, and the subsequent 'Basic Agreement' of 1991/92. The reference to 'outside force or its interference', and the date, American Independence Day, is significant and is a clear reference to the United States. The year 1972 was that of Nixon's famous visit to China, and détente was in the air.

The Republic of Korea was not the only US ally to harbour thoughts of more independence. Relations between America and Western Europe were not without their frictions, though nothing in comparison with the venom of the Sino–Soviet schism. However, in the early 1970s there were developments which were to have repercussions on the Korea peninsula 30 years later. In 1970 Britain, Germany and the Netherlands agreed in the Treaty of Almelo 'to develop centrifuges to enrich uranium jointly, ensuring their nuclear power industry a fuel source independent of the United States'. It is said that this technology was subsequently transferred by a Dutch company to Pakistan and from there, in the 1990s, by Pakistan's 'Father of the A-bomb', Abdul Qadeer Khan, to the DPRK.[33] Ironically, if the DPRK does have an enriched uranium programme it may be not so much for weapons, which is the usual assumption, but for the same reasons as the Europeans – to produce an independent source of fuel for nuclear power stations.[34] This possibility was reinforced by a statement of Ri Gun (DPRK deputy chief delegate to the Beijing Six-Party talks 2003/04) at a conference in the US in August 2004: 'Asked whether North Korea has a uranium enrichment program for peaceful purposes, however, Ri only replied, "We are entitled to have it for peaceful purposes".'[35]

1973–84: A DECADE OF FALTERING STEPS

The DPRK made repeated attempts to break out of US encirclement during this period as its economic strength vis-à-vis the ROK began to wane. At some stage during this decade, according to calculations by Professor Hwang Eui-gak of Korea University in Seoul, the per capita GNP of the South began to exceed that of the North.

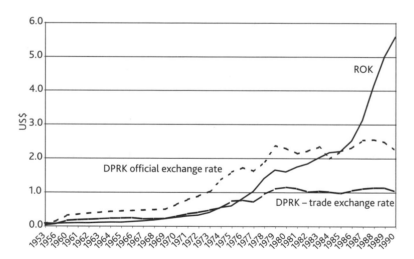

Source: Appendix I, Table A1.1

Figure 2.1   Per capita GNP, North and South Korea, 1953–90

Exactly when depends on the exchange rate chosen. If the trade rate between US$ and DPRK won is used the crossover comes in 1976, and if the official rate is used the date is 1984. The reasons for this reversal of fortune are complex, and there are some very differing opinions, but in many ways it was a reflection of the unequal competition between the Soviet Union and the United States. The ROK was in the right camp, and because of the existence of the DPRK (and China) it had sufficient leverage to reap the benefits while avoiding the dangers of peripheralisation, as evidenced by Latin America. The Soviet bloc was, for a variety of reasons, a poor economic partner for the DPRK, despite the advantages of oil at below world-market prices. Pyongyang tried, without success, to normalise relations with Washington and there is one report that in September 1980 Kim Il Sung offered 'to abandon 1961 treaties with China and Russia if the United States begins negotiations for a peace treaty'.[36] This proposal came, it will be noted, a year after the United States established diplomatic relations with the People's Republic of China, relegating Taiwan to unofficial status. However, China was big and could not be ignored forever. It was also a useful card to use against the Soviet Union. The DPRK was not in this league. There was a period of hope, and perhaps missed opportunity, in the early years of the Carter presidency. In 1976 Jimmy Carter announced plans to withdraw US forces from Korea, but he was not able to overcome bureaucratic and military opposition and not much came of it. Whether a positive response from Pyongyang would have swung the balance is an unexplored issue.

Pyongyang tried to outflank Washington by establishing relations with its allies, and with international organisations. Relations with the Nordic countries in 1973 were followed by diplomatic relations with Australia in July 1974. This latter one did not last long, and the DPRK closed its embassy in Canberra in October 1975 over an argument about an Australian vote in the UN.[37] The DPRK joined the World Health Organization (WHO) in 1973, the International Atomic Energy Agency (IAEA) and the Food and Agriculture Organization (FAO) in 1977. Although the relationship with IAEA has been difficult those with WHO and FAO seem to have been less troubled. The FAO, in particular, has been deeply involved in the DPRK since the food crisis of the mid 1990s.

The opening to the West was not confined to the diplomatic front. There was an attempt in the early 1970s to break into economic ties with Western Europe but this ran foul of the 1974 oil shock and the drop in demand for DPRK exports, and Pyongyang was left with substantial debts which it has not been able to renegotiate.

Timeline 5   1973–84

1973

30 March	Nordic foreign ministries announce that their countries will establish diplomatic relations with North Korea
18 April	DPRK exports cement to Japan for first time
17 May	DPRK joins World Health Organization (WHO)
8 August	South Korean opposition leader Kim Dae-jung kidnapped in Tokyo and brought to Seoul; DPRK suspends talks in protest

1974

20 March	DPRK proposes a peace treaty with US
31 July	Australia and North Korea establish diplomatic relations
15 August	Assassination attempt on Park Chung-hee by pro-North Korean from Japan. Park's wife killed
16 September	DPRK joins the International Atomic Energy Agency (IAEA)

1975

April	Fall of Saigon to North Vietnamese forces. Kim Il Sung visits Beijing

1976

9 March	US President Jimmy Carter announces plan to withdraw US forces from Korea
18 August	Axe affair in Joint Security Area at Panmunjom
9 September	Mao Zedong dies

1977

14 November	DPRK joins Food and Agriculture Organization (FAO)

1978

April	ROK's first nuclear power station comes into operation; by early 1980s a further eight are under construction

1979

January	US and China normalise relations
26 October	Assassination of Park Chung-hee by head of Korean Central Intelligence Agency
12 December	General Chun Doo-hwan stages coup and arrests Martial Law Commander General Chung Sung-hwa

1980

27 May	Kwangju massacre, hundreds killed

1981

12 January	Chun Doo-hwan proposes a North–South summit meeting

1983

9 October   Rangoon bombing; attempted assassination of Chun Doo-hwan

1984

10 January   Joint meeting of Central People's Committee and SPA proposes a non-aggression pact with ROK and peace treaty with US

8 September   DPRK Joint Venture Law promulgated. It consists of 26 articles dealing with foreign investment

29 September   Arrival of North Korean flood-relief goods in South Korea

15 November   First round of North–South economic cooperation talks at Panmunjom

Although the ROK was moving ahead fast economically (its first nuclear power station came into operation in 1978) it had more than its share of political violence. In August 1974 there was another assassination attempt on Park Chung-hee while he was giving an address, by a Korean Japanese. Park escaped by hiding behind the armour-plated rostrum, but his wife (and Park Geun-hye's mother) were fatally wounded. Apparently Park continued his address while his wife's body was carted away. He did not survive the third attempt, by KCIA director Kim Jae-kyu, in October 1979. This was followed shortly afterwards in December by another coup, led by Chun Doo-hwan. In May the following year there were demonstrations in the southern city of Kwangju, which were brutally suppressed by Chun. It is not known how many were killed, but even the official accounts say hundreds. In comparative terms it was a far greater massacre than China's Tiananmen Incident in 1989, but whereas China still refuses to condemn the crackdown, the National May 18 Cemetery in Kwangju has become a place of pilgrimage for politicians across the spectrum.[38] Chun Doo-hwan (and his successor Roh Tae-woo) were put on trial by Kim Young-sam in 1996, and convicted on charges of treason, mutiny and corruption. Chun was sentenced to death but this was commuted.[39] The United States, whose permission was necessary before troops could be used, has not apologised for its complicity.

In October 1983 there was a major assassination attempt on Chun Doo-hwan and many of his entourage in Rangoon where he was on the first stage of a six-nation Asian tour. Chun escaped but 17 Koreans and four Burmese were killed. Although Kim Il Sung dismissed the accusation against the DPRK as 'a preposterous slander', the Myanmar government caught three North Koreans – one was killed at the time, another hanged and the third, Kang Min-chol, is according to a report, happy in Insein gaol in Myanmar, where he is serving a life sentence and studying English and Buddhism.[40] Myanmar broke off relations with the DPRK and they have not been restored. The bombing followed just a month after the downing of Korean Airlines flight KE007 by Soviet fighters when it infringed airspace (about which there are countless conspiracy theories), and the two incidents proved valuable for both Chun and the US. 'The Rangoon bombing and the airline incident silenced those who had claimed that Chun exaggerated the Communist threat for his political purposes', says a Western diplomat. 'There are few doubters now. The threat from North Korea is very, very persuasive and gives the government a certain leeway.'[41]

The Rangoon bombing remains a mystery because it was so predictably counter-productive and was out of kilter with the general thrust of DPRK foreign policy. On 8 October 1983, one day before the bombing, Pyongyang passed a 'secret proposal via Chinese officials to the United States, suggesting [a] North, South and US meeting'.[42] The following January there was a high-level, public proposal for a non-aggression pact with the ROK and a peace treaty with the US, which it repeated in October.

In September of that year the DPRK signalled its desire for direct foreign investment by promulgating its first joint venture law. The same month it sent relief goods to the South, which was suffering from heavy flooding and by the end of the year Red Cross and economic meetings had been held between North and South.

1985–92: THE LOOMING CRISIS

Any moves towards peace were disrupted, once again, by joint US–ROK military exercises and the DPRK response. On 9 January 1984 the DPRK postponed Red Cross talks in protest again the joint US–ROK Team Spirit military exercises. These exercises have varied over time but there have traditionally been four: Team Spirit, Ulchi Focus Lens, RSOI (Reception, Staging, Onward moving and Integration) and Foal Eagle.[43] These exercises are considered by North Korea, reasonably enough, as threatening. The KPA has its own exercises but none, as far as is known, with allies such as China. Team Spirit was the major one, involving 200,000 troops – not so far below the 300,000 which the US deployed in the invasion of Iraq in March 2003. Team Spirit was suspended each year from 1994 to 1996 and cancelled from

1997. It was one of the main points of friction between the civilian government of President Kim Young-sam and the US.[44] It may be presumed that the ROK military tended to side with the US on this. However, in 1985 General Chun Doo-hwan was still in power and the exercises went ahead. These joint exercises have a significance that extends far beyond the mechanical military functions of training and testing the operability of weapons systems. They legitimise the US military presence and the huge role the ROK military plays even in contemporary South Korean society – the large military budget and standing army, and the military service imposed on young males – by creating a physical manifestation of the 'threat from the North'. Given, as we shall see in Chapter 6, the huge imbalance between the DPRK and the combined US/ROK military, there is a need to present some tangible display that a credible enemy threat exists and the well-publicised exercises are one of the ways in which this is done.

On 12 December that year the DPRK signed the Nuclear Non-Proliferation Treaty (NPT), a move that was to have momentous consequences, as is discussed in Chapter 7. They signed the NPT because that was the condition imposed by the Soviet Union for the construction of nuclear power stations, stations which in the end were never completed.

In 1985, the Soviet Union promised to give North Korea nuclear power for peaceful use, by constructing three 635 MWe LWRs in exchange for the DPRK's accession to the non-proliferation treaty and ratification of the IAEA safeguards regime. Pyongyang bought into this promise and joined the nuclear non-proliferation regime in the late 1980s–early 1990s. But the collapse of the USSR left the North without the much promised and long expected nuclear power industry and [saddled] it with the newly acquired nuclear non-proliferation obligations.[45]

The NPT is much misrepresented, with a virtually exclusive focus on the obligations of the non-nuclear-weapon states. The treaty was signed in 1968 (coming into force in 1970) by the five declared nuclear-weapon states (NWS) – US, USSR, UK, France and China – and a large number of non-nuclear-weapon states (NNWS), including ROK but excluding DPRK, India and Pakistan. India and Pakistan subsequently went on to become nuclear-weapon states outside the NPT. Israel is widely considered to have nuclear weapons and delivery systems. The NPT was basically a deal between the two groups of states in which the spread of nuclear weapons technology was to be stopped in exchange for assistance with the peaceful use of nuclear technology and a commitment by the NWS to

> ... pursue negotiations in good faith on effective measures relating to cessation of the nuclear arms race at an early date and to nuclear disarmament, and on a treaty on general and complete disarmament under strict and effective international control. (Article VI)[46]

The preamble reiterates that 'in accordance with the Charter of the United Nations, States must refrain in their international relations from the threat or use of force against the territorial integrity or political independence of any State ... '. The treaty explicitly allows withdrawal:

> Each Party shall in exercising its national sovereignty have the right to withdraw from the Treaty if it decides that extraordinary events, related to the subject matter of this Treaty, have jeopardized the supreme interests of its country. (Article X)

This article enabled the DPRK to join the NPT in 1985 because it was an exit clause that could be invoked if circumstances demanded it. That was to happen in January 2003 when it finally withdrew from the NPT, invoking Article X.

Concomitant with the prohibition on the use of force was the development of the concept of the strangely worded Negative Security Assurances (NSA). This is an undertaking by nuclear-weapon states not to use, or threaten to use, nuclear weapons against non-nuclear states. China, for one, has strongly advocated NSA, along with declarations of 'no first use', that is, nuclear weapons would only be used in retaliation for a nuclear attack.[47] The United States has shied away from commitment to 'no first use' but since 1978 has accepted NSA. The acceptance was partial and hedged:

> ...the United States has pledged not to use nuclear weapons against non-nuclear-weapon states that are members of the Nuclear Non-Proliferation Treaty (NPT), except if attacked by such a state that is allied with a state possessing nuclear weapons. At the same time, successive administrations have maintained a policy of 'strategic ambiguity' by refusing to rule out nuclear weapons use in response to attacks involving biological or chemical weapons.[48]

Since the DPRK has (nominally) a mutual defence treaty with China, a nuclear-weapon state, then it might be argued that the NSA does not apply. However, that legal loophole was not necessary because 'Iraq and North Korea are members of the NPT, but both have violated its terms by pursuing nuclear weapons and are not considered to be in good standing with the treaty'.[49] Interestingly that appraisal from the US NGO Arms Control Association was published in July 2002, at a time when the State Department was publicly stating that the DPRK was in compliance with the Agreed Framework, and hence with the NPT.

Nuclear non-proliferation is a laudable aim but if nuclear disarmament and adherence to UN principles forbidding the use, or threat of use of force, are ignored by nuclear-power states then it becomes a hollow and empty promise. The NPT is increasingly seen as a mechanism by which nuclear-power states, principally the US, maintain a monopoly on nuclear weapons. No country has a god-given right to nuclear weapons, denied to others. Countries, such as Pakistan or Libya may be cajoled, threatened and bribed into giving ostensible support to US anti-proliferation efforts, but there will be no real commitment. If the possession of a rudimentary retaliatory nuclear capacity is seen as the best defence of small states against the predations of large, then no amount of coercion couched in sanctimonious hypocrisy will avail. It is still uncertain whether the DPRK has been able to develop a deliverable nuclear weapons system, but that is its intention now, and the events of the last decade have made that inevitable. Other states will follow.

Timeline 6   1985–92

1985

9 January	North postpones full-scale Red Cross talks because of joint South Korea–US exercise Team Spirit
18–23 September	Exchange of North–South artistic troupes/home visit groups
12 December	NK signs the Nuclear Non-Proliferation Treaty. The Soviets require this as a condition of nuclear technology assistance. NK agrees to open new 30 mw experimental reactor to inspection by International Atomic Energy Agency.

1986

October	Kim Il Sung visits Moscow for talks with Soviet President Mikhail Gorbachev

1987

1 January	Third Seven-Year Plan (1987–93) begins
July	In July, SK President Chun resigns, appointing former general Roh Tae-woo his successor. SK adopts its 6th constitution (12 October). In December, Roh is elected president in SK's first direct election
11 November	North proposes five-point plan for reunification, including co-hosting 1998 Olympics
29 November	Korean Air Flight 858 blown up over Andaman Sea
14 December	Chief Command of the KPA announces that DPRK has reduced the number of its military personnel to (sic) about 100,000
16 December	Roh Tae-woo wins election (37 per cent); opposition split between Kim Young-sam (28 per cent) and Kim Dae-jung (27 per cent); Conservative Kim Jong-pil gets 8 per cent

1988

12 January	DPRK Olympic Committee announces it will not participate in 1988 Seoul Olympics
20 January	US State Department adds North Korea to its list of terrorist states because of the November 1987 aircraft bombing

1989

1 January	Kim Il Sung propose an Inter-Korean Consultation Conference for National Reunification in his New Year's address

1990

1 January	Kim Il Sung in New Year's address proposes a consultation conference involving top government authorities and leaders of political parties of North and South
4 September	First round of North–South prime ministers' talks in Seoul
28 September	A Joint Pyongyang–Tokyo communique for normalising diplomatic relations is announced in Pyongyang
2 November	Pyongyang and Moscow sign an accord to settle two-way trade in hard currency, discontinuing barter trade between the two countries

1991

17 September	DPRK and ROK simultaneously enter UN
27 September	US President George H. Bush announces worldwide withdrawal of US tactical nuclear weapons
13 December	North–South Agreement on Reconciliation, Non-aggression, Exchanges and Cooperation. North–South Joint

	Declaration on Denuclearisation of the Korean peninsula (came into effect in January 1992)
25 December	Soviet Union replaced by Russian Federation and Commonwealth of Independent States

The year 1987 saw the launch of the Third Seven-Year Plan (1987–93), a plan that was destined to be abandoned after the collapse of the Soviet Union. This year was notable for two major events. Firstly, in the South there was the transfer of power from Chun Doo-hwan to Roh Tae-woo, from one general to his subordinate, though both by this time were downplaying their military positions. Roh was very much a transitional figure, in preparation for civilian rule which came with his successor, Kim Young-sam. One of the many ironies of the Korean situation is that Park Chung-hee, Chun Doo-hwan and Roh Tae-woo, who were generals, hastened to shed their military titles at first opportunity, and were known as 'President', whereas Kim Jong Il, who has no military background, is known as 'General', the title of president being reserved in perpetuity for his father.

Roh won the election in December, partly because the opposition vote was split between Kim Young-sam (who won next time) and Kim Dae-jung (who won the time after that). However, Roh was also boosted in the polls by the explosion of Korean Air flight 858 over the Andaman Sea, off Myanmar, in which all 115 persons on board perished. Two 'North Korean agents' were apprehended in Bahrain; one committed suicide on the spot, the other, Kim Hyon-hee, known also by the Japanese name Mayumi, was brought to Seoul, arriving the day before the election. She was sentenced to death, this was commuted and she was released. Again theories abounded. It was a private killing masquerading as North Korean terrorism, just like the case of Suzi Kim, a Korean in Hong Kong whose murder was blamed on North Korea, but the villain turned out to be her husband. It was part of a deal between low-level operatives North and South, part of a pattern where DPRK agents would be bribed to create an incident at a convenient point in the ROK electoral calendar. It was personally ordered by Kim Jong Il, who was in charge of external terrorism. It was a special operation by the National Agency for Security Planning (ANSP; formerly the Korean Central Intelligence Agency) in order to bolster Roh's chances in the election; one estimate was that it garnered him 1.5 million votes. Whatever the truth, the doubts lingered and on 3 February 2004 a Seoul court ordered the disclosure of the prosecutor's investigation records. How long this investigation will take, or its outcome, remains unknown.[50] On 20 January 1988 the US State Department added the DPRK to its list of 'terrorist states' because of the KAL bombing, and it is still on that list despite repeated efforts to be removed; in fact it is one of the major demands of the DPRK. Since the State Department concedes that the DPRK '... is not known to have sponsored any terrorist acts since the bombing of a Korean Airlines flight in 1987', a revisiting of the issue could have important repercussions.[51]

Kim Hyon-hee claimed that the purpose of the bombing was to disrupt the forthcoming Seoul Olympics, the other main event of the period. As a motive this was very suspect since Pyongyang had put forward a new five-point plan for reunification, which included co-hosting the Olympics, on 11 November, a fortnight before the bombing. Wrangling over co-hosting continued into 1988 but the proposal was rejected and the DPRK boycotted the Olympics which started on 17 September. Holding the Olympic Games has become the rite of passage for emerging nations; the Tokyo Olympics in 1964 was widely regarded as marking Japan's postwar ascendancy. The same held for the ROK. The Seoul Olympics proved that it had made it and the exclusion of the DPRK demonstrated that the North had not. However, both Koreas ultimately suffer from the division and it was unfortunate that the Korean Olympics did not draw on the origin of the games: a way of bring warring states together.

Every year, in his New Year's Address, Kim Il Sung would reiterate calls for unification talks. How genuine those calls were must remain open to conjecture, and certainly each side would blame the other for any breakdown in talks. Negotiations never achieved a breakthrough, but they have continued, on and off, over the years with increasing frequency. There was also some progress on the Japan front, with a joint communiqué on normalising diplomatic relations issued on 28 September 1990, but that, so far, has still not happened.

COLLAPSE OF THE SOVIET UNION

What did happen, with awful and irrevocable effects on the DPRK, was the collapse of the Soviet Union, and the system of 'Socialist states' in Eastern Europe. This had a profound impact on the DPRK economy and on its security and political standing in the world, especially vis-à-vis the United States. If the DPRK did attempt to develop nuclear weapons capability in the 1990s, as alleged by the US, then this must have been in no small measure due to the removal of Soviet power, not so much as a bulwark against invasion or military action (because the USSR could not be depended upon to do that) but as a general counter-vailing and restraining force. It seems unlikely that the dismemberment of Yugoslavia and the invasions of Afghanistan and Iraq would have taken place if the Soviet Union had still been in existence. Clearly the DPRK felt much more vulnerable although whether this led to a nuclear weapons programme is another matter, which will be discussed shortly.

The relationship between politics and economics was illustrated by Russia's establishing of diplomatic relations with ROK on 30 September 1990, which was followed a little over a month later with its forcing the DPRK to sign an accord that trade would be conducted henceforth in hard currency and at world prices. The effect of this was catastrophic and Russian–DPRK trade plummeted. China followed suit in January 1992, though 'friendship prices' were continued, at least for a while. China also established diplomatic relations with ROK, on 24 August 1992, and the economic effects of that were astounding – over the next ten years trade increased seven-fold, ROK investment in China increased 80-fold, and the number of visitors in both direction, 23-fold.[52] What negative effect this had on the DPRK economy is unclear, but there could not have been much diversion effect. In the long term, especially with the reconnection of rail and road links, ROK–China economic interaction will be to the benefit of the DPRK.

The DPRK had long been resisting the individual entry of the two Korean states into the United Nations, on the ground that this would hamper reunification, but eventually it gave way and they both joined simultaneously on 17 September 1991. This had the important consequence that it gave the DPRK a de facto embassy in New York.

DENUCLEARISATION OF THE KOREAN PENINSULA?

In September 1991 US President George H. Bush announced worldwide withdrawal of US tactical nuclear weapons, and this included Korea. The Korean peninsula became, in theory, 'nuclear-free' and in December the North and South signed an 'Agreement on Reconciliation, Non-aggression, Exchanges and Cooperation' and the following January a 'North–South Joint Declaration on Denuclearisation of the Korean Peninsula'. The reconciliation promised many things which have not yet come to pass, though progress has been made. The denuclearisation agreement carried a clause which was to assume great importance a decade later – 'South and North Korea shall not possess nuclear reprocessing and uranium enrichment facilities'. In October 2002 the Bush administration charged the DPRK with having an enriched uranium programme and proceeded to dismantle the Agreed Framework signed, as we shall see in a moment, by the Clinton administration in 1994. The DPRK denied the charge, and was still denying it in September 2004 when the ROK admitted that it had itself been clandestinely working on uranium enrichment.[53] Actually, both Koreas have a common interest in having a home-based programme for enriching uranium as fuel for nuclear reactors.

'Denuclearisation of the Korean peninsula' was, and continues to be, a rather meaningless phrase not so much because of cheating – and both the US and the DPRK accuse each other of that – but because US nuclear weapons capability is global. Withdrawal of tactical weapons *from* the peninsula did not diminish their ability to use nuclear weapons *against* the peninsula. It would seem to have been a mistake of the DPRK not to get recognition of that built into the agreement.

Timeline 7   1992–94

1992

10 January	North Korea signs International Atomic Energy Safeguards Agreement
26 January	DPRK and China sign in Pyongyang an accord for hard currency payment in their mutual trade beginning that year
30 January	DPRK and IAEA sign in Vienna the nuclear safeguard accord
11 May	IAEA Director Hans Blix visits DPRK to tour research facilities at Yongbyon
5 October	The SPA adopts the Law on Foreign Investment, the Law on Foreign Enterprises, and the Law on Contractual Joint Ventures
18 December	Ruling party candidate, former opposition leader Kim Young-sam, elected president of South Korea
8 March	Order no. 34 is issued by Kim Jong Il, as supreme commander of KPA, to place the entire country of a 'semiwar footing' in response to US/ROK joint military exercises Team Spirit

1993

25 March	North Korea announces its withdrawal from the Nuclear Non-Proliferation Treaty

2–11 June	NK suspends withdrawal after US agrees to talk, talks last a bit more than a week. Joint statement says the two agree to 'principles of assurances against the threat and use of force, including nuclear weapons', peace on a nuclear-free peninsula, and support for the peaceful reunification of Korea.

1994

1 January	The Three-Year Stopgap Plan (1994–96) begins under a policy of agriculture first, light industry first, and foreign trade first
27 January	US evangelist Billy Graham makes second visit to North Korea
13 June	DPRK Foreign Ministry announces decision to withdraw from IAEA
15 June	Former US President Jimmy Carter in North Korea to discuss nuclear issue
28 June	North–South preliminary contact on summit agrees that Kim Young-sam will visit North Korea 25–27 July
8 July	Kim Il Sung dies of a heart attack at 82
10 September	Led by Lynn Turk, first US diplomatic mission to North Korea since the Korean War
11 October	A dedication ceremony of the Tomb of Tangun, legendary founder of Korea, is held in Pyongyang
21 October	North Korean and US delegates in Geneva sign an Agreed Framework on the supply of light-water nuclear reactors to North Korea
28 November	IAEA confirms that North Korean nuclear programme is halted

Despite the official withdrawal of tactical nuclear weapons, the nuclear weapons issue took on a new lease of life in the early 1990s and has dominated DPRK–US relations, and by extension, relations with Japan and ROK, since then. This is so central to the issues that it is covered in great detail in Chapter 7, with an extensive and detailed chronology in Appendix IV.

The story is complicated and few facts go uncontested. We are in a world of complex double and triple bluff and nothing is as it seems; it is not simply a matter of one conceals and the other reveals. Pyongyang has good reasons to deny having nuclear weapons if it has them, in order to avoid sanctions or other coercive action, but it might also claim to have weapons when it does not, in order to deter attack. The United States line is even more convoluted because it is a more open society. The US may claim that DPRK has nuclear weapons when it knows it does not, in order, for instance to justify Missile Defense, or to keep Japan on the diplomatic leash. On the other hand, it may deny that North Korea has nuclear weapons when it in fact believes it has them in order to hide a failure of containment. This may have been what has been happening in the runup to the 2004 presidential election. A major weapon in election campaigns, and US domestic policy generally, is the use of the media leak or planted story. David Sanger of the *New York Times* would write stories based on his sources in 'the intelligence community' and Glenn Kessler of the *Washington Post* would file stories from his sources. And behind the journalist can be discerned the shadows of bureaucrats, spooks, politicians and analysts seeking to change or confirm policy. On top of all this there is misinterpretation of messages between Pyongyang and Washington so even when deliberate deception is not in play cultural incompatibilities and arrogance may do just as well.

What is well established is that US satellites in 1989 detected that the research reactor at Yongbyon had been shut down for a period which, because there was no IAEA monitoring at the time, would have allowed plutonium to be extracted. There was no evidence, let alone proof, that the DPRK had actually produced nuclear weapons – merely a calculation based on assumptions about technological capability (and political commitment). Russian experts to whom I have spoken say that the Koreans do not have the technical resources to weaponise, a point that is corroborated by Selig Harrison, who has written probably the best book on the DPRK–US confrontation.[54] Further corroboration has recently come from an unlikely source. On 8 January 2004 Dr Siegfried Hecker, senior fellow at Los Alamos National Laboratory, was invited by the DPRK to visit Yongbyon in order to demonstrate that they now had a nuclear 'deterrent' from the reactor which had been reactivated following the collapse of the Agreed Framework in October 2002 (discussed below). He was part of a three-man unofficial mission led by Professor John W. Lewis of Stanford University. Hecker said in his testimony to the Senate Committee on Foreign Relations:

> So the last day I had several discussions with Ambassador Li Gun and also with the vice minister, when they said, once again, that 'Okay, we've demonstrated our deterrent'. And I went through the following. And I said, 'No, you haven't', because to me, it takes at least three things to have a deterrent. The first one is, you got to make plutonium metal. The second one is, you have to make a nuclear device. And the third one is, you have to integrate that nuclear device, weaponize it, into a delivery system of some sort. ...

The response was, 'Well, you know, you saw our people at Yongbyon. From their technical competence, can't you tell, and from the facilities?'. And I said, 'Absolutely not'. You know, what I saw was pretty good reactor physics and a lot of good chemical engineering to extract the plutonium, and maybe a little bit of metallurgy. But the next step takes a lot of physics, a lot of computation. It takes a lot more metallurgy. It takes the understanding of high explosives. You have to do some high explosives, non-nuclear testing, and then it takes the rest of the materials, and you have to know how to assemble it.

And so I had actually told them late on Friday morning, 'Look, bring me somebody that I can talk to about this, so that I can get a better sense. By dinner that night, they told me that's – it wasn't possible, there wasn't enough time to do so. And I said, 'Well, that's fine, but you'll have to understand that then I did not see a deterrent. I'm not able to make a judgment as to whether you either have built nuclear weapons or you know how to build nuclear weapons'.[55]

Hecker is implying that he gave the Koreans the opportunity to prove to him that they had a nuclear deterrent, but they did not and so we can assume that they could not. So when the DPRK was very anxious, in 2004, to convince the United States that they *had* nuclear weapons, they could not. And if they did not have the capability to weaponise in 2004, it seems unlikely that they had it in the early 1990s.

Nevertheless, the possibility was enough to ignite a crisis. This had probably more to do with the flammability of the US political system, where politicians constantly strive to outdo each other as 'patriots', and the need to generate enemies and threats in the post-Cold War world, than the issues themselves. Certainly the elevation of the DPRK into such a threat was preposterous, and yet is accepted without demur across the mainstream political spectrum (and deep into the Left for that matter). When the claims are examined dispassionately, as we do in Chapters 6 and 7, we see that North Korea's ability to project military power is very limited, and a tiny faction of that of its adversaries. We also see that even after the declaration of 10 February 2005 when the DPRK claimed that it had a nuclear deterrent it was highly unlikely that it had, in fact, a deliverable nuclear weapons system; certainly the South Korean National Intelligence Service was dismissive.[56] Similarly, General Leon J. LaPorte, commander of American forces in Korea (and hence of ROK forces as well), said in testimony in Washington in March 2005 that the North Korean long-range rocket Taepodong could be operational by 2015, and capable of reaching the west coast of the United States.[57] LaPorte was putting an alarmist spin on things for Congressional, and public, attention; as any general would. However, what he was also saying was that it was unlikely that the DPRK could deliver a nuclear weapon against the continental United States within ten years.

Despite the evidence, the 'North Korean threat' is too tempting for politicians to ignore. Senator Lugar, Chair of the Foreign Affairs Committee, regularly claims that 'The North Korean regime's drive to build nuclear weapons and other weapons of mass destruction poses a grave threat to American national security'.[58] On the hustings, presidential candidate Senator John Kerry, while promising to unveil 'specific plans to build a new military capable of defeating enemies both new and old' singles out the DPRK – 'North Korea poses a genuine nuclear threat'.[59]

In 1993 the CIA estimated that the DPRK had 'produced enough plutonium for at least one, and possibly two, nuclear weapons'. This was later amended, under political pressure it would seem, to an assertion that 'North Korea had produced one, possibly two, nuclear weapons'.[60] In 1993 the Clinton administration was contemplating airstrikes on the Yongbyon reactor. It seems that two people prevented the outbreak of war, and brought about negotiations which led to the signing of the Agreed Framework in 1994. Firstly, there was ROK President Kim Young-sam who told the Americans he would not tolerate it; it would have been the Korean peninsula, South and North, which would have suffered, not the US. Secondly, former President Jimmy Carter made a trip to Pyongyang, met Kim Il Sung, and with some deft footwork, outmanoeuvred the administration by giving a press conference outlining prospects for a negotiated settlement. Once it was in the open, the administration had no option but to go ahead.[61]

DEATH OF KIM IL SUNG

While the preliminary negotiations were going on the DPRK was struck by another blow. Kim Il Sung died on 8 July 1994, just a month after his meeting with Carter. He was 82, so his death was not unexpected, but it led to two surprises and one major setback. The world was taken aback by the manifest outpouring of grief in North Korea. The unknown number who felt no grief kept their feelings to themselves, but the public trauma was evident. It was in contrast to

Park Chung-hee's funeral where, although there were huge crowds, there was little mourning; US Assistant Secretary of State Richard Holbrooke observed 'There wasn't a wet eye in Seoul.'[62] Kim had dominated the landscape since the 1940s. The summit meeting that Kim Young-sam of South Korea was scheduled to have with Kim Il Sung on 25 July was a month too late. That in itself would have been a setback for the peace process, but not a major one. Negotiations with the US continued after Kim Il Sung's death. However, the North was very annoyed when President Kim did not send condolences and relations soured, not to be restored until Kim Dae-jung came into office.[63]

The big surprise, and one that has disconcerted many observers over the last decade, is that the regime survived the death of its founder. Despite the traumatic crises of this decade, and in particular the unremitting hostility of the Bush administration, the DPRK has survived.

3

Creation of the Agreed Framework and the Flowering of Détente

THE AGREED FRAMEWORK

The Agreed Framework, which was signed in Geneva on 21 October 1994, seemed to be the breakthrough that the DPRK had been striving for. True, the nuclear programme was suspended, and with it both the drive to develop an indigenous nuclear energy programme let alone the prospect, however distant, of developing a nuclear deterrent that would make an attack too expensive. However, the benefits, if achieved, would far outweigh this. The problem, as it turned out, was that the benefits were not delivered.

The Agreed Framework is a short document with four main clauses, each with three or four subclauses. It was signed by Bob Gallucci on behalf of the United States and Kang Sok Ju for the DPRK. It was the same Kang whom James Kelly was subsequently to confront in Pyongyang in October 2002 in the meeting which led to the collapse of the agreement. Although South Korea and Japan were saddled with the bulk of the cost of the reactors to be provided under the agreement, they were not party to its negotiation, nor indeed to its demolition.

The reactors, two light-water reactors (LWR) with a total generating capacity of approximately 2,000 MWe, were to replace the DPRK's graphite-moderated reactors and related facilities. They were to be provided by an international consortium led by the US. The energy forgone by the suspension of the DPRK facilities was to be replaced by heavy fuel oil (HFO) of up to 500,000 tons a year. Although the US was often to be close to default on delivery of oil, because of opposition from the by-then Republican-dominated Congress, this was the one provision that was fulfilled.

In return the DPRK was to freeze its reactors and to dismantle them once 'the LWR project is completed'. This sequencing was crucial and became one of the main bones of contention in later negotiation with the Bush administration which wanted the complete, verifiable and irreversible dismantlement (CVID) of the Korean nuclear programme before concessions.[1] It also invalidates the point, that the DPRK did not fulfil its obligations under the Agreed Framework, as sometimes alleged: 'Pyongyang promised ultimately to dismantle its nuclear facilities and leave the Korean Peninsula free of nuclear weapons but did neither.'[2] The DPRK was under no obligation to dismantle until the LWRs were operational, and that never happened. It was also agreed that the spent fuel would not be reprocessed. The DPRK complied with this and reprocessing only started after the collapse of the Agreed Framework.

Clause II promised that both sides would move to full normalisation of political and economic relations. This involved 'reducing barriers to trade and investment', opening liaison offices in each other's capitals and finally upgrading of bilateral relations to ambassadorial level. The US relaxed some sanctions the following January.

Under Clause III the Americans promised to 'provide formal assurances to the DPRK, against the threat or use of nuclear weapons by the U.S'. Not only was this not done, but the first use of nuclear weapons remained on the US agenda even during the Clinton period. Clinton himself, on the DMZ in July 1993, had nearly derailed US–DPRK negotiations by publicly threatening nuclear annihilation.[3] As late as 1998 the US had 'active contingency plans ... to drop up to 30 nuclear warheads on North Korea', and bombers were practising simulation missions.[4] Bush's Nuclear Posture Review of 2002 was to push nuclear weapons, especially in the form of tactical weapons such as 'bunker busters' back into mainstream military planning.

Clause III also had a reference to the North–South Joint Declaration on the Denuclearisation of the Korean Peninsula which, in turn, prohibited the maintenance of an enriched uranium programme. This was to surface, tangentially, in October 2002.

Clause IV committed both sides to 'work together to strengthen the international nuclear non-proliferation regime'.

The problem, from the North Korean point of view, was that its concessions were given immediately – the IAEA confirmed on 28 November, just over a month after the Agreed Framework had been signed, that the nuclear programme had been halted. However, apart from the annual supply of heavy fuel oil, the US concessions were all in the future and by the time George W. Bush tore up the Agreed Framework at the end of 2002 none of them had been delivered. The light-water reactors, due to go on stream in 2003, were years behind schedule. Sanctions had only been partially lifted and the constraints that continued to be in place, including being on the Terrorism List, were sufficient not merely to stifle US–DPRK trade, but to make North Korea's participation in the international economy very difficult.[5]

Timeline 8   1995–99

1995

20 January	Partial lifting of US sanctions
November	In response to DPRK appeal for aid following natural disasters, World Food Programme opens resident office in Pyongyang
21 December	Indictment of former presidents Chun and Roh on a variety of charges, including mutiny

1996

15 June	US–North Korean agreement on joint searches for those missing in action (MIA) remains
20 July	DPRK participates in the 1996 Summer Olympics in Atlanta
17 August	First joint venture between North Korea and a South Korean company begins operation at the North Korean port of Nampo

1997

12 February	Hwang Jang-yop, a secretary of the KWP CC in charge of international affairs, seeks asylum in Seoul while staying in Beijing
6 August	Rumsfeld commission on 'current and potential missile threat' to US established
19 August	Ground-breaking ceremony for the light-water reactors to be built in North Korea by KEDO (Korean Peninsula Energy Development Organization)
8 October	Kim Jong Il becomes Secretary General of KWP
9–10 December	Four-party talks begin in Geneva
18 December	Election of veteran opposition leader Kim Dae-jung as president of South Korea

1998

16 June	South Korean industrialist Chung Ju-yong (Hyundai) delivers 501 head of cattle and other relief goods; he also reaches agreement on opening tourist traffic between South and North Korea (Kumgangsan)
15 July	Rumsfeld Commission submits its report to Congress. The report warns of a threat from North Korea, Iran and Iraq
31 August	Kwangmyongsong-1 rocket launched over Japan into Pacific
18 November	First South Korean tourists visit Kumgangsan on Hyundai ship

1999

22 January	Fourth round of the Four-Party peace talks closes in Geneva
March	Armitage report, *A Comprehensive Approach to North Korea* published
March	US officials inspect alleged nuclear site at Kumchangri and find nothing
May	Defense Secretary William Perry visits North Korea and delivers a disarmament proposal
17 September	Bill Clinton agrees to the first significant easing of economic sanctions
24 September	NK formally announces that it will not test missiles while the DPRK–US talks continue
12 October	Perry report published
21 October	North Korea establishes its first Internet website, 'Korea Infobank'
1–3 December	Murayama delegation visits the DPRK, calls for negotiations to normalise diplomatic relations

It is commonly felt that the US was relaxed about its promises under the Agreed Framework (AF) because it was presumed that the DPRK would not be around long enough to collect. Indeed, the underlying assumption that whatever was given under the AF, specifically the LWRs, would sooner or later revert to the US under one form or another still prevails; Jack Pritchard, the former special envoy for North Korea who had resigned in protest at Bush's policies, in testimony to the Senate Foreign Relations Committee in July 2004 argued that

> My assumption is that ... a reunified peninsula will be ruled by a democratic government allied to the United States. That reunified nation, let alone the projected needs of the current Republic of Korea, will have vastly greater energy requirements. It stands to reason that some of that energy might well be supplied by nuclear facilities yet to be built. In that regard, I can see value to preserving the current LWR work at Kumho or even advancing it.[6]

Despite the persuasive logic of Pritchard's argument the US failed fully to implement the LWR commitment, and other promises except for heavy fuel oil, and that often only lethargically. One reason was the widespread animus against the DPRK within the elite (of both parties). Carter's action in broadcasting from Pyongyang was viewed as 'almost traitorous'. Another was the fact that the Democrats lost control of Congress just after the AF was signed, which impeded fulfilment of obligations even if they had wanted to. There was also a basic flaw in the agreement in that once the DPRK had frozen its nuclear programme, there would be little incentive for the US to honour the agreement with any vigour. Some, accepting the existence of the HEU programme alleged by the Bush administration, argue that it was a reaction to the failure of the Clinton administration to deliver its promises.[7]

The HEU issue aside, Sigal's[7] general thrust nicely summarises US–DPRK relations before, during and since the Agreed Framework: '[The DPRK] was playing tit for tat, cooperating whenever Washington cooperated and retaliating when Washington reneged, in an effort to end enmity.'

The search for an end to enmity, and for the termination of the US hostile policy continues to this day.

MISSILE DEFENSE AND THE SEARCH FOR ROGUE STATES

In June 1996 a DPRK–US agreement was reached on the search for the remains of US troops missing in action (MIA) during the Korean War. This agreement paralleled other such agreements in Indochina, and these searches have continued intermittently ever since. Despite these conciliatory gestures, relations between Washington and Pyongyang showed little signs of thawing. Clinton, under attack for financial and sexual improprieties at home (the Lewinsky affair), and being focussed on Europe and the Middle East to the relative neglect of Asia, did not formulate a proper Korean policy, at least not until the Perry report of late 1999. In the background the Republicans were busy. It is difficult to pin down to what degree ostensible differences between Democrats and Republicans are due to ideology and what is really just partisan politics.

In August 1997 Rumsfeld was appointed to head a commission on 'current and potential missile threats' to the US and the following July duly reported that:

Concerted efforts by a number of overtly or potentially hostile nations to acquire ballistic missiles with biological or nuclear payloads pose a growing threat to the United States, its deployed forces and its friends and allies. These newer, developing threats in North Korea, Iran and Iraq are in addition to those still posed by the existing ballistic missile arsenals of Russia and China.[8]

This emerging threat established, it was claimed, the political case for Missile Defense. This programme is a hugely profitable enterprise, not least because of its technological challenges, which would require a never-ending stream of dollars to address. However, it needed a plausible enemy, and North Korea seemed to fit the bill perfectly. Being small and impoverished it was assumed, by some strange twist of logic, that it would be prepared to commit suicide for the satisfaction of killing Americans. This would later come to be confused with the quite different rationale of suicide bombers. These are individuals who sacrifice their lives in striking the enemy knowing that the ability to retaliate is limited, precisely because they are individuals and not a state. Indeed, most of the people involved in 9/11 were Saudis, from a state allied to the US. Nation states do not have anonymity and so are constrained from attacking larger states, however they might want to, for fear of retaliation. States might make miscalculations, such as Japan did when it attacked Pearl Harbor, but they do not deliberately commit suicide.

Whatever the speciousness of the concept of a missile threat from a 'rogue state', North Korea had another advantage in being cast for the role. It seemed to have the greatest capability out of the three states which would later be labelled the 'Axis of Evil'. As it turned out Iraq had no substantial missile force (what little it had was destroyed on the eve of the invasion in March 2003 and in any case no missiles were fired). Whilst the Rumsfeld commission decided that Iran had a more sophisticated missile infrastructure than North Korea, Teheran's missiles were at the most of intermediate range and so posed no threat, as yet, to the continental United States.[9] North Korea, on the other hand, has a certain amount of proven expertise, and missiles are one of its exports. Meaningful statistics and authoritative, impartial assessments are rare, perhaps non-existent. The (US) Arms Control Association, for instance, in its *Worldwide Ballistic Missile Inventories* gives a list of countries by type of missile, range, payload and place of manufacture, but does not give numbers (nor extraneous controls).[10] To the innocent eye, India would appear to have a greater missile arsenal than the United States.

North Korea, for its part seemed to give credence to the role of 'growing missile threat' by launching the Kwangmyongsong-1 on 31 August 1998. This was billed as a long-range missile (Taepodong-2) by the Americans and caused much hysteria in Japan because it had been launched over Japan into the Pacific. North Korean scientists said that it had been aimed to pass between the islands of Honshu and

Hokkaido, with destruction devices in case it went off course.[11] North Korea would scarcely need an ICBM to hit Japan, and its existing missiles, the Nodong-1 and -2, already had the range for that (if not necessarily the payload or accuracy). What caused the Japanese over-reaction was the fact that the launch came as a surprise, and that all their information about it came from the Americans, reinforcing a sense of vulnerability.[12] The DPRK claimed that this had been not a missile, but the launch of an artificial satellite; the US later agreed that it had been a satellite launch but said that it had failed to orbit. Whether the satellite had orbited or not was clearly of less consequence than the demonstration that Pyongyang had a rocket flying deep into the Pacific; not quite to the continental United States, but getting close.

Some have argued that the launch was a commercial for North Korea's missile exports, and this indeed it may well have been, although the Taepodong does not seem ever to have been exported. More important, it was a message to Washington which was dragging its feet over the implementation of the Agreed Framework. It appeared the message got home because Clinton, under criticism that his North Korea policy was 'incoherent' appointed William Perry to conduct a review. The charge of 'strategic incoherence' was later to be levelled at Bush, and he was urged to establish a latter-day Perry.[13] He did not follow suit, probably because he already had his own 'Perry report' in the form of the Armitage report, *A Comprehensive Approach to North Korea*, published in March 1999.[14] This was a Republican critique of Clinton policy, and we may presume it served as the blueprint when Armitage subsequently became Assistant Secretary of State.

THE PERRY REPORT

The Perry report was not published until October of 1999, and followed Perry's visit to the DPRK in May. Preceding the Perry visit there had been long negotiations between Washington and Pyongyang on access to a site at Kumchangri which the US alleged was a nuclear site. In March US inspectors were allowed in, in return for food aid, and found nothing. The Kumchangri fiasco, along with the initial denial of the satellite launch, was later to be itemised by Jack Pritchard as one of a series of US 'intelligence failures', of which the latest was a botched assessment of Pyongyang's ability to remove spent fuel rods from the Yongbyon reactor after the collapse of the Agreed Framework in 2002.[15]

Perry, in his public report at least (Clinton got a private version) had four main conclusions:

- The overwhelming military superiority of the 'allied forces' in Korea could be upset if the DPRK developed nuclear weapons, especially if deliverable on ballistic missiles (which could make the US vulnerable)
- There had been no production of fissile material at Yongbyon since the Agreed Framework, but if it were aborted production would be re-started within months, and this would be 'the surest and quickest path for North Korea to obtain nuclear weapons'
- Support in the US (and Japan) for the Agreed Framework was unsustainable with DPRK missile developments
- The regime was not going to collapse.

Perry's argument basically was that the United States had to accept the DPRK as it was, not as what it would wish it to be.[16] The implication was that the US had to honour the Agreed Framework but negotiate with Pyongyang over missiles. The Armitage approach to 'the missile problem' was different, not only because he advocated a 'comprehensive approach' as against a 'prioritised' one, as had been employed by Gallucci in negotiating the AF.[17] More important as it turned out when he was in office, Armitage thought that the US could get its way without negotiations, by applying pressure on Pyongyang, directly and indirectly, via South Korea, Japan, China and Russia (the so-called 'multilateralism').

When Bush aborted the Agreed Framework in 2002 in line with Armitage's policy, Perry's prediction proved correct.

Perry's allusion to the reopening of the Yongbyon reactor as the 'surest and quickest path' is significant because it suggests that there is another path. In other words, enriched uranium, although this is not mentioned in the unclassified report. It is clear that there was talk in Washington at the time of an enriched uranium programme because the House of Representatives' North Korea Advisory Group report ('Gilman report') released on 3 November 1999 specifically mentioned 'North Korea's efforts to acquire uranium technologies, that is, a second path to nuclear weapons'.[18] Did Perry decide in 1999 that intelligence reports on enriched uranium did not justify aborting the Agreed Framework and pushing North Korea to reactivate

Yongbyon? Would that assessment have been different in 2002, if he had been in the shoes of Powell and Armitage? Probably not.

Perry's conclusion that the US should both accept the Agreed Framework and negotiate with Pyongyang was strongly reinforced by developments within South Korea. In December 1997 Kim Dae-jung had been elected president and the political climate in Seoul underwent a sea-change; this in turn helped to mould the climate in Washington among policy makers and policy persuaders.[19] To some extent his victory was a manifestation of change in South Korean society and its attitude towards the North. Kim Young-sam had won the 1992 election as the anointed successor of the military regimes and was assisted by 'Red baiting' against Kim Dae-jung.[20] In 1997 Kim Dae-jung narrowly defeated, by 40.3 per cent to 38.7 per cent, the conservative candidate Lee Hoi-chang (who was to lose out to Roh Moo-hyun five years later) on a platform that included a promise of meaningful talks with the North.[21]

KIM DAE-JUNG AND THE SUNSHINE POLICY

Kim Dae-jung's victory did not represent a radical break with the past. His running mate was Kim Jong-pil who had assisted Park Chung-hee in seizing power back in 1961. The policy of engagement with the North had long roots, certainly back to Park Chung-hee; the joint declaration of 15 June 2000 between Kim Dae-jung and Kim Jong Il was not markedly different from the joint statement of 4 July 1972. However Kim Dae-jung best articulated the logic of engagement and the popular name it acquired – the Sunshine policy – might well have been dreamt up by a marketing manager. The term was not used in his inaugural address on 25 February 1998 but he employed it in a speech at the School of Oriental And African Studies (SOAS) in London in April.[22] However, it was at a speech at the Free University in Berlin the following March that he put some real meat onto the bones. In his inaugural speech he had said:

Here, I will define three principles on North Korea:

- First, we will never tolerate armed provocation of any kind
- Second, we do not have any intention to harm or absorb North Korea
- Third, we will actively push reconciliation and cooperation between the South and North beginning with those areas which can be most easily agreed upon.[23]

In Berlin, cognisant of the similarities between the German and Korean experiences and the lessons to be drawn from German re-unification, to which he referred at length, he added three promises and three demands:

> In the same vein, the Republic is making three important promises to Pyongyang – to guarantee their national security, assist in their economic recovery efforts, and actively support them in the international arena. In return, the Republic wants three guarantees from Pyongyang: first, the North must abandon any armed provocation against the South once and for all; second, it must comply with its previous promises not to develop nuclear weapons; and third, it must give up ambitions to develop long- range missiles.[24]

The promise to 'guarantee their national security' was certainly beyond his powers. The United States was the main threat to DPRK national security and a ROK president, however well-regarded in Washington, only had limited influence. The meeting with incoming President George W. Bush in March 2001 was to show how inadequate that influence could be. Moreover, Pyongyang would always be sceptical of the control the president in Seoul had over the military. Firstly, because the military was ultimately under the control of the American general in charge of the Combined Forces Command. Secondly, because the ROK military had a history of stoking up tension when it suited, a charge also levelled at its counterpart to the North. For instance, the ROK military had taken the lead in 1992 in pressing for a renewal of the Team Spirit exercises with the Americans which caused a rupture in North–South relations and contributed to the nuclear crisis, as well as assisting Kim Young-sam's defeat of Kim Dae-jung.[25]

Even though he was overstating his hand, Kim Dae-jung's advocacy of the Sunshine policy was persuasive enough not merely to inspire much of South Korea, and the world, earning a Nobel Peace Prize in the process, but also to convince Pyongyang cautiously to respond.

Kim Dae-jung's rationale for the Sunshine policy was, and remains, compelling. War would be catastrophic for all concerned. One US estimate in the early 1990s calculated 1 million dead, North and South, including 80,000–100,000 Americans, $100 billion in direct costs to the US and $1,000 billion in costs of destruction and interrupted business to countries involved and the region.[26] Figures like that had stopped Clinton in 1994, and Bush in his turn, and few have openly advocated war, although the 'neocons' are accused of pressing for it.[27] However, Kim Dae-jung took this analysis further. Crucially, he also recognised that a collapse of the DPRK would be devastating for the ROK as well.[28] Gradual, peaceful and consensual economic integration as a precursor offers not merely the least cost but benefits for the South Korean economy increasingly overshadowed, as it is, by China.[29]

Kim Dae-jung came to the role of mediator between Pyongyang and Washington with strong credentials. From the perspective of Pyongyang he was perhaps the least antagonistic of all major South Korean politicians, and he had fallen foul of their enemies, from Park Chung-hee through to Kim Young-sam.[30] He had spent much of his early political life either in gaol or in exile and he was the personification of the struggle against the military regimes. At the same time he was broadly acceptable to the Americans. Indeed, of all South Korean leaders, from Syngman Rhee through to Roh Moo-hyun, he was the one most attuned to America and if anyone could persuade the Americans it would be him. He was Catholic, socially conservative, and owed various personal debts of gratitude to the United States. American (and Japanese) protests had saved him from murder at the hands of the Korean CIA after being kidnapped in Tokyo in 1973.[31] The US later had put pressure on Chun Doo-hwan to commute a death sentence although Alexander Haig, then US Secretary of State thought that Seoul should be free to dispose of political prisoners, including Kim Da-jung, as it wanted.[32] Kim was subsequently allowed to go into exile in the United States where he stayed for over two years. However, Kim must have been aware of the deep ambivalence in US policy, which was basically supportive of the military dictatorships, and intervention on his behalf was either prompted by fears of adverse publicity (less prominent dissidents received no such succour) or by individual initiatives running counter to official policy; the kidnapping rescue being a case in point.[33] Nevertheless, if anyone could ameliorate US policy, it was Kim Dae-jung. He succeeded to some extent with Clinton, but failed with Bush.

KIM JONG IL TAKES THE REINS IN PYONGYANG

In the North things were going badly, though perhaps not as disastrously as most outside observers thought, and many hoped. Firstly there was an apparently smooth transfer of power to Kim

Jong Il who over the years had already picked up several of his father's positions, but not that of president which was reserved, in perpetuity, for Kim Il Sung. Whilst power through inheritance, whether in politics or business, has familiar problems, it also has advantages, especially in times of crisis. Inheritance is stultifying of talent, is conducive to sycophancy and makes the correction of past mistakes, or the amendment of out-of-date policies, more difficult. On the other hand, it makes for continuity of policy which provides confidence to bureaucrats and stable expectation to the populace. It also makes it easier for foreign governments to negotiate, if they so desire, being reasonably confident that what is agreed today will not be disavowed tomorrow. One of the problems that Pyongyang, and others, have had with Washington has been the reversals of policies between administrations (e.g. from Clinton to Bush) and the shifts of policies within administrations, as happened when Clinton lost control of Congress in 1994.

Curiously, whilst it has become commonplace for journalists to talk of Pyongyang being 'unpredictable', in reality it was Washington which was erratic, and Pyongyang consistent. This was partly a matter of perception; policy debate and struggle in Washington being visible and much commented on. Indeed, one of the main weapons in that struggle is the leak of privileged information to favoured, and favourable, journalists. In Pyongyang whatever happens takes place behind closed doors, with decisions only becoming known when the battle is lost or won. How much happens is matter of conjecture. Philip Yun, a Korean-American diplomat who accompanied Perry to North Korea in 1999 observed:

> This trip revealed to many of us the existence of a generational divide in North Korea and put to rest any notions I had of a monolithic leadership. Youth usually connotes freedom. But the North's leaders in waiting – now in their late 40s, and 50s – are more isolated than their elders ever were, promising to be all the more hostile to the West.[34]

From personal experience it is clear that there is tension between those involved in exterior linkages, either cultural or business, and the security forces. Beyond these simple observations our vision becomes blurred. But there seems to be consensus that Kim Jong Il has effective control of the state and military apparatus and that there has been no overt challenge to that.[35] Certainly many states, and companies, have been destroyed by struggles of succession after the demise of a strong leader and the DPRK avoided that fate in the 1990s.

A fascinating insight into Kim Jong Il's relationship with the military was provided during a lunch he had with South Korean media on 14 August 2000, shortly after the summit. In response to a question about direct air links between North and South he replied:

> Direct air routes are no problem for our government, but the military has some problems with direct air routes. I have to approve direct routes. Large groups may come directly from Seoul to Pyongyang. Both North and South have to import oil and why should we waste our gas and spend our money in China?
>
> Some military commanders fear that direct air routes would allow South Koreans to photograph sensitive military sites, but I have told them that spy satellites have been taking pictures of every square inch for some time now and worrying about airplanes taking pictures is nonsensical.[36]

His confidence was due not merely to the strength of his inheritance, but also his deliberate courting of the military through the *Songun* ('army-first' policy) which is now touted as the hallmark of his regime.[37] It remains unclear how much extra power and resources this afforded the military beyond what the changed geopolitical situation demanded. The DPRK was much more vulnerable in the 1990s than it had been in earlier years, when the Soviet Union had provided some sort of bulwark against the US so it might be expected that the military would make greater claims which would be difficult to refuse, although Kim Il Sung would have been in a stronger position. The Agreed Framework had dampened the immediate danger of attack, but it would still lurk until it had been fully implemented, with security guarantees and normalisation, and that was not forthcoming. There has been talk of cutting back the size of the armed forces but this will depend not merely on an easing of the security situation but also an increase in the civilian demand for labour. If those conditions come about we will get some indication of the strength of the military lobby. Plans in 2003 for a substantial demobilisation appear to have been scuppered by the collapse of the Agreed Framework.[38]

FOOD CRISIS AND THE APPEAL FOR INTERNATIONAL AID

The economy deteriorated very badly during the mid 1990s, and with it the food situation, exacerbated by natural disasters.[39] It is unknown how many people died at the height of the food shortage. The latest estimates by a South Korean scholar suggest somewhere between a low of 25,000 to 69,000 and a high of 250,000 to 1.2 million.[40]

The DPRK called for international aid in 1995 and in November of that year the World Food Programme opened a resident office in Pyongyang, leading to a cluster of UN agencies setting up offices in the former East German embassy. Pyongyang has been criticised for being slow in appealing for aid, and that is probably so.[41] It must have been a difficult decision, not merely because of loss of face, at home and abroad, but because of the fear of espionage. Secrecy is one of the DPRK's main lines of defence and there must have been strong objections to letting in foreigners, many of them citizens of 'hostile' countries. There was also the question of subversion, though this might have been a less explosive issue than is commonly thought. Many consider the system rigid and unwilling to accept setbacks and change but in fact, as the economic reforms of July 2002 indicated, considerable change and reversal of policy can be accommodated as long as the fundamentals of power remain intact. There are parallels here with other authoritarian structures, such as China and the Catholic Church. What are seen by outsiders as necessarily system-disturbing ideas may be taken up but neutralised by the power of culture and ideology. Interestingly, this question of foreign impact worked both ways. Many in the aid community agonised over whether their intervention was propping up a system which they saw as the root of the problem. The French NGO, Médicins sans Frontières (MSF), made a well-publicised withdrawal from the DPRK in 1998. A more balanced take on the dilemmas facing humanitarian agencies is that of Hazel Smith, the British academic who has worked with the World Food Programme in Pyongyang.[42] We return to these issues in Chapter 5.

THE PYONGYANG SUMMIT OF JUNE 2000

All this left Kim Jong Il with good reasons to respond to overtures from Kim Dae-jung, albeit with circumspection. The initial response to the 'Berlin declaration' of the Sunshine policy was dismissive, calling for actions rather than words. Specifically there were demands that Seoul stop joint military exercises with the Americans, repeal the National Security Law and allow 'pro-reunification activities'.[43] Secret negotiations in Beijing appeared to have persuaded Pyongyang that a genuine offer was on the table even though, in the end, Kim

Dae-jung never did really satisfy those demands. A surprise joint announcement was made on 10 April that a summit would take place in June. How much this was influenced by sweeteners in the form of money circuited from Hyundai as business expenses is unclear, obscured as it is by becoming an anti-government scandal in Seoul.[44] Once it became the stuff of partisan politics and scandal mongering in the media it became difficult to disentangle fact from embroidery. It seems unlikely that it was, in itself, a major consideration since the summit was a reprise of the projected one between Kim Il Sung and Kim Young-sam in 1994.

There were many other factors encouraging a sense of detente. In June 1998 Hyundai founder Chung Ju-yong (a Northerner by birth) brought a symbolic 501 head of cattle, and other relief goods, as a gift. Five hundred would have been a valuable gift; the extra one was a cultural gesture to show deep sincerity. This led to the development of various Hyundai activities in the North, principally the Kumgangsan tourist complex (the first Southern tourists went in November 1998) and later the Kaesong industrial park.[45] Internationally a flurry of diplomatic relations broke out between DPRK and Western countries, helped in no small measure by encouragement from Seoul. Italy led the way in January 2000 and by March 2001 Australia, the Philippines, Britain, the Netherlands, Belgium, Canada, Spain, Germany, Luxembourg, Greece, and New Zealand had followed suit.

Not all was sweetness and light. The US decided on 25 April to keep the DPRK on its list of terrorism-supporting states but whatever private misgivings it might have had, it publicly supported the summit. Kim Jong Il made an unofficial visit to China in May, meeting President Jiang Zemin and Premier Zhu Rongji.

The summit was a stunning success, and a wave of euphoria swept Korea. In his speech in Pyongyang, Kim Dae-jung was effusive:

> Chairman Kim Jong-il and I have successfully concluded the summit. For the first time, the Korean people can see a bright future as a dawn of hope for reconciliation, cooperation and unification is breaking.
>
> ... Cooperation would expand if we could broaden understanding and trust through continuing dialogue and exchanges. Then, peace will spread from Mt Paektu [in DPRK] to Mt Halla [in ROK] and waters of prosperity would fill Han River [Seoul] and Taedong River [Pyongyang]. And then, the unification for which we have been yearning will be realized at last.[46]

The rest of the year was an exhilarating time in Korean affairs. There were setbacks and incidents, such as a minor naval clash in November, but the overall feeling was a sense of progress and movement towards a resolution of the division and hostility that had bedevilled the peninsula since 1945.[47] Family reunions on 15 August, Liberation day North and South, were very emotional and very symbolic. Parallel with the course of inter-Korean relations, and ultimately more important, were developments abroad, particularly in respect of the United States.

Putin signalled a more focussed attention upon East Asia, and a desire to correct the neglect of the Yeltsin period with visits to Beijing, Japan (for a G-8 meeting), and Pyongyang. The DPRK joined the ASEAN Regional Forum (ARF) at its meeting in Bangkok in July where their Foreign Minister, Paek Nam Sun, had a string of unprecedented bilateral meetings with counterparts: ROK's Lee Joung-binn, Japan's Yohei Kono, Canada's Lloyd Axworthy, China's Tang Jiaxuan, Thailand's Surin Pitsuwan, Australia's Alexander Downer, and New Zealand's Phil Goff amongst others. Most important was the one with US Secretary of State Madeleine Albright, who described their meeting as 'modest but historic', going on to croon at the closing dinner: 'Just had my first handshake with Foreign Minister Paek. Used to think he was a rogue, but here at ARF, he's so in vogue.'[48]

There was potentially a major hiccup in US–DPRK relations when, in September, American Airlines staff at Frankfurt airport wanted to strip search Kim Yong Nam, President of the Presidium of the Supreme People's Assembly (and head of state), on his way to attend the UN Millennium Summit in New York.[49] He went back home and Pyongyang complained of the 'misbehaviour of world's largest rogue state':

> This happening clearly convinces us that though the United States is proposing a number of talks at present, talking about 'improved relations' with us and the like, it is, in fact, displeased with our opening of relations with other countries.
>
> The recent happening goes to clearly prove that the U.S. is the world's biggest state of hooligans and rogues.[50]

There was embarrassment in Seoul and Washington but a letter of apology from Albright seems to have been accepted in Pyongyang. Vice Marshal Jo Myong Rok, first vice-chairman of the National Defence Commission, was despatched to Washington as Kim Jong

Il's special envoy in early October. He met with Bill Clinton and issued an invitation to visit Pyongyang. The DPRK press hailed all this as a breakthrough that marked the end of the 'Arduous March', US hostility was coming to an end.[51] Secretary Albright made her historic visit to Pyongyang later in the month where she received star treatment.[52]

But Clinton's term of office was coming to an end and the 'hanging chads' of Florida brought in a successor who had no desire to bring the hostility to an end. Clinton did not officially abandon plans for a visit until the last moment, 28 December, but when the Supreme Court had decided that George W. Bush had won the election, the die had been cast. A new administration, determined to overturn whatever Clinton had done, was due to come into office.

4
Crisis Reignited: Economic Reform, Regional Accord, Washington Discord

THE CLOUDING OF THE SUNSHINE POLICY

During the final months of the second Clinton administration US–DPRK relations seemed to be on the verge of a breakthrough. It looked as if the enmity that had lingered for half a century was to be replaced by some sort of normal relationship and by 'peaceful coexistence'. That in turn would have opened the way for rehabilitation of the North Korean economy, and accelerated economic and perhaps political reform. Good, or at the least non-confrontational, Washington–Pyongyang relations would have encouraged the improvement in relationships between all the countries in Northeast Asia. Japan–DPRK relations would probably be normalised and Japanese reparations, imports and investment would have done much to stimulate the North Korean economy. The economic integration of the North and South Korean economies would have moved ahead faster, and North–South linkages of all sorts would have accelerated.

Four years later, at the beginning of George W. Bush's second administration, relations between Washington and Pyongyang were extremely bad. Officials made little secret of their antipathy for the government in Pyongyang, and their desire to bring about 'regime change'.[1] During that period the Bush administration destroyed the Agreed Framework, negotiated by its predecessor, and the DPRK responded not only by reactivating its nuclear power programme but also eventually developing, it claimed, a nuclear deterrent. The deterioration in US–DPRK relations has had a knock-on effect throughout the region, exacerbating and fostering Tokyo's confrontationalism. Japan–DPRK relations are frigid and Tokyo is seeking ways to ratchet up economic warfare against Pyongyang.[2] Japan's relations with China are plummeting, and those with South Korea are strained.[3] How, and why, was crisis snatched out of the jaws of peace?

The why is part of the overarching theme of this book. A North Korea which can be portrayed as hostile and threatening has been a staple of postwar American foreign policy despite all attempts, maladroit or not, by Pyongyang to build bridges. It can be argued that the warming in Washington's stance towards Pyongyang in the final months of the Clinton administration may be seen as an aberration, largely brought about by pressure from Seoul and that the Bush policy is merely a reversion to long-term strategic fundamentals. There is an underlying strategic imperative to keep Japan, and South Korea, alienated from China and continued crisis with North Korea plays a role in that. The 'North Korean threat' also serves to justify the Missile Defense programme. We return to these themes in Chapter 8; this chapter describes the process by which the crisis was reignited.

It was clear that both Kim Dae-jung and Kim Jong Il were hoping for an Al Gore victory in the US elections of 2000.[4] They were not alone in that; in Britain, for instance, there was talk of the government bracing itself for a cooling of the 'special relationship' when it became evident that Bush would become president.[5] Mr Blair, as we know, quickly made new friends and the 'special relationship' blossomed as never before. Things were different in Korea. So concerned was Kim Dae-jung that the new administration would undo his 'Sunshine policy' that he made an urgent request for a meeting with the incoming president.[6] He attempted to reinforce the message not only by sending Foreign Minister Lee Joung-binn to arrange the 7 March summit, but also by dispatching at short notice Lim Dong-won, director of the National Intelligence Service (NIS) and his key handler of North Korean affairs, for meetings with Secretary of State Colin Powell, CIA director George Tenet, and National Security Advisor Condoleezza Rice. It did not work. Kim Dae-jung was treated in a perfunctory manner – so much so that the opposition Grand National Party took some delight in complaining that Secretary Powell had 'insulted the nation' by giving a press conference while the two leaders were still talking, saying that Bush had 'forcefully told' Kim that he wouldn't continue missile talks with the DPRK. The GNP also said that Bush had 'hurt the pride of the Korean people' by his 'derogatory reference' to Kim Dae-jung as 'this man' during the postsummit press conference.[7]

Whilst Kim Dae-jung put a brave face on things it was apparent that he had been rebuffed. Even segments of the American press were highly critical of the Bush team for treating a 'close ally' in this way, confused by conflicting messages (Powell being seen as more 'pragmatic') and exasperated by the administration's attitude towards negotiations. For example, Thomas L. Friedman, writing in the *New*

York Times, after having excoriated Kim Jong Il as a 'wild man who understands only force', concluded:

> You have to wonder whether Mr. Bush knows. He declared Wednesday that when it comes to North Korea, 'We're not certain as to whether or not they're keeping all terms of all agreements'. But as the *Times* reporter David Sanger pointed out, the U.S. has only one agreement with North Korea — the 1994 accord that froze its plutonium processing. And Bush aides admitted there was no evidence that this deal was being violated. Later a White House official, trying to clean up for the president, said Mr Bush was referring to concerns about whether North Korea would comply with a future deal, even though he didn't use the future tense. 'That's how the president speaks', the official said. O.K.
> Well, if that's how he speaks, is that how he thinks? Confused?
> Which approach Mr. Bush adopts depends in part on how he understands North Korea's past behavior. But if he doesn't understand that, or he hasn't applied himself to understanding it, or he is so wedded to his own Star Wars missile shield he doesn't want anything to get in the way, or he is so worried about being accused by Republican hard-liners, as his father was, of being a 'wimp' that he'll never take yes for an answer from the North — then, Houston, we have a problem.[8]

Friedman was right about the problem, and it went beyond Bush's apparent confusion of thought. Basically he wanted to scrap the Agreed Framework, and to dismantle the Clinton inheritance in Korea, and in general; the ABC – Anything But Clinton – policy as it was dubbed. The problem was that the DPRK was keeping to its agreement to freeze plutonium processing, so another reason had to be found, and that was to be revealed in October the following year.

Timeline 9   2000–01

2000

4 January	Diplomatic relations are established between DPRK and Italy
10 March	Kim Dae-jung's 'Berlin Declaration' outlines 'Sunshine policy'. Soon after, secret North–South talks open in Beijing
10 April	SK and NK simultaneously announce plans for June summit in Pyongyang.
25 April	US decides to keep DPRK on its list of terrorism-supporting states

29 May	Kim Il Jong makes unannounced visit to China, meeting Jiang Zemin and Zhu Rongji
13 June	Kim Jong Il and Kim Dae-jung meet in Pyongyang for summit and sign joint declaration
19 July	Russian President Putin becomes the first to Kremlin leader to visit DPRK
15 August	The first North–South family reunions since 1985 take place
9 October	Vice Marshal Jo Myong Rok visits Washington and meets President Clinton
23 October	US Secretary of State Madeleine Albright visits DPRK and holds talks with Kim Jong Il
12 December	UK and DPRK establish diplomatic relations

2001

4 January	New Year editorials report Kim Jong Il stresses 'economic renovation' with 'new thinking'
16 January	Kim Jong Il makes surprise visit to China, visiting hi-tech industries and stock exchange in Shanghai
20 January	President George W. Bush assumes office
6 February	Canada and DPRK establish diplomatic relations
1 March	Germany establishes diplomatic relations with DPRK
7 March	Kim Dae-jung meets George W. Bush in Washington to press for Sunshine policy
2–3 May	High-level EU delegation (Persson, Solana, Patten) visits Pyongyang and Seoul
6 June	George W. Bush announces completion of NK policy review, says US will now begin discussions with Pyongyang
16 July	Kim Jong Il begins a trip to Russia by train
3 September	Chinese President Jiang Zemin visits DPRK
11 September	Terrorist attacks against US; Twin Towers destroyed, Pentagon damaged
12 September	DPRK issues statement denouncing the terrorist attacks; sends secret cable to Washington
14 December	Congress approves Bush's $343 billion defence bill that gives full funding to his Missile Defense program

BUSH'S REVIEW OF NORTH KOREA POLICY

By mid year, after six months of 'malign neglect' with no formal talks with Pyongyang, the Bush administration had completed a review of its North Korea strategy and this was announced on 6 June 2001. President Bush declared, in his statement, 'I have directed my national security team to undertake serious discussions with North Korea'.[9] The Independent Task Force on Korea of the Council on Foreign Relations, chaired by Ambassadors Abramowitz and Laney, and drawing in many of the great and good from the political elite, in a report released at the time commented favourably on 'the recently stated willingness of the Bush administration to begin talks with Pyongyang' and offered a number of earnest recommendations.[10] All to no avail. When Bush said 'discussions' he did not mean negotiations, but rather the tabling of unilateral demands that offered little, if any, inducement to Pyongyang to respond. This was to be the formula for the next three years, though in mid 2004 there was, under concerted pressure from within the US and abroad, some slight softening of posture.

The review, according to Sigal, 'reneged on past U.S. commitments and reinterpreted agreements with the North unilaterally.' Specifically:

- It did not reaffirm the pledge of no hostile intent towards the DPRK
- It wanted 'improved implementation of the Agreed Framework', meaning inspections without offering anything in return
- It required North Korea to reduce its conventional military posture, again unilaterally and without reciprocity
- It tied progress on missile production and exports with that in 'other areas of concern'.[11]

Meanwhile, in Pyongyang, the 2001 joint New Year editorials, presaging the economic reforms of the following year, had quoted Kim Jong Il stressing 'new thinking' as the key to 'economic renovation'. 'Things are not what they used to be in the 1960s. So no one should follow the way people used to do things in the past'.[12] Kim himself made another unannounced visit to China on 16 January, this time being escorted round Shanghai by Premier Zhu Rongji (a former mayor), visiting hi-tech foreign joint ventures and the stock exchange.[13] In July Kim Jong Il balanced the China visit by one to Russia, travelling by special train to St Petersburg, and Moscow, where he signed a declaration with President Putin, but snarling up the Russian railway system in the process.[14] President Jiang Zemin made a return visit to Pyongyang on 3 September, suggesting China–DPRK relations were on the mend.

9/11: DPRK CONDEMNS TERRORISM

September saw the terrorist attacks on the Twin Towers in New York, and on the Pentagon, and brought '9/11' into the international lexicon. It was the defining moment of George W. Bush's first term and was put to good account. In somewhat the same way the Falklands War rescued Margaret Thatcher from potential oblivion, it turned a floundering leader into a 'war hero'. It was used with despatch to advance a range of policy initiatives which had been a long time brewing in conservative and neocon think tanks. The invasions of Afghanistan and Iraq were the most visible and spectacular results of the re-energized administration and have tended to overshadow the less dramatic hardening of Korea policy which led to the destruction of the Agreed Framework.

Pyongyang's condemnation of the attacks was swift, but not swift enough for Washington. On 12 September KCNA carried a brief factual account of the incidents, with no hint of glee or criticism.[15] On the same day it carried a brief statement from the Foreign Ministry:

> Terrorists' large-scale attacks made on the US by blowing themselves up in planes on Tuesday have caught the international community by great surprise.
>
> The very regretful and tragic incident reminds it once again of the gravity of terrorism.
>
> As a UN member the DPRK is opposed to all forms of terrorism and whatever support to it and this stance will remain unchanged.
>
> The DPRK approaches the incident from this point of view.[16]

Had this happened the year before, when relations with Washington were rapidly improving, there would probably have been expressions of sympathy rather than regret about a 'very regretful and tragic incident'. In February 2005, for instance, on the occasion of the assassination of former Prime Minister Rafik Hariri, the DPRK sent a message to the Lebanese government, with whom its ties must be very limited despite having diplomatic relations since 1981, which 'condemned the brutal terrorism in Beirut and hoped that the Lebanese government and people would overcome sorrow and achieve success in the work to eradicate the aftermath of the incident as early as possible and protect the stability and sovereignty of the country'. Pyongyang was criticised for having missed a 'golden opportunity' to sign a joint statement with Seoul on the issue.[17] This criticism was unfair given the quite different nature of the relationship that Seoul had with Washington. It would have been extremely difficult to craft a message suitable for both capitals.

Nevertheless, over the next few months the DPRK signed a number of anti-terrorism conventions and indicated its readiness to sign more.[18] Most important of all, it sent, according to South Korean reports, a cable to Washington '... immediately after the Sept. 11 terrorist attacks on New York and Washington, D.C., telling its archrival that it regretted the attacks and didn't have anything to do with them'.[19]

Although the South Korean press carried various reports that the terrorist attacks would not affect US attitudes to negotiations with North Korea, it did seem to harden attitudes. Some observers, including me, thought that faced with such a growing, and unpredictable, threat of 'Islamic terrorism', the United States might sensibly comes to terms with enemies in other quarters, a war on too many fronts having been the downfall of other empires. It was not to be. Rumsfeld, for instance, was later when flushed with excitement over the invasion of Iraq to boast that he could take out both countries:

> Mr Rumsfeld now considers North Korea a 'terrorist regime teetering on the verge of collapse' and which is on the verge of becoming a proliferator of nuclear weapons. During a bout of diplomatic activity over Christmas he warned that the US could fight two wars at once – a reference to the forthcoming conflict with Iraq. After Baghdad fell, Mr Rumsfeld said Pyongyang should draw the 'appropriate lesson'.[20]

Subsequently Rumsfeld was to withdraw troops from South Korea to send to Iraq, which had turned out to be a tougher proposition than he had anticipated.[21]

NUCLEAR POSTURE REVIEW

North Korea policy was part of a wider framework to re-vitalise the military spending and posture that had been blunted by the end of the Cold War. On 14 December Congress approved a $343 billion defence bill that included Missile Defense. Later that month the Nuclear Posture Review was sent to Congress. The report remained confidential but a summary was given at a Pentagon press briefing on 9 January 2002.[22] However it was not until two months later that it was leaked to the *Los Angeles Times*, appearing on 9 March.[23]

Substantial excerpts were subsequently posted on the GlobalSecurity. org website.[24] These revealed that North Korea was the first amongst a string of (non-nuclear) countries that could be target of a nuclear strike – 'North Korea, Iraq, Iran, Syria, and Libya are among the countries that could be involved in immediate, potential, or unexpected contingencies'.[25]

There was an angry response from Pyongyang on 13 March, showing that whatever the lack of detail in US attention to North Korea, the Koreans themselves kept a keen eye on the US press:

> The DPRK will not remain a passive onlooker to the Bush administration's inclusion of the DPRK in the seven countries, targets of US nuclear attack, but take a strong countermeasure against it.
>
> The present political and military situation where the US is openly threatening the DPRK with nuclear weapons proves once again how just it was when it exerted tremendous efforts to increase its capacity for self-defence.[26]

What exactly this meant is unclear. What were the 'strong countermeasures'? How was the DPRK to 'increase its capacity for self-defence'? Did this mean that North Korea was turning to an enriched uranium programme? Or already had one?

We do know that the plutonium programme remained frozen. CIA Director Tenet admitted as much to a Senate hearing on 19 March.[27] Yet the following day the White House revealed that the administration was refusing to certify to Congress that the DPRK was adhering to the Agreed Framework.[28]

Timeline 10　2002

2002

9 January	US Nuclear Posture Review (sent to Congress, 31 December 2001) includes contingency plans for possible nuclear attacks against seven countries, listing NK first (followed by Iraq, Iran, Syria, Libya, China, and Russia)
29 January	President George W. Bush gives his State of the Union address – North Korea, Iran and Iraq labelled an 'Axis of Evil'
13 May	Park Geun-hye meets Kim Jong Il in Pyongyang
17 September	Japanese PM Junichiro Koizumi makes a surprise trip to Pyongyang, signs 'Pyongyang Agreement'

3 October	Assistant Secretary of State Jim Kelly visits Pyongyang, alleges HEU programme
16 October	Press conference in Washington reveals HEU allegation and claims that NK admitted it
18 October	Five Japanese citizens abducted by North Korea visit Japan as agreed by Pyongyang Agreement but are 'persuaded' not to return to their families
25 October	DPRK Foreign Ministry denies HEU programme and calls for non-aggression treaty with US
11 November	The United States and its key Asian allies, Japan and South Korea, decide to halt oil supplies to North Korea promised under the 1994 deal
14 November	South Korean Unification Minister Jeong Se-hyun suggests Kelly may have misunderstood 'admission' because of 'cultural differences'
18 November	BBC reports 'N. Korean nuclear "admission" in doubt'
9 December	Spanish and US forces intercept a NK ship carrying missiles to Yemen. Ship released after Yemeni protest. US admits action illegal
12 December	North Korea says the US decision to halt oil shipments has left it with no choice but to reactivate nuclear facilities for energy generation
19 December	Roh Moo-hyun is elected president of South Korea
31 December	North Korea threatens to pull out of the Nuclear Non-Proliferation Treaty

AXIS OF EVIL

All this was taking place against the backdrop of the furore caused by Bush's 'Axis of Evil' speech on 29 January 2002, the annual presidential State of the Union address. In this he had lambasted North Korea, Iraq and Iran:

> Our second goal is to prevent regimes that sponsor terror from threatening America or our friends and allies with weapons of mass destruction. Some of these regimes have been pretty quiet since September the 11th. But we know their true nature. North Korea is a regime arming with missiles and weapons of mass destruction, while starving its citizens.
>
> Iran aggressively pursues these weapons and exports terror, while an unelected few repress the Iranian people's hope for freedom.

Iraq continues to flaunt its hostility toward America and to support terror. The Iraqi regime has plotted to develop anthrax, and nerve gas, and nuclear weapons for over a decade. This is a regime that has already used poison gas to murder thousands of its own citizens – leaving the bodies of mothers huddled over their dead children. This is a regime that agreed to international inspections – then kicked out the inspectors. This is a regime that has something to hide from the civilized world.

States like these, and their terrorist allies, constitute an axis of evil, arming to threaten the peace of the world.[29]

This curious concoction of untruths and deception, wrapped in purple prose is as divorced from reality as anything that Pyongyang churns out. It is however much more skilful in the way that it manages to convey impressions that are quite at variance with reality without explicit statements that can be proven as lies. Many people, and most Americans, took it to mean that North Korea, Iraq and Iran were somehow linked, and that they were all 'regimes that sponsor terror'. To Americans that meant 9/11 and al-Qaeda. The American radical journalist and media analyst Robert Parry describes how it is done, in discussing a *Washington Post* poll in September 2003 that found that seven out of ten Americans 'still believe that Iraq's ousted leader Saddam Hussein was involved in the Sept. 11 terrorist attacks although U.S. investigators have found no evidence of a connection':

> While downplaying the WMD case, however, Bush continued to work the subliminal connection between the Sept. 11th murders and Iraq.
>
> Indeed, after listening to Bush on Sunday juxtapose references to the Sept. 11th murders, their al-Qaeda perpetrators and Iraq, it shouldn't be surprising how seven out of 10 Americans got the wrong idea. It's pretty clear that Bush intended them to get the wrong idea.
>
> In speech after speech, Bush has sought to create public confusion over these connections. Though no Iraqis were involved in the terror attacks two years ago – and though Osama bin Laden and most of the attackers were Saudis – Bush and his top aides routinely have inserted references about Iraq and the Sept. 11 terror attacks in the same paragraphs. They often used unsubstantiated assertions that Iraq was sharing or planning to share WMD with Osama bin Laden's al-Qaeda as the connection.[30]

The problem for Pyongyang here was not merely the vituperativeness of the language – there were other examples of that – but the tying together of three countries whose links were either limited, or in the case of Iraq and Iran, actually hostile. When the United States invaded Iraq, Pyongyang did not need to be paranoid to see itself as next in line, or at best following Iran.

This message of threat was to be hammered home. On 6 May John Bolton, Undersecretary of State for Arms Control, and a noted hawk, accused both Iraq and North Korea of having 'covert nuclear programs, in violation of the nuclear Nonproliferation Treaty'.[31] A few months later, when the country was in American hands, his assertions about Iraq were shown to be untrue. Whether he, and other senior members of the administration were deliberately lying, or merely grasping at ambiguous intelligence reports to support a policy they wanted to happen is a matter of conjecture. I tend to agree with Monbiot that we have deliberate lies.[32] Others, more generously, or gullibly, incline to think in terms of convenient 'intelligence failure', an overenthusiastic embracing of dubious evidence. Jon Wolfsthal for instance, writing in the *Christian Science Monitor*, anguishes, 'If the US was wrong – or manipulated intelligence – in Iraq, how can it be completely trusted in North Korea?'[33] Since Bolton has been prone to making accusations of covert nuclear, chemical and biological weapons programmes against a number of countries, Iran and Syria also being high on his target list, it is unclear how much this was a considered attack on the DPRK as such. It should be noted that Bolton appears to have to no objections to weapons of mass destruction as such, merely their possession by other countries, especially those not amenable to US 'guidance'.[34]

On 1 June President Bush announced his doctrine of 'pre-emptive war', a statement that the US was not to be bound by international law but was free to attack whomever it felt possibly to be a future threat, a doctrine which was to be put into practice the following year with the invasion of Iraq.[35] It should be noted that what is at issue is not so much the fact that the charges against Iraq were trumped-up but that even these trumped-up charges by themselves were insufficient to justify war, which in theory is only allowable in self-defence.[36]

PYONGYANG SEEKS COUNTERVAILING LINKAGES

Pyongyang was not idle in face of these threats. Attempts to build new diplomatic linkages and to repair old relationships with Russia and China proceeded apace. Two developments deserve special note because they may have been the catalyst that generated the crisis of October 2002.

Firstly the European Union, worried perhaps by Washington's adventurism, had been taking a more active role. A top-level delegation – Joran Persson, President of the European Council and Prime Minister of Sweden, Javier Solana, high representative for common foreign and security policy of the EU, and Chris Patten, commissioner for external relations of the European Commission, had visited Pyongyang on 2–3 May 2001 for talks with Kim Jong Il and his government.[37] Although the EU said publicly that the visit had nothing to do with Bush's Korean policy it clearly was meant as an unequivocal message that the European Union was very concerned and wanted to play a role as peace maker. This was well understood in both Pyongyang and Seoul. The delegation flew from Pyongyang to Seoul to have discussions with Kim Dae-jung and brought with them two messages from Kim Jong Il. One was that Pyongyang would unilaterally continue with the moratorium on missile testing until 2003 and the other was that Kim Jong Il's reciprocal visit to Seoul, promised at the 2000 summit, was still definitely on, if the Americans came back to the table. On 14 May it was announced that the EU and the DPRK were to establish diplomatic relations.[38] The ball was in the US court and Bush's statement of 6 June of resuming discussions was the response.[39] Pressure from the EU was not the only factor. The president's father, George H. Bush, also intervened by passing on a memo from Donald P. Gregg, president of the Korea Society, and former ambassador to Seoul advocating negotiations.[40] It has been suggested that this fatherly advice was related to his business interests in Northeast Asia through his involvement with the Carlyle Group, the Washington private equity company with large investments in Korea and Japan.[41]

KIM-KOIZUMI SUMMIT THREATENS US POLICY

A year later the DPRK celebrated the anniversary of the EU visit.[42] However, even if the opening to the EU had helped propel the US into discussions, they had not in fact led to meaningful negotiations. Something bigger was on the horizon and this was to have a dramatic effect on US policy. On 30 August 2002 there was a virtually simultaneous announcement in Tokyo and Pyongyang that Prime Minister Junichiro Koizumi was to visit Pyongyang on 17 September for a summit with Kim Jong Il.[43] The announcement took observers by surprise and even the Americans had only a few days' notice.[44] The summit was reportedly put together, after an initiative from Pyongyang, through extensive secret negotiations by Hitoshi Tanaka, the then director general of the Asian-Oceanian Affairs Bureau of the Japanese Ministry of Foreign Affairs.[45] The fact that Washington was kept in the dark suggests that the Japanese were worried what the reaction would be, and thought that if the plans were known, the US would put a stop to things, and therefore went for a virtual fait accompli. They were right about the reaction, but wrong in thinking that the Americans would accept the summit, and the possibility of a Tokyo–Pyongyang rapprochement without demur. Publicly, the United States welcomed news of the meeting and if it had ended in disaster concerns would have been allayed and Washington might not have acted with the despatch it did.

However, the summit was successful. Kim Jong Il gave Koizumi what he had come for and more – he apologised for the abductions of Japanese in the past and agreement was made for survivors to be free to travel back to Japan. Koizumi, for his part, apologised for Japanese colonialism, and looked set to move forward on normalisation, which would have yielded the DPRK virtual reparations, perhaps in the region of $8 10 billion, and would have lifted the restraints on trade and investment.[46] The Japanese rightwing, always ready for a spot of (North) Korea bashing, was not pleased and unleashed a wave of hysteria about the abduction issue that has not died down, to the detriment of the hapless abductees themselves.[47]

Washington had tried to scupper Koizumi's trip to Pyongyang by briefing him on allegedly new information about a covert enriched uranium programme. Bush also read the riot act on the issue when Koizumi visited on 12 September, a week before going to Korea. Koizumi, it appears, was either not convinced by the American 'evidence' or thought the issue not of great importance, and according to US scholar Jonathan Pollack did not bring it up with Kim Jong Il, despite American desires that he should 'raise vigorously the nuclear issue'.[48]

The summit left the United States facing real problems in its Northeast Asia policy. Pollack argues that

In the aftermath of the Japan–North Korea summit, the Bush administration confronted the prospect of abrupt and unanticipated changes in the Northeast Asian political and security environment. The United States believed that Pyongyang had defaulted on fundamental policy commitments to Washington, at the precise moment when the DPRK had opened the door to a new relationship with America's most important Asian ally and, prospectively, a major aid donor to the North.[49]

In reality what was at stake went beyond that, because a Japan at peace with North Korea would be less amenable to US leadership, let alone a US military presence, and more liable to be seduced by China.

Pollack, who accepts the validity of the allegations about an enriched uranium programme (though he is doubtful about the practical importance of it) sees the summit as the 'trigger' which brought forth the visit to Pyongyang of James Kelly in October, which in turn led to the collapse of the Agreed Framework and the subsequent crisis.

THE DESTRUCTION OF THE AGREED FRAMEWORK

When James Kelly, Assistant Secretary of State for East Asian and Pacific Affairs, visited Pyongyang on 3–5 October 2002 this was the first substantive meeting that the Bush administration, nearly two years in office, had had with the DPRK. Kelly was a middle-ranking official with no authority to negotiate, merely to read the script, though he may have had a hand in writing it. Kelly had a military background, and had served as an assistant on security to Reagan, and in the Pentagon, before spending the Clinton years as president of the Pacific Forum Center for Strategic and International Studies (CSIS) of Honolulu.[50]

What exactly passed at this meeting has become a matter of great controversy. The official US position, as expressed by State Department spokesman Richard Boucher on 16 October was that Kelly

advised the North Koreans that we had recently acquired information that indicates that North Korea has a program to enrich uranium for nuclear weapons in violation of the Agreed Framework and other agreements. North Korean officials acknowledged that they have such a program. The North Koreans attempted to blame the United States and said that they considered the Agreed Framework nullified. Assistant Secretary Kelly pointed out that North Korea had been embarked on this program for several years.[51]

There are some curious things about this account. Firstly, Boucher refers to 'recently acquired information', yet stories of an enriched uranium programme had obviously been widespread in Washington at least since the Gilman report in 1999. In that year a Department of Energy report had claimed that North Korea 'is in the early stages of a uranium enrichment capability' in cooperation with Pakistan.[52] The Pakistani connection was an important one and formed the basis of most of the information leaked to the press over the next few years.[53] How much new information the US actually got from Pakistan remains suspect. Following 9/11 Washington put great pressure on the Pakistani leader, General Pervez Musharraf, to join 'the war on terror', abandon the Taliban and cooperate in the US occupation of Afghanistan. Pakistan and America had worked together in the past over Afghanistan, when the US was funding the Taliban and other Islamic groups in order to destroy the Soviet-backed government in Kabul, but had drifted apart after the Taliban victory. The stakes were huge; Washington offered a military and economic package of $3 billion as an inducement with a threat of reimposition of sanctions if Islamabad did not toe the line.[54] The line was toed, but not crossed and there has been plenty of evidence of Pakistani reluctance to cooperate fully. Musharraf has refused to hand over to the CIA Abdul Qadeer Khan, the 'father of Pakistan's bomb', and a national hero, who reportedly provided North Korea with the technology and equipment for a uranium-based programme.[55] What we see in the public domain has been passed from Pakistani intelligence to US intelligence, and then on to dependable journalists such as David Sangster of the *New York Times*. Plenty of opportunity and motivation for filtering and distortion, let alone the planting of misinformation. Sangster does admit, however, that 'American intelligence agencies still cannot locate the site or sites of any North Korean uranium enrichment facilities', in other words they have no direct knowledge (or evidence) of the programme or what it can deliver.[56]

Secondly, Boucher must have been well aware that such a programme would not be a violation of the Agreed Framework itself, a point made by the Gilman group in 1999 when they wanted to attack the Clinton administration.[57] An enriched uranium programme would however have been a violation of the North–South Joint Declaration on Denuclearisation of the Korean Peninsula, which the Agreed Framework had pledged to uphold. Did the Americans know that the South Koreans had already violated that agreement as the North had charged?[58] It seems unlikely, not so much because of any compunctions about lying (and they would in any case argue that the good South Koreans had committed a peccadillo whereas the bad

North Koreans had perpetrated an egregious violation), but because the South has good reason to keep secrets from the Americans.

Thirdly, and this was the big one, was the statement that 'North Korean officials acknowledged that they have such a program.' If this was a deliberate lie, it was a master stroke. If it was an honest misinterpretation of what Kang Sok Ju had said, as the South Korean press has suggested, it was extremely fortuitous.[59] The Americans have not hurried to clarify what was said, and have not admitted to any doubt – Pritchard, for one, has said, he 'heard what he heard'.[60] Oberdorfer, who had visited Pyongyang after the Kelly confrontation and spoken to officials involved, suggested that the Koreans hadn't admitted but hadn't denied.[61] Kelly has remained adamant, suggesting that they did admit, but later denied it: 'Kelly said the change of heart resulted when the North realized the admission was a major tactical error that was resulting in massive international criticism.'[62]

That does not seem plausible because they had a night to ponder the response, so it was not a spur of the moment thing, later to be regretted. There would be no good reason to admit to a programme in the circumstances of the Kelly confrontation, and as the South Korean press pointed out, 'it was hard to believe North Korea confessed. Pyongyang is seen as the last country in the world to admit doing wrong, even if caught red-handed'.[63] The North Koreans themselves gave a transcript later to John Lewis, which reportedly 'contained no such admission', but this does not appear to have been published, and in any case would scarcely prove anything, although it might indicate a plausible explanation for misinterpretation.[64]

Not being privy to the discussions it is impossible to be sure but it seems likely to me that the Koreans did not admit to a uranium enrichment programme but talked in rather rhetorical terms, angry at the American bluster, and the Americans heard what they wanted to hear. It may well have been leaks to the US press, in mid October, which precipitated the US statement of 16 October, forced their hand and made them more adamant about the conversation than they might otherwise have been.

Be that as it may, the US statement of 16 October established the admission as a sort of urban myth, widely believed, seldom challenged but easy to disprove for those who looked. Few did. Had the US just made the allegations that would have been one thing. Saying that the Koreans admitted to it was a double whammy, and the story has been repeated many times, as if it were established and irrefutable fact. It gave rise to a raft of articles trying to explain why Pyongyang would 'confess'; 'North Korea's nuclear programme: analyzing "confessional diplomacy"' and 'North Korea's Confession: Why?' were typical.[65] The Americans were lucky with the timing. A year later, when the hollowness of the accusations against Iraq became glaringly apparent there may have been more scepticism. But perhaps not. The website of the Campaign for Nuclear Disarmament (CND), which of all organisations might be presumed to be cautious at taking US assertions as fact, does just that: 'Towards the end of 2002 the DPRK revealed that it had produced highly enriched uranium.'[66]

PYONGYANG'S DENIALS FALL ON DEAF EARS

DPRK attempts to establish their account did not get much coverage until the visit of Lewis, Hecker and Pritchard in January 2004, although the BBC, for one, in some of its stories did mention that Pyongyang had denied the allegations. The BBC also ran a story about a mistake that had occurred in the monitoring of a North Korean broadcast; a South Korean

> unification ministry official was reported as saying that the North Korean announcer's accent had confused Southern listeners monitoring the broadcast. Just one syllable had turned 'is entitled to have' (*kajige tui-o-itta*) into 'has come to have' (*kajige tui-otta*), the official explained.[67]

The official Korean Central News Agency (KCNA) published an implied but ambiguous denial of an HEU programme on 25 October 2002 (and this was what was reiterated to Oberdorfer) when reporting the DPRK's call for a non-aggression treaty between the two countries.

> Producing no evidence, [Kelly] asserted that the DPRK has been actively engaged in the enriched uranium program in pursuit of possessing nuclear weapons in violation of the DPRK–US agreed framework. He even intimidated the DPRK side by saying that there would be no dialogue with the U.S. unless the DPRK halts it, and the DPRK–Japan, and north–south relations would be jeopardized.
>
> The U.S. attitude was so unilateral and high-handed that the DPRK was stunned by it. ...
>
> Its reckless political, economic and military pressure is most seriously threatening the DPRK's right to existence, creating a grave situation on the Korean Peninsula. Nobody would be so naive as to think that the DPRK would sit idle under such situation.

That was why the DPRK made itself very clear to the special envoy of the U.S. President that the DPRK was entitled to possess not only nuclear weapon but any type of weapon more powerful than that so as to defend its sovereignty and right to existence from the ever-growing nuclear threat by the U.S.

The DPRK, which values sovereignty more than life, was left with no other proper answer to the U.S. behaving so arrogantly and impertinently.

The DPRK has neither need nor duty to explain something to the U.S. seeking to attack it if it refuses to disarm itself.[68]

The following January (2003) the *People's Korea* published an interview with DPRK Foreign Ministry Director O Song Chol in which he said that Kelly's story that they had admitted an enriched uranium programme was 'a sheer lie' and that the DPRK had flatly denied having such a programme.[69] After the Lewis visit, where the DPRK strenuously denied having an HEU programme, the mainstream US media discovered what the Koreans had been saying for over a year; for example the *Washington Post*: 'But, in a curious twist, they now deny that they ever had a uranium enrichment plant or had ever suggested that they did.'[70]

UNRELENTING AMERICAN PRESSURE

Using the 'admission' of an HEU programme as justification the United States announced on 11 November 2002 that it was halting oil shipments and the following month the DPRK responded by saying that this left it no choice but to reactivate its nuclear reactors for electricity generation. The US kept up the pressure, intercepting a North Korean ship carrying missile exports to Yemen on 9 December. The Yemeni government complained and the US was forced to step down, admitting that the action was illegal and allowing the ship to go its way. The Spanish, who had been deployed to carry out the actual seizure of the Korean ship, were angry that their men had been endangered in such a way.[71] This may have contributed to the anti-American feeling that helped sweep Aznar from power in April 2004, after the Madrid bombings, and that led to the rapid extraction of Spanish troops from Iraq.

Anti-Americanism was also taking its toll in South Korea, where Roh Moo-hyun, defying earlier predictions, narrowly defeated the conservative candidate, Lee Hoi-chang, to succeed Kim Dae-jung as president. Anti-Americanism was widely recognised to be a major factor in the election, and this had been building up especially since mid year when two Korean girls had been accidentally killed by a US army vehicle.[72] Since a crisis with the North had often erupted prior to elections in the past, to the benefit of the conservative candidate, such as Roh Tae-woo in 1987, the calculation may well have contributed to Washington's despatch of the Kelly mission and the creation of the crisis. For creation it certainly was. Kelly was not sent to seek a solution of a dispute with Pyongyang, but to bring things to a head. This was probably precipitated, as Pollack suggests, by the Kim–Koizumi summit, but the expected effect on the South Korean election may well have entered into calculations. Less pressing, the crisis would also serve to dent any rapprochement between the DPRK and the EU, and freeze relations with other countries such as Canada and New Zealand.

Whilst it is plausible to suggest that the Bush administration purposefully engendered a crisis, it is not clear whether the consequences were fully anticipated. Some hawks were undoubtedly happy to see anything that might lead to military confrontation with Pyongyang; Richard Perle for instance called for 'bold action' when he resigned from the Pentagon's Advisory Board (having been forced to do so by revelations of conflict of interest).[73]

Perhaps it was thought that the Koreans would buckle and yield, as the Iraqi government had done, and the Libyan government was about to do. If so, these hopes were dashed. Pyongyang responded to the American challenge with a series of graduated steps that would allow Washington to resolve the crisis at any time without undue loss of face. The responses all took place within the structure of the Agreed Framework itself. When the Americans beefed up their military presence around the Korean peninsula, Pyongyang complained but did not attempt to follow suit.[74] Significantly the moratorium on missile testing stayed in place and there was no threat to lift it, although Pyongyang did say, in November 2002 when Koizumi was reneging on the September summit agreement that it was having second thoughts.[75] And when Beijing managed to get talks going, first the Three-Party talks in April 2003 then the subsequent Six-Party talks, the DPRK turned up, albeit reluctantly.

DPRK UNPACKS ITS OBLIGATIONS

However, when it came to the provisions of the Agreed Framework, things were different. When the US abrogated the AF in November

2003 by halting the oil shipments the DPRK moved, step by step, to unpack its own obligations under the agreement. The Yongbyon reactor was reactivated a month later, when the US had showed no sign of being willing to negotiate it announced that it would complete its withdrawal from adherence to the NPT that had been suspended in 1994. However, it explicitly said in its statement of 10 January 2003 that it had no intention of making nuclear weapons:

> Though we pull out of the NPT, we have no intention to produce nuclear weapons and our nuclear activities at this stage will be confined only to peaceful purposes such as the production of electricity.
>
> If the U.S. drops its hostile policy to stifle the DPRK and stops its nuclear threat to the DPRK, the DPRK may prove through a separate verification between the DPRK and the U.S. that it does not make any nuclear weapon.
>
> The United States and the IAEA will never evade their responsibilities for compelling the DPRK to withdraw from the NPT, by ignoring the DPRK's last efforts to seek a peaceful settlement of the nuclear issue through negotiations.[76]

Timeline 11   2003

2003

10 January	NK announces it plans to withdraw from the Non-Proliferation Treaty effective the next day. NK says it doesn't intend to make nuclear weapons and all of its nuclear development efforts 'will be confined only to power production and other peaceful purposes'.
18 January	DPRK Foreign Ministry official says Kelly produced no evidence of HEU programme and 'fabricated' an admission; claims HEU was 'flatly denied'
17 February	US and South Korea announce that they will hold joint military exercises in March
25 February	Roh Moo-hyun inaugurated as president of South Korea. Outlines 'Peace and Prosperity policy', a continuation of the 'Sunshine policy'
26 February	US says North Korea has activated its five-megawatt nuclear reactor at its main nuclear complex in Yongbyon
20 March	US and allies invade Iraq
9 April	Announcement that US forces in South Korea will relocate south of Seoul

23–25 April	US, North Korea, and China hold trilateral talks in Beijing. US later says NK privately claimed to have nuclear weapons but no independent verification of this
18 June	DPRK announces that it is 'increasing its nuclear deterrent force for self-defence'
30 June	Ground breaking for Kaesong industrial complex, Hyundai's industrial park for SK companies in NK
22 August	Charles 'Jack' Pritchard, US special envoy for negotiations with North Korea resigns in argument over administration policy on eve of Beijing talks
27–29 Aug	First round of Six-Party talks are held in Beijing, no significant progress

There was no response from Washington bar an announcement of forthcoming joint military exercises with South Korea. It talked of interdiction under the Proliferation Security Initiative (PSI) and harassment, as laid out in Operations Plan (OPLAN) 5030, it increased its military presence and spending in Korea, and invaded Iraq in March 2003.[77] By June the DPRK was talking of its 'nuclear deterrent'. At the same time it stressed that 'any contention that the DPRK may secretly sell nuclear substance and missiles to terrorist groups is a mockery of its firm stand against terrorism'.[78] Pyongyang had long ago decided that appeasement would be no solution, and pointedly and frequently referred to the Iraq experience: 'As the Iraqi situation showed, arms inspection is followed by disarmament and war.'[79] However, it also signalled its desire to 'open up' as part of the process of economic reform and marketisation embarked upon in July 2002: 'The DPRK wishes to receive as much cooperation as possible from other countries including expert training and experience as it is the first time for it to run such markets.'[80]

Furthermore, a nuclear deterrent would allow it to decrease its conventional forces (which the US had been demanding) and shift the demobilised soldiers to civilian production:

> The DPRK's intention to build up a nuclear deterrent force is not aimed to threaten and blackmail others but reduce conventional weapons under a long-term plan and channel manpower resources and funds into economic construction and the betterment of people's living.[81]

However this mixture of olive branch and talk of a nuclear deterrent had no effect on the US position. Despite the rhetoric, marketisation without regime change, on the lines of China, was not at all appealing. No more than democratisation, in Iraq or elsewhere, without US dominance. But if the carrots of marketisation, opening-up and demobilisation were ineffective, so was the threat of a nuclear deterrent. This was partly because, whatever the brouhaha, even if Pyongyang possessed a handful of atomic bombs and the missiles with which to hit the continental United States, they could only be used as a retaliatory last resort, and the decision to bring that about could only be Washington's. However, there was another reason for their apparent unconcern. As Jack Pritchard revealed after he resigned, the administration did not believe that the Koreans could in fact process the spent fuel rods from the Yongbyon reactor before 'diplomatic pressure' would force them to stop: 'American intelligence believed that most if not all the rods remained in storage, giving policymakers a false sense that time was on their side as they rebuffed North Korean requests for serious dialogue … .'[82]

This was a curious business, because the administration had claimed that it had to act with urgency in respect of the HEU programme, although there was a general consensus that the uranium route was longer and that the quickest way for the Koreans to develop a weapons capability was through the reprocessing of plutonium.[83]

DPRK, SIX-PARTY TALKS AND US STRATEGY

The message that Washington was unconcerned about the spent fuel rods must have got through to Pyongyang which is why Pritchard, along with Stanford professor John Lewis and Los Alamos nuclear scientist Siegfried Hecker were invited to visit Yongbyon in January 2004.[84] Pritchard has been ringing the alarm bells ever since, and stories that the DPRK now has eight warheads (and more) became commonplace during 2004. Even Kelly was forced to admit that the arsenal may be increasing.[85] On the other hand Hecker, it will be recalled, was unconvinced that Pyongyang was able to develop a meaningful weapons and delivery capability.[86]

Timeline 12   2004
2004

January	US private delegation – Lewis, Hecker and Pritchard – visit Yongbyon
25–28 February	2nd round of Six-Party talks in Beijing
12 March	Impeachment of Roh Moo-hyun

23 March	Park Geun-hye elected leader of Grand National party
1 April	Chung Sun-dok, last Communist guerrilla from the Korean War dies in Seoul. She was captured in 1963
15 April	Roh Moo-hyun's Uri party makes sweeping gains in South Korean election
12–14 May	Working-party meeting for Six-Party talks in Beijing
14 May	Impeachment of Roh Moo-hyun overturned by Constitutional Court
23–26 June	Third round of Six-Party talks; slight progress

It seems likely that the administration judged that the possibility of Pyongyang possessing and demonstrating a nuclear weapons capability was sufficiently low for it to pursue the strategy that it did. It shrugged off the criticism from various quarters that this strategy was giving the DPRK time to become a nuclear weapons state.[87] The strategy had three components.

1   Raising of the HEU issue both to force Pyongyang out of the Agreed Framework, opening up the 'comprehensive solution' that Armitage had drafted in 1999, and also to provide a mechanism for intrusive, thorough and potentially unending inspection of DPRK territory, thus negating the secrecy of its defences and putting pressure on its security apparatus
2   Multilateralism with as little bilateral contact as it could get away with. The argument was that the DPRK had violated the Agreed Framework, and the NPT, and that it was a matter for the 'international community', and not the US alone to force it into compliance with the NPT. Powell and Armitage thought that they could exert sufficient pressure on others, especially China, South Korea and Russia, to pressure North Korea to comply.
3   Talks without meaningful negotiations. No step-by-step approach as in the Agreed Framework, but a demand that North Korea agree to 'complete, verifiable and irreversible dismantlement (CVID) of its nuclear programme before the US would allow South Korea and Japan to provide energy aid. Furthermore, the US added a long string of other issues that would have to be settled to its satisfaction – human rights, missile testing and exports, conventional armed forces, religious freedom – before there could be talk of normalisation of relations.

Faced with this stand, there was precious little Pyongyang could do. No doubt its public relations could have been better but there was slim chance that coverage in the Western media would actually improve. It made concessions in the course of the Six-Party talks – the demand for a treaty of non-aggression seems to have been watered down to an acceptance of security guarantees – but there was a sense that whatever it agreed, the United States would move the goalposts. The DPRK initiated, or responded to, moves to improve relations with ROK, Japan, China, Russia, and indeed the US public. It reiterated time and again: 'The DPRK will make sustained efforts for the peaceful settlement of the nuclear issue between the DPRK and the U.S. And the DPRK is ready to render necessary cooperation to this end.'[88]

It was like a replay of the US invasion of Iraq in that, despite the rhetoric from Washington, there was nothing the other side could do, bar surrender, to bring about a change in American policy, and outsiders had limited impact.[89]

The US strategy was not without its critics and dangers. If Pyongyang demonstrated nuclear weapons capability then this would give ammunition to domestic critics, and would probably be taken up by the Democratic presidential contender Kerry himself. The Chinese, in particular, would be unhappy with a nuclear North Korea because it would give impetus to pressure for Japan to go nuclear, and stimulate the whole re-militarisation campaign. The administration had shown itself comfortable with Japanese re-militarisation because it believed it could constrain and control it. Indeed Armitage has publicly said that Japan would not get US support for becoming a permanent member of the UN Security Council unless it removed the peace clause from its constitution.[90] However a Japan re-armed to a level commensurate with its economy and one that was furthermore nuclear-armed might be less amenable to American direction than in the past, and certainly many Americans would be concerned about that possibility. A nuclear North Korea would put pressure on Seoul to go nuclear. The US had stopped that in the 1970s, but might not succeed this time.[91]

The HEU issue, once raised, had become something on which neither Pyongyang, nor Washington, could compromise.

For Washington, certainly while Bush is in office, HEU is non-negotiable not so much because of its inherent importance in terms of weapons potential, but for its political implications. Ralph

Cossa, Kelly's successor as president of Pacific Forum CSIS, put it succinctly:

> North Korea knows – or should realize –that President Bush cannot yield on this point: to turn a blind eye toward the uranium program now does more than 'reward bad behavior'; it says that the whole crisis was unnecessary in the first place. Both election year politics and sound strategic reasoning preclude such a step.[92]

It would clearly have been easier for Kerry, if he had been elected, to move on and enter into meaningful negotiations with Pyongyang on issues that were negotiable. But he would have had to disown to some extent the actions of his predecessor and he was unlikely to have had the political courage to do that.

It is equally difficult for Pyongyang to compromise. If it has no programme, then that cannot be relinquished. If it has a programme and now admits to it, after having vehemently denied it, there is a loss of face. But there is more to it than that.

Richard Armitage, in a somewhat cavalier and probably disingenuous manner, has said in an interview to the Japanese newspaper, the *Asahi Shimbun*:

> Q: Will you also ask for the dismantlement of highly enriched uranium (HEU)?
> A: Well, don't you think it would be reasonable to expect that if they don't have it they'll have to be able to show the international community they don't have it? They say they don't have it. Let them prove that. If they have it, then of course it would have to be dismantled, as we talk about the complete, irreversible and verifiable dismantlement of the nuclear program.[93]

The problem is, as Armitage no doubt knows, and as his senior colleague Donald Rumsfeld said when asked about high-level Pakistani government involvement in exporting nuclear technology, 'You can't prove a negative.'[94] On the other hand, the administration is secure in the knowledge that as long as the DPRK exists, no one can prove that an HEU programme does not exist. The Chinese, and others, may not believe the US, but it cannot disprove the American claims.[95] The crunch would only come, as in Iraq, with a US occupation.

None of the other major powers involved – China, Russia, Japan and South Korea – were happy with the US strategy, though public criticism was naturally muted. To some extent they voted with their feet by supporting the multilateral forum for bilateral talks that China had started with the Three-Party talks in April 2003, and the series of Six-Party talks that commenced in August that year. In addition Koizumi made another visit to Pyongyang in May 2004, and Roh pushed ahead, despite the setbacks, with improving relations with the North. By August 2004 there were rumours that the long-delayed second North–South summit would take place before the US elections.[96] In the event, no summit took place and Roh, in his European tour in December 2004, 'barnstorming for negotiations', ruled out a summit before a deal was reached in the Six-Party talks.[97]

All these countries would, to varying degrees, suffer from a collapse of the DPRK, and all would benefit, not merely from a peaceful resolution of the nuclear crisis, but from a consensual, gradual and economically stimulating reunification of the Korean peninsula. The Chinese might have worried about a reunified Korea making irredentist claims in the future on its northeast on grounds of the ancient kingdom of Koguryo, but a collapse of the DPRK, or worse still hostilities, would drive still more Koreans into the area and exacerbate the danger.

How are we to interpret this American strategy? What drives it and what are the desired outcomes?

There is an inherent contradiction in long-term US East Asia policy. There is a general, if unarticulated, desire to keep China, Japan, and Korea separated from each other and amenable to American 'leadership'. A North Korea viewed either as a threat, irritant or liability, has been the centrepiece of that policy. It has thus been necessary to keep the DPRK isolated, threatened and impoverished. A consensual, gradual and economically stimulating reunification of the Korean peninsula would remove that element in the strategy. However, so would a destruction of the DPRK. Moreover, there would be other consequences, difficult to calculate. An economically and socially fractured Korean peninsula might well fall under greater Chinese political and economic influence.

If this assessment of American policy is correct then the core of it must be balance. Sufficient pressure on North Korea to keep the tension of the last 50 years in place, but not too much so as to provoke a crisis that will lead to a costly, and probably disadvantageous, resolution. The policy may be morally indefensible, but it does have its own logic. Whether it is sustainable is another matter.

The continuing North–South rapprochement, and the faltering but not defunct normalisation process between Japan and the DPRK, threaten US hegemony. The Bush administration of 2001–04 reacted with the hesitant impulsiveness, and lack of strategic foresight (perhaps a consequence of its notorious internal divisions), that has also characterised its Middle East policy. The second Bush administration might act with greater circumspection. But the past cannot be undone, either in Iraq or in Northeast Asia.

We can hope that peace, and prosperity, will prevail, but we cannot be confident. All we can be sure of is that the decision will be made in Washington. Not without outside constraints and influences, to be sure, but ultimately the power for Korean peace or war, for continued privation or for economic growth and transformation, lies with the United States. And that is where the responsibility rests as well.

Part II

The Pillars of Confrontation

Introduction to Part II

The first four chapters of this book have given a survey in rough chronological order of North Korea's struggle to survive. In its approximately 60 years of existence it has fought one hot war and endured virtually unremitting cold war. At times the pressure has lessened, as during Jimmy Carter's presidency or the final months of Clinton's and at other times, most recently under George W. Bush, it has intensified.

It is not surprising within this context that the DPRK has developed characteristics that many outsiders find abhorrent and most find difficult to understand. We have two sets of problems to tackle. Firstly, we must try to disentangle what is inherent in the system, and would continue whatever happened outside, and what is caused, exacerbated, or ameliorated by exterior forces and pressures. For instance we can look at figures for military expenditure, number of people under arms and length of compulsory military service and say this is the most militarised nation in the world because that is its nature. That is the line taken, for example, by Nicholas Eberstadt, who argues that

> The Democratic People's Republic of Korea (DPRK) is a state unlike any other – a political construct especially and particularly built for three entwined purposes: to conduct a war, to settle a historical grievance and to fulfil a grand ideological vision.[1]

Alternatively we can examine the threats facing the DPRK, first and foremost from Dr Eberstadt's America, and the balance of military power between the DPRK and its adversaries and decide that self-defence makes a more credible explanation. Furthermore we can look at the historical process of cycles of arms buildup and demobilisation and correlate those with the state of tension on the Korean peninsula. In other words we can look at the DPRK as a state in its essentials similar to any other. When threatened it will bristle and when not threatened it will become more relaxed. Clearly this is a complex process. Military establishments have their own vested interests – and this is as marked in the US as anywhere else – and countries find it easier to mobilise than to demobilise. Nevertheless, we can, I would argue, look at North Korea with understanding, identifying causes and seeking ways to improve things.

The other problem facing us is to disentangle truth from falsehood, fact from propaganda and that is no easy task. However, it is not impossible to clear away some of the more egregious misrepresentations to get at, if not that elusive animal the truth, at least some idea of the complexity and contradictoriness of reality. Often it is possible to disprove assertions but not to be able to establish what is actually happening.

Chapter 5 looks at what might broadly be called human rights in the DPRK covering allegations about public executions, experiments on prisoners, and prison camps. It also surveys the food position and examines the question of aid, and NGOs and refugees. The following chapter turns to issues which relate to North Korea's impact on the outside world; allegations of drug running, and questions of missile exports, terrorism and the military. Chapter 7 discusses the nuclear issue, for over a decade the centrepiece of the US–DPRK relationship, and this is accompanied by a detailed chronology in Appendix IV.

Chapter 8 concludes the book by bringing these issues together and examining the situation at the beginning of the second administration of George W. Bush.

5
The Human Rights Record: Complexities, Causes, Solutions

This chapter looks at the issues of human rights, international aid and refugees. There is a near universal international perception that the human rights record in North Korea is the worst in the world, and that the outflow of refugees is a manifest indication of that. However, the situation is much more complex and equivocal than that, as we shall see. Moreover, when we look into causes we discover that much is due to, or at a minimum exacerbated by, outside forces, principally the United States whose economic, political and military pressure contributes so much to the privations suffered by the people of the DPRK. The other side of that coin is that it is the United States more than any other actor which can bring about an improvement in the situation. However, there are serious dangers that genuine popular concern about human rights, and specifically about refugees, will be used by those in Washington pressing for 'regime change' and that this will lead to a worsening of the situation, South as well as North, and perhaps the devastation of the peninsula.

HUMAN RIGHTS

The currency of human rights is much debased. It was used, after the event, to justify the invasion of Iraq when the 'weapons of mass destruction' line was no longer sustainable, but it proved to be used just as fraudulently. Tony Blair, for instance, was forced to admit that his claim that '400,000 bodies had been found in Iraqi mass graves' was untrue and that only 5,000 bodies had been unearthed.[1] Since he alleged that the bodies *had* been found, rather than asserting that they *would* be found, we can fairly describe it as a deliberate falsification. That is not to justify human rights abuses in Iraq (after the occupation as well as before) nor anywhere else, North Korea included, but it does mean that we have to watch the lips of the accuser, and bear in mind what they have said in the past, and what their motivations might be. Saddam Hussein may well have been responsible for the 5,000 bodies, but Tony Blair was responsible for the lie.

The point here is not whether human rights are violated in North Korea, not even the degree of that, but the motivation of the accusers, the way they use concern over human rights as a camouflage for less disinterested purposes and to set a climate of opinion. When Tony Blair or the State Department talk of human rights, in Iraq or the Sudan, what drives the matter is oil and strategic interest.[2] There is no appreciable oil in North Korea, but there is certainly strategic interest. The coexistence of genuine moral fervour over crimes committed by others with a readiness to commit one's own is not uncommon. The road to empire is paved with good intentions.

It is because human rights are so important that we must be scrupulous in examining the evidence and be alert to the possible motivations of the accusers. We must also set out to make things better, rather than worse. Threatening a first nuclear strike is hardly a way to save victims of human rights abuses. And finally, in dealing with the DPRK we need to take special account of its incredible ineptitude in presenting its case. For in this, as in other fields, the DPRK is very poor at international public relations.

Just to give one example. Every year the US State Department releases a report on human rights around the world, though not in the United States. It also tends to touch lightly on countries where the US is in a dominant position, which is quite a number now, or skips over the relationship it has with the local government. It is an important part of the armoury of America's 'soft power'. This is the phrase coined by Joseph S. Nye, Dean of Harvard University's John F. Kennedy School of Government (and a former Assistant Secretary of Defense) to describe what we might think of as national brand image, in contradistinction to things like military power. He defines it as America's 'ability to attract others by the legitimacy of US policies and the values that underlie them', and he has criticised the Bush administration for depleting that power and fuelling anti-Americanism.[3] The US has traditionally had a competitive advantage in human rights; it was perceived to be better than its opponents such as the Soviet Union, China or North Korea. This reputation has become rather threadbare in recent years, along with the overall decline in its soft power. Glenn Kessler, writing in the *Washington Post*, was moved to point out that:

The State Department's annual human rights report released yesterday criticized countries for a range of interrogation practices it labeled as torture, including sleep deprivation for detainees, confining prisoners in contorted positions, stripping and blindfolding them and threatening them with dogs – methods similar to those approved at times by the Bush administration for use on detainees in U.S. custody.[4]

Secretary of Defense Rumsfeld had publicly approved methods which the State Department was condemning. 'Iran and North Korea, both labelled part of an "axis of evil" by Bush, also used techniques similar to those employed in U.S. terrorism detentions', he noted.[5] Actually, the position is rather worse that Kessler suggests because the US is increasingly outsourcing interrogation to countries like Egypt where prisoners can be interrogated under torture without infringing American law, though presumably the results are sent back to Washington.[6] None of this lets North Korea off the hook but it does mean that there is growing scepticism about the motivation behind American accusations and the legitimacy of America's self-appointed role of prosecutor. There is an increasing backlash from amongst the 190 countries criticised. The president of the Mexican Human Rights Commission, for instance, 'compared Washington's criticism of Mexico's record to "the donkey talking about long ears" – the Spanish-language equivalent of "the pot calling the kettle black" – because the United States violates human rights, especially those of our countrymen'.[7] He was referring to US treatment of illegal immigrants, the economic refugees who sneak across the border in much the same way, and for much the same reasons, as North Koreans into China. China has been taking a particularly robust stand again US 'double standards' and is now issuing its own annual report on the US human rights record.[8]

The DPRK's reaction to the State Department's 2004 human rights report was incredible. In the past it has scathingly counter-attacked the US which it has termed the 'world's biggest human rights abuser' because it is

> ... the most ferocious violator of sovereignty and abuser of human rights. It does not hesitate to threaten and blackmail those countries which incur its displeasure and destroy them by mobilizing armed forces under absurd pretexts. In recent years it waged several wars of aggression against those countries.[9]

That did not answer the accusations, but it did make a point about the accuser that many would accept. In its response to the 2004 report however, the DPRK Foreign Ministry under a headline which claimed it 'refutes U.S. Report on human rights' said:

> The U.S. ballyhoo about human rights practices every year does not deserve even a passing note. This can be made only by the Bush group, a mastermind of swindling and deception.
>
> The DPRK does neither pay heed to it nor listen to it. It is nothing surprising for the Bush administration to utter such words as it has inveterate enmity toward the system in the DPRK.
>
> It is, therefore, not interested at all in dealing with Washington.[10]

Retreating into a hermit shell in high dudgeon is not refutation, and clearly gives the impression that Pyongyang has much to hide. This is unfortunate because, as we shall see, the human rights situation is less certain and more complex that is commonly thought. The problem with the US human rights stand, of which the State Department's annual report is a major component, is that by hypocritically debasing and exploiting the debate on international human rights it exacerbates violations rather than facilitating improvement. But Washington's duplicity does not justify Pyongyang's intransigence, though it contributes to it. The DPRK needs to engage better on the human rights issue with the international community (in the real meaning of the word, not as a euphemism for the US government). The international aid community in the DPRK perhaps offers the best way of doing this, although it will not be easy.

Koreans are very proud, and very prickly in a situation where that pride and self-respect are perceived to be threatened. One of the lessons of the NGO experience in North Korea is that, over time, if both parties have the proper attitude, bridges can be built, trust established and dialogue can take place. To give charity with humility is as difficult as receiving it with self-respect.

Current human rights abuses, or alleged abuses, in North Korea cover a wide range. In this chapter I can only touch on the main ones

- Public executions
- Experiments on prisoners
- Prison camps and human rights, North and South
- Religion
- Using concern over human rights as a weapon
- Economic deprivation (the major infringement).

This is a difficult subject and one over which it is all too easy to indulge in sanctimonious hand wringing. It is important at the outset to establish the objectives, and to select objectives which are attainable within the context of this book.

The purpose here is not an academic assessment of the scope and extent of human rights abuses. It is trying to say, that given that there are no exact empirical measures, a lot of our perception is from second-hand reporting by people and agencies with anti-DPRK agendas. In painting this context and raising critiques of the data, analyses and assessments, I am saying that we must be reflexive and cautious. A writer on this subject has a special right and duty to do this, given the awesome example of the Iraq invasion which was based on a year of relentless media and politician propaganda about what turned out to be non-existing weapons and greatly exaggerated human rights abuses. But Iraq was not an isolated example. To give just one more, evidence is accumulating that the dismemberment of Yugoslavia was sold on the basis of a similar campaign of misinformation. John Pilger argues that:

> Lies as great as those of Bush and Blair were deployed by Clinton and Blair in their grooming of public opinion for an illegal, unprovoked attack on a European country. Like the buildup to the invasion of Iraq, the media coverage in the spring of 1999 was a series of fraudulent justifications ...
>
> One year later, the International War Crimes Tribunal, a body effectively set up by NATO, announced that the final count of bodies found in Kosovo's "mass graves" was 2,788. This included combatants on both sides and Serbs and Roma murdered by the Albanian Kosovo Liberation Army. Like Iraq's fabled weapons of mass destruction, the figures used by the U.S. and British governments and echoed by journalists were inventions along with Serb "rape camps" and Clinton's and Blair's claims that NATO never deliberately bombed civilians.[11]

Often images are fixed as a result of false claims which even if subsequently corrected (frequently in small print) remain pinioned to our minds. Mud sticks, as proponents of black propaganda fully realise. We should be aware that misinformation is a crucial part of war and politics. For instance, even though Rumsfeld was forced to disband the Office of Strategic Influence, whose function was, inter alia, to feed false stories to journalists, the debate goes on:

The Pentagon is engaged in bitter, high-level debate over how far it can and should go in managing or manipulating information to influence opinion abroad, senior Defense Department civilians and military officers say ...

Pentagon and military officials directly involved in the debate say that such a secret propaganda program, for example, could include planting news stories in the foreign press or creating false documents and Web sites translated into Arabic as an effort to discredit and undermine the influence of mosques and religious schools that preach anti-American principles.[12]

According to the *New York Times* story, the Pentagon plans only to lie to foreigners, not to Americans, though how, in a globalised world, that could be achieved, even if they really attempted it, is unclear.

But another purpose of this chapter is to unravel the causes of the human rights situation. Even if the human rights abuses do exist and exist on the scale that they are alleged to do, the question remains: who is responsible? Can it be laid entirely at the door of the regime in Pyongyang or is it also the consequence of external forces? The question of causes then leads immediately into the solutions.

Public Executions

Public executions are a common allegation but the charges are difficult to assess. For instance the Washington-based group Human Rights without Frontiers claims that it is 'independent of all political, ideological or religious movements'. Yet for all this lofty 'objective' moral high ground, it has the same myopia as the State Department. It looks in all parts of the world except the United States. Its standards of dispassionate investigation – verifying where possible and admitting to uncertainty elsewhere are open to question. It does indeed have horrifying stories about North Korea, many of which may well be true. But not all.

For example, in one rather infamous, much-rehearsed and broadcast case, it reports the public execution of one Yu Tae-jun, a defector who, it is said, went back to North Korea to rescue his wife:[13]

In June of last year [2000] he travelled to China and was not heard from since. However, in the beginning this year [2001] he is known to have been executed in the South Hamgyong Province in North Korea.

It is known that the North Korean government executed many former North Koreans, however this is the first time that the victim has actually been identified. In addition, due to the fact that Mr. Yu was a South Korean citizen, the repercussions for this incident are expected to be large.

> Mr. Yu was publicly executed in front of a group of North Korean citizens. It is known that he was charged with going to South Korea and committing treason against the Pyongyang government.[14]

'By all accounts', noted Aidan Foster-Carter, 'he's now very dead – at just 33.'[15] Fortunately for Mr Yu, public executions ain't what they used to be, and despite his execution being reported ten times by the conservative *Chosun Ilbo*, he gave a press conference in the North on 12 June 2001.[16] He subsequently turned up in South Korea in 2002 having, according to his mother, been pardoned by Kim Jong Il.

> 'I heard from my son that the North Korean leader directed my son's pardon on April 30 last year by saying that a man who loves his wife also loves the fatherland', Ahn Chong-suk, Yu's mother, was quoted as saying by the Yonhap News Agency.
> Ahn said she talked her son into lying about the circumstances of his escape out of fear that 'it might make Kim Jong-il look good'.[17]

Although he had been resurrected from the dead, Mr Yu was not out of trouble yet. In May 2003 he hit the news again:

> The Seoul District Court yesterday sentenced Mr. Yu to six months in prison for violating the inter-Korean exchange law. His crime: returning to the North without government permission in hopes of finding his wife and bringing her back.
> The court acknowledged yesterday that Mr. Yu had no improper motive, but it said the law must be obeyed ... The court said yesterday that a period of isolation from society would help to calm Mr. Yu down.[18]

It would also give Mr Yu the opportunity to meditate on the fickle nature of fame (he thought he was going to be treated like a hero), the uncertain, but usually hostile, reception given to asylum seekers, and human rights in general. He might also consider himself lucky because there was speculation he might be a double agent and the consequences then would be much worse.

'Double agent' has echoes of a chilling story that emerged in October 2000. Representative Kim Seong-ho of the ruling Millennium Democratic Party revealed in a report at a parliamentary audit session that some 10,000 'spies' had been sent North between 1953 and 1972. Some 7,726 did not return, and those that did were given little or no compensation, nor public recognition, because to have done so would be an admission that the South was breaking the Armistice Agreement.[19] However, according to one story, those who were infiltrated into the North and managed to return successfully three times were deemed to have been 'turned' into double agents and promptly arrested.[20]

These events, and these stories, are significant irrespective of whether they are true or not, because they give a flavour of the times. Of terrible things done, but also of accusations and rumours which by their very nature are difficult to verify or disprove. This is an added reason for being scrupulous with the facts. Yu Tae-jun was not publicly executed though this was widely, and confidently, reported in various media. Some of the earlier reports might have been genuine mistakes but there is no excuse for the later ones. While Andrew Gilligan and Dan Rather lost their jobs because they were not careful enough in checking their criticisms of the powerful, no one gets into trouble for writing accusations which are subsequently invalidated against North Korea, and other unpopular places. Such double standards are bad for journalism.

North Korea does not publish statistics on executions, public or otherwise, and might not be believed in any case. Amnesty International, in its survey of capital punishment worldwide, does not even conjecture a figure for North Korea.[21] It is impossible therefore to make any international comparisons. Singapore has officially the higher per capita execution rate in the world.[22] On the basis of published statistics the United States is 'ranked alongside world's most repressive regimes' being 'one of just four countries responsible for 84 per cent of executions around the world [in 2003]. The others are China, Iran and Vietnam.'[23] How does North Korea rank in this grisly league table? We just don't know but it is probably towards the top, certainly in per capita terms.

Experiments on Prisoners

On 1 February 2004 a BBC reporter, Olenka Frenkiel, presented a programme entitled *Access to Evil* which alleged that 'chemical experiments [were] being carried out on political prisoners in specially constructed gas chambers' at prison camp 22 which she said was in Haengyong, an isolated area near the border with Russia. The programme broadcast interviews with Kwon Hyok, who had been head of security at the camp. He was later transferred to the North Korean embassy in Beijing as an intelligence agent from where he subsequently defected. Olenka Frenkiel described how she had travelled to Seoul and had also met Kim Sang-hun, 'a distinguished human rights' activist, who gave her documentation, notably a Letter of Transfer, authorising human experimentation on prisoners. She showed this letter to 'a Korean expert in London who examined it and confirmed that there was nothing to suggest it was not genuine'. She asked Kwon Hyok what sort of paperwork accompanied victims, and he replied that there would be a Letter of Transfer.[24]

This horrific story was corroborated in a long article in the *Observer* by Antony Barnett. In it Kwon Hyok was described as former military attache at the DPRK embassy in Beijing. Barnett quotes a Letter of Transfer as saying 'The above person is transferred from ... camp number 22 for the purpose of human experimentation of liquid gas for chemical weapons.' He quotes Kim Sang-hun as confirming the document is genuine.[25] So here we have evidence that is repeated and circulated. Evidence, not merely of horrible crimes, but also of chemical weapons. Given the fact that the world had just gone through a lengthy period of media speculation and fabrication full of satellite pictures supporting defectors' reports of chemical weapons being held in Saddam Hussein's arsenal, only to discover that they were bogus, we should be very cautious and sceptical.[26] Here they go again perhaps, spreading the lies and the deceptions, this time in respect of another member of the Axis of Evil.

In the North Korea case the stories began to fall apart relatively swiftly. First, it was revealed that South Korean officials said that Kwon had not been military attache in Beijing as claimed.[27] Next, the attention was focussed on the Letters of Transfer which the South Korean intelligence community decided were forgeries; there were problems with nomenclature, size of the seals and type of paper.[28] When pressed by the opposition Grand National Party to be 'less lenient' towards North Korean human rights abuses the government countered that these particular accusations were groundless, 'saying they [refugees] often make unauthenticated statements'.[29] Joseph Koehler, an American working in Seoul as a newspaper translator, and a virulent critic of the North, thought the National Intelligence Service (the successor to the Korean CIA) 'seems to be spending more time trying to keep defectors quiet and blowing Sunshine up our asses', and was quite likely to want to squash 'yet another unflattering report about the North'. Yet even he came to the conclusion that 'the document looks like a fake'.[30]

More information about the Letter of Transfer seeped out. Worried by the doubts being expressed about the authenticity of the document, the Citizens' Coalition for Human Rights of Abductees and North Korean Refugees held a press conference in Seoul on 12 February 2004 at which they gave more information about its provenance. They said it had been one of three smuggled out of North Korea the previous August (2003) by Kang Byong-sop, 'who had worked as an engineer at the Hamhung plant where the testing allegedly took place'.[31] This later turned out to be the Vinalon textile fibre plant, which has long figured in US accusations of chemical weapons.[32] According to the press conference the prisoners were held at camp 22 but were transferred to the factory for the tests. This seems to be in conflict with the BBC documentary which placed the gas chambers in camp 22. Frenkiel also states that she was told that the documents had been 'snatched' from camp 22, and does not mention the factory.[33]

The Citizens' Coalition argued that Kang Byong-sop and his family had been arrested while trying to cross the border from China into Laos in January and feared that they had been sent back to North Korea. It is unclear whether the BBC knew of Kang's arrest before they showed the documentary. It is also uncertain exactly when the Kangs were returned to DPRK; a statement by the US Wiesenthal Center on 11 February called on China not to deport them because that 'would be tantamount to death sentence'.[34]

On 31 March it was reported that Kang Byong-sop and his family had given a press conference the previous day in Pyongyang.[35] KCNA carried a lengthy description of the testimony of Kang Byong-sop and his second son Kang Song Hak.[36] The elder Kang was reported to have confessed that the whole thing was a money-making scheme by his eldest son, Kang Song Guk, who had defected to the South seven years before. They had all met at Yanji in China where it is claimed that Song Guk told his father:

'Father, you can say that experiments of chemical weapons on human bodies have been made there'. 'If we say that we have brought important information about an "experiment of chemical weapons on human bodies" in a workshop in the February 8 Vinalon Complex where my father was working, we would be given a huge sum of money by human rights organizations in South Korea', Song Guk said.

When I said, 'There is no chemical plant in the complex, much less is it thinkable that the plant produces chemical weapons', my son said that he would prepare a document about a chemical plant, insisting that human rights organizations in South Korea would simply believe that the complex would have a chemical factory and might produce such weapons.[37]

Kang Song Guk was not present at the Pyongyang press conference and it is not clear what has happened to him. If he had handed the documents over to the Citizen's Coalition in Seoul he might have stayed there rather than return to his father in China, but he does not seem to have surfaced. However, there is another twist. According to the Melbourne Age he was, in fact, Kwon Hyok:

> Much of the evidence in the program came from a defector given the new name of Kwon Hyuk (sic) (called Kang Song Guk by the North Koreans), described as a former military attache at the North Korean embassy in Beijing and who had also managed the camp.[38]

Olenka Frenkiel on the other hand, says the document she received from Kim Sang-hun had been 'given to him by someone else completely unrelated to Kwon Hyok. He told me the man had recently snatched them illicitly from camp 22 before escaping'.[39]

The forgeries and inconsistencies of the camp 22/Vinalon plant story do not prove that North Korea does not have chemical weapons, nor conducts experiments on prisoners. Sadly there have been many documented cases of experiments on humans over the last century. Nazi Germany is one obvious example, and Japan's infamous wartime unit 731 is another. This unit carried out experiments on Chinese and Korean prisoners nicknamed 'maruta' (logs) because they were viewed as insensate beings of no consequence, and its experts were inherited by the US occupation.[40] The British, we know, carried out experiments on national servicemen at Porton Down in the 1950s.[41]

Olenka Frenkiel reasonably claims that she did her best to get at the truth:

> So I haven't seen these gas chambers. I haven't seen these prisons myself. So the next best thing you have is testimony and what documentary evidence you can find.
>
> Now of course we know from Iraq that testimony from defectors can be suspect, can be exaggerated, and we went to some considerable lengths to filter it through, check it with others, corroborate it with other people's testimony, and check the credibility as far as was possible of eye witnesses.[42]

She argues that North Korea is sensitive to bad publicity and will stop doing things if pressured:

... that the North Koreans do respond when they are accused of, for example, counterfeiting money, which is what they were doing, for (sic) manufacturing pharmaceuticals. There was clear evidence that they stopped doing it or that they scaled it down, and there is a strong belief, I think, among significant people in South Korea, that this film will force them to look at their human rights and start to – well, to stop doing what they're doing. ...

... They need friends in the world. They want diplomatic relations with the United States. They have diplomatic relationships with Britain. They want to expand those. They want cultural exchanges. All of those expansions of their diplomatic status in the world could be made conditional on an improvement of the human rights record, and with any luck we can only do a little, small amount as journalists. That will help. It will feed into the agenda and it will put a bit of pressure on them to improve that.[43]

There is much to agree with there, but the problem is that false accusations might be counter-productive.

Ms Frenkiel has been undeterred by the South Korean scepticism and returned to the attack with another documentary in July 2004 in which she 'quoted a defector identified only as Dr. Kim as saying he had experimented on prisoners with a cyanide-based gas since the late 1970s'.[44]

Reuben Staines, writing in the *Korea Times*, noted that

The BBC reporter, Olenka Frenkiel, in February presented a similar story featuring another defector who said he witnessed atrocities in prison camps, including human experiments. Those claims were dismissed by South Korea's National Intelligence Service, prompting Frenkiel to search for other defectors to back her story.[45]

However, a South Korean government official was reported as saying,

'It's hard to check the authenticity of the North Korean defector's allegation', the official told The Korea Times on condition of anonymity. 'But unless the claims can be clarified, we will not take up the issue with North Korea'.[46]

The attitude of the Seoul government has been criticised but its policy of working within the political context, and refraining from statements which damage the improvement of North–South relations, already under such strain from US policy, offers the best way forward. Despite what Ms Frenkiel says, unsubstantiated accusations about secret experiments, even if they were true, would not be a restraining influence. It is more to likely to make those responsible for experiments ensure that there are no witnesses and no survivors. Changing the environment so there is less incentive, or hopefully a disincentive, for anyone to do such a thing, is more productive.

Prison Camps and Human Rights, North, South, and Elsewhere

North Korea is often portrayed as a vast gulag, with large numbers of political prisoners and the rest of the population living in daily fear of being sent off, arbitrarily, to a prison camp. However, once we look into it we find that this picture is suspect. For instance, as we shall see in a moment, few people who flee to South Korea from the North give political repression as the reason.

The figure invariably given for the number of prisoners in North Korea is 200,000 although the 2004 State Department Human Rights report gave an estimate of 150,000–200,000.[47] Where these figures come from, and how dependable they are, are unknown. Certainly, standard official sources such as the British Home Office *World Prison Population List* do not give estimates for DPRK. It is also unknown whether the estimate of 200,000 excludes criminals, and in any case, the dividing line between a 'criminal' and a 'political prisoner' is very much a contested one.

However, for comparison, we should note that according to the British Home Office, the United States has the largest prison population in the world, not merely absolutely (2.0 million in 2001) but also as a proportion of population, at 686 per 100,000 population. According to other sources, 5.6 million Americans have spent time in prison, and 30 per cent of black American males go to gaol sometime in their lives. Table 5.1 puts these figures together. If there are 200,000 people in prison in the DPRK then this is a high rate by world standards, and much higher than the ROK, but not much higher than the United States. It is, however, considerably lower than the rate for Afro-Americans and other ethnic groups such as Latinos in the United States.

There are also satellite photos of camps.[48] We know that George W. Bush has seen them because he refers to them in his discussion with Bob Woodward.[49] Exactly what they really indicate or prove is another matter. Colin Powell, it will be recalled, showed satellite photos to the UN that purported to prove Iraq's WMD.

Table 5.1   Imprisonment rates, US, DPRK, ROK, 2001

Country	In prison	Total	Prisoners per 100,000 population	Source
	Millions		Number	
US				
Prison population	2	293	683	1
Some time in prison	5.6	293	1,911	2
Black males			33,333	2
DPRK				
Prison population	0.2	22	909	3
ROK				
Prison population	0.063	47	134	1

Sources:
1 Walmsley, Roy. *World Prison Population List*, fourth edition. London: Home Office, 2003.
2 Younge, Gary. '30% of black men in US will go to jail'. *Guardian*, 18 August 2003.
3 Usual estimate, see text.

Lack of hard data from disinterested sources aside, it is important to approach this subject within the historical and comparative context. Basically, political and social systems are not fixed in concrete. They are products of historical and situational forces and these we must attempt to understand if we are going to arrive at ways of making things better. The South Korean experience, and the inter-Korean comparison, is instructive. Amnesty International estimated that there were 300 political prisoners in South Korea in 1999.[50] By 2004 it considered the situation had greatly improved but it said that at least 16 were still being held under the National Security Law, and at least 493 conscientious objectors were in prison.[51]

To attempt to tally up human rights abuses in the two Koreas as a way of excusing the situation in one part or the other is morally untenable, but a comparison is important nonetheless if we are to understand the causes and help improve the condition of the Korean people.

The human rights situation in the South at one time was very bad, and for much of the same reasons as in the North, namely, a perceived threat within the framework of an authoritarian culture and political system. It is much better now, with the onset of civilian democracy but it still carries too many vestiges of the past. Until recently South Korea had the unenviable reputation of having the world's longest-serving political prisoners.[52]

One of those political prisoners, Suh Sung, is the author of a book, *Unbroken Spirits: Nineteen Years in South Korea's Gulag*, published in 2001.[53] Coincidentally, the same year saw the publication of a book by a former prisoner in a North Korean gulag, Kang Choi-Hwan, called *The Aquariums of Pyongyang: Ten Years in a North Korean Gulag*. Gavan McCormack, the noted scholar of Northeast Asia from the Australian National University did a radio review of the two books in which he was able to compare and contrast the experiences and the analyses.[54] He faults both authors for focussing on the awful situation in the part of Korea in which they were imprisoned, without being aware of the crimes in the other part. There is, in other words, a lack of historical and political context:

> Kang and Rigoulot present their picture of wickedness and cruelty, roguishness or 'evil', in simple terms that even George W. Bush would understand. What is missing is any sense of Korean history, the half century of Japanese colonialism, the externally imposed division, the terrible civil war, turned by external intervention into a catastrophe, the prolonged Cold War. Paradoxically, the picture presented by Suh Sung is almost the reverse image of this: of brutality and oppression under anti-communism. Even writing in 2000, ten years after his release, Suh can focus only on his South Korean gulag, seemingly blind to the problem of North Korea's gulag system. Both accounts, in other words, remain steeped in Cold War thinking.[55]

The Frenchman Jean Rigoulot, who is credited as joint author of *The Aquariums of Pyongyang* is a contributing editor to the *Black Book of Communism*.

Kang Chol-hwan comes from a Korean Japanese family who emigrated to North Korea in the 1960s, as did many others helped, it has since transpired, by a Japanese government keen on 'ethnic improvement'.[56] His grandmother became a deputy to the Supreme People's Assembly but for some reason the family ran foul of the authorities in 1977. Young Chol-Hwan was sent, aged nine, to a camp at Yodok where he spent the next ten years before, again for an unknown reason, he was released. He eventually found his way to South Korea in 1989 where he encountered a society that had just moved into democracy.

One result of this democracy was the release from prison the following year of Suh Sung:

... who endured not 10 but 19 years of horror under even worse conditions including torture, before being released just a little after Chol-Hwan, in 1990. This account, however, is of a gulag in South Korea. *Unbroken Spirits: Nineteen Years in South Korea's Gulag* tells the story of a political prisoner in South Korea, Suh Sung, now a professor at a University in Kyoto, who was convicted on trumped-up political charges in 1971 and not released from prison till 1990. When Kang arrived in Seoul, which seemed the epitome of freedom, Suh was still in his gulag.[57]

McCormack concludes his review by wishing for a book that would offer a dialogue between Kang and Suh so that 'When each can feel grief and outrage over the brutality and violence inflicted on the other, perhaps then Korea north and south will be able to move towards its democratic future, one without gulags of any kind'.[58]

Gavan McCormack is absolutely right to tie the two parts of Korea together. Human rights, and prosperity, in the one half are linked to those in the other.

Human rights in the South have much improved since the departure of the military dictatorships but there is still plenty of criticism, and much to criticise.[59] It is expected that the situation will improve further under President Roh Moo-hyun who is a former human rights lawyer, but the National Security Law still imposes restrictions that would be considered unacceptable elsewhere. A recent cause celebre has been the case of Professor Song Du-yul.

Song Du-yul fled Park Chung-hee's Korea in the mid 1960s ending up in Germany where he became a professor of sociology at Muenster University. In September 2003 he returned to Korea after 37 years of exile at the invitation of the Korea Democracy Foundation as part of its programme of inviting 'Foreign activists who fought for democracy in South Korea in the 1960s–80s'.[60] On arrival he was promptly arrested for having carried out 'pro-North Korea' activities in Germany. He was given a seven-year jail term in March 2004 but in July this was overturned on appeal and the sentence was reduced to three years, suspended for five years. The high court rejected the charge that Song had been a member of the politburo of the Korean Workers' Party – an allegation vouched for by defector Hwang Jang-yop – but upheld the charge that he 'secretly visited North Korea'.[61] He was subsequently allowed to return to Germany for his teaching but it was suggested that he would come back to South Korea after that.[62]

The Song case has come to be a symbol of the National Security Law and a poll of National Assembly members conducted by the liberal daily *Hankyoreh* reportedly showed 87.7 per cent wanting to revise or abolish the law.[63] The *Korea Times* worried that

> ... the ruling is likely to embolden the Presidential Truth Commission on Suspicious Deaths, which recently triggered a controversy with its recommendation that two Northern spies be recognized as fighters for democratization because they struggled to abolish undemocratic laws until their deaths from hunger strike during their second imprisonments.[64]

The response of the 'international human rights community' to the case was muted, compared with what would have happened if this had been North Korea (or China) handing out the sentences. Amnesty International, for one, did issue a letter of protest.[65]

Both Koreas had violent births, with foreign midwives. This led, perhaps inevitably, to the Korean War and that in its turn further embedded polarisation and repression in both societies. The repression took different forms, and evolved in different ways. In the North political orthodoxy was imposed largely through political mobilisation, with straightforward military force being a lesser instrument. In the South there was also political mobilisation, but because it inherited the Japanese policing apparatus there was a greater tendency towards conventional army-led repression, as on Cheju island and in Kwangju. With the demise of the military dictatorships South Korea has undergone a rapid and profound transformation, as yet unmatched in the North, but residues of the past, such as the National Security Law, still linger.

North Korea is a much more repressive and authoritarian society than *contemporary* South Korea. However, it is important to consider the reasons for that and the forces, such as US hostility, which reinforce those characteristics rather than facilitate change. Paradoxically, visible signs of repression are less evident in the North than in the South, where even today baton-wielding riot police are a frightening sight, especially the plain-clothes ones. In fact, police or security presence in Pyongyang is very light, most of the police seen being female traffic police. Social control in North Korea, as in many other countries or institutions, is internalised so external force is less necessary. This raises the old conundrum whether repression accepted as natural and unchallengeable through custom and socialisation, indoctrination, and education is better or worse than that imposed through external, visible, power.

Religion

South Korea is unusual in Asia having a large Christian minority.[66] It has been described as 'one of Christianity's most strategic centers in Asia'.[67] Things are different in the North, but the situation is more complex, and less repressive, than alleged by evangelical Christians.[68] The standard line is that Christians are persecuted. Antony Barnett, writing of prison camps, claims, 'Many are Christians, a religion believed by Kim Jong-Il to be one of the greatest threats to his power.'[69] Mr Barnett does not give any evidence for Kim Jong Il's alleged fear of Christians. It is more plausible to suggest that although there is a large element of ideological competition between *Juche* and Christianity, the latter is tolerated (and increasingly so) in so far as it supports the state rather than opposing it, and allying itself with the enemies of the DPRK. Indeed one can go, as I have done on a couple of occasions, to Pongsu church in Pyongyang and see a building, and a service, familiar to Christians elsewhere. The Rev. Don Borrie, a Presbyterian minister whom I accompanied, wrote,

> ... we joined in an Easter Communion service along with two hundred Koreans, a smattering of foreign visitors and members of the diplomatic service. Despite being in Korean the Order of Service was familiar as were a number of the hymns which were sung with the same energy and conviction found in Pacific Island acts of worship. The congregation was a balance of women and men, a number of whom assisted the ordained male minister in the conduct of worship. Communion was with individual cups with communicants coming to the Communion Table.[70]

There were no portraits of the Kim family in the church, or indicative presence of the state, though the adjoining offices of the Korean Christian Federation did have portraits, as does any public building, from offices to schools. Pongsu church is a showcase, but it is not alone. The Korean Christian Federation, the state-sanctioned protestant body, has '500 house groups, two churches, involving 12,000 members, a theological seminary catering for 10 students in a 5 year program'.[71] Kathi Zellweger, who heads the DPRK aid effort of the Catholic charity Caritas, and who by June 2004 had notched up 46 visits to North Korea, describes going to Mass:

A surprise was to find a delegation from South Korea at the Changchun Catholic Church. With priests in the visiting group, a proper Mass in Korean and with communion took place and moreover, the South Koreans also explained the work of Caritas in North Korea to the community.[72]

One of the more intriguing developments of recent years has been the building of a Russian Orthodox Church in Pyongyang, expressly ordered it is said by Kim Jong Il after a visit to Russia in August 2002:

It was reported that during his visit, Chairman Kim viewed the churches in Khabarovsk and Vladivostok and said, 'It would be good to have a church like these in N.K. in the future'.[73]

The provincial government of Primorskii Krai, the Russian Far East, has donated $10,000 towards the construction of the church, Saint Trinity Church, and two North Koreans are studying theology in Moscow.[74]

Many Christian writers have noted the similarities between the 'Kim cult' and Christianity. Thomas Belke, an American evangelical, for instance, views *Juche* as a religion that attempts to supplant Christianity – 'North Koreans need the real Jesus Christ of the Bible, not a counterfeit'.[75] Tony Namkung writes of Kim Il Sung's 'deeply Christian background', coming from his parents and their milieu:

[Kim Il Sung's father] Kim Hyong Jik, who was undoubtedly a devout Christian by virtue of his admission to the Presbyterian Sungsil Academy, the most prominent mission school established by American Presbyterian missionaries in Pyongyang, [his mother] Kang Ban Sok, the daughter of a prominent Presbyterian elder of a church in Chilgol near the district called Mangyongdae today. In Daedong County, of which Pyongyang was the center, there were no less than 40 churches in 1911. This was why Pyongyang in those days was known throughout the Christian world as the 'Jerusalem of the East'.[76]

The historical interaction between leftist Korean nationalism (within which we might place Kim Il Sung and his family) and Christianity is a complex one. Christians were allies against the Japanese, but also rivals for Korean hearts and minds. After 1945 Christianity became increasingly identified with American imperialism and a hostile South – Syngman Rhee made much of his Christian connections. Even today there are vestiges of it as an anti-DPRK symbol. Along the

DMZ, besides the famous loudspeakers of both sides that used to blare propaganda, the North Koreans had slogans carved on rocks and the South Koreans illuminated Christian crosses.[77] But there have also been counter-currents, especially the activities of church-based NGOs, such as Caritas or the South Korean Good Neighbours International, in DPRK. Christians have also spearheaded the democratisation movement in South Korea which led to the removal of the military regimes and led to the Sunshine policy. Kim Dae-jung is himself a Catholic, and now the illuminated crosses on the DMZ are being turned off.

There is an aura of change. The Rev. Borrie comments that when he first had a meeting with the Korean Christian Federation in 1975 it 'took place semi secretly late at night in a Pyongyang hotel' whereas his meeting on Easter Sunday 2004 took place after a well-attended church service, and in front of a video camera operated by me.[78] Change in attitudes is a constant theme in Kathi Zellweger's reports, or in conversations one has with aid workers in North Korea.

Change implies conflicting forces and contradictory messages. Evangelical Christians see one harsh reality, other Christians, such as Borrie and Zellweger, see a rather more nuanced and hopeful one.

The Manipulation of Honest Concern

The Secretary General of Caritas, Duncan MacLaren, in a press release commemorating ten years of involvement with the DPRK noted that 'The Caritas programme is a good example of humanitarian engagement devoid of political manipulation'.[79] Whilst the aid agencies operating in North Korea, both the religious such as Caritas and international, such as WFP, have steered clear of 'political manipulation' in their 'humanitarian engagement' this is unusual. Elsewhere there has been blatant manipulation of humanitarian concern to advance political agendas. In particular, concern over human rights has been used as a weapon with which to try and dismantle the DPRK. James Kelly, amongst others, has stated that the US will not normalise relations with the DPRK until it is satisfied with its human rights situation.[80] This is a violation of the concept of the United Nations which assumes that nations will have normal diplomatic relations with each other, this not necessarily implying either approval or friendship. The American habit of judging human rights records of other countries has, as we have seen, come under increasing criticism from around the world, but this has not deterred either the US government, or Congress.

Mid year 2004 a bill entitled North Korea Human Rights Act 2004 was making its way through Congress, on the heels of another bill of the previous year, the North Korean Freedom Act of 2003.[81] Under the Human Rights Act funding was to be allocated for refugees (of which more below) and for broadcasting to North Korea, but there was no attempt to develop a relationship with DPRK that might lead to an improvement of human rights, rather the reverse. This was the fear expressed by many Koreans in the US and in South Korea. A coalition of a dozen NGOs grouped under the umbrella of Korean Civil Society issued a statement in April 2004 expressing concern. The statement identified five 'Issues to consider':

1   Right to food is a human rights issue
2   Engagement is more effective than isolation
3   Prevent making of refugees by continuing humanitarian assistance
4   Human rights should not be used to undermine the North
5   The North Korean Freedom Act and North Korean Human Rights Act affect the South Korea–US relationship.[82]

These NGOs were not alone in being concerned about the effect and implications of the bills. South Korean National Assembly Representative Chung Bong-ju of the ruling Uri party thought there were worrying precedents in that the US had invaded Iraq after passing a similar bill.[83] There was a general apprehension that these bills would exacerbate the human rights situation, rather than improve it, and would hamper moves to develop North–South relations.[84] The South Korean government was circumspect, treading carefully, caught as it so often has been between Washington and Pyongyang. In August 2004 I asked the South Korean Foreign Minister, Ban Ki-moon, what the official government position on the bill was and he said that there had been no official approach to Washington but they had 'made suggestions' in private.[85]

Hazel Smith has pointed out that the North Korea Freedom Act of 2003 (the 'Brownback Bill' after the Republican Senator Samuel Brownback, who introduced it) is counter-productive in that it exacerbates the human rights situation that it purports it wants to improve:

Instead, Brownback's proposals further threaten the basic freedoms of North Koreans by providing conservatives in the country an opportunity to restrict the openings to the West that have occurred since the late 1990s.[86]

Economic Deprivation

Despite improved harvests and a partially reviving economy, North Korea still remains afflicted by a cruel food shortage. The 'Arduous March' is not hyperbole. A joint news release (23 November 2004) from the World Food Programme (WFP) and the Food and Agriculture Organization (FAO) spelt it out:

> Despite its best harvest in ten years, the Democratic People's Republic of Korea (DPRK) will post another substantial food deficit in 2005 and require external aid to support more than a quarter of its 23.7 million people, two United Nations agencies said today.
>
> A report by the Food and Agriculture Organization (FAO) and the World Food Programme (WFP) projected domestic cereals availability in the 2004/05 marketing year (November–October) at 4.24 million tonnes, including milled rice and potatoes – a 2.4 per cent increase on 2003/04.
>
> However, it warns that insufficient production, a deficient diet, lower incomes and rising prices mean that 6.4 million vulnerable North Koreans – most of them children, women and the elderly – will need food assistance totaling 500,000 tonnes next year.[87]

As the Korean Civil Society coalition pointed out, the right to food is a human right. Indeed malnutrition, privation and economic deprivation are the major infringement of human rights for most North Koreans. The US North Korea Human Rights Act 2004 repeats the familiar charge that

> More than 2,000,000 North Koreans are estimated to have died of starvation since the early 1990s because of the failure of the centralized agricultural and public distribution systems operated by the Government of North Korea.[88]

This is a simplistic travesty of the complex forces that brought economic crisis to North Korea in the 1990s. Crucially it ignores the impact of external factors over which the DPRK government has little influence and the major current efforts on its part to reform and expand the domestic economy and to integrate into the global economy. As the executive director of the UN Environmental Programme said at the launch of the UNEP report on the State of the Environment in DPR Korea in August 2004:

> The Democratic People's Republic of Korea has shown its willingness to engage with the global community to safeguard its environmental

resources and we must respond so it can meet development goals in a sustainable manner.[89]

As with environmental resources, so across the board from a growing space for religion to joint ventures and special economic zones, there has been a definite shift in North Korean policy towards engagement.

The WFP/FAO echo the call for engagement:

> To deal with the chronic, structural food deficit, the FAO/WFP report recommended that the international community enter into a dialogue with the DPRK government toward the eventual mobilization of the economic, financial, and other resources needed to promote sustainable production and overall food security.[90]

Unfortunately, the 'international community' really means, in effect, the United States and the American government, which, especially since the presidency of George W. Bush, has been the major impediment to that engagement which is essential for the long-term and sustainable rehabilitation of the DPRK economy. Moreover, the nuclear crisis initiated by that administration and the hostility exemplified by the Axis of Evil speech have had an impact on short-term humanitarian aid, '... with North Korea listed in Washington's Axis of Evil, aid for the state has been cut by 80 per cent since 2001'.[91]

Much of the responsibility for malnutrition and privation in North Korea lies with the US government and Congress. There is a paradox here, since the US is also a large donor of aid to the DPRK via international agencies such as the WFP. But one reality, the giving of aid, should not blind us to the bigger reality. Moreover the cynic would suggest that US food aid can also be seen as a subsidy to American farmers.

Assessing the degree of responsibility of the United States for the lingering economic crisis in North Korea is a difficult and complex task that, as far as I know, has not been attempted. To begin with Pyongyang blames its very severe electricity shortage on US pressure to mothball its graphite-moderated reactors followed by failure to implement the Agreed Framework.[92] Next, sanctions and the inclusion on the Terrorism List seriously hamper attempts to increase exports and attract foreign investment. Then there is the unremitting military pressure on the DPRK. It is accompanied by demonstration of the devastating global power of America; the 100,000 casualties, mainly women and children, in Iraq in the 18 months after the US invasion, for instance.[93] This military threat persuades Pyongyang to keep a large number of people under arms, and away to some extent from production, although since the military spends much of its time on economic activities, a strict head count gives a misleading picture.[94] In addition, imports of arms reduce the ability to import food, medicines and civilian goods while building strategic installations underground must add considerably to the cost. American pressure on South Korea and Japan to restrict economic relations with North Korea is another factor, and one of which Pyongyang has bitterly complained. American interference, utilising the Wassenaar Arrangement, has slowed the transfer of alleged 'dual-use' technologies to the small South Korean garment and other labour-intensive companies setting up in the Kaesong Industrial Park.[95] The impact of politics is manifest in North Korea's foreign trade. In the first nine months of 2004 trade with China surged 40 per cent while that with Japan actually declined slightly. The growth in trade with China was due to economic forces, primarily the increasing demand of China for raw materials such as steel and zinc, but the decline in trade with Japan was due to politics. In this case domestic politics aligned with US policy.[96]

A comparison with Iraq is instructive in illustrating the effect of economic warfare on the vulnerable, especially children. Estimates of mortality and malnutrition vary, but all are horrifying. One FAO study in 1995 estimated that sanctions had caused the death of 567,000 children. In 2000, Richard Garfield of Columbia University arrived at a figure of 350,000 over the decade.[97] Child malnutrition peaked in 1996 at 11 per cent before declining to 4 per cent in 2002; it has doubled to 7.7 per cent since the US invasion.[98] Children are the major victims, but not the only ones. The World Food Programme in September 2004 calculated that a quarter of the Iraqi population was dependent on food rations and vulnerable to food insecurity.[99] It so happened that the following month the WFP announced that the same proportion of the North Korean population, 25 per cent, was partly dependent on international aid.[100] Whilst there can be dispute about responsibility – to what extent Saddam Hussein brought about and exacerbated the situation – there is little doubt about the effect. Before 1990 oil exports provided Iraq with considerable revenues which were largely extinguished by sanctions with demonstrated results. Before sanctions the biggest nutrition problem facing Iraqi children was obesity, now Iraq's malnutrition rate equals that of Burundi.[101] Cause and effect are fairly clear. However, with North

Korea things are more complicated. The immediate precipitating cause of the economic crisis in the DPRK was the collapse of the Soviet Union and the trade based on the DPRK's relations with the Soviet Union and Eastern Europe. The policy and actions of the United States and its allies have undoubtedly damaged the North Korean economy and hampered attempts at rehabilitation and reform, but the degree of responsibility is unclear. That is the sin of commission; there is also the sin of omission. Different, non-hostile, policies could have greatly facilitated the restoration and growth of the North Korean economy, and the life of its people, and that remains a continuing option.

AID

North Korea has been a major recipient of international aid since the mid 1990s. In 2003 it was the sixth largest recipient of aid from the World Food Programme but figures that year were distorted by the US invasion of Iraq, which propelled its share of WFP assistance from 2 per cent to 33 per cent. North Korea's share fell from 13 per cent ($234m) in 2001 to 3 per cent ($102m) in 2003 (Table 5.2). How much this fall was directly due to American pressure is unclear, but since the US is by far the major donor to the WFP – $1.5b in 2003 – it is difficult to avoid that conclusion.[102] The WFP is not the only source of aid and there has been substantial bilateral aid from China although the amount is unknown.

Table 5.2   Major recipients of WFP assistance, 2000–03

Country/year	2000		2001		2002		2003	
	US$m	*%*	*US$m*	*%*	*US$m*	*%*	*US$m*	*%*
Angola	79	7	95	5	109	7	149	5
Ethiopia	180	16	171	10	128	8	230	7
Sudan	54	5	122	7	100	6	136	4
Afghanistan	43	4	119	7	136	9	141	4
Korea, DPR	113	10	234	13	103	6	102	3
Iraq	18	2	28	2	32	2	1,092	33
World	1,158	100	1,776	100	1,592	100	3,275	100

Source: *Annual Performance Report for 2003*. Rome: World Food Programme, 2004, Annex VIII, Table 2.

International aid is a major topic, touched on throughout the book, but here I will briefly address four overlapping issues: aid as a hindrance to system reform, the diversion of aid to the military, the efficacy of aid, and the bridge building of aid agencies.

Aid, Regime Change and the Aftermath

There are many who argue that the problem in North Korea is 'the regime', and that the only real solution is to replace it ('regime change'). International aid, according to that argument, bolsters the regime and delays the happy time of transformation. This is a deeply flawed argument for a number of reasons. A collapse of the DPRK would not merely impose terrible additional hardship on the population of the North, and impose huge economic and social problems on the South, and to a lesser extent other countries, especially China. Ah, some counter, this would only be temporary and the generosity of the United States, whose Marshall Plan transformed Western Europe after the Second World War would put things right. Not so. The experience of Afghanistan and Iraq suggests otherwise. Even in the unlikely event of there not being armed resistance to the US/ROK occupation, it is doubtful that substantial American aid would be forthcoming. The Marshall Plan was driven by the fear of Communism and the need to restore markets for US exports. Neither of these conditions obtains in Korea. As Paul Krugman has pointed out, 'This [Bush] administration does martial plans, not Marshall Plans: billions for offense, not one cent for reconstruction.'[103] As with KEDO (Korean Peninsula Energy Development Organization) the bulk of the cost would fall on South Korea.[104] Moreover, it is not commonly realised how modest South Korean aid has been so far. In the five years of Kim Dae-jung's term of office, according to the ROK Unification Ministry, the South provided $462.8 million in humanitarian aid to the North. That worked out to just $2 per capita per year.[105] Leaving aside the question of resistance, the amount given so far is just a drop in the bucket to what would be required if Seoul was faced with the necessity of administering the North. Kim Dae-jung himself has been reported as saying that, 'South Korea has no financial capacity to cover the huge unification cost in case the communist North suddenly collapses.'[106]

Diversion of Aid

It is frequently alleged that international aid is 'diverted' to the North Korean military or the elite and that little, if any, reaches the hungry ordinary people. One of the most vociferous supporters of this position is the aid agency Médicins sans Frontières (MSF), which withdrew from DPRK 'due to a lack of access to people in need and no independence to carry out its programs'.[107] The DPRK responded to that withdrawal by saying, 'Humanitarian assistance should be given from the humanitarian point of view in the true sense of the word. If donor organisations give us humanitarian assistance, we will accept it gratefully, and if not, we will not beg for it.'[108]

MSF researcher Fiona Terry, writing in the *Guardian* in August 2001, forcefully argued that since food aid was not getting through to the needy it was counter-productive – 'Food aid to North Korea only props up Kim Jong-il's grotesque regime. It should be stopped.'[109] Martin Woollacott, reviewing an MSF book followed the same line. In North Korea, he wrote, 'huge resources are being expended in humanitarian aid, but that aid has not reached many of those for whom it was intended because, MSF says, it has largely gone to the party and the army'. International aid, he continued, was a 'policy aimed at calming and containing the North Korean regime – a policy which may be rational but, says MSF, let's not pretend it has anything much to do with feeding ordinary people, who have continued to starve to death in large numbers'.[110]

Most aid workers on the ground in North Korea disagree with this analysis and with this conclusion. World Food Programme officials frequently state in public what I have heard from them in private; they are not happy with their limited access but are broadly confident that aid gets through and is effective. Masood Hyder, UN Humanitarian Coordinator in North Korea, writing in the *Washington Post* in January 2004, gave a perceptive, and authoritative, analysis of the situation:

We have been in North Korea for nine years. During that time there has been a very substantial donor response to the humanitarian crisis. Millions of tons of food have been distributed, and a variety of health care, agriculture, nutrition, water and sanitation programs have been implemented.

How, then, can we say that things are still bad, that basic assistance is needed? Did we fail?

We did not fail. Lives were saved; we are helping turn the situation around. The malnutrition, stunting and maternal mortality rates, while still high, have fallen. Above all, we have established preventive capacity: another famine cannot happen while we are here and properly supported.

Some critics advocate ending humanitarian aid to North Korea and passing the burden to the government. If we did not help, resources would have to be diverted from more aggressive purposes to take care of the vulnerable, they argue. This is a dangerous assumption. Let us not place unrealistic expectations on the ability of the humanitarian imperative to dictate national security priorities.[111]

On the specific issue of diversion of aid to the military, Hyder commented,

We must also address the allegation that WFP assistance is diverted to the North Korean military. While we cannot guarantee that every sack of grain goes where it should, there are good reasons to believe – foremost among them the impressive results of last year's nutritional survey – that the great bulk of it does.[112]

Hyder was right to allude to the latest nutritional survey as the firmest evidence we have that aid is getting through to the vulnerable, specifically children. There have been two major nutritional assessment surveys conducted in North Korea with funding from UNICEF and WFP. They have been conducted with statistical rigour, involving randomly selected households and computerised statistical analysis. The first was in 1998 and the second in 2002. This one, which was conducted with technical support from the Institute of Child Health, London, and Thailand Health Foundation, Bangkok, sampled '6,000 randomly selected households located in 200 randomly selected Ri and Dong of seven provinces and three cities'.[113]

The survey was both thorough and intrusive:

The selected households were those that had children aged under seven years of age. In each such household selected, the youngest child was weighed and measured and information collected on household food. In those households that the child was under two years of age, the mother was also interviewed concerning maternal and child health care practices, infant feeding practices, and maternal feeding practices. The mothers of children under two years old were also weighed and measured, and invited to have a haemoglobin examination.[114]

Although child malnutrition was still far too high, the survey showed that, 'The nutrition situation has certainly improved dramatically since 1998.'[115] The UN Office for Co-ordination of Humanitarian Affairs (OCHA) concurred:

- The proportion of children underweight (weight-for-age) had fallen from 61 per cent in 1998 to 21 per cent in 2002

- Wasting, or acute malnutrition (weight-for-height), had fallen from 16 per cent to 9 per cent
- Stunting, or chronic malnutrition (height-for-age), had dropped from 62 per cent to 42 per cent.

The improved nutrition cannot be credited entirely to international aid, because the North Korean economy was recovering over the years, as were harvests, but it must have played a considerable, probably major, role. OCHA reported that 'The Government of DPRK attributed the improvement in part to the substantial humanitarian assistance provided by the international community in recent years.'[116] By contrast we should recall that child malnutrition doubled in Iraq after the US invasion.[117]

Professor Hazel Smith, who has closely studied the issues, and has had personal experience working with WFP in Pyongyang concludes,

> Soldiers desperate enough to steal food may also be stealing food aid but there is no evidence of systematic food aid diversion to the army as public or government policy. On the other hand, no international aid agency that has been involved in the regular delivery and distribution of food aid to North Korea has ever reported systematic diversion of food aid.[118]

More disturbing and morally more offensive is the deliberate withholding of aid in order to apply political pressure. This takes various forms. Sometimes aid is tied to a particular concession, such as the inspection of the underground facility at Kumchangri. The Japanese are more overt than the Americans, who are more conscious of the danger of ethical opprobrium.[119] However, US aid often has restriction written in by law to appease lobby groups. One example is the 'Foreign Operations, Export Financing, and Related Programs Appropriations Act' of 2004 which expressly states that 'None of the funds made available ... as a United States contribution to the Global Fund to Fight AIDS, Tuberculosis and Malaria may be made available for assistance for the Government of North Korea.'[120]

Building Bridges and Facilitating Reform

Returning to the question of system reform, it could be argued that the 'safety net' provided by international aid facilitated the introduction of the marketisation measures of July 2002. However, while marketisation may produce general benefits in the long term, in the short terms it privileges those with access to money, and disadvantages those, especially the unemployed in the hard-hit industrial cities, who look to the state for support, but see that support wither away. Kathi Zellweger of Caritas probably provides the best ongoing analysis, generous, dispassionate, and informed, of the complex and evolving reality. She sees the need for partnership and engagement, and the aid agencies as bridge builders. The situation, she argues,

> ... calls for engagement – dialogue, talks, listening, proper respect for the views of others, patience, consensus building – all basic and essential components of any partnership.[121]

There are a lot of issues revolving around international aid, but diversion is not a major one. On the contrary, what is important is the continuing effect of US economic and political warfare on the ordinary people of North Korea, and the way it hinders attempts to rehabilitate the economy. Zellweger maintains that

> Domestic reforms to increase production and profitability are one side of the story, trade with, and investment from, other countries is the other crucial element. Opening up the economy can only work if the international community is willing to help.[122]

Unfortunately, the 'international community' is unlikely to participate in the rehabilitation and internationalisation of North Korea unless there is a change in US policy. Nevertheless, NGOs and religious groups do persevere, making small but significant improvements. Major Seth Le Leu, of the Salvation Army, for instance, in writing of their project to install a yogurt packaging machine on a dairy farm, noted how one step led to another, not only in the economic sense, but also in building mutual knowledge:

> The packaging for the yoghurt has the Salvation Army red shield logo on it, and this will be the first thing the Salvation Army will be known for in North Korea. In other dairies we visited we tried some excellent local cheeses and butter, but yoghurt is the preferred product and at each dairy they requested a packaging machine. Another benefit of the project is that when the yoghurt is packaged the value of the product increases and the farmers are able to benefit from the added value. As an anti-famine strategy the industry has a logical basis that should be engaged with.[123]

He concluded, 'When a country like North Korea engages with the outside world we need to respond at its pace. Such constructive engagement will reap positive results.'[124]

REFUGEES – VOTING WITH THEIR FEET?

An issue which brings together both the human rights situation in North Korea, broadly defined, and international concern, often genuine but misinformed, sometimes duplicitous and calculating, is the question of refugees. At first sight this seems all very straightforward. Here we have people at considerable cost and danger voting with their feet. Isn't this an obvious indictment of the appalling human rights situation in North Korea? Again, the real situation is more complex, and our knowledge of it less certain, than the media stereotype would lead us to believe. Bearing in mind the ease with which valiant seekers for freedom and a better life can be transformed so quickly, when political needs change, into 'illegal immigrants' who are not entitled to our sympathy we should approach the matter with caution. This is a highly politicised subject. The South Korean press always uses the term 'defectors'. The Chinese press calls them 'economic refugees'. The US Human Rights Acts refers to 'refugees', and that is the term I will use because it is more neutral.

Firstly it is indisputable that there has been considerable privation, malnutrition and even death caused by the economic crisis of the 1990s and, as noted, we have plenty of data from international agencies on the extent of that.[125] However, what is debatable are the causes and solutions. Was the crisis inherent in the system, as many would argue? Or was it something that was caused and/or exacerbated by exogenous forces, namely the collapse of the Soviet Union on the one hand and US hostility and economic warfare on the other? This is roughly the position of the UN agencies, though naturally no mention is made of the role of the United States:

> In the 1970s, the DPRK made substantive progress on many of the main development indicators compared to its regional partners. The country was economically more advanced than most regional countries, and a net provider of development aid to some smaller developing economies. The DPRK reportedly had a comprehensive and inclusive social sector infrastructure. This progress towards human development continued until the onset of the decline of the former Soviet Union and Eastern Bloc economies in the 1980s, which resulted in the disappearance of guaranteed markets for

DPRK production and reduced aid inflows. The effect on the country was devastating – energy production reduced sharply with negative spill-over effects on industrial operational capacity and agricultural production.[126]

If we believe the first explanation then helping people flee makes sense. If we tend to the second explanation then we would favour measures that produce an improvement in the economic situation in North Korea so that people's lives are better, and there is less incentive to leave.

The first school of thought is represented by various South Korean Christian evangelist groups, by initiators and supporters of the US Congress North Korea Human Rights Act of 2004 and by the German doctor Norbert Vollertsen. Vollertsen worked in North Korea for 18 months (his account, other reports say three years) before being expelled in 2000.[127] Since when he has become an anti-North Korean activist, arranging protests and publicity stunts. Vollertsen argues that

> Kim Jong Il has to fight for survival like the leader of a religious cult – he can only do so by blackmailing the world: 'Feed me or I will kill you with my nuclear weapons'. He will never abandon these weapons, his only real 'security guarantee'. (There is only one security guarantee for the starving children in North Korea: When there is no more security for Kim Jong Il and his evil regime!)
>
> The only way to get rid of the nukes is to get rid of Kim Jong Il, and the best way to do that is by creating an inner collapse of the North Korean regime started by a flood of refugees – just as in the former East Germany.[128]

Diametrically opposed to this strategy is former South Korean President Kim Dae-jung who explicitly drew on the German example in his famous speech in Berlin in March 2000, on the occasion of the international launch of the 'Sunshine policy'.[129] President Kim argued then, and has reiterated since, that a collapse of North Korea would inflict considerable damage on the South, far greater than the economic dislocation caused by the sudden integration of the two Germanys. President Kim was not alone in that analysis and whilst Dr Vollertsen is lionised in much of the international media he has had a lot of trouble in South Korea where he claims he has been beaten up by police, and bombarded by 1,400 hate emails a day.[130]

Apart from the question of whether refugees should be encouraged or discouraged, there are a number of other areas of dispute. We do not know how many there are, what China will do, what the motivations of the refugees are, and what should be done to help them.

There are reportedly some 6,000 in South Korea, and a handful elsewhere.[131] Elsewhere other than China that is. How many are there in China? Estimates vary considerably. Some say 500,000, others put the numbers more credibly at 100,000 and again others lower still.[132] Illegal immigration is, by its nature, not officially recorded. However, a lot of movement across the border is legal, with people going to study or do business abroad.

Many people are worried that the politicising of the refugee situation by people such as Vollertsen will force the Chinese to crack down, just as surely as would a substantial increase in the number of refugees. In addition there are fears in Seoul, Beijing, and presumably also in Pyongyang, of the ghost of Koguryo should there be a major crisis. This ancient kingdom which occupied much of modern North Korea and China's Northeast until 668 AD was, depending on the source, either Korean or a sinicised state on the periphery of China (see Chapter 1). The Chinese fear that it might form the basis of an irredentist claim to large swathes of the Northeast from a future unified Korea, especially if the area's Korean population had been swollen by refugees.[133] Some South Koreans, on the other hand, have suggested that China's position on Koguryo is a dastardly plot to set up a pro-Chinese regime in the North in the event of a collapse of the DPRK.[134] Pyongyang, for the moment, contents itself with asserting the Korean-ness of Koguryo and its contribution to East Asia.[135]

The motivations of the refugees are also the subject of conflicting claims. The Chinese see them as economic refugees, most of whom will return home when the economic situation in the DPRK improves. Others – the evangelicals, Vollertsen, the US Congress, and much of the international media – see them as people fleeing oppression who would only return, if at all, after a change in regime. 'Asylum seekers' in other words. The truth is difficult to pin down because it would be a very witless economic refugee, Korean, Afghan or Albanian, who did not claim to be escaping from tyranny.

Increasingly, however, the movement of refugees is becoming, according to South Korean sources, a commercial enterprise, and a very profitable one at that. In late 2004, a ROK official in Beijing was quoted as saying, 'The recent asylum bids are all masterminded by brokers. Brokers are involved in the defectors' decision to try and reach the South.' One such case was that of Park Myeong-suk who reached South Korea in 2003. On arrival she was entitled to a government grant of 35.9 million won ($33,850), 14.63 million ($13,800) of which was given as a lump sum. Some 4.5 million ($4,200) of this was immediately turned over to her broker for engineering her journey. She then invested another 6 million won ($5,700) to arrange for her brother and his wife to join her, because 'they will also receive settlement funds from the government. So, we can live on that money.'[136] How much of an inducement is $33,850? According to South Korean government estimates, the per capita national income in North Korea was $818 in 2003, so the settlement grant was worth about forty times that.[137]

Refugees are increasingly a 'commodity in a profitable business', noted a *JoongAng Ilbo* article, with a regular scale of charges (there are approximately 1,000 won to the US$):

Brokers say a trip from China to South Korea can cost between 2 million and 12 million won, depending on the routes and means of transportation. If a broker provides the opportunity for a defector to seek asylum at foreign missions and international schools in China, the bill ranges from 2 million to 5 million won per person. Leaving China to enter the South by way of a third country, usually a Southeastern Asian nation, costs about 3 to 6 million, they said. Direct air travel with a forged passport is the most costly means, adding up to 12 million won per defector.[138]

One of the ironies in this sorry business is that no government really wants the refugees. The Americans have been posturing, with the North Korea Human Rights Act 2004, but an American official, when pressed, said that although they would in principle accept them, 'the most appropriate solution' was for them to go to South Korea.[139] The fine print of the act conveniently excludes those 'who have already gained South Korean citizenship'.[140]

The South Korean government, for its part, has to offer haven – and the constitution of the Republic of Korea guarantees citizenship to anyone born on the peninsula – but in reality is loth to receive them. They don't fit in, and they find it difficult to adapt, with 75 per cent remaining on welfare.[141] Efforts have been made to persuade Mongolia to become a temporary, or perhaps semi-permanent, staging post and the Mongolian government has, so far, balked at this.[142]

And what of the refugees themselves? They complain of discrimination in South Korea and most appear to be unhappy with their new life. It appears that few want to stay in South Korea:

A poll conducted by a South Korean daily in September on 100 defectors showed 69 percent would prefer emigrating to Western countries such as the U.S., Canada and Australia over staying in the South. Thirty-three percent of those surveyed said they would return to North Korea if they could.[143]

Many refugees are attracted by America and want to get there, even illegally, because of a 'false belief that they will receive a large amount of resettlement money from Washington'.[144] The fact that a third of them wanted to return to North Korea suggests that the portrayal of it by evangelists and much of the media as a 'human rights abyss' is perhaps much exaggerated. This scepticism is reinforced by another survey, this time conducted by the South Korean Ministry of Unification in late 2004:

The survey of 4,075 North Koreans who entered South Korea from 2000 to June this year, showed that 2,263 defectors, or 55.5 percent, escaped their homeland because of poverty, the ministry said.

'More than half of the defectors left North Korea to avoid destitution and starvation', a ministry official said. 'Political oppression is not playing as big a role as we thought'.

Around 367 people, or 9 percent cited 'political dissatisfaction' as a reason for defection, the ministry said.[145]

The Ministry of Unification survey can be viewed as very authoritative. It covered all of the refugees over the period, rather than just a sample, and they constituted two thirds of the refugees since the Korean War.

It seems clear that the best solution is to ameliorate the economic situation in North Korea so that the pressure on people to leave is lessened. That to a large extent requires the cessation of US economic warfare and political and military pressure; in other words the abandonment of the 'hostile policy' of which Pyongyang complains so constantly and so bitterly. It seems likely, though not guaranteed, that such a change in US policy would bring about an improvement in the political and human rights situation.

This solution is basically the thrust of the 'Appeal to the American People' issued by the US-based Korean Peace Network in October 2004, just prior to the election.[146] In the event, the appeal by this group of Korean-Americans was unsuccessful, and may well have been so whatever the outcome of the election. Nevertheless, it is evident that a significant improvement in the humanitarian situation in North Korea hinges, as the appeal put it, on 'a major rethink' of US foreign policy.

THE WAY FORWARD

To write about human rights in North Korea is difficult because it is a subject much shrouded in hypocrisy, misinformation and uncertainty. It is an emotive subject but we must be dispassionate if we are to understand the situation, its causes and what might make things better.

Any human rights situation is the result of a complex interplay of historical, political and cultural factors. The cultural aspect is a particularly difficult one to come to terms with because we tend to look at things from our own perspective and with our own values, which we tend to elevate into universals. Whilst we should not condone inhumane action on the specious grounds that it is culturally sanctioned we should still be cautious, empathetic and humble, recognising that what we see as clear-cut may not seem that way to others, even those we see as victims. Perhaps especially the victims.

The human rights environment is not merely moulded by the inertial forces of the past but also by the current situation. Societies tend to be more authoritarian and less tolerant of diversity the more they are under stress and threat. This is not an automatic process but one subject to the efforts and manipulation of the powerful, as well as the acquiescence of the public. Post-9/11 America is a graphic illustration of this. So too in North Korea, which has been under siege and threat for most of its history. Removal of the external threat will not automatically result in a more free and a less oppressive society, but it is an essential first step. China is a case in point. As China has become stronger and as relations with the US, and the Soviet Union/ Russia improved, the perception (and reality) of threat lessened and the social and political environment loosened up. Not completely, as the Tiananmen incident demonstrates, but significantly nonetheless. The same process can be seen in South Korea as the threat from the North abated after the Korean War and the political structure gained legitimacy. The move from military dictatorship to civilian democracy had to be fought for, and could be reversed, but it is unlikely that the struggle would have succeeded in an atmosphere of external threat.

One of the main signs in North Korea, visible to the observer, of political repression is the constraint on movement around the country. People can't live where they like and have to pass through military checkpoints, on main roads at least. These controls seemed to have lost a lot of their effectiveness during the famine, when people did move, but they are still in place. This has its roots in security concerns, including those 10,000 southern agents sent north before 1972. If US special forces are operating in Iran 'selecting sites for future air strikes', as alleged, then clearly this is a possibility in North Korea.[147] It is unlikely that the security forces will relax their control over movement while that danger exists.

Those who argue for continuing to keep up pressure on North Korea do so on the grounds that it would bring about 'regime change'. There is much talk of 'regime change' but little recognition that if there were to be a coup, it would be likely to come from the military (who else mounts coups?) opposing Kim Jong Il's programme of economic reform and engagement with Washington. In other words, the human rights situation, by this measure, would probably get worse, rather than better. Regime change brought about by collapse and some sort of military intervention would lead to chaos and probably a war of resistance which might well continue a long time, causing devastation and sapping the strength of the peninsula. It should be remembered that the last armed resistance in the South was not put down until 1963, nearly 20 years after Syngman Rhee was first installed in power.[148] The fate of Iraq, with its 100,000 deaths and soaring child malnutrition, is a warning of some the consequences of 'regime change'.[149]

We should also recognise the linkage between the human rights environment in the North and that in the South. Basically, as in long-term economic development, the two parts of Korea will either swim together, or sink together. The current moves to abolish the draconian National Security Law in the South are affected by perceptions of the situation in North, and by North–South relations. Those who want an authoritarian society in the South want one in the North to justify it and they also want a continued state of tension.[150] One thrust of the US neocon scenario is to engineer regime change in the South, to bring in hardline conservative forces, in order to get a free hand to apply military pressure on the North.

Human rights is a rather amorphous concept, lacking in the concreteness that moves people. This is where the issue of refugees comes in. They appear to be an unambiguous manifestation of the flight from a despised, unjust society. They arouse genuine concern and sympathy, and so they should. They offer to the media stories of human interest and pathos. The fact that they are coming to us, at considerable cost, reinforces the media message about the superiority of our society and their frequent disappointment tends to get less coverage, though it should be noted that it is reported to some extent in the South Korean press. But most of all there is the danger of them being used as pawns by those who have more sinister agendas. The Korean-American academic Yuh Ji-yeon, who is well placed to see what is going on, offers a trenchant critique:

> The human rights issue is being callously used by the right to justify regime change, which in practice is simply a misnomer for U.S. military intervention and attempted imposition of a U.S.-dominated political structure. We need only look to Afghanistan and Iraq for the latest examples.[151]

This theme is taken up again in Chapter 8 when we look at neocon prescriptions for regime change. For neocon ideologues sitting in the comfort of their Washington offices this is merely a matter of re-shaping the world to what they see as America's interest. For Koreans, and Korean-Americans, it is different, as Ms Yuh argues:

> The stakes are high, and for Korean Americans there are very personal consequences. Promoting or supporting regime change in North Korea all too quickly segues into supporting U.S. military action against the North – that will turn into another Korean War, and our relatives in Korea will die, become war refugees, and then be subject to who knows how many more years of political and economic chaos. In such a scenario, human rights for everyone goes out the window, more people than ever before will try to leave Korea, and instead of a trickle of North Koreans fleeing starvation, we'll see a flood of Koreans – north and south – fleeing war.[152]

6

Drugs and Generals: Some Surprising Facts on Narcotics, Missiles, Terrorism and Military Confrontation

INTRODUCTION

The previous chapter looked at issues such as human rights which are primarily domestic to North Korea, notwithstanding the United States' claim that it has a role as global moral arbiter. These next two chapters turn to issues which really do have an impact beyond the borders of North Korea and which can fairly be considered to be of concern to other countries.

The picture the media prints for us, based so often on tasty titbits supplied by officials, is stark and unambiguous. North Korea is the very model of a rogue state, flouting international law at every turn. The headlines, and stories, are sensational:

Drugs and forgery 'sustain North Korean economy'
The threat from North Korea may be more insidious than the mere possibility of a nuclear attack, it was claimed yesterday. The regime is shoring up what remains of its economy by racketeering, according to US officials quoted in the magazine *US News and World Report*.

They believe North Korea is producing 40 tonnes of opium a year, huge quantities of high-quality amphetamines and millions of dollars worth of 'supernotes' - beautifully made counterfeit $100 bills.

The magazine says the US has seen videotape of Kim Jong-nam, the son of the dictator Kim Jong-il, using the fake notes at a casino in Macao.[1]

It gets worse. On 9 June 2003 the Asia edition of *Time* magazine blazoned a less than flattering photo of Kim Jong Il on its cover with the caption 'The Racketeer: How Kim Jong Il makes his billions'. The lead story gave the horrific details:

Kim's Rackets
To fund his lifestyle – and his nukes – Kim Jong Il helms a vast criminal network
...

Much may be mysterious about hermetic North Korea, but some facts are well known. Kim has weapons-capable missiles and a million-strong army breasting the 38th parallel. He has the material for nuclear weapons, might have several nuclear bombs, and threatens to destroy Seoul – South Korea's capital – if anyone tries to forcibly take them away. Beyond the security threat North Korea poses to its neighbors militarily, however, is another clear and present danger: Kim Jong Il props up his destitute failed state with international criminal enterprises that would be the envy of any Mafia don.[2]

The evidence is overwhelming because it comes from so many sources; the 'facts are well known'. The Global Security Newswire of the NTI (Nuclear Threat Initiative) organisation founded by CNN's Ted Turner and former Senator Sam Nunn ran a story 16 May 2003:

North Korea: Pyongyang funds WMD programs by selling drugs, counterfeit currency
Since the late 1970s, North Korea has produced and trafficked millions of dollars worth of heroin and methamphetamines throughout Northeast Asia to gain badly needed hard currency to help fund its military, a high-ranking North Korean defector told a Senate Governmental Affairs subcommittee yesterday ...
'North Korea is essentially a criminal syndicate with nuclear bombs', said subcommittee Chairman Peter Fitzgerald (R-Ill.). 'The role of a government is to protect its citizens from criminals. But, in the case of North Korea, it appears the government is the criminal', he said.[3]

With so many people saying the same sort of thing can there be any doubt? Well, here's a clue. On the same day the NTI posted that story about North Korea it recycled, approvingly, an article in the *New York Times* headed 'U.S. Analysts Link Iraq Labs to Germ Arms'.[4] The story told us how US officials had concluded that mobile 'laboratories' captured in Iraq were 'mobile units to produce germs for weapons'. They came to these conclusions even though they found no evidence because they could see no other plausible explanation for the trailers. Before long, other plausible explanations surfaced when other experts decided that they had been used to inflate artillery balloons, which is perhaps why no evidence of biological agents was found.[5] A year later the editors of the *New York Times* published their famous, if rather self-serving, apology 'The Times and Iraq' for all the stories they had printed which had later been shown to be false (they were not complicit with US officials in misleading the American public; they just 'fell for disinformation' from devious foreigners).[6]

So much certainty which vaporises when put to the test. We are not in a position to put allegations about North Korea to that sort of test, but we can examine the evidence and the accusations carefully and critically. And that is what we will do in these two chapters.

We shall distinguish between two sets of issues which are conceptually different and which we shall call the mercenary and the military. The first is the alleged export of narcotics. This is done, it is claimed by the Americans, not out of some malevolent intention, such as to destroy the moral fibre of American youth, but only to make money. The other set of issues are concerned with the development of nuclear weapons and other weapons of mass destruction, missiles and conventional arms. These can be construed as posing a deliberate threat. Straddling the two is the question of missile exports. These, the Americans themselves agree, are intended merely to earn foreign exchange, but do pose a danger, not so much to the United States, but to its allies, such as Israel.

Curiously enough, the only allegation which is not contested by the North Koreans themselves is that of missile exports, although estimates of the actual value of sales vary considerably. Because it makes more sense to discuss missile exports along with missile production and domestic deployment, this will be covered in the second part of this chapter. However, there is one aspect that needs to be noted here and that is the question of economic incentives, disincentives and options.

North Korea denies exporting narcotics (as a state activity) but readily acknowledges missile exports, which are not illegal under international trade rules. Be that as it may, if we accept for the sake of argument that North Korea is exporting both narcotics and missiles, and for money, then clearly one remedy is to facilitate the earning of foreign exchange from other, more acceptable, sources. Yet the United States does precisely the reverse. It imposes sanctions that impede the expansion of North Korea's foreign economic relations, such as exports of goods and the attraction of foreign investment. For instance, the Kaesong Industrial Park being developed in North Korea by Hyundai for small South Korean companies, and with strong support from the South Korean government, is constantly being hampered by American restrictions.[7] It bars the DPRK's access to international financial institutions such as the World Bank, and hence to international loans. Instead of applauding North Korea's moves towards a market economy, as we might naively expect, it studiously ignores all the myriad ways it could assist that process.

DRUGS

We are bombarded with 'facts' about North Korea's alleged high-level involvement with international narcotics but they are often of dubious validity or credibility. For instance, much is made of the charge that

> North Korea has become a major drug producing and trafficking nation, using diplomatic channels to market heroin, opium, and methamphetamine ... At least 34 documented incidents, many involving arrest or detention of North Korean diplomats, directly link the North Korean government to drug production and trafficking. Such events provide credible allegations of state-sponsorship of drug production and trafficking.[8]

However, many of these 'documented reports' are from newspapers such as *US News and World Report* and yet, when we go to the official (US government) sources that they quote, such as the State Department's annual *International Narcotics Control Strategy Report*, we find that this is littered with phrases such as

> 'Uncertainty and speculation characterize much of the reporting concerning narcotics cultivation and production within North Korea'
> 'no concrete evidence of illicit opium cultivation ...'
> 'The credibility of regular allegations that North Korea engages in state-sponsored drug trafficking and other forms of criminality (e.g., counterfeiting) for profit and to fund state programs, such as weapons development, is difficult to evaluate with certainty, given the inaccessibility of reliable information from and about North Korea.'[9]

Murky and uncertain territory. Yet the *US News and World Report* seems to take a special interest in the subject, claiming that drugs and counterfeiting 'sustain North Korean economy'.[10]

Another important source of information on these issues are Congressional hearings. Since these are bipartisan there is perhaps a presumption that they are objective. However, the experts called to these hearings tend to be of a predictable persuasion and are usually serving or retired bureaucrats, or staffers at rightwing think tanks – and defectors.

One such was the hearing of the Senate Subcommittee on Financial Management, the Budget, and International Security entitled *Drugs, Counterfeiting, and Weapons Proliferation: the North Korean Connection* in May 2003. They heard testimony from officials (one from Defense and one from the State Department), rightwing think tanks (Nick Eberstadt of the American Enterprise Institute and Larry Wortzel of the Heritage Foundation), former diplomat Robert Gallucci (who was the US signatory to the Agreed Framework), and two North Korean defectors. The lumping together of drugs and counterfeiting with 'weapons proliferation' is significant. As we see below, North Korea's exports of arms are tiny compared with those of the US, but more pertinent here is that such exports are *not* illegal.

In these Senate Subcommittee hearings Larry Wortzel claimed that

> North Korea's exports from *legitimate* businesses in 2001 totaled just $650 million, according to *Wall Street Journal* reports of April 23, 2003, citing South Korea's central bank. Income to Pyongyang from illegal drugs in the same year ran between $500 million and $1 billion, while missile sales earned Pyongyang about $560 million in 2001. North Korea is producing some 40 tons of opium a year, according to officials from US Forces Korea cited in *The Guardian* on January 20, 2003, and earns some $100 million a year from counterfeiting currency. (Emphasis added)[11]

In fact, Dr Wortzel is mistaken about the figure for 'legitimate' exports of $650 million which excludes intra-Korean exports. His figure for counterfeiting of $100 million here (presumably for 2001) contrasts with a statement elsewhere in his testimony of $15 million for 1999. If Dr Wortzel is loose with figures, he is equally slipshod when it comes to legal concepts. Here he implies that missile sales are illegitimate but elsewhere he confesses that he is vexed by the fact that 'the sale of these missiles does not violate international law'. Lumping legal and illegal, legitimate and illegitimate together is done with a purpose and does have an effect. It passes into the discourse and it is automatically replicated by officials, politicians and journalists, thereby reinforcing the propaganda ploy. For instance, Australia's ambassador to Seoul was reported as saying that 'Australia was taking a tough stance on illegal trafficking of missiles and drugs by North Korea'.[12] It so happened that the following year the Australian government unblushingly participated in a little 'trafficking in missiles' itself by announcing a A$450 million purchase of American Cruise missiles.[13] This purchase may have been unwise or provocative, but it was not illegal. No more than DPRK's sales are, as is discussed below.

Dr Wortzel is also vexed with the State Department not being able to 'to confirm the extent of North Korea's opium production':

> If United States space surveillance assets cannot find and confirm the existence of opium poppies, which are brightly colored, seasonal, and grow above ground, we will never get adequate intelligence on North Korea's underground missile and nuclear weapons programs.[14]

One can share his surprise because, according to defectors, North Korea is awash with opium production:

> In the late 1997, the central government ordered that all local collective farms must cultivate 10 Chungbo [Jungbo] (Korean land unit equal to approx. 25 acres) of poppy farm beginning in 1998.[15]

Perhaps US surveillance satellites are not what they are cracked up to be, or farms are not obeying central government. Or perhaps the reports are somewhat untrustworthy. In fact, defector reports in general are notoriously undependable.[16] It is said that Machiavelli, who must have been an authority on such matters, viewed them with distrust.[17] The two defectors who testified at this particular hearing were apparently spirited out of South Korea by the Americans without the South Korean government being told.[18] One of them subsequently got into a public dispute with another defector, each accusing the other of embroidering stories. They also complained that South Korean intelligence suspected they were lying or withholding information. Both wanted to settle in the United States.[19]

The media tends to lap up stories from defectors and one can see why. It makes for good, lurid reading, which newspapers and magazines find irresistible.[20] *Time* magazine, for instance, drawing on defector reports ran a collection of articles on 9 June 2003 informing us that, 'to fund his lifestyle – and his nukes – Kim Jong Il helms a vast criminal network'.[21] Such articles are then quoted by officials and others as evidence, and so the process continues. It makes for good tub-thumping politics too; 'North Korea is essentially a criminal syndicate with nuclear bombs', said subcommittee Chairman Peter Fitzgerald (R-Ill).[22]

The latest report from the US State Department's Bureau for International Narcotics and Law Enforcement Affairs, *International Narcotics Control Strategy Report 2003*, concludes that it is 'highly likely, but not certain, that Pyongyang is trading narcotic drugs for profit as state policy'.[23] Two incidents are described to back up this claim. One incident 'occurred in June [2003] in Pusan, South Korea, where customs authorities seized 50 kilograms of methamphetamine from a Chinese vessel that had stopped at the port of Najin [Rajin], North Korea, before arriving in Pusan'. However, on the very next page we read:

> The container had apparently been packed in China, shipped by rail to the North Korean port of Najin, and loaded there aboard the Chinese freighter 'Chu Xing' before it arrived in Pusan and was seized by South Korean Customs. Initially, the drugs were said to be North Korean in origin.

Methamphetamine had apparently been found on the same vessel in Pusan in 2001. To instance Chinese smuggling of Chinese drugs as evidence of North Korean state policy might be seen to be stretching things a bit far but the Bureau pushes gamely ahead arguing that these events 'suggest collusion between Chinese drug traffickers and elements in North Korea and indicate that North Korea is a trans-shipment point for illicit narcotics intended for distribution in the region'. Not much evidence of 'state policy' here, it would appear.

The other incident, and one held up as the most damning evidence that North Korea was engaged in the state-sponsored export of narcotics, was the *Pong Su* affair. The North Korean ship *Pong Su* was boarded by the Australian navy on 20 April 2003, presumably after a tipoff from the Americans, although the Australian government claimed that it only discovered the ship was Korean after the event.[24] It happened at a time when the US administration was gearing up its Proliferation Security Initiative as a possible prelude to a blockade of the DPRK. The ship was seized by Australian Special Air Service troops after a four-day chase on the high seas. Why the heroin was not ditched during that period remains a mystery. There was also some doubt about the legality of interception; 'there are questions concerning the legality of undertaking searches and seizures in international waters. North Korea is not a signatory of any treaty that requires states to not produce drugs or to prevent the transport of narcotics.'[25]

The Narcotics Bureau report does not explicitly state that the *Pong Su* incident proves state policy but it tries to establish this by a sort of guilt by association. They made a point of saying that on board the ship was 'a North Korean identified as a "Political Secretary" of the ruling Communist Workers' Party in North Korea'. Apart from getting the title of the party slightly wrong – it is the Korean Workers' Party – the report did not elaborate on whether this was unusual or not, but it went on to draw the conclusion that, 'The "Pong Su" incident seemingly signals a further shift in North Korean involvement in drug trafficking. It is the first indication that North Korean enterprises and assets are actively transporting significant quantities of illicit narcotics to a designated destination outside the protection of DPRK territorial boundaries.'[26]

The report omits to say what happened at the trial. In testimony, the Australian Federal Police said that the heroin was being smuggled by a Macau organised crime syndicate, and that there was no evidence of North Korean government involvement.[27] Moreover, the US journalist Cam Simpson wrote,

A federal magistrate in the Australian state of Victoria on Friday dismissed drug charges against 27 of the ship's 30 North Korean crew members, including a 'political secretary' whose presence aboard the ship was highlighted by the State Department in its case against the Pyongyang regime. ...

Other evidence, records show, also suggests the heroin was produced in the Golden Triangle region of Southeast Asia, not in North Korea.[28]

Confronted with this testimony by Mr Simpson the State Department stuck to its guns. 'The Pong Su narcotics seizure occurred within the context of a range of criminal activities perpetrated by North Korean officials', the agency said.[29]

An Australian reporter went even further. Not fazed by the police testimony she brought in familiar witness from defectors ('Two defectors confirm what most serious Korea watchers already know – nothing at all happens in North Korea without the imprimatur of the all powerful leader, Kim Jong Il') and concluded by asking,

Why has the Australian government chosen to tread so softly? And is diplomacy and fear of North Korea's nuclear capability proving more important than cracking the strange case of the Pong Su?[30]

The idea that the Australian government might pressure police to commit perjury for fear of a North Korean nuclear attack might sound far-fetched but I have heard stories of academics earnestly discussing the possibility that Pyongyang might expend one of its then supposed arsenal of two nuclear bombs on Darwin as a warning to the Americans. There must be a word for that; paranoia doesn't quite seem to suffice.

Despite the US government's fulminations about state participation in drug dealing in general, and by the North Korean state in particular, we should not forget its own long involvement. For many years there have been many stories, seemingly well-documented, of CIA connections with international narcotics trafficking.[31] More recently there have been reports of friction between the British and Americans on drug policy in Afghanistan. It will be recalled that the Taliban banned opium production but after the US-led invasion opium growing has flourished again. The British government is unhappy because much of this finds its way to Britain. The United States, it appears, gets its heroin from other sources so is less concerned about drug warlords whom it needs to keep on its side against the Taliban in the 'war on terror'.[32]

The drugs charges serve a dual purpose. They are used to denigrate the DPRK but also serve as an excuse for sanctions and harassment of North Korean ships. Drugs, as we have seen, are elided with missiles to extend the framework of the virtual blockade.

One of the terrible ironies of the situation is that, if Afghanistan is anything to go by, a collapse of the DPRK may well result in a great expansion of narcotics production and trading. Opium production, which had been severely curtailed by the Taliban, is now reportedly Afghanistan's major crop.[33]

TERRORISM

'Terrorism' is a very emotive and much abused word and it is not appropriate to get into a discussion about what it is, whether it is justified, and under what conditions. The FBI says:

> There is no single, universally accepted, definition of terrorism. Terrorism is defined in the Code of Federal Regulations as '... the unlawful use of force and violence against persons or property to intimidate or coerce a government, the civilian population, or any segment thereof, in furtherance of political or social objectives'.[34]

Interestingly, and ominously, this implies that it is not the act that is at issue, but whether it is 'unlawful', and that begs the question, 'who determines what is lawful?'. Does it include or exclude acts committed by people in uniform such as the firing of rockets from Israeli helicopters at religious leaders outside a mosque or the napalming of Fallujah by US forces?[35] Let it suffice to say that this is contested territory.

Suspending moral judgement, but noting that the 'use of force and violence' for political objectives is widespread (including, for instance, the invasion of Iraq) let us examine two issues or events that are particularly pertinent to our discussion of North Korea – assassination and the bombing of KAL 858.

Focussed Violence – Assassination

Assassination has played an important role in modern Korean history. The assassination of the Japanese colonial administrator Ito Hirobumi by Korean An Chung-gun in 1908 was a significant event in the anti-Japanese struggle.[36] Kim Ku, the nationalist leader, was so taken with the efficacy of assassination as a means of resistance to the Japanese that he earned the nickname 'the Assassin'.[37] In 1946 Kim Ku sent a team to assassinate Kim Il Sung, but in 1949 when he had softened his stance on the Communist leader and moved closer to a pro-unification position, he himself was assassinated by his former comrades.[38] In fact, according to Professor Park, Kim Il Sung was by no means the only target;

> Anti-communist terrorist gangs from the south also targeted Ch'oe Yong-gŏn, Kim Ch'aek, Kang Ryang-uk, and others for assassination ... [and as a result the North Koreans were furious, claiming in an article that] through the primary fascist means of terrorism, they hope to destroy the North Korean People's Committee as well as the communist party, which serve as the democratic leaders of North Korea and the Korean democratic movement.[39]

What other assassination attempts against Northern leaders were made over the years is unclear. We know that many agents (some 10,000 according to some reports) were sent North between 1953 and 1972 but whether assassination was on the agenda is unclear.[40] Assassins on the ground are not the only way of doing things and the American press reported that in the buildup to the invasion of Iraq, Kim Jong Il 'went into seclusion ... because he feared that he too might be the target of attack'. The Pentagon did not deny the possibility.[41]

In 1968 there was a commando-like attempt to kill Park Chung-hee. The North credited Southern partisans, but Park thought it was a Northern attempt and set up Unit 684 in preparation for a retaliatory attempt on Kim Il Sung. However, relations with the North improved before the hit squad was ready to go and it was planned to kill the commandos off. They escaped from their training island of Silmido in August 1971 and headed for Seoul and Park Chung-hee. Most were killed before reaching the Blue House and the survivors were subsequently executed. The event was made into a very popular film, *Silmido*, in 2003.[42]

In 1974 there was a further attempt on the life of Park Chung-hee, this time by a Japanese-Korean (who reportedly confessed to North Korean connections before being executed). Finally, Park Chung-hee was successfully assassinated in 1979, but by the head of the Korea CIA, Kim Jae-kyu. Kim was subsequently executed but by 2004 the circle had turned and the government's Democratisation Rewarding Committee was deliberating whether to award him a posthumous honour for his 'promotion of democracy' by killing Park.[43] There have been suggestions that the Americans, unhappy with Park's flirtation with the North were complicit in his assassination.[44]

Park's assassination was a traumatic event in peninsula history and Kim Jong Il, in his discussion with the South Korean media in 2000 commented, 'I have been watching South Korean TV programs since the third anniversary of Park Jung Hee's assassination'.[45]

There was a major attempt on Chun Doo-hwan and leading members of his government during a visit to Yangon (Rangoon) in 1983. Chun described it as 'tenacious provocation by the band of Communists in North Korea' but the DPRK dismissed the accusation as 'preposterous and ridiculous'.[46] South Korean sources have accused Kim Jong Il of being personally behind the attempt, and in general being the mastermind for such activities.[47] By the nature of such things, impartial evidence is scanty.

Ironically, the other president of the Republic of Korea to survive assassination attempts was Kim Dae-jung. In his case the perpetrators were agents of the Korean CIA, acting on the orders of Park Chung-hee, who was later to be killed by its director. Kim was abducted in a hotel in Tokyo and was to be eliminated by being dropped out of a helicopter but was rescued as a result of US and Japanese pressure.[48]

Terrorism as Indiscriminate Violence

Apart from the alleged attacks on Park Chung-hee in 1968 and the more serious one on Chun Doo-hwan in 1983, there are two incidents linking DPRK with terrorism.

The first issue is, in reality, only partially connected with terrorism in the usual meaning of the word. It is the granting of asylum to the Japanese Red Army members who hijacked a plane in 1972, with no loss of life, in protest against Tokyo's support of America's Vietnam War.[49] There have been intermittent reports of them returning to Japan but this seems to have run foul of the abductee imbroglio.

The main instance has been the allegation that North Korea was behind the bombing of KAL 858 in 1987, as described in Chapter 2. The incident, it will be recalled, helped win Roh Tae-woo the election and put the DPRK on the United States Terrorism List. Doubts that North Korea was behind the incident soon surfaced, partly because of unexplained oddities in the investigation and its aftermath, but principally because the obvious beneficiary was Roh Tae-woo. These doubts have, if anything, increased over the years, and at the 17th and most recent anniversary of the incident, on 29 November 2004, relatives of the victims again called for a new investigation.[50] The matter is currently a political football between the ruling Uri party and the conservative opposition Grand National Party. At the time of writing the mystery continues, with the lead witness, 'self-confessed North Korean agent' Kim Hyon-hee, apparently in hiding:

> There has been a suspicion that some spy agents loyal to Roh and his predecessor Chun Doo-hwan had plotted the bombing to bounce back the popularity of the then ruling camp in the lead up to the 1987 presidential election.
>
> It was common for the past regimes in the South to use the North's potential military threat as a bait for the public to vote for the ruling party candidates, who argued they had strong and stable power to protect the country.
>
> The Supreme Court sentenced Kim Hyon-hee to death in March 1990. But Roh, the then head of state, gave her a special pardon the next month. In December 1997 she married a secret agent who had guarded her.
>
> Many domestic media, including *The Korea Times*, had tried to contact her for an interview, but she declined.
>
> Her testimony is considered a key to solving the current controversy over the truth of the KAL accident because there has been a strong argument that Kim was not a North Korean spy at all.[51]

In an interesting twist, the National Intelligence Service (NIS), the successor to the Korean CIA, was ordered in August 2004 to reinvestigate 13 cases alleged covered up by the military regimes, including the KAL bombing. The NIS made the original investigation and conceivably was behind the actual bombing. The other main incident to be reopened was the execution in 1974 of eight student activists:

> Both cases are considered to have the potential to deliver a serious blow to the reputation of the NIS if its alleged cover-up attempts are revealed to the public.
>
> In case of the KAL bombing, which claimed 115 passengers, the NIS concluded that two North Korean agents, including Kim Hyon-hee, blew up the Boeing 747 under direct orders from North Korean leader Kim Jong-il to thwart the opening of the Seoul Olympic Games in 1988.[52]

Clearly if investigations reveal that operatives loyal to Roh and Chun were behind the bombing this would be explosive and divisive in South Korea, even if no direct links to the generals were established. It seems unlikely that fresh, credible proof pointing in the other direction, that is towards Kim Jong Il, will be found, so at the least doubts will remain.

All this makes the inclusion of the DPRK on the US Terrorism List look increasingly threadbare. The then Secretary of State George Shultz added North Korea to Section 6(j) of the Export Administration Act of 1979 (50 USC. App. 2450(j)), which in March 2004 also included Iraq, Sudan, Syria, Cuba and Libya, on the sole grounds of its involvement in the KAL bombing.[53] What the State Department would do if it were proven that it was South Korea, not North Korea, that was responsible is an intriguing thought. In any case, the prevailing doubts, and the time elapsed, suggest that on grounds of US law alone, it would be prudent to remove the DPRK from the list.

The State Department's annual report *Patterns of Global Terrorism 2003* noted that the DPRK 'is not known to have sponsored any terrorist acts since the bombing of a Korean Airlines flight in 1987'.[54]

The report grudgingly continues,

> Following the attacks of September 11, Pyongyang began laying the groundwork for a new position on terrorism by framing the issue as one of 'protecting the people' and replaying language from the Joint US–DPRK

Statement on International Terrorism of October 2000. It also announced to a visiting EU delegation that it planned to sign the international conventions against terrorist financing and the taking of hostages and would consider acceding to other antiterrorism agreements.[55]

In fact, as we saw in Chapter 4, Pyongyang made a number of public and private overtures to an unresponsive Washington after 9/11. It frequently reiterates that it has no connection with terrorist groups, and none, as far as is known, have been established. None of this stops the accusations flowing freely, and North Korea is commonly charged with being ready to sell missiles, or nuclear materials, to whomever knocks on the door with a fistful of dollars. Not merely is there no evidence of this, it doesn't really make much sense. Selig Harrison, describing conversations in Pyongyang in April 2004, reports:

Here's foreign minister Paek Nam Soon: 'Let me make clear that we denounce Al Qaeda. We oppose all forms of terrorism and we will never transfer our nuclear material to others. Our nuclear program is solely for our self defense. We denounce Al Qaeda for the barbaric attack of 9-11, which was a terrible tragedy and inflicted a great shock to America. Bush is using that shock to turn the American people against us. But the truth is that we want and need your friendship'.[56]

Pyongyang has been very careful in its dealing with Washington. It has been firm, believing that weakness would be fatal, but although the media often likes to portray it as provocative, it has in reality studiously avoided being confrontational. Any connection with terrorists would give strong excuse in Washington to those who advocate military action. But it goes beyond that. North Korea does indeed need America's friendship, or at least its non-hostility, and that is the central thrust of its foreign policy which it is not likely to abandon for a mess of pottage.

WEAPONS OF MASS DESTRUCTION AND EXPORTS OF MISSILES

North Korea is portrayed as a highly militarised country, a threat to its neighbours and to the peace of the world, and a proliferator of weapons of mass destruction (WMD). How valid are these allegations, and to the degree that they are valid, what are the explanations?

Possession and Proliferation of Weapons of Mass Destruction

Four general points need to be made about WMD before we look at the DPRK in detail. This chapter looks at delivery systems, namely missiles, and the next chapter focusses on nuclear weapons per se, but these introductory remarks cover both. I also touch below on the issue of chemical and biological weapons (CBW).

Firstly, although the potential casualties from WMD are huge, in reality by far the majority of people killed are in fact killed by weapons of selective destruction (even when these are used indiscriminately). Iraq is a case in point. The US has not used any WMD but an estimated 100,000 Iraqis have died since the invasion, and sanctions before that killed many more.[57] The same holds true wherever we look, whether it be Chechnya or the Sudan. It is the violence that is the issue, not so much the mode. We should not let an undue focus on WMD obscure the weapons that are actually causing destruction in the world about us, and who is using them.

Secondly, aggressor states don't usually use WMD, partly for fear of retaliation (the fear that kept chemical warfare under control in European wars after the initial use in the First World War) but mainly because they might destroy the booty, whether it be oil, land, or workers. On the contrary, WMD are basically weapons of defence, a deterrent against attack, and often one of last resort. This is best exemplified by the Mutually Assured Destruction (MAD) of the Cold War. The unstated reason for the objection to WMD from large and powerful countries such as the US, who have, let us not forget, by far more WMD than any of the countries they criticise, is the possibility of horrific equalisation. To be specific, with conventional weapons alone North Korea could not retaliate against the United States, any more than could Iraq. It could kill Americans in Korea (and perhaps in Japan) but no further than that. The gap in destructive power is so far unbridgeable. If, on the other hand, North Korea could detonate an atomic weapon on Los Angeles then that gap would become bridgeable. The discrepancy would still be huge – the US has more nuclear weapons than there are targets in North Korea – but the US would no longer be invulnerable, and that is the key. But we should also realise the limitation of that potential Korean capability. It could only be used as a weapon of the very last resort. It could not be used for 'blackmail' as is frequently alleged ('blackmail' in this context is a malapropism, but let that pass). Pyongyang cannot say to Washington, 'Give us $100 billion and normalise relations or we will drop one of our eight atomic bombs on Los Angeles.' That really is not feasible. What is feasible for North Korea, if it had the capability, is to threaten to retaliate if attacked. In other words, a deterrent and no more than that.

Thirdly, the United States has less and less need to threaten WMD, even in defence, precisely because of its overwhelming military superiority in weapons of selective destruction. The Strategic Missile Defense Programme, if successfully implemented, would further lessen the need. Furthermore, it is so advanced in military technologies that it is constantly transforming WMD technologies to make them more selective. 'Bunker-buster' nuclear weapons are the foremost example of that. These are designed to destroy deep underground facilities (including bomb shelters), of which there are many in North Korea, as in other countries. The DPRK is noteworthy both for the extensive use of underground facilities, which include factories, and also for its artillery, dug into the hillsides along the DMZ. In particular, the artillery, which can threaten Seoul, is the main element of Pyongyang's retaliatory capacity, so the ability to destroy it is a valuable prize.[58] However, transformation of the technology is only one aspect. Just as important is the metamorphosis in popular perception, so that the use of nuclear weapons by the United States (and the US alone) becomes sanitised and acceptable.[59]

Fourthly, perhaps in order to hide these realities, talk of WMD is often couched in terms of high hypocrisy and double standards. A listening Martian would have assumed that Iraq, Iran and North Korea were awash with WMD, and the US would never touch such things with a bargepole. WMD are not presented as a global problem, threatening mankind with great destruction, perhaps extinction, but as something uniquely connected with 'evil regimes'. The solution is for them unilaterally to disarm, or be disarmed. The thought of multilateral disarmament is not seriously entertained, though that is, in theory, one of the pillars of the Nuclear Non-Proliferation Treaty. As the *Japan Times* put it in an editorial in February 2004 in response to President Bush's statement on non-proliferation:

> The failure of the nuclear weapons states to live up to their part of the NPT fatally undermines the entire nonproliferation regime. As long as they cling to their arsenals – and continue to update and modernise them – they reinforce the notion that such weapons have utility and are worth pursuing. Moreover, their inaction confirms the belief that the NPT is a hypocritical agreement

that perpetuates nuclear apartheid. That mentality erodes the legitimacy of the NPT, and underscores Japan's commitment to nuclear disarmament.[60]

In September 2004 the junior British Foreign Office minister Bill Rammell flew to Pyongyang to 'ask North Korea to cease its programme and destroy any existing weapons, or else face continued isolation from most of the rest of the world'.[61] We can be sure that he was not planning to announce that Britain would show the way by unilaterally getting rid of its nuclear weapons, and would urge the US to do likewise.

The Indian scholar Brahm Swaroop Agrawal put it succinctly. '[If] the United States, Russia and China can have nuclear weapons, why not India, Pakistan and Korea?'[62]

The word 'proliferation', as used in agreements such as the Nuclear Non-Proliferation Treaty has a legal definition. The United States and Britain, for instance, are legally in violation of the NPT by virtue of their mutual nuclear weapons treaty.[63] However, the term 'weapons proliferation' is usually used, especially in the Western media, to describe arms exports from, or to, countries of which the United States disapproves. This convenient definition means that the US, which is by far the largest arms exporter in the world (64 per cent in 1999 according to the US government) escapes the opprobrium of being a weapons proliferator like North Korea.[64] This is helpful because, again according to US government figures, North Korea's exports of arms are roughly 0.4 per cent that of the United States ($0.1 billion against $33 billion), and considerably smaller than those of such peace-loving countries as Sweden, Australia and Canada (see Appendix II).

Chemical and Biological Weapons

Chemical and biological weapons are by their nature, difficult to pin down. They are easy to conceal, compared with say nuclear reactors, or missile sites, and no country likes admitting to possessing them. Whatever research is admitted is always done, so it is said, purely for defensive purposes. For instance, a British government website for Porton Down claims 'The UK gave up its offensive capability in the 1950s and now carries out research and development on defensive measures only'.[65] The DPRK does not admit to CBW research or production, defensive or otherwise, but presumably something goes on. Certainly there are plenty of accusations. The Republican Party's North Korea Advisory Group report of 1999 (the one that said that

DPRK did have a uranium programme but that this did not violate the Agreed Framework) was quite adamant about CBW:

- North Korea possesses biological weapons production and dispensing technology, including the capability to deploy chemical or biological weapons on missiles.
- The DPRK is generally credited with possessing a full range of chemical warfare agents ...[66]

American military websites speak with confidence if imprecision of the DPRK CBW programme. The Center for Defense Information, for instance, says North Korea 'is suspected of possessing a relatively large chemical and biological weapons (CBW) stockpile, though the exact size and scope of North Korea's CBW program is unknown'.[67] The Henry L. Stimpson Center, in 2000, reported that

On 12 October 1999, the South Korean Ministry of Defense issued a White Paper that concludes North Korea has enhanced its capacity to wage chemical and biological warfare in the last several years. Not only does Pyongyang have a significant stockpile of poison gas and germ weapons, but South Korean authorities identified six chemical weapons storage areas, three chemical production facilities, and eight chemical research centers scattered across the northern half of the peninsula.[68]

The Stimpson report makes the intriguing comments that

Fears about chemical and biological weapons production are not new to the Korean Peninsula. In 1992, North Korea took the unusual step of distributing gas masks to its entire population.[69]

This implies that Pyongyang was seriously worried about the possibility of a chemical attack. Seoul, on the other hand, is only reported as establishing a 'Chemical and Biological Defense Command' in 1998, and no mention is made of the general issuance of gas masks, which suggests that they were not so concerned about an gas attack on them.

John Bolton, the then American Undersecretary for Arms Control and International Security, routinely fulminates against North Korea's alleged chemical warfare programme. In 2002, for instance, he said, 'With regard to chemical weapons, there is little doubt that North Korea has an active program. This adds to the threat to the people of

Seoul and to Korea–U.S. frontline troops.' Citing recent reports, he said, 'North Korea is capable of producing and delivering warheads using a wide variety of chemical agents and has a minimum of 2,500 tons of lethal chemicals.'[70]

A more cautious line is taken by the London-based International Institute for Strategic Studies which judged:

> Estimates of North Korea's chemical and biological weapons programmes are extremely uncertain. On balance, we assess that North Korea has probably produced and stockpiled a variety of chemical weapons agents and munitions, including artillery shells, aerial bombs, rockets, and missiles, but we cannot hazard an estimate of the amount and type of agents and munitions. ...
>
> There is general agreement that North Korea has conducted research and development on biological agents, but it is not known whether it has decided to produce and weaponise biological agents.[71]

A more muscular approach was taken by CNN which ran a story curiously entitled 'N. Korea's bio-chem warfare threat' on 3 March 2003. Curious because nowhere in the article does it say that North Korea admitted to having CBW, let alone threatened to use them. Be that as it may, CNN confidently reported that '... the maturity of North Korea's bioweapons (BW) program is at such a level that the United States ranks it just behind Iraq's germ warfare capability'. Just over two weeks later the United States invaded Iraq, and found no germ-warfare capability.

There is one particular irony to the accusations about North Korea's alleged CBW programme. According to many reports, most notably by the Canadian scholars Stephen Endicott and Edward Hagerman, the United States employed an operational biological weapons system during the Korean War.[72]

It is difficult to speak with any surety on the issue of CBW. As we have seen in Chapter 5, reports of chemical warfare experiments have been unsubstantiated. It seems likely that the DPRK, along with other countries, does what it can in respect of CBW research production and defence. After all, the anthrax used in the attacks in Washington in October 2001 came from American laboratories, and probably government ones at that.[73] It is also likely that estimates of capacity and intention are much exaggerated if for no other reason than vulnerability to retaliation. The DPRK response to the SARS epidemic in China in 2003, when it virtually sealed its borders for three months, something no other country did, was an indication, according to one World Health Organization official, of how conscious they were of the fragility of their health structure and the vulnerability of the population.

Missile Exports

Much is made of missile exports. US Assistant Secretary of State for Nonproliferation, John S. Wolf, at a press briefing in February 2003 claimed: 'They're kind of Missiles-R-Us. Anybody who has money can buy missiles.'[74] In fact, total North Korean arms sales are a tiny fraction of those of the US – 0.3 per cent in 1999 according to the State Department itself.[75] However, there is a continual insinuation that DPRK arms sales (unlike those of the US) are somehow illegal. US sales of missiles, and other armaments, to countries such as Britain, Australia or South Korea are seen as both less newsworthy and as somehow benign and peaceful. To take just one example, in November 1999 the US Department of Defense (DoD) announced that the ROK had 'requested' to buy Patriot Advanced Capability 3 (PAC-3) missile fire units with ancillary equipment, totalling $4.2 billion.[76] That sale alone was over four times as much as the $1 billion that, according to the ROK's Korea Institute for Defense Analyses, the DPRK is spending annually on all of its defence, including exports.[77] The DoD release noted that the sale would 'enhance [South Korea's] defense capability against hostile neighbours', implying that North Korea was not the only adversary. Indeed, given the parlous state of North Korean military equipment South Korea's hi-tech defence capability probably only makes sense if China is considered the likely antagonist, or perhaps Japan. The DoD release went on to say that 'The proposed sale of this equipment and support will not affect the basic military balance in the region.' At first this seems nonsensical. Why spend $4.2 billion if it has no effect? However, it is probably doublespeak, meaning that since the sales are to ROK, rather than to Taiwan, China will not protest. Alternatively, but still in the realms of doublespeak, they may be using the line that since PAC-3 is a surface-to-air guided-missile air-defence system, a component of Theatre Missile Defense (TMD), and hence of Missile Defense in general, then somehow it is non-threatening.

North Korea's missiles exports are sometimes quoted as being worth $1 billion a year.[78] However, as mentioned in Chapter 3, lack of dependable, comprehensive statistics is a problem. The (US) Arms Control Association, for instance, in its factsheet on missiles focuses solely on ballistic ones but excludes cruise missiles.[79] This is an important exclusion because cruise missiles, not ballistic ones, are what the United States has used, for instance in Sudan, Afghanistan and Iraq. It is also a major, almost certainly the major, exporter of cruise missiles:

> General Tome Walters Jr., who directs the Pentagon agency overseeing arms sales to foreign governments, claimed the United States only sells weapons to friends and that U.S. exports are not the problem. Walters, who said his agency has not exported any UAVs (unmanned aerial vehicles), asserted that the Pentagon has exported or agreed to export almost 200 fewer cruise missiles during the reviewed period than GAO (General Accounting Office) claimed. Past cruise missile deliveries went to the United Kingdom, Canada, Denmark, and Taiwan, according to Walters. He said there are pending deliveries to Oman, South Korea, and the United Arab Emirates (UAE). Among others, GAO identified Egypt, Kuwait, and Israel as additional U.S. cruise missile recipients.[80]

The concept of legality in the missile business comes from the rules of the Missile Technology Control Regime (MTCR) described by US Army Lt. Col. Alvin Perkins as 'a voluntary, informal arrangement among 33 member nations, including the world's most advanced suppliers of ballistic missiles and its related technology'.[81] Clearly the MTCR has no problem with exports of ballistic missiles as such, but rather to whom they are sold, and by whom. Perkins notes that 'The actionable word is "control" rather than "prohibit" weapons of mass destruction systems'.[82] He does not mention, and really does not need to, that the US government attitude towards the sellers and buyers is the key criterion in all this. Be that as it may, since the DPRK is not a member, its sales of missiles are not 'illegal'. The US has attempted to bring the DPRK into the MTCR but negotiations have faltered on the issue of compensation for sales foregone. North Korea has reportedly asked for $500 million.[83]

Many writers, perhaps deliberately, confuse export of missiles with export of nuclear material, technology or bombs. For instance, the Democratic Platform Committee, in the runup to the 2004 US presidential election, had this to say:

> North Korea has sold ballistic missiles and technology in the past. The North Koreans have made it clear to the world – and to the terrorists – that they are open for business and will sell to the highest bidder.[84]

In reality, Pyongyang has been at pains to distinguish between missile and nuclear exports. Selig Harrison, reporting on his discussions in Pyongyang in early 2004, wrote,

> On April 13, Richard Cheney, US vice-president, gave a speech in Shanghai branding North Korea a proliferator of nuclear and missile technology. Mr Cheney warned specifically that Pyongyang might sell nuclear material to al-Qaeda.
>
> These allegations evoked categorical denials. 'We make a clear distinction between missiles and nuclear material', declared Kim Yong-nam. 'We're entitled to sell missiles to earn foreign exchange. But in regard to nuclear material our policy past, present and future is that we would never allow such transfers to al-Qaeda or anyone else. Never'.[85]

The idea of non-state actors ('the terrorists') attacking the United States with a ballistic missile is the stuff of nightmares, but equally fanciful. It was noticeable that the report of the Rumsfeld commission of 1998 (Commission to Assess the Ballistic Missile Threat to the United States) focusses virtually entirely, in its unclassified published version at least, on *states*. In particular it looked at Russia, China, North Korea, Iran, Iraq, India and Pakistan.[86] One of the unclassified working papers in Appendix III exposed the central flaw of the Rumsfeld analysis of threat. It was written by John M. Myrah of Thiokol Corporation which modestly describes itself as 'the world's leading developer and producer of solid rocket motors': 'If there were a launch of these WMD by ballistic missiles on the territory of the U.S., an immediate response from the U.S. could be expected with devastating consequences for the aggressor.'[87]

Which is the obvious reason why the alleged threat of a missile attack from a 'rogue state' such as North Korea is palpable nonsense. For a state, ballistic missiles could only be used against the United States as a retaliatory weapon of last resort.

Myrah then moves on to the dilemma facing the United States:

> That is, if we knew with certainty, who the aggressor was. Wherein lies, in my opinion, the problem. With the demise of the Cold War, identifying our enemies has become a serious problem. ... Who launched the ballistic missile, if it comes from a non-terrorist state? Our eyes and ears (what few we have left) are now pointed at 'the bad guys', but what if it comes from the territory of 'a good guy'. As we dig out of the rubble or treat the thousands of chemical

burns or overload our hospitals with anthrax victims – who do we punish? There will be cries from many Americans to punish someone.[88]

However, almost by definition, most 'terrorists' come from 'non-terrorist states'. They come from Saudi Arabia or Jordan rather than Iran or North Korea, for two basic reasons. The Saudi and Jordanian terrorist 'non-state actors' are protesting against what they see as the dominance of their state by America. On the other hand, states that are not under US dominance, such as Iran and North Korea, take good care to restrain their citizens for fear of retaliation. One of the consequences of the US invasion of Iraq is that it removed the restraining influence of the state.

Unfortunately, Myrah does not address the vital question of whether non-state actors could actually launch a substantial ballistic missile at the United States from, in his language, the territory of 'a good guy'. That seems to remain uncertain. All we know is that when the United States was attacked on 9/11 it was by Saudis wielding box-cutter knives rather than ballistic missiles.

Missile Development and Capability

The usually level-headed Selig Harrison suggests that

> North Korea's missile development programs are primarily motivated by a desire on the part of the military factions in control of this program to earn foreign exchange through exports for their own profit and for the perpetuation of their power internally.[89]

This is really not very plausible. Exports of missiles are an off-shoot of the production for domestic military purposes. This is common elsewhere where governments off-set the costs of developing and producing armaments by selling them internationally. Japan is currently the exception for constitutional reasons. It is difficult to see North Korea going into the ballistic missile business primarily as an export venture. It is much more likely that missiles are developed for defensive purposes and that had there been no perceived threat from the United States then the DPRK would not have embarked on their development. Once a missile industry has been established, then the attraction of earning foreign exchange comes into play and this could conceivably be a factor in continuing development and production even if the perceived threat diminished. Indeed, this is the likely main reason for Missile Defense and a wide range of hi-tech weapons systems such as the Virginia-class attack submarine, costing $2 billion apiece, which are evidently profitable weapons in search of an increasingly implausible enemy.[90]

It is this search which makes an assessment of North Korea's missile capabilities difficult. Most of the estimates we have come from sources who have good reason to err on the side of exaggeration. The Rumsfeld commission, with its desire both to embarrass the Clinton administration (the commission was appointed by the Republican-controlled Congress, not the President) and also to promote Missile Defense and associated arms spending is a case in point. The commission admitted that the long-range Taepodong-2 had not yet been tested, and that the shorter range Nodong had only been tested once, in 1993. It also conceded that the 'Intelligence Community [had] encountered [considerable difficulties] in assessing the pace and scope of the Nodong missile program'. It therefore concluded that the DPRK had deployed the (scarcely tested) Nodong and would deploy the (untested) Taepodong-2.[91]

The warnings of the commission seem to have been justified with the launch of a Taepodong-1 in following month, on 31 August 1998. This was billed by Pyongyang as the launch of 'the first artificial satellite of the DPRK' which 'demonstrates the might of science and technology of Juche and proves the high level of the technology of development and manufacture of the carrier rocket'.[92] Some saw it as vindicating the Rumsfeld commission, others thought it was a way of the North Korean missile industry advertising its wares, and again others considered it a message to the Clinton administration to revive the failing implementation of the Agreed Framework. Gary Samore argues,

> In the brief period between the Taepodong-1 missile test of August 1998 and the end of the Clinton administration, the missile issue became the main focus of U.S. diplomacy towards the DPRK. As a result, Washington and Pyongyang reached agreement in September 1999 on a moratorium on additional long-range missile tests and came close to negotiating a framework for freezing major elements of North Korea's indigenous missile program and ending all missile-related missile exports. The clock ran out on the Clinton administration, however, before this comprehensive missile deal could be completed.[93]

Interestingly, the moratorium survived the advent of the Bush administration and was extended beyond its original agreement date of

2003. In November 2002, when Koizumi was reneging on the summit agreement of September, Pyongyang warned that it might 'reconsider the moratorium', but the threat was not implemented.[94]

One explanation is that the DPRK did not have the resources to sustain a development programme. In 1999 the Federation of American Scientists (FAS) obtained and published photos of the Nodong launch site taken by the IKONOS commercial satellite. The FAS commentary noted that

> The newly available commercial IKONOS satellite imagery reveals the vaunted Nodong test site as a facility barely worthy of note, consisting of the most minimal imaginable test infrastructure.
>
> It is quite evident that this facility was not intended to support, and in many respects is incapable of supporting, the extensive test program that would be needed to fully develop a reliable missile system. ...
>
> The North Korean missile program has always been distinguished by the disparity between the extremely modest and protracted North Korean test activities and the vast scale of the American response to this program.[95]

The Times reported that

> John Pike, director of the Federation of American Scientists, a private organisation in Washington that bought the pictures from the space company in Denver, Colorado, said: 'These photographs make a nonsense of American foreign policy, which has been dominated in recent years by the perceived ballistic missile threat from North Korea.
>
> 'All you can see is a shed, a dirt road, a launch pad and rice paddy. They don't seem to have any permanent tracking facility or any accommodation for launch crews. It's a temporary encampment from where you could launch the odd missile but not carry out a real test programme'. Mr Pike added that the US carried out 'dozens' of missile tests before deciding whether a weapon system was reliable. Yet US foreign policy was based on the fear that North Korea might attack American territory.
>
> He said that Washington was prepared to tear up the Anti-Ballistic Missile Treaty in order to spend billions of dollars on building a defence system to counter the North Korean threat, yet the Nodong site, he claimed, could not support a test programme for the three types of Taepodong missiles being developed.[96]

In September 2004 the South Korean, US and Japanese press carried stories of an imminent test of a medium-range No Dong missile, capable of hitting Japan.[97] No such test took place and the stories might have been a ploy to divert attention from recent revelations about South Korea's nuclear experiments.

The moratorium continues, for the moment. When Selig Harrison was in Pyongyang in April 2004 he brought up the question of when the DPRK would conduct a long-range missile test or a nuclear test:

> Asked how long North Korea could wait before conducting such tests, [head of state] Kim Yong-nam replied: 'There is no deadline in the negotiations. We're patient. But if the United States doesn't alter its position, we can't foresee what will happen and we'll have to decide about testing when the time comes'.[98]

That is where things stood in early 2005. No one knows the state of North Korea's missile capabilities, though unsubstantiated reports abound. General LaPorte claimed in Congressional testimony in March 2005 that the Taepodong would be operational by 2015 but whether this was based on a real intelligence estimate is unknown. Significantly, in the same testimony, he cited press reports about the intermediate-range missile, rather than anything from the intelligence community.[99] No one knows when, or if, they will conduct another test of a ballistic missile. The only thing we can be really sure about, is that it is all negotiable.

CONVENTIONAL FORCES

The DPRK is frequently referred to as the most heavily armed country in the world with the highest proportion of its population in the military.[100] And sometimes journalists get rather carried away; the otherwise admirable Seymour Hersh breathlessly claimed, obviously without thinking about it, that North Korea has 'more than forty per cent of its population under arms'.[101] When in Pyongyang in 1998 I was told in informal discussions with our guides that 60 per cent of young people go into some form of military training after graduation from high school, 30 per cent go on to higher education and 10 per cent are rejected on health or education grounds 'and go into the workforce'. They said that military service lasts for five to six years.[102]

On paper the DPRK does have an inordinately large army, though that was not so in the past and there were plans, before the present crisis, to reduce numbers drastically. There are five major explanations for the large numbers.

Table 6.1   World's largest military forces, 1999

Rank	Country	Number (thousand)	Rank	Country	Number (thousand)
1	China	2,400	6	Turkey	789
2	US	1,490	7	South Korea	665
3	India	1,300	8	Pakistan	590
4	North Korea	1,000	9	Vietnam	485
5	Russia	900	10	Iran	460

Source: *World Military Expenditures and Arms Transfers*, Vol. 28, 6 February 2003. Washington, DC: US State Department.

One is that the military threat facing North Korea, properly measured, is so huge compared with its own military resources. The invasion of Iraq confirmed, once again, that the number of men nominally under arms is not a good indicator of military capability. Expenditure is not a perfect measure of that; it is said, for instance, that Japan's expenditure exaggerates its capability partly because Japan, for constitutional reasons, is not able to export military equipment to offset development and production costs. As with GNP calculations, the exchange rate used can affect comparative costs by a factor of two. Nevertheless, expenditure is the best measure available. As Tables A2.2 and A2.3 in Appendix II indicate, North Korea's expenditure, whilst large in terms of its economy, is tiny in world terms and dwarfed by that of South Korea alone (see also Table 6.1, Figure 6.1 and Map 4).

Secondly, a straightforward comparison of military capacity in terms of tanks and planes, North and South, as is commonly done, is meaningless. Certainly the United States, and probably Japan, have to be brought in to the equation. The same reasoning applies to military forces measured in numbers. The US currently has some 37,000 ground troops stationed in South Korea, but it can rapidly deploy more. Bearing that in mind, the disparity between the North's 1 million and the South's 665,000 is not so great.

A third reason for the large armed forces is that North Korea, like other developing countries, has to substitute men for technology. The fourth reason is that it can be fairly conjectured that North Korea is preparing for 'people's war' in the case of invasion. Mandatory military service is long with the result that not merely is a large percentage of the population under arms at any given time, but the level of military training in the society is very high. The first Korean War was, as Cumings has pointed out, a people's war, like that in Vietnam.[103] It is likely that a second Korean War would be the same.

The fifth reason is that the numbers under arms, and the military equipment and capabilities, are inflated by those with a vested interest in portraying North Korea as a threat. Oberdorfer recounts that during the Carter administration, when the President was trying to implement his campaign promise to withdraw US troops from South Korea,

> New US intelligence estimates claimed that NK had substantially greater military forces than previously known. In tanks and artillery it was said that it had a 2-1 advantage over the South, the ground forces were now put at 680,000 rather than 485,000. For the first time, the North was estimated to have more men under arms than the South ... one out of every twenty-six was on active duty in the army, the highest proportion of any major nation.[104]

These new estimates were leaked to the press and this put a stop to the withdrawal. Years later Carter wrote to Oberdorfer,

> I have always suspected that the facts were doctored by DIA [Defense Intelligence Agency] and others, but it was beyond the capability even of a president to prove this.[105]

Similar new estimates of greatly increased North Korean military strength surfaced in South Korea in October 2004, in case President Roh Moo-hyun should be lulled into thinking of peace too much and were part of an opposition attack on the government's performance, so there was a large element of inter-party jousting.[106] They also came at a time when there was much talk of US forces being downsized because of Iraq and other commitments.[107]

MYTHICAL THREATS AND REAL DANGERS

Much was made in the National Assembly about a report by the Korea Institute for Defense Analysis (KIDA) which concluded that 'The South Korean Army and Navy's strengths were calculated to be 80 percent and 90 percent of those of the North, while its Air Force capability was 103 percent of the North's.'[108] It was said that Seoul would fall within 15 days (some versions had 16) if South Korea 'has to defend itself without U.S. troops'.[109] Since a war in Korea without US involvement (of which ground troops, certainly in the short term, would be a minor factor) is inconceivable there was a degree of artificiality about the debate. But apart from that, there was something a bit amiss about the estimates of relative North–South military capability. The Republic of Korea has about the tenth largest arms budget in the world.[110] In absolute terms the South spends about ten times as much on defence as the North.[111] And since the Russians have been trying to pay off their debt to South Korea through arms sales, it now even has much later model Russian tanks than the North.[112] Somehow, South Korea doesn't seem to be getting value for money.

Or is it? Calculations of military balance are both inherently difficult and subject to agendas of self-interest. Where would defence establishments be without frightening enemies? The general line in respect of North Korea seems to be that the South, and the US, need strong forces, indeed ever stronger forces, to deter an attack from the North, but such an attack would not be sustainable. One authoritative US assessment is that

> Although the North has no real prospect of prevailing in an armed conflict with the South, it nonetheless maintains the offensive capability to hold the Republic of Korea (ROK), and especially Seoul, hostage to the threat of a massive, short-warning attack that could inflict an unacceptable level of damage.[113]

In other words, even without the United States, the Republic of Korea is stronger but the DPRK might attack. Why it should, other than in retaliation, remains unexplained.

There are frequent reports about the poor state of North Korean equipment, and the lack of resources for training, which are in marked contrast to the KIDA assessment:

> The majority of its tanks, for example, were acquired from the now defunct Soviet Union. Visitors to the country say jeeps and other military vehicles are commonly seen broken down by the side of the road. A senior officer who defected from the Korean People's Army says there isn't enough fuel for military exercises and soldiers are told not to waste bullets during training. Food is also in short supply. Troops eat better than the country's

starving citizens, but some units raise cabbages and pigs to keep from going hungry.

North Korea's navy is small and its air force is dysfunctional. Because of chronic fuel shortages, pilots are limited to less than 10 hours of flight training a year, compared with the 200 to 300 hours that U.S. air-force pilots receive.[114]

Since any attack on South Korea would inevitably bring in the United States, and probably Japan, all this raises serious doubts about the likelihood of such an attack. The odds against North Korea are staggering. Taking expenditure on arms as a rough indicator of military capacity then the ratio between North Korea and its three possible adversaries is 266 to 1. Given the asymmetry of power, this only gives a partial picture. The United States can bomb and devastate Pyongyang, but the DPRK, at the moment at least, cannot touch Washington. On the other hand North Korea could inflict serious damage on South Korea and Japan, and US forces and citizens in both countries.

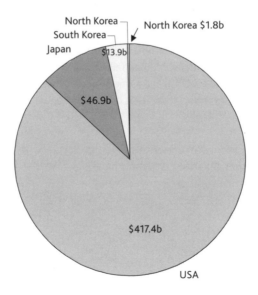

Source: Stockholm International Peace Research Institute. *Military Expenditure Database 2004*. Stockholm: SIPRI, 2004. Available from http://web.sipri.org/contents/milap/milex/mex_data_index. html (accessed 11 October 2004)

Figure 6.1   Comparative military expenditure, North Korea and its enemies, 2003

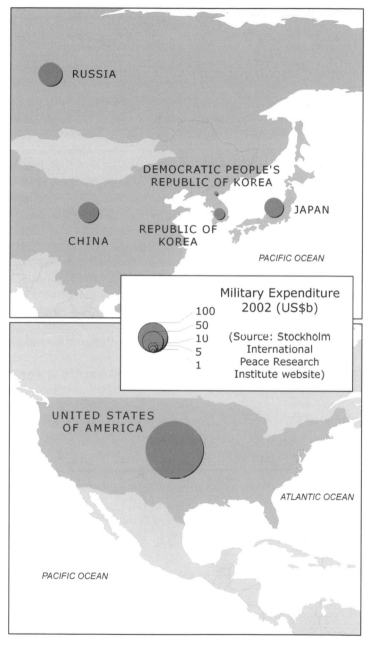

Map 4 A dwarf among giants: North Korea's military expenditure
in comparative perspective

The disparity of military capacity does suggest that the idea of North Korea mounting an invasion to take over the South is very far-fetched. Although the rhetoric continues, Selig Harrison argues, 'The United States and South Korea do not, in fact, base their military strategy on the premise that North Korea is still dedicated to unifying the peninsula by force.'[115]

The possibility of war, by miscalculation or by design, still remains however. The most probable scenario is an American airstrike that would cause a Northern retaliation. Representative Park Jin of the Grand National Party has said that 'South Korea should map out measures to prevent the United States from launching surgical strikes against North Korea'. He referred to the 1994 OPLAN 5026 in which US aircraft would strike 756 targets in the North. Amongst other things South Korea would be imperilled from radiation released by strikes at nuclear installations.[116] Also on the cards in the runup to the US 2004 election, according to press rumours denied by US ambassador Christopher Hill, were suggestions that the US might create an 'October surprise' to boost Bush's election prospects. He dismissed 'Media speculation that North Korea might provoke a crisis on the peninsula this month and that the United States might retaliate with a surprise surgical strike against the North and its nuclear facilities'. He did not explain why North Korea should give an election present to George Bush when it was widely assumed that it preferred Kerry. There were echoes here of the bombing of KAL 858 in 1987 which did so much to assist Roh Tae-woo's election.[117]

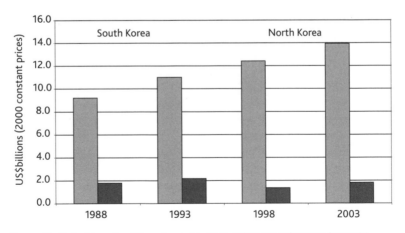

Source: Stockholm International Peace Research Institute, *Military Expenditure Database 2004*.

Figure 6.2   The two Koreas: comparative military expenditure, 1988–2003

Meanwhile the North complained that Seoul's plan to increase the military budget by 10 per cent was an 'intolerable criminal act to increase the tensions on the Korean peninsula and bring the inter-Korean relations back to a military confrontation and a phase of war'.[118]

Illustration that South Korea does not take a Northern military victory seriously, but anticipates the reverse, was given by revelations in the National Assembly in 2004 of contingency plans *Chungmu 9000*, for an 'emergency administrative headquarters in the North' and *Chungmu 3300* for coping with refugees (facilities were provided for 200,000) and 'a possible civil war'.[119] Whether this 'civil war' meant resistance in the North to southern occupation, or civil disturbances in the South was not clear.

Actually, there was nothing particularly new about talk of the northern threat being more of a propaganda ploy than something which was a real concern. Certainly the southern forces were no match for the North in the 1950s but even aside from the fact that the Korean War anchored the United States to the Korean peninsula and made any attack by the North (though not perhaps the South) unthinkable, the ROK armed forces were greatly strengthened in the postwar period. Not merely were they larger, and probably better equipped than the DPRK forces, they also had considerable war experience in Vietnam. The Vietnam War was not merely profitable for the South Korea of Park Chung-hee – in the late 1960s it provided 40 per cent of the foreign exchange earnings – but gave hundreds of thousands of ROK troops war experience.[120] The current expeditionary force to Iraq is far smaller, just a few thousand, but again there is an element of experience of a real war zone (some no doubt see fighting the Iraqi resistance as useful preparation for activities closer to home). In between the real wars there have been the massive, and frequent, war games such as Team Spirit. North Korea cannot compete with any of this. Despite the warlike image the North Korean armed forces have had virtually no war experience in 50 years. A number of fighter pilots fought in Vietnam against US bombers, and there have been a handful of military advisors abroad, especially in Africa. In fact, there are few countries with less war-fighting experience over the last half-century than North Korea, certainly compared with the US, Britain, France, China, Russia, South Korea, Australia and New Zealand amongst others. Even Germany and Japan have sent troops abroad to areas of conflict.

Before the government of Kim Dae-jung it was normal for governments to utilise the bogey of the northern threat; especially in the runup to elections. However, when more important things happened they seemed to find the threat less than pressing. In 1979 General Roh Tae-woo withdrew his units from the DMZ to help General Chun Doo-hwan's coup in Seoul (much to the annoyance of the US military because he didn't ask permission).[121] As for Chun, according to Oberdorfer, although he was adept at using the North Korean threat as a card against dissident students, and the Americans, he did not take it seriously himself.[122]

When US commentators decide that it would be wise to move US troops out of South Korea, for whatever reason, they soon come to the conclusion that the threat from the North is no problem after all. Charles Krauthammer argues that the long-established rationale of US troops as a 'tripwire' makes no sense. 'This invitation to suicide might have made sense when South Korea was weak, impoverished and war-ravaged. Today it is an industrialized tiger with a large and superbly equipped army.'[123] In an interesting twist, some argue that US should remain, or at least be withdrawn slowly, to prevent the South invading the North.[124] Given the real disparity in military and industrial strength between North and South, as well as population, and the strength of conservatism in political, civil and military circles, a southern invasion is by no means improbable. There have been rumours for some time that the Americans keep the South Korean forces short of critical ammunition in order to restrain any such ideas. Lending support to these rumours, Representative Park Jin has complained that supplies for the Multiple Launch Rocket Systems will last for just one day, that for K1A1 tanks ten days and K-9 self-propelled guns, five days leading to doubts 'whether Seoul can take up a self-reliant defense posture against Pyongyang'.[125]

It is clear that the sustainable offensive conventional military strength of North Korea is less than that of South Korea alone, and the balance is constantly moving against it. Once we add the United States, and perhaps Japan, into the equation, the force deployed against it is overwhelming. It can retaliate against attack, and it would probably put up a fierce, and sustained, resistance to invasion. However, to suggest that it poses a threat of unprovoked aggression is the stuff of neocon fantasy. It is also the stuff of military self-interest. Eisenhower is well remembered in his valedictory speech in 1961 for having warned against the military-industrial complex.[126] Few readers will need convincing of the relevance of that to contemporary America, from Missile Defense to Iraq. However, the interest of the US and ROK military, in sustaining a sense of threat from North

Korea and continuing crisis should not be under-estimated. The struggle between the civilian presidents Kim Dae-jung and Roh Moo-hyun, who wish to build a peaceful relationship with the North, and the military forces opposing that, is mainly kept behind the scenes, though occasionally it surfaces. One example was the incident between North and South in the West Sea in July 2004 where the ROK navy opened fire on a northern boat, ignoring a protocol signed by the two sides, and then tried to cover it up, leading to suspicions that 'this accident was intentionally caused by individuals disgruntled with the currently amicable military relationship between the two Koreas'.[127]

That particular incident has been papered over, but the lines of fissure remain and the struggle between civilian democracy and the military, supported by allies on the right, will probably become an increasingly major issue in South Korea especially if neocons strengthen their influence in the second Bush administration. This civil–military struggle will be replicated in the North, thus exacerbating confrontation, but it is in the South we might discover the most surprises.

Kim Jong Il's Songun or 'army-first' policy is arguably partly a way of keeping his generals on-side while he attends to other matters, such as negotiating with the Americans, developing ties with the new leaderships in Russia and China, and reforming and revitalising the economy.[128] In the South, Roh Moo-hyun faces similar problems. For instance, the military budget is jumping a whooping 30 per cent over the period 2005–08, going from 2.8 per cent of GDP to 3.2 per cent.[129] This despite the massive increase in US military spending on the peninsula, $11 billion over three years, announced in June 2003.[130] Despite, also, the stagnant or declining North Korean military expenditure (Figure 6.2). It is claimed that the increased ROK spending is needed both to counter an attack from the North and to make the military more 'self-reliant'. Yet President Roh publicly discounts the possibility of such an attack.[131] There is also an ongoing tussle between progressives and conservatives, civilian and military, over the designation of the DPRK as the 'main enemy'.[132]

Thus both Kim Jong Il and Roh Moo-hyun have problems with their generals, whose policies are at variance with theirs, though neither can admit to this. However, there is one crucial difference in their dilemmas. Roh's generals, unlike Kim's, have powerful friends, and increasingly powerful ones at that, in Washington. This friendship may exert a profound influence on Korean affairs in coming years.

7

The Nuclear Confrontation

The nuclear issue has become the main bone of contention between the DPRK and the US for the last decade and more. It also impacts upon, and sometimes virtually submerges, relations between North and South and, to a lesser but still important extent, relations between DPRK and other countries. Inevitably it is discussed extensively throughout this book. Moreover, Appendix IV gives a detailed chronology of developments, mainly over the last ten years, but stretching back to August 1945, when the first atomic bomb was exploded over Hiroshima. Here it is a matter of tying the threads together and highlighting the main points. North Korea's nuclear confrontation with the US takes place against a backdrop of historical, cultural, ethical, and practical premises and realities that need to be taken into account in any serious and thoughtful attempt to understand the issues.

DYNAMIC, INTERACTIVE, HISTORICAL PROCESS

Nuclear weapons are an emotive issue, and one which nuclear powers attempt to invest with as much obfuscation and hypocrisy as possible, so it is important that we approach the subject dispassionately and with care. Condemnation of nuclear weapons, or more usually the acquisition by non-nuclear states of such weapons ('proliferation') is insufficient. We need to fit things together so causes and consequences can be identified.

The chronology in Appendix IV is different from other chronologies on the subject such as, for example, those by the Arms Control Association or by the Nautilus Institute, in one important respect. *They* give events from an American perspective in which the DPRK is invariably cast in the role of either transgressor or initiator. The events are portrayed against a blank background, and if the US appears it is primarily as a standard and would-be enforcer of international probity. Often the International Atomic Energy Agency (IAEA), or the cant phrase 'the international community' is used as a virtual surrogate for the United States. My own chronology, by contrast, sees all this as a dynamic, interactive, historical process. If the DPRK is developing weapons it is primarily because it feels threatened, and mainly by the US. We can trace the process. It includes not merely negotiations between Pyongyang and Washington, but other impacting events such as threatening war games, Missile Defense, new policies on so-called 'pre-emptive war' and using nuclear weapons ('Nuclear Posture Review'), and the invasion of Iraq. The purpose of weaving a chronology using a number of threads is not to construct a simplistic picture of an innocent and hapless North Korea as victim to an overbearing, predatory US, as some sort of corrective to the prevailing stereotypes, but to remind us of the complexity and historicity of the nuclear issue; events have causes as well as consequences, and the linkages can be convoluted and misunderstood. On top of which we need to be aware of the uncertainty or contestability of much of the information in the public domain. Misinformation, deception and secrecy are, after all, all major weapons in this game.

DOUBLE STANDARDS AND HYPOCRISY

It is often overlooked, either on purpose or because we are all so buffeted with propaganda, that no country has any particular right to nuclear weapons to the exclusion of others. Much of the discussion on the issue automatically assumes that it is natural for the US to have nuclear weapons, so natural that its possession of them is not even mentioned, while on the other hand it is presumed that it is immoral and threatening for North Korea to develop them. Such double standards are unacceptable but it is unusual for anyone to point that out, which makes ElBaradei's statement, quoted below, quite an exception.

IAEA'S Dubious Role

The International Atomic Energy Agency has played a dubious role in all this. In theory it is, like the United Nations of which it is part, a neutral body that serves 'the international community' composed of sovereign and equal states. However, power talks. With the United Nations that is partly reflected in its structure, for example with the special status and rights given to the permanent members of the Security Council. But extraneous power, principally but not exclusively that of the United States, goes beyond that formal structure to affect the voting of states and the actions of UN officials. US power and influence are not absolute, by any means, as the hostility amongst many Americans towards the UN attests. But the IAEA seems to have been a pretty well-behaved animal. Its website, for instance, could well be run by the State Department. Its 'In focus' section has pages on Iran, Libya, DPRK and Iraq, but no special attention paid to the nuclear weapon states (except a page on Chernobyl!) or to the issue of nuclear disarmament.[1] Indeed, so anxious have its bureaucrats been at times to serve the cause that they have embarrassed the Americans themselves. During the 1993/94 crisis, according to Oberdorfer, Hans Blix, the Director General of the IAEA, drawing on unchallenged US satellite intelligence made demands for unprecedented intrusive inspections that went beyond American demands.[2] Wit, Poneman and Gallucci, US officials involved with the negotiations that led to the Agreed Framework, later complained that the IAEA

> kept shifting the goalposts by adding new conditions for 'continuity of safeguards' inspections, making it difficult for the United States and North Korea to return to the negotiating table. Some U.S. officials felt the IAEA was piling on the pressure too much, and that the need to ensure that there would be no diversion of North Korean nuclear material required fewer activities than it was demanding.[3]

Hans Blix and ElBaradei – the Dilemma of the International Civil Servant

In general, the Americans seem to have been well pleased with Blix's tenure at IAEA, with his focus on non-proliferation, and 'the need to confront countries such as Iraq and North Korea'.[4] He was later to fall out with the US, or specifically the Bush administration, over Iraq.[5] His successor at the IAEA since 1997, Mohamed ElBaradei, shows no signs of doing that, although he did sail close to the wind in an article for the *New York Times* in February 2004 when he wrote:

> We must abandon the unworkable notion that it is morally reprehensible for some countries to pursue weapons of mass destruction yet morally acceptable for others to rely on them for security – and indeed to continue to refine their capacities and postulate plans for their use.

However, the United States was not mentioned by name, and there appear to have been no howls of outrage in the US media ('Nuclear watchdog savages US over double standards') so his job was secure. Job security for an international civil servant, as his fellow countryman, Boutros Boutros-Ghali found out, depends on being well regarded in Washington.[6] There was a telling incident in October

2004, just after the revelation about South Korean covert nuclear experiments. ElBaradei went to Seoul where, according to Reuters, he was to launch his campaign for a new term at the agency.[7] The newspaper headlines say it all. 'Nuclear Agency Chief Goes Easy on Seoul',[8] 'ElBaradei Discounts Seoul's Nuclear Lab Test',[9] and 'IAEA Chief Says World Getting Impatient with N. Korea'.[10] The second term beckons although there were stories that he wasn't tough enough on Iran for the Americans' liking and they were working to get rid of him. However, revelations in the *Washington Post* that they were bugging his phone may have rebounded on the US plans.[11]

PRACTICAL AND ETHICAL REASONS

There are good practical reasons why North Korea should not have nuclear weapons. One is the huge expenditure, which could be put to other uses. Another is that it will provide justification, an excuse or a reason, for Japan and perhaps South Korea to weaponise, thus stimulating a further arms race in Northeast Asia. However, there is no moral reason for North Korea to sacrifice its interests.

THE NUCLEAR NON-PROLIFERATION TREATY

The NPT was a compromise whereby non-nuclear weapon states were to forgo the security of nuclear weapons in exchange for help in developing peaceful uses of nuclear energy, not being threatened by nuclear weapon states (NWS), and by a global move to nuclear disarmament. The NWS, particularly here the United States, have not kept to their side of the bargain. The United States has failed to ratify the Comprehensive Test Ban Treaty, has withdrawn from the Anti-Ballistic Missile Treaty, has routinely threatened the use of nuclear weapons (in particular in the Nuclear Posture Review), is developing new generation nuclear weapons (bunker-busters) and is militarising space, through Missile Defense and other programmes.[12] Brazil, for one, has made it clear that it sees its own commitment to the NPT contingent on 'total nuclear disarmament', to the 'concern', it is said, of the IAEA.[13]

NUCLEAR ENERGY

This is very important for North Korea, as it is for countries in the region, and most parts of the world. According to statistics compiled by the IAEA, the country with the highest proportion of its electricity coming from nuclear power is Lithuania (80.1 per cent) with France (78.0 per cent) close behind. Globally, in 2002, some 16 per cent of the world's electricity came from nuclear power. Although the United States is the biggest generator of nuclear power, its proportion (20.3 per cent) is relatively modest, just behind Britain's 22.4 per cent and quite a way behind Japan (34.5 per cent) and South Korea (38.6 per cent).[14] Although some nuclear energy is reportedly being generated in North Korea it is too small to register in the statistics. DPRK complaints that the US had objected to a peaceful nuclear programme during the course of the Six-Party talks in June 2004 reflect a recognition on both sides of how important nuclear power is to North Korea if the economy is to recover.[15] Other sources of energy, such as coal, and Russian gas, are important but have their drawbacks. A gas pipeline project has been blocked by the US.[16]

Security of Energy Supply

Secure sources of energy supply are a major concern of any government, not least the United States. The invasion of Iraq was to a large extent driven by this. If there is a uranium enrichment programme in North Korea, it is likely that one reason would be to provide feedstock for the projected light-water reactors.[17] DPRK negotiators have hinted at such.[18] Moreover, the enriched-uranium technologies which it is claimed were passed to North Korea by A. Q. Khan, came in turn from European efforts in the 1970 to provide their 'nuclear power industry a fuel source independent of the United States'.[19] By the same argument, although attention has been focussed on the weapons aspect, it is likely that one of the reasons for South Korean experiments on uranium enrichment is to develop the capability to produce energy feedstock. Although South Korea, according to IAEA statistics has only modest deposits of uranium, there are estimates that the North has 26 millions tons, which would be an important resource for a reunified Korea.[20] Whilst the desire of the US, shared with other NWS, to keep a monopoly over nuclear weapons and delivery systems is well known, less explored is the way it seeks to dominate global supply of nuclear fuel also. Russia, with its nuclear heritage appears thus far to have been a junior partner.

THE STRANGE WORLD OF NUCLEAR ASSESSMENTS

US assessments during the 1980s tended to discount the possibility of North Korea acquiring nuclear weapons. A report by the US

Directorate of Intelligence in May 1983 noted that, 'We have no basis for believing that the North Koreans have either the facilities or materials necessary to develop and test nuclear weapons [some 15 letters excised].'[21] An appended document from October 1986 reprinted 'key judgements' for an intelligence assessment produced by the Office of Scientific and Weapons Research suggests that the Yongbyon facility is civilian because it was thought unlikely that North Korea would locate a military reactor at a known research centre, open to international inspections (others have noted that there has been no attempt to hide Yongbyon). The report outlines a number of good reasons why North Korea should refrain from embarking 'on a venture as costly, hazardous and politically sensitive as a nuclear weapons program', and gives some not very convincing ones why it might nonetheless want to do so. The first CIA study of North Korea's nuclear programme publicly available, *North Korea's Nuclear Efforts*, written in 1987, focusses on energy production.[22] Although some parts of the report are still classified, it does not appear that the CIA was overly worried about weaponisation. It says, ' In our opinion, the [Yongbyon] reactor also could produce weapons-grade plutonium ...', and then the rest of the sentence is blacked out. Later in the document the CIA says, 'The North's expanded nuclear program could include an effort to develop nuclear weapons.' Here the rest of the paragraph is blacked out. We can only speculate why the CIA wants to keep these paragraphs and sections of the document secret. One reason, and the usual excuse for such secrecy, is to safeguard sources of information. However, another reason might be that opinions were expressed that became embarrassing in the light of further developments, either in the DPRK nuclear programme or in the CIA assessments of it. Who knows, it may well be that the CIA analysts concluded that North Korea was unlikely to have the capabilities or commitment to develop nuclear weapons.

Political Pressures and Sexing-Up

That these assessments change in the 1990s and beyond might have as much to do with political pressures on the intelligence community as with anything happening in North Korea. Jonathan Pollack, amongst others, has noted how CIA estimates were hardening up from 2001 onwards, often retrospectively. The CIA assessment of 1993 that 'North Korea ... had produced enough plutonium for at least one, and possibly two, nuclear weapons', becomes, in a statement to the Congress on 19 November 2002 (i.e. in the aftermath of the

Kelly confrontation in Pyongyang), 'The U.S ... has assessed since the early 1990s that the North has one or possibly two [nuclear] weapons using plutonium it produced prior to 1992.'[23]

Election Claim and Counter-claim

During 2004, following the visit of Lewis, Pritchard and Hecker to Yongbyon, and as the election campaign heated up, there were leaks to the press that 'the intelligence community' estimated DPRK now had eight nuclear weapons.[24] This became, as clearly intended, part of the election battle. Kerry, in his first TV debate with Bush, charged:

> With respect to North Korea, the real story: We had inspectors and television cameras in the nuclear reactor in North Korea. Secretary Bill Perry negotiated that under President Clinton. And we knew where the fuel rods were. And we knew the limits on their nuclear power ... [after the ending of the Agreed Framework] And for two years, this administration didn't talk at all to North Korea. While they didn't talk at all, the fuel rods came out, the inspectors were kicked out, the television cameras were kicked out and today there are four to seven nuclear weapons in the hands of North Korea. That happened on this president's watch.[25]

The *Washington Post* came to President Bush's rescue in an editorial:

> While the CIA concluded that North Korea may have built one or two nuclear weapons before Mr. Bush took office, and while U.S. intelligence agencies believe the fuel rods have been reprocessed into plutonium, there is no certainty that North Korea has built more nuclear weapons.[26]

The writer was correct in saying there was 'no certainty'. However, since the methodology was the same – knowing how much time the Koreans had to work on the fuel rods, and making assumptions about their technological capabilities – then there was 'no certainty' about the earlier estimates either. Indeed, if we assume that Korean technology had improved over the decade then weapons would be more likely now than in the early 1990s. However, as Charles Kartman, the American director of the virtually defunct KEDO (Korean Peninsula Energy Development Organization) said in an interview after the Bush–Kerry debate, 'The number of proven weapons is zero.'[27]

STRATEGIC AMBIGUITY AND ASSERTION

It is often claimed that the DPRK employs 'strategic ambiguity' about is nuclear intentions and capabilities in order to keep its adversaries guessing and uncertain. There is truth in this, and it is to be expected from any country (that is what 'neither confirm nor deny' is all about), but especially one faced with far more powerful enemies. However, it is important also to note the assertions and public statements. The DPRK has frequently over the years called for a nuclear-free Korean peninsula. It was not until the early 1990s when the US, for its own reasons, in theory withdrew tactical nuclear weapons from South Korea though not thereby rescinding its ability to use nuclear weapons against North Korea.[28] Pyongyang also frequently said it had no nuclear weapons programme. When it finally withdrew from the NPT in January 2003, after the US had conclusively reneged on the Agreed Framework by refusing to deliver fuel oil, it continued to say that its nuclear programme 'at this stage will be confined only to peaceful purposes'.[29] It was only after the US refused to negotiate and continued with its 'hostile policy' that in July 2003 the DPRK publicly said it was developing a nuclear deterrent. 'Going public' is an important step in diplomatic negotiations and this marked a new stage. There was a further escalation when Vice Foreign Minister Choe, in his speech to the UN General Assembly on 27 September 2004, said that 'the DPRK is left with no other option but to possess a nuclear deterrent [because the Bush administration] ... has been attempting to eliminate the DPRK by force while designating it as part of an 'axis of evil' and a target of pre-emptive nuclear strikes'.[30]

DECISION TO WEAPONISE

We do not know when Pyongyang decided to go for nuclear weapons. Many argue that it has been a long-term aim, but there is no substantial evidence to back this up. We do know that the plutonium programme, the immediate source of any nuclear weapons, was suspended over the period 1994–2002 during the Agreed Framework. It is likely that there have been continuing low-level experiments over the years, as there were in the South, but this is different from a commitment to weaponise. There are no certainties but it seems fair to say that the evidence suggests that Pyongyang has been more than willing to renounce nuclear weapons in exchange for quite modest 'concessions' from the United States. Non-aggression, normalisation of relations and refraining from economic warfare is, after all, behaviour that is assumed by the Charter of the United Nations. It is not the fruit of blackmail. If North Korea has, or will soon have, nuclear weapons it is because this has been forced upon it by the United States. It was by no means inevitable.

ENRICHED URANIUM: SMOKING GUN AND EVIDENCE

The alleged existence of a enriched uranium programme has been the cornerstone of the Bush administration's revocation of the Agreed Framework. There are two aspects of this. One is the alleged 'admission' to such a programme, and the other is the question of the existence of the programme itself.

The Smoking Gun? 'Admission' Issue

James Kelly made his allegations when in Pyongyang 3–5 October 2002. As we have seen in Chapter 4 he gave press conferences in Seoul and Tokyo on his way home but made no mention of the allegation or the admission. This only surfaced, after an unexplained hiatus of two weeks, in a State Department press briefing on 16 October. By 25 October the DPRK Foreign Ministry had implicitly denied both the 'admission' and the programme. It then appeared that the South Koreans were dubious about the admission, suggesting that the Americans 'might have misunderstood'. At about the same time there were reports that Kelly claimed that the North Koreans had admitted 'storing bio-weapons' but Armitage later admitted this was a misunderstanding. On 18 January 2003 a DPRK official in an interview accused Kelly of deliberately making up the admission and said that that they had expressly denied the programme at that meeting. This has been the line ever since. For their part, the Americans (Kelly and Pritchard) have remained adamant that Kang Sok Ju did acknowledge the programme. Pritchard, even after having broken with the Bush administration, says that he heard correctly.[31] John Lewis, who was given a transcript of the discussion by the North Koreans in January 2004 thought there had been a confusion between the Koreans saying 'we are entitled to have a nuclear program' and the Americans (or presumably their interpreter) hearing them say 'we have a program'.

The Enriched Uranium Programme – Evidence

Whilst the admission might have been instrumental in having a gullible media accept that the programme existed, we need to see what other evidence existed. Pritchard, in his discussion with Vice Minister Kim Kye-Gwan in January 2004 made the point that 'it really didn't matter to the United States whether they admitted or not. That was not why at the time the U.S. took action. They did that based upon reliable information that we had about the program.'[32] What was this 'reliable information'? It seems to have been a mixture of information from Pakistan (the 'Khan connection') and satellite photos.[33] The North Koreans have frequently said that the Americans, whatever information they might have, in fact produced no evidence.[34] Although IAEA Director General ElBaradei seems to have accepted the US line, at least before Iraq, there does not seem to have been any presentation of evidence to the IAEA as there had been in the early 1990s.[35] The American case against DPRK, as with Iraq, seems to have rested on what they said they knew, rather than what they could demonstrate to impartial and expert opinion.

CREDIBILITY AND THE IRAQ FACTOR

The invasion of Iraq, and the failure to substantiate any major US allegation, dealt a huge blow to US credibility – 'Crying wolf on Iraqi WMD costs US credibility on North Korea', as Jon Wolfsthal, deputy director for non-proliferation at the Carnegie Endowment for International Peace, put it. Wolfsthal said that

> the US must be more open with South Korea, Japan, and even China about its intelligence on North Korea. While this carries the risk of North Korea learning more about what the US knows and how it collects intelligence, the risk of letting doubts linger may be greater.[36]

Whether the Americans have been more open or not, it is generally agreed that the other countries in the Six-Party talks are sceptical about the US allegation and the Chinese, in particular, have made this known, much to American annoyance.[37]

EVIDENCE, WHO NEEDS EVIDENCE?

Selig Harrison, one of the foremost American writers on Korean affairs, gave an authoritative assessment of the issue in the January 2005 edition of the prestigious mainstream journal *Foreign Affairs*, which is worth quoting at some length. He wrote:

> Two years ago, Washington accused Pyongyang of running a secret nuclear weapons program. But how much evidence was there to back up the charge?

A review of the facts shows that the Bush administration misrepresented and distorted the data ...

Much has been written about the North Korean nuclear danger, but one crucial issue has been ignored: just how much credible evidence is there to back up Washington's uranium accusation? Although it is now widely recognized that the Bush administration misrepresented and distorted the intelligence data it used to justify the invasion of Iraq, most observers have accepted at face value the assessments the administration has used to reverse the previously established U.S. policy toward North Korea ...

Relying on sketchy data, the Bush administration presented a worst-case scenario as an incontrovertible truth and distorted its intelligence on North Korea (much as it did on Iraq), seriously exaggerating the danger that Pyongyang is secretly making uranium-based nuclear weapons ...

The CIA says that it cannot reveal all that it knows without exposing 'methods and sources'. This argument would be more persuasive if the agency had at least made a credible case to congressional committees in executive session or to U.S. Asian allies. But since the report came out, no evidence to support it has been supplied to South Korea or Japan – or to China and Russia, the other countries participating in the ongoing six-party negotiations. (This assessment is based on off-the-record conversations with past and present government officials in these countries, including officials in South Korea and Japan who participated in the intelligence exchanges with the CIA that preceded the Kelly visit.) China alone has gone public on the issue. Deputy Foreign Minister Zhou Wenzhong told a New York Times reporter on June 7, 2004, 'So far, the United States has not presented convincing evidence of the uranium program. We don't know whether it exists'.[38]

State Department Denies Sexing-up, but Produces no Evidence

Adam Erili, deputy spokesman at the State Department answered a question about Selig Harrison's *Foreign Affairs* article in the daily press briefing on 10 December. There were no surprises. He claimed that the US possessed 'clear and compelling evidence, a wealth of clear and compelling evidence about North Korea's uranium enrichment program'. However, he offered no comment on why, if they have such evidence, they do not show it to 'congressional committees in executive session or to U.S. Asian allies'.[39]

UNRELIABILITY OF US INTELLIGENCE

There is widespread scepticism about the quality of US intelligence, and not merely in relation to Iraq. Russians and Iranians, for instance, with whom I have discussed Afghanistan, have been very scathing about American professionalism, an opinion corroborated by the Western press.[40] Of particular relevance is a very long and detailed article which appeared in the *New York Times* in October 2004. This describes the disagreements between the Energy Department and the CIA about Iraq's alleged enriched uranium programme. The intelligence agencies would compete for the ears of senior officials and politicians, who in turn accepted what best served their political agendas. In this case, according to the *New York Times*, the best man lost; the US went to war claiming the existence of such a programme and the hollowness of the claim, and the intelligence on which it was based, was revealed.[41] There is no reason to suppose that US compilation, analysis and utilisation of intelligence on North Korea is any better.

MUTED RESPONSE FROM SEOUL

It has been pointed out in Chapter 4 that an enriched uranium programme would not in itself breach the Agreed Framework, a point made by Republican Representative Gilman back in 1999. However it would infringe the North South Joint Declaration on Denuclearization of the Korean Peninsula (1991/92) and so we might expect Seoul to take a vigorous position on the issue. But it did not. There appears to have been no high-level formal complaint, as one might expect, though the issue did reportedly come up in meetings. There are three possible reasons for this muted response. The South Koreans might not have believed the Americans, and were offered no real information to make them change their minds (complaints that the Americans do not share intelligence periodically surface[42]). They may have thought there was substance to the allegations but the issue was not critical enough to jeopardise the Agreed Framework, and the movement towards peace on the peninsula. And thirdly, they may have been worried that their own enriched uranium programme would come to light.

REASONS FOR DPRK TO HAVE AN HEU PROGRAMME

Whilst there is no publicly available compelling evidence that North Korea had, and has, a substantial enriched uranium programme, there are nevertheless good reasons for supposing that it might have one of some sort. Firstly there are the stories from Pakistan, though these are of dubious reliability; the IAEA does not appear to have found much in Libya to substantiate claims about a Pakistani-provided enriched uranium programme there.[43] Secondly, it would be sensible for DPRK to have a second string to its bow. The Agreed Framework had cut off the plutonium route to nuclear protection but a prudent government might decide to explore the other route. Pressure to do this would have mounted as the United States failed to implement its side of the Agreed Framework (apart from the fuel oil). This is the position taken by people such as Leon Sigal who sees the DPRK as 'playing tit-for-tat to induce the United States to end enmity'.[44] Thirdly, they may have been working on ways to utilise their substantial deposits of uranium as feedstock for the promised LWRs.[45] This is Harrison's argument.[46] On the other hand, it seems unlikely that they would do anything that would imperil the Agreed Framework in which they had invested up front, by freezing the plutonium programme, and which, if the Americans delivered, would offer such important results.

REASONS FOR THE US TO DISCOVER A HEU PROGRAMME

For the Bush administration the situation was quite different. They did not like the Agreed Framework and wanted to get out of it. Armitage thought that he could have done much better than Gallucci. The problem was that Gallucci had signed the Agreed Framework and the North Koreans were both keeping to their side of it, and were pressing for the Americans to deliver on their side of the bargain. Bolton might fulminate against North Korea and threaten that its 'non-compliance' would force the US to withdraw from the Agreed Framework and he might allege that North Korea and Iraq have 'covert weapons programs' and Bush might refuse to certify compliance, but when CIA director Tenet had to give testimony before Congress he admitted that the DPRK plutonium programme remained frozen, and this was the core Korean obligation. The HEU allegations offered a way out of this impasse and it seems likely that the threatened rapprochement between Tokyo and Pyongyang following the Kim–Koizumi summit in September 2002 provided the trigger. This does not prove that the administration concocted or even 'sexed-up' intelligence, but it does indicate that they had good reason to. Just as telling is the fact that they made no effort to negotiate and save the Agreed Framework. Kelly went to Pyongyang in October 2002 to deliver demands, not to seek solutions.

DPRK OBJECTIVES AND STRATEGY

Pyongyang's objectives in 2004 were pretty much what they were a decade earlier, although the need was more urgent and the commitment more obvious. It was security from attack, normalisation of relations with the US, the ending of US economic warfare, and energy aid. Selig Harrison argues, with justification, that the economic reforms, which are socially and politically de-stabilising, make a resolution of the crisis even more important than ever.[47] The DPRK strategy to achieve this remains consistent – bilateral negotiations with the United States, offering complete and verified dismantlement of the nuclear weapons programme in a step-by-step process. This is basically the Agreed Framework Mark II.

US ADMINISTRATIONS: VARYING POSITIONS

The US position under Bush marks a significant departure from the Clinton period. No bilateral negotiations this time, but 'multilateral diplomacy'. That means, in effect, putting pressure on regional countries (South Korea, Japan, Russia and China) to put pressure on North Korea so that it succumbs to US demands without any step-by-step concessions. When, or if, the United States is satisfied that North Korea is suitably disarmed and controlled, then it will, in generosity, allow Japan and South Korea to provide energy aid, and perhaps more. But this would be largesse, not part of a negotiated agreement.

The Strengths of Multilateral Diplomacy

This strategy has a lot going for it. North Korea is very anxious to make progress on relations with the South. It needs energy, investment and the easing of tension that would allow a degree of demobilisation. Similarly it needs to achieve normalisation of relations with Japan to release Japanese reparations, aid and investment, and to remove the measures which have stifled its exports to Japan. There is probably an additional, personal, reason in that Kim Jong Il has been willing to suffer loss of face over the abductees issue, but has little to show for it. The United States wields immense influence over the region, although to varying degrees in respect of different countries. Both Russia and China see good relations with the United States as the highest priority, for economic, security and political reasons. South Korea is the most susceptible to American wishes, with its armed forces ultimately under US command. Japan comes in between, not quite a client state, but not quite independent either.

The Limits of Multilateral Diplomacy

Although the pressure the United States can exert through these relationships is immense, it has its limits. China, for instance, might well be willing to sacrifice North Korea for its own interests, but it is not willing to surrender Chinese interests to those of the United States. The basic flaw with the US strategy is that, in order to be effective, it requires all the participants to yield more than they gain. It requires them to sacrifice their welfare, or to expose themselves to danger, to no great benefit, other than the advantage of Washington. And often American aims and desires are either not shared by the region, or are actively opposed. Take 'regime change', for instance. Many in Washington, and not merely neocons, would like to see the collapse of North Korea and not a few are actively labouring to bring that about, but for the region, especially South Korea and China, it would be a potential disaster. The North Korea Human Rights Act 2004, passed by Congress, is widely seen in Pyongyang, Seoul and Washington as a tool with which to undermine the DPRK. For this very reason it has been opposed by the government and ruling party in Seoul, and by many Korean, and Korean-American, NGOs.[48]

SIX-PARTY TALKS

The Six-Party Talks, brokered by China as a compromise have achieved little. The US has refused to enter into meaningful bilateral negotiations, the DPRK has refused to surrender and the other parties have had little effect on the policies of the two main protagonists. China, as chair and host, has gained in stature but the limits of its influence were illustrated at the conclusion of the second round of Six-Party talks in February 2004 when a Chinese-drafted joint statement was scuppered by direct intervention from the White House.[49] The incident was also revealing about Bush administration politics; the intervention was engineered by Vice President Cheney and Secretary of State Colin Powell only found out the following day when 'fielding anguished calls from his Asian counterparts'.[50]

TWO CONFLICTING WORLD VIEWS

What we see at the Six-Party talks is much more than a disagreement on nuclear issues, it is a conflict between two views of the world.

The first, represented by the DPRK, is the Westphalian system which sees the world as comprised of sovereign states, who are equal in their sovereignty. Crucially this sovereignty includes the right to self-defence, prohibits the intervention of other states in internal affairs, and only allows a country to go to war when directly threatened. This is the system which is enshrined in the Charter of the UN, if not in its structure and operations. The other view is the imperial one, which sees the world as centred on a state representing civilisation and good governance, surrounded by subordinate states. If the legitimacy of the rulers of these states is endorsed by the imperial power then they are allowed arms (but not so much as could threaten the centre) and are considered as 'members of the international community'. The others, whose legitimacy is not recognised are called, in contemporary parlance, 'rogue states'. Clearly the United States' foreign policy uncomfortably straddles both views, exhibiting a continuing and unresolved tension between the two with the associated questions of whether or not to have bilateral negotiations and normal diplomatic relations a key indicator of this unresolved tension.

DPRK'S PR INADEQUACIES AND THE NUCLEAR CONFRONTATION

North Korea has not handled the confrontation with America as well as it might have. It has not managed its relationship with the IAEA, the United Nations, and the international media successfully. It has not tried hard enough to communicate with the people in the United States, Japan and, crucially, South Korea. In particular it has not been very effective in supporting progressive and engagement forces in the South, whether government, business, religious, community or academic, and has often played into the hands of hostile elements. Its hesitancy in participating in the Six-Party talks allows the United States to portray itself as being open to discussion 'any time, anywhere' and the DPRK as being belligerent and confrontational. It allows rightwing American academics such as Victor Cha to claim that further pressure is required, rather than negotiation, because '... North Korea doesn't really want to give up its nuclear program', even though the evidence points in the other direction. Having said that, the real problem is not so much what North Korea is saying, but what is heard. What is heard depends on what is reported, and how that is done. One example, amongst many, was a Reuters story carried in the *New York Times* on 18 September 2004. The headline read, 'N. Korea Vows Will Never Dismantle Its Nuclear Arms'. No ambiguity there; clearly the DPRK was hell-bent on developing nuclear weapons come what may. However, the very first paragraph revealed the headline as completely misleading when it was reported that what the Koreans had said was that they would not give up nuclear weapons while they were being threatened by the United States and its 'hostile policy'.[51]

BUSH ADMINISTRATION AND THE IMPERIAL POSTURE

The neocons in the administration of George W. Bush did not invent the imperial reluctance to negotiate. Clinton was manoeuvred into negotiating the Agreed Framework by Carter publicising his discussions with Kim Il Sung. In general, as Boutros Boutros-Ghali remarked on the Clinton administration, 'Diplomacy is perceived by an imperial power as a waste of time and prestige and a sign of weakness.'[52] A cable from then Secretary of State James Baker to then Secretary of Defense Richard Cheney, during the administration of Bush senior, reads very much like a dry-run of the policy followed a decade later. Baker says that the US might raise the level of contact with the DPRK but will 'not negotiate peace issues'. Rather it will focus on 'orchestrating international pressures'. He notes that because of the nuclear issue 'Tokyo's terms [on normalising relations with Pyongyang] have hardened considerably' despite opposition from some 'Japanese bureaucrats'. He harbours the same illusions that the US and China have 'shared concerns about the nuclear problem on the peninsula' and so would bring sufficient pressure to bear.[53]

The next, and concluding, chapter returns to these issues, surveying the state of play at the end of the first administration of George W. Bush, and the beginning of the second one. The nuclear issue remains the most prominent part of the confrontation between Washington and Pyongyang, but the confrontation is wider and deeper than that alone.

8

On the Precipice:
Options, Positions and Dangers at the
Start of the Second Bush Administration

On 2 November 2004 George W. Bush was elected to a second term of office. Shortly thereafter Secretary of State Colin Powell tendered his resignation and so did Richard Armitage, the architect of the administration's Korea policy. Whilst there was widespread speculation that the administration would move to an even more confrontational posture, not only towards North Korea but also to the world in general, there was no certainty that this would actually happen or, more to the point, that it would be effectively implemented. Despite the 'political capital' that Bush claims the election has given him, there still remain substantial restraints on his freedom of action. The election has not made Iraq go away, nor has it substantially altered the global geopolitical framework. This final chapter looks at the state of play in the closing days of 2004. We look at the position of the other countries in the Six-Party talks, and survey some of the more important options being presented to the administration as it gears up for its second term.

RUSSIA AND CHINA

These two countries can be taken together, at least initially, because they have so much in common in their approach to the Korean peninsula. Both were traditional allies of the DPRK though relations were seldom smooth, and often became strained, especially in the 1990s. In its search for independence, the DPRK played off one against the other, and distanced itself from both. The ROK, by contrast, with a single patron, did not have this possibility. Whatever disagreements there have been between Seoul and Washington in the past or at present, the relationship has been more intimate, and mutually beneficial (in, for instance, economic affairs), than Pyongyang's relations with Moscow and Beijing.

For both Russia and China a good relationship with the United States is the necessary foundation of foreign policy. Whatever they

might privately think of US policy they are not in a position to
openly oppose it. American military and economic power makes
them reluctant to resist US moves, except when they consider them
too damaging to their own national interests in general, and even
then opposition is cautious – a procedure they share with probably
all governments around the world (including, crucially, Pyongyang).
Since 9/11, the United States has discovered a common interest
with both countries in opposing Islamic-articulated nationalism;
in Chechnya and adjacent regions for the Russians, in Xinjiang
for the Chinese and globally for the Americans. Nevertheless, the
three still compete for influence within the Islamic world, especially
central Asia.

The ROK has become a significant economic partner, especially for
China.[1] For both, and again, most particularly China, a war centred
on the Korean peninsula or a collapse of the DPRK would have
very serious consequences. Similarly, both have an interest in the
peaceful economic integration of the Korean peninsula. For Russia,
such integration would help establish Russia as a land bridge between
Europe and the eastern littoral of Asia. China also would benefit from
land access to South Korea (and through to Japan), and might expect
to participate in land trade with Europe.

Both Russia and China are worried about Missile Defense and
the opinion expressed by Alexander Zhebin, Director of the Center
for Korean Studies of the Russian Institute of Far Eastern Studies is
probably representative:

> a final reconciliation between North and South Korea would deprive
> Washington of its last more or less serious argument justifying creation of
> both the Theater Missile Defense (TMD) in NEA and the American NMD. If
> the so-called North Korean missile threat were to be removed, the true plans
> of the U.S. leadership to neutralize the nuclear missile means of deterrence
> of China and Russia would be exposed.[2]

Although they hold common hopes and fears for the Korean
peninsula, Russia and China clearly differ in their level of involvement.
Their approach to Iraq illustrates their differing perspectives. Russia
took a much stronger line than China, which was rumoured to have
adopted a soft stance in the Security Council in exchange for a US
promise not to attack the DPRK.[3] China stands both to suffer much
more from a DPRK collapse, and a resulting flood of refugees, and
to gain more from peaceful economic integration. Although South

Korean investment in the event of such collapse might be diverted from China to the North, that loss would be offset by other benefits such as a larger market on China's doorstep, and one to which China is the main entry point from the Eurasian landmass. Neither Russia nor China would be happy about the stationing of US troops in what is now North Korean territory, but the effect, which would be largely symbolic with little military significance, would weigh more heavily on China. Mao Zedong was not the only Chinese to have lost a son there.

While Putin has taken a more forceful and personal interest in East Asia than Yeltsin did, the Russian role in the present crisis has been fairly limited compared with that of China. Deputy Foreign Minister Losyukov led a mission to Pyongyang in January 2003, Foreign Minister Sergei Viktorovich Lavrov went in July 2004 for talks with Kim Jong Il and Sergey Mironov, Chairman of the Russian Council of Federation visited Pyongyang in September 2004. Also in September 2004 Roh Moo-hyun visited Moscow for talks with Vladimir Putin, and there was even speculation that Putin might host a summit between Roh and Kim Jong Il.[4] This has not yet happened but it would make sense. Both Koreas, conscious of China's past and future centrality in the region might prefer Russia as a venue. The Russians, for their part, are anxious both to play a larger role and also to be seen as even-handed between Seoul and Pyongyang, and good friends to both.[5]

The appointment of Losyukov as chief Russian delegate to the talks was in indication of Russian commitment. Russia has remained peripheral but has continued to press for negotiation; Losyukov has been quietly critical of the American 'hardline stance'.[6]

However, the Six-Party talks, and the Three-Party talks that preceded them in April 2003 were China's achievement.[7] China, as broker of the talks, as well as host and chair, has continued to edge the talks forward with limited success. That they have continued is perhaps achievement enough under the circumstances. Beijing has also had to contend with a resurgence of the Taiwan issue, which could easily lead to a serious deterioration in US–China relations, and seems to have played the game with quiet diplomatic finesse and patience.

The talks were rich in historical symbolism. They posited Beijing once more as the arbiter of disputes between a tributary state and encroaching barbarians. One of the interesting consequences of the Powell/Armitage Korea strategy has been this elevation of China on the diplomatic stage. This has been mirrored on the economic front with China's booming economy becoming a major partner for trade and outbound investment for South Korea, Japan and the United States itself (Table 8.1). In particular, China accounts for 12.2 per cent of Japan's exports and 19.7 per cent of its imports. South Korea sends 18.1 per cent of its exports to China, and sources 12.3 per cent of its imports from it. This economic rise was nicely symbolised by IBM's sale of its personal computer division to the Chinese company Lenovo (formerly Legend), 'in a deal that reflects the profound changes taking place in the economic world order and marks the end of an era for one of America's most iconic companies'.[8]

Table 8.1   China as trading partner, 2003

Country	Exports		Imports	
	%	rank	%	rank
Japan	12.2	3	19.7	1
South Korea	18.1	1	12.3	3
USA	5.8	2	5.7	4
North Korea	50.9	1	38.9	1

Note: Statistics for USA give EU as single partner so the rank of China in terms of country is uncertain.
Sources:
JP, SK, US: *Long-term trends – world exports, production, GDP, from 1950*. World Trade Organization, 2003. Available from www.wto.org/english/res_e/statis_e/its2002_e/section2_e/ii01.xls (visited 20 May 2003)
NK: Cho, M. A. 'North Korea's 2003 foreign trade (abstract)'. KOTRA, 13 August 2004.

The huge economic, diplomatic and security importance of China to the DPRK needs no emphasis. Whilst Pyongyang tries to off-set this by, for instance, attempting to expand trade with Japan and other countries, ironically US policy hampers this and tends to drive North Korea into China's arms. For its part, the DPRK was keen to claim that relations with China, and Kim Jong Il's personal relationship with the new leader of the Chinese Communist Party, Hu Jintao, were excellent. The year 2004, it declared, was a 'Year of Epochal Significance in DPRK–China Friendship'.[9]

JAPAN

Whereas the position and policies of Russia and China have been broadly consistent and predictable, those of Japan have been marked in the last couple of years by a dramatic double volte-face, the result of a continuing struggle between what may be conveniently labelled the peace movement in Japan and the forces pressing for remilitarisation abetted by US pressure, with a good measure of domestic demagogy thrown in. While the past has not been entirely laid to rest, the ROK and Japan have managed to achieve good neighbourly relations, in distinct contrast to the lack of formal diplomatic ties and the mutual hostility that have marked Japan's relationship with the DPRK. After the 2000 summit Seoul put increased pressure on Tokyo to mend its bridges with Pyongyang, but there seemed to be little progress.[10] Indeed, by 2001–02 relations had distinctly deteriorated; in December 2001 raids were carried out on the offices of Chongryon, the pro-Pyongyang association of Korean-Japanese and a North Korean 'spy' ship was sunk, outside Japanese territorial waters and, in fact, inside the Chinese economic zone.[11] The saga of the raising of the 'spy boat', and the crackdown on Chongryon continued into 2002 when, suddenly, on 31 August, it was announced that Prime Minister Koizumi would go to Pyongyang on 17 September for a summit with Kim Jong Il. The Japanese press said that the historic, and unprecedented, meeting was 'aimed at making a breakthrough ... in the deadlocked negotiations between the countries to normalize diplomatic relations. The talks, which started in 1991, have been suspended since 2000.'[12]

The summit, while not warm, was businesslike, and both sides seemed to arrive at a reasonable compromise, in which they pledged themselves to 'establish diplomatic ties at an early date'.[13] In respect of the abductee affair the DPRK side declared that it would take a proper measure to prevent the recurrence of such 'regrettable things', and privately, according to Japanese sources, Kim Jong Il apologised and agreed that they would be allowed to return to Japan; a face-saving formula seems to have been achieved. Kim also said that the moratorium on missile tests would extend beyond 2003. Koizumi, for his part, 'keenly reflected on and sincerely apologized for the historical facts that Japan had inflicted huge damage and sufferings upon the Korean people during its past colonial rule over Korea'.[14] Koizumi agreed to discuss reparations, though no figures were mentioned and the phrasing was vague. The DPRK climbdown over abductees, as discussed in Chapter 4, was widely seen as a remarkable concession and an indication of their eagerness to establish normal relations with Japan. It would yield vital economic benefits, both in terms of disguised reparations (often estimated at US$8–10b) and trade.[15] Politically it would outflank Washington.

Therein lay the problem and this led, we have argued in Chapter 4, to the Kelly visit in October 2002 that brought about the present crisis.[16] It is unclear what pressure the US placed on Koizumi after the Pyongyang visit, and it may be that he was genuinely surprised at the media hysteria over the abductions. Whatever the reason, another abrupt change in policy occurred. The abductees who had been allowed by North Korea to visit family in Japan were not now allowed to return, thus effectively scuppering what had been a settled issue. By 17 September 2003, a KCNA statement could note that 'bilateral relations are much worse' than before the summit.[17]

The role of Japan is perhaps the most difficult to pin down, but that may be due to Koizumi's flair for theatre as he attempts to cope with waning popularity, and US and domestic pressure to send troops to Iraq despite popular opposition, in an emotional atmosphere of anti-(North) Korean hysteria. Having reneged on the October 2002 deal with Kim Jong Il, he has allowed himself to be swept along the path of suspension of aid and economic sanctions, which have exacerbated the situation. His dramatic May 2004 return visit to the DPRK, at which Pyongyang, anxious to improve relations with Tokyo both for economic reasons (trade, remittances, aid and reparations) and to outflank Washington, was conciliatory, seems to have done little to bolster his electoral standing; the abduction issue was reportedly a waning factor in the July 2004 elections.[18] Nevertheless, the abduction issue ostensibly remains at the heart of Tokyo–Pyongyang negotiations, though why this should be so requires explanation. The DPRK says it is cooperating fully to clear up any outstanding cases, including providing DNA of dead abductee Megumi Yokota and holding on-the-spot inspections.[19] Japan says the remains are not of Megumi, but of two other people. Tokyo lodged a strong protest and there was talk of freezing aid and increasing sanctions because of Pyongyang's 'stonewalling'.[20] Since there is no conceivable reason for Pyongyang to stonewall, given that Kim Jong Il admitted and apologised for the abductions at the meeting with Koizumi in September 2002, the affair has all the hallmarks of a contrived crisis.

Why has the abductee issue, which appeared to have been basically resolved in 2002, continued to stoke the flames of confrontation? In addition to US pressure on Japan, two other factors deserve mention. First, the abductee question, however inflamed it might have been by the media, is clearly an emotional issue in Japan, resting on deep racialist roots from Japan's colonialist past. A strong line on North

Korea sells papers and wins votes. Second, hostility towards North Korea should be seen against the backdrop of the continuing struggle between those who want a non-militaristic Japan, at peace with its Asian neighbours, and those who argue that Japan, which already has the fourth largest arms budget in the world, should become a 'normal' nation with the legal armed forces to match.[21] The DPRK provides a very convenient 'threat' to support the cause of re-militarisation.[22] Meanwhile, Armitage has said that unless Japan renounces its 'peace constitution' the US will not support its drive to become a permanent member of the UN Security Council.[23] Japan is perhaps on the brink of becoming a nuclear power.[24] The problem with North Korea acquiring nuclear weapons is not so much what it would do, because given its technological infrastructure they would not be much more than of symbolic deterrence. More important is the impetus it would give to Japanese nuclearisation, which in turn would stimulate tension and an arms race in East Asia, with profound consequences for the region and the world.

REPUBLIC OF KOREA

Any government in Seoul needs to pay a great deal of attention to Washington, and a continuing theme of South Korean politics from Syngman Rhee to Roh Moo-hyun has been the attempt to wrest as much independence from the United States as possible. President Roh put it diplomatically in his inauguration speech: 'We will foster and develop this cherished [US–ROK] alliance. We will see to it that the alliance matures into a more reciprocal and equitable relationship. We will also expand relations with other countries, including traditional friends.'[25]

He also said, in the same speech, 'South and North Korea are the two main actors in inter-Korean relations.' Roh's remarks can be interpreted as addressed to both Pyongyang and Washington. The DPRK, as is well known, has always stressed that security issues (including the present crisis) are primarily a bilateral matter between it and the United States. So Roh is claiming a role for the ROK. But he is also telling Washington that where divergence occurs, ROK interests in the Korean peninsula should take precedence over those of the United States.

The Sunshine policy of Kim Dae-jung, which has been taken up by Roh has, in my reading, worked to secure the survival of the DPRK and the lessening of tension and animosity within the peninsula.

This, as was planned and as is happening, led to the beginnings of economic integration between the two halves of the country. The ROK has also sought to facilitate the DPRK's diplomatic and economic engagement with the capitalist world. The idea was that this process would lead, over time, to a relative equalisation and harmonisation of the southern and northern economies (and perhaps polities) that would make peaceful and consensual reunification feasible.

There is little debate that war on the peninsula would be disastrous both in the short and long term. Japan, even if it did not initiate a strike, would be a legitimate target as the host of US bases. Despite the American solipsistic brouhaha about 'the North Korean threat', the DPRK's ability to retaliate against the continental United States is unlikely. The DPRK would be a harder nut than Iraq to crack, as the main danger to the US would be a prolonged resistance war, a war that the ROK would be drafted into fighting. The political and social consequences need no elaboration.

A peaceful collapse of the DPRK would have very serious consequences for the ROK, far outweighing the impact of the demise of the DDR. The heritage of the Korean War and its aftermath had no parallel in Germany, of course. Furthermore, the current economic state of the DPRK is well known; the latest estimate from the Bank of Korea is that the Gross National Income (GNI) of the DPRK was 1/28 that of the ROK, and the per capita GNI approximately 1/13.[26] Indications are that the South would be left to foot the bill for the reconstruction of the North with very modest support from the United States and its 'international community'.[27] Calculations vary, but the costs would be formidable.[28] Professor Sohn Hong-keun has warned that

> The potential collapse of the economy in North Korea must be avoided at all costs, as this will only bring instability, both politically and economically, first to the North Eastern region of Asia and, subsequently, to most regions of the world.[29]

The ROK's frequently reiterated call that the 'North Korean nuclear issue be resolved peacefully through dialogue' and that the DPRK forgo the 'development of nuclear weapons' in exchange for 'guarantees for the security of its regime and international economic support' is essentially code that the ROK opposes the confrontational policy of the Bush administration.

Seoul continues to be buffeted by currents, international and domestic, but the overall effect has been that the forces for engagement have been strengthened. The failed impeachment of Roh Moo-hyun and the concomitant success of the Uri party in the polls are widely seen as pushing South Korean politics to the left, a more positive attitude towards the North, and greater resistance towards the US.[30] Less noticed, however, was that these trends have also been mirrored to some extent within the opposition Grand National Party with the election (and subsequent re-election) of Park Geun-hye as leader. Ms Park, daughter of Park Chung-hee, has attempted to position herself as a mediator with the DPRK, which she visited in 2002 for discussions with Kim Jong Il.[31] Parallel to, and interacting with, US pressure on ROK to conform to its policy towards the DPRK has been the issue of troops to Iraq; 3,000 have been promised, earning the thanks of Condoleezza Rice.[32] Despatch is increasingly unpopular with the electorate as dangers mount (one Korean has already been executed in Iraq), the intelligence scandal deepens, and opposition to the war grows even within the US, as exemplified by Michael Moore's film *Fahrenheit 9/11*, released in Seoul 23 July.[33] Clearly Roh has promised troops as part of a deal to get Washington to soften its position on the North. The US position during the third round of the Six-Party talks indicated that Roh had been having some success, though less than the Seoul media may claim.[34] The gains from the modest impact on US policy could be wiped out by even minor casualties in Iraq.

Roh's difficulties with Washington and Pyongyang have been exacerbated by incidents with his own military. In June an agreement was signed, to some fanfare, between the military of North and South on procedures to avoid the clashes over crab-fishing grounds in the West Sea that tend to erupt every year. In 2002 a southern naval vessel was sunk with loss of life and in 1999 a northern ship went down. On 14 July 2004 a ROK warship contravened the agreement by ignoring radio messages from a DPRK ship, and fired warning shots. The ROK navy initially tried to cover up, but a protest from Pyongyang brought the affair into the open. Embarrassed by this defiance Roh instigated an enquiry, and there was talk of a major shakeup, with a civilian being put in direct command of the armed forces. In the event Roh seems to have backed down, not punishing the military but merely issuing a reprimand.[35] This leniency, however, may turn out to diminish his bargaining power with the military establishment, and with Pyongyang.

Whatever his weaknesses at home, Roh Moo-hyun has put up strong fight on the international stage. He has developed good relations, despite some setbacks, with all the major players, and a good deal of the minor ones. His reaction to the re-election of George W. Bush makes an illuminating contrast to what his predecessor did at the time of Bush's first victory. Kim Dae-jung, anxious to preserve the Sunshine policy got himself head of the queue to have an audience with President Bush in 2001. He was rebuffed and embarrassed.[36] Presumably learning from this, Roh has taken a different approach, imaginative and adroit. Whilst he did meet with Bush after the election it was in the context of a bilateral meeting at the APEC leaders' meeting in Santiago in Chile in November 2004. Predictably the media echoed the official line that Bush and Roh 'agree on how to handle North'.[37] Predictably also, a close reading of the text revealed that this was not so:

> ... with the news that the new Bush administration would be filled with more hawkish officials, including Condoleezza Rice as the new secretary of state, some Koreans expressed concern that Washington may take tougher measures against Pyeongyang.
>
> According to Mr. Ban's statements, the two leaders' meeting may have removed such concerns.
>
> When Mr. Roh told Mr. Bush, 'For smooth progress in the six-party talks, Pyeongyang, our negotiating partner, should not be made nervous, and that officials should refrain from making any remarks that appear to cause unease in the security situation of the Korean Peninsula'.
>
> Mr. Bush replied that he completely understood Mr. Roh's points, Mr. Ban stated.[38]

This scepticism about Bush and Roh seeing eye-to-eye is reinforced by what came next. President Roh, in a whirlwind tour of parts of Asia and Europe in early December, articulated strong, if coded, criticism of US policy. He was, as the South Korean paper *JoongAng Ilbo* put it, seeking 'allies beyond the U.S'.[39] Seoul claimed it was all very successful:

> He succeeded in winning support from the regions for a peaceful resolution to the North Korean nuclear standoff, aides said.
>
> While having summit meetings with international leaders, including British Prime Minister Tony Blair and French President Jacques Chirac, Roh made an

active effort to explain his firm belief regarding a peaceful resolution to the diplomatic impasse.

He hardly passed a day without commenting on the issue during his successive visits to Britain, Poland and France.[40]

In London he cautioned against using the refugee issue in an attempt to bring about 'regime change'. He said,

The most important thing at hand is for the world to assist North Korea on a course of reform and greater openness, and I feel that this would be the most rational solution to the North Korean human rights situation.[41]

In Poland he warned against expecting the DPRK to collapse and pointed out that South Korea neither wanted that, nor would tolerate it.[42] In Paris, he was, again according to the *JoongAng Ilbo*, 'even more outspoken, declaring 'that Seoul should have the leading say on the issue' of talks with the North.[43] Moreover, he explicitly contrasted US policy with that of South Korea and China:

... he said relevant parties in the nuclear talks will have to narrow differences between China and South Korea, which do not want a North Korean 'regime change' and the countries that do.

His remarks, apparently targeting some hawkish Americans represented by the 'neocons', were understood to be in line with a speech he gave in Los Angeles last month, in which he urged the U.S. not to take a hard-line attitude toward the North.[44]

Whether the European leaders really were won over to Roh's side is uncertain; they may not quite have realised what the coded messages meant. They may have thought they were just agreeing with the usual platitudes about peace, motherhood and dialogue, not realising that Roh was calling on Washington to abandon the Powell policy, to give up the goal of collapse and regime change and engage in substantive negotiations with Pyongyang. Back in Seoul there was less confusion. A leading member of the opposition Grand National Party, Kim Deog-ryong complained, 'His language explicitly supports North Korea and criticizes the policies of the United States.'[45]

On his way back to Seoul Roh pulled off a master stroke. He made an unannounced visit to South Korean troops in Iraq and posed for photographs, attired in a camouflage jacket over his shirt and tie, surrounded by cheering soldiers. As a symbolic gesture it was brilliant. A civilian president (as evidenced by his tie) at one with the army. More than that, of course, it was a gesture to Washington. The ROK, with the third largest contingent of troops in the occupation force (after the US and Britain) was there as a loyal ally. The Iraq commitment which had been deeply unpopular in South Korea, as well as fraught with danger, had been the subject of acrimonious horse trading between then Foreign Minster Yoon Young-kwan and Secretary Colin Powell in September 2003, a meeting at which it was reported that 'Mr. Powell became extremely angry'.[46] Roh's troop visit in December 2004 was a pointed reminder to Washington of the deal.

Adroit and forceful though this diplomatic foray was, it is uncertain what effect it will have on post-Powell US Korea policy. Significantly, Roh explicitly ruled out a summit with Kim Jong Il before there was progress in the Six-Party talks.[47] In other words, a summit could take place after the Americans had started negotiations, as part of a reward package for North Korea, rather than as a device to force the US into negotiations. This revealed the dilemma of Roh's position, or perhaps his indecisiveness. Either not strong enough or not courageous enough to stand up to Washington, he risked the danger of being both impotent and vulnerable. He has not been able, so far, to change US policy but he is presumably becoming increasingly unpopular in Washington. One indication of that was the attack by Michael Horowitz, a former official who played a leading role in drafting the US North Korea Human Rights Act. Horowitz claimed that 'President Roh Moo-hyun's government is alone in its opposition to regime change in North Korea.'[48] That is not true, but one can see that if the idea gained currency in Washington so too would the thought that a change in government in Seoul would open the way for American power to prevail.

Perhaps conscious of the danger, Roh built another bridge to the United States with the appointment, in December 2004, of a new ambassador to Washington. This was Hong Seok-hyun, publisher of the conservative South Korean newspaper *JoongAng Ilbo*. In addition, Mr Hong has close ties with Samsung and started his career, before inheriting the paper from his farther, at the World Bank. He was, as is virtually inevitable amongst the South Korean elite, a graduate of Seoul National University. However, he also did a Masters and then a PhD at Stanford, the university at which Condoleezza Rice was provost.

The description, in his own paper, put it delicately:

> Mr. Hong's aide quoted him as saying, 'The president's request for help in resolving North Korea's nuclear problem peacefully was too earnest to turn down'. Mr. Hong also said he was confident he could use his personal connections developed over many years in the United States to enhance ties between the two countries.[49]

The *JoongAng Ilbo* was too discrete to mention that the boss had spent 66 days in jail during Kim Dae-jung's term of office for tax evasion. That will probably not be held against him in Washington.[50]

DEMOCRATIC PEOPLE'S REPUBLIC OF KOREA

In contrast to the ROK, the DPRK position is fairly straightforward and easy to describe. Its stated position accords reasonably well with what we can surmise to be its self-perceived, and actual, national interests. Whilst the DPRK engages in bargaining, it has shown itself capable of flexibility in the past if such flexibility is reciprocated, and its statements need little decoding.[51] The DPRK basically pursues two (or perhaps three) main goals:

- National survival
- The opportunity to engage in the international economy without US hindrance.

Or, in the words of the statement by the DPRK Foreign Ministry on 25 October 2003, the DPRK

> clarified that it was ready to seek a negotiated settlement of this issue on the following three conditions: firstly, if the U.S. recognizes the DPRK's sovereignty, secondly, if it assures the DPRK of non-aggression and thirdly, if the U.S. does not hinder the economic development of the DPRK.[52]

Not 'hindering the economic development' refers to the US veto on the DPRK joining international financial institutions, sanctions (including restrictions on access to information technology through the Wassenaar Arrangement)[53] and claims that the US has disrupted DPRK relations with ROK and Japan.[54]

The third demand is a package whose composition shifts slightly from time to time but includes at a minimum that the United

States comply with the promise in the Agreed Framework (AF) to provide light-water reactors (LWRs). Occasionally compensation for the electricity generation forgone by the late building (and now suspension) of the reactors has been demanded. A Foreign Ministry statement on 25 October 2003 mentions 'economic and humanitarian aid from the U.S'.[55]

Substance aside, the main concern of the DPRK, and a crucial matter of contention with the United States, is the question of sequence and simultaneous action. The DPRK position has hardened somewhat since the Agreed Framework. For instance, Clause II of the AF said 'The two sides will move toward full normalization of political and economic relations'. Now establishment of diplomatic relations is no longer downstream, to be moved toward, but one of the 'simultaneous actions'. 'Simultaneous' is a key word in current DPRK statements:

> In a comment as regards the U.S.'s recent expression of its intention to provide the DPRK with assurances of non-aggression, the spokesman said, 'we are ready to consider Bush's remarks on the 'written assurances of non-aggression if they are based on the intention to co-exist with the DPRK and aimed to play a positive role in realizing a proposal for a package solution on the principle of simultaneous actions. 'What we want is for both sides to drop guns and establish normal state relationship to co-exist peacefully.[56]

The statement conveniently and clearly brackets what the DPRK wants, and what it will give:

> The DPRK has previously said that 'simultaneous actions' include economic and humanitarian aid from the U.S., opening diplomatic ties, and building nuclear reactors. Pyongyang has also said it must include a nonaggression treaty which the Bush administration has refused.
>
> In exchange, the DPRK has said it would declare its willingness to give up nuclear development, allow nuclear inspections, give up missiles exports and finally dismantle its nuclear facilities.[57]

The inner workings of policy making in Pyongyang remain opaque, but it is safe to surmise that constant discussions takes place over how to approach both the Six-Party talks and the countries involved. At the time of writing the 'softliners' appear in the ascendancy, with Pyongyang conciliatory to Tokyo and Seoul (consider, e.g., the North–South military agreement in mid 2004), and careful to give no provocation, or excuse for being provoked, to the US. The response to the proposals advanced by the US at the third round in June 2004 was not as dismissive as it might have been. The DPRK Foreign Ministry statement, released by KCNA on 28 June, was studiously emollient; there was, it read, a ' sincere atmosphere' at the talks, and 'positive progress'. Indeed, Pyongyang leaned over backwards in suggesting it was also at fault: 'What merits a serious attention is that substantial negotiations could not start among the parties concerned for the settlement of the issue as the DPRK and the U.S. failed to wipe out the bilateral mistrust and misunderstanding.'[58]

But in truth there are no serious decisions to be made until the Americans put a serious proposal on the table. Until that point Pyongyang has no choice but to continue as before. The danger will come when (or if) Washington makes an offer that provides a way out and requires difficult choices and careful evaluation of American intentions and capabilities.

The argument, often advanced, that Kim Jong Il was 'waiting for Kerry' does not hold water. The outcome of the election was uncertain up to the last day. If Kerry had won there was no guarantee that he would have taken a radically different line from Bush; he said that, in contrast to Bush, he would negotiate, but he has also criticised the administration for a lack of determination.[59] Beyond that lay the question of delivery. Pyongyang would have remembered that Clinton did not fulfil the Agreed Framework and that losing control of Congress was only part of the story. Pyongyang would probably have preferred a Kerry victory, and they are hardly alone in that. But it seems unlikely they were pinning great hopes on it. When Pak Gil Yon, North Korea's ambassador to the United Nations, said at a peace forum in Washington in July 2004 that Pyongyang had no favourite in the presidential race ('It's entirely a U.S. internal affair', he told reporters) he was being diplomatically correct but also probably not straying too far from the truth.[60]

Shortly after the election Han Song-ryol, DPRK deputy ambassador to the United Nations was reported by the South Korean newspaper, *Hankyoreh Shinmun*, as saying,

I have watched the Bush administration's North Korea policy over the past four years, and I am doubtful that there will be any policy shift in the future. Unless there are substantial changes in U.S. policy, we will not attend the six-nation talks.[61]

On 13 November 2004 a Foreign Ministry spokesman denied that it was insisting on bilateral talks with the United States and said that it would continue with the Six-Party talks if the US accepted coexistence:

> For the U.S. to make its policy switchover is the key to finding a solution to the issue.
>
> If the U.S. drops its hostile policy aimed at 'bringing down the system' in the DPRK and opts for co-existing with the latter in practice, it will be quite possible to settle the issue.[62]

This reiteration of the demand for an end to the 'hostile policy' was consistent and it is difficult to see it being dropped. As long as the US stays on its present course then there is no incentive for the DPRK to drop the demand.

UNITED STATES

The Clinton administration, as we have seen, was manoeuvred into engaging in bilateral negotiations with the DPRK. The result was the Agreed Framework, under which the North Koreans froze their graphite-moderated reactors in return for a promise of two light-water reactors, annual deliveries of heavy fuel oil as an interim measure to compensate for the electricity forgone, and most crucial, security guarantees and a movement towards normalisation of relations. The American side never fully implemented their side of the bargain, partly because the Democrats lost control of Congress. American foreign policy is often a by-product of adversarial domestic politics and the relationship with North Korea was no exception. In many respects the Republicans opposed Clinton foreign policy not so much because they had strong alternatives, but because it was Democrat policy.

In 1999 a team of Republicans led by Richard Armitage and including Paul Wolfowitz, both later to become prominent in the Bush administration, produced a critique of the Clinton policy entitled *A Comprehensive Approach to North Korea*. The report identified three assumptions on which the Agreed Framework had been built, and challenged them:

- The first is the assumption made by some senior administration officials that the Agreed Framework had ended North Korea's nuclear program

- The second is that North Korea is a failed state on the verge of collapse and that a 'hard landing' – collapse perhaps accompanied by aggression – should be avoided
- The third is that the Agreed Framework would induce North Korea to open up to the outside world, initiate a gradual process of North–South reconciliation, and lead to real reform and a 'soft landing'.[63]

The report also challenged a fourth assumption, not bulleted, that time was on the American side and that North Korea would disappear; the North would solve the US's problems by ultimately reconciling or uniting with the South.

The report was correct in some respects. North Korea did not disappear. On the issue that North Korea had a 'covert nuclear program' the report curiously did not mention uranium but merely alluded to 'at least one suspect site'. That was Kumchangri which, on inspection, yielded no indication that it was nuclear-related.

In some respects the report presaged what would happen when Armitage was Deputy Secretary of State. The report talks of interdicting missile exports at sea (on the patently untenable grounds that the US would be acting 'under the UN Charter's right of self-defence'). But it also said that 'Washington should table an offer that meets Pyongyang's legitimate economic, security, and political concerns', and that did not happen. Was Armitage overruled by Cheney and Powell, or was his definition of what was 'legitimate' for a country of which the US disapproved somewhat different from the normal?

A key part of the criticism of the Agreed Framework was that it was not 'comprehensive' and crucially did not include missiles. However, the US–DPRK agreement of September 1999 did address this question and, according to Gary Samore of the International Institute for Strategic Studies in London, it basically laid the foundation for putting the matter to rest.[64] However, Clinton was not able to complete the deal and the new administration took a different approach. Samore argues:

Rather than pick up where Clinton left off, the Bush administration decided in June 2000 to adopt a different diplomatic strategy, seeking North Korean concessions on nuclear and conventional arms issues, as well as the missiles, and offering fewer inducements for North Korean good behavior.[65]

The missile issue was not the only area where the Armitage report had been overtaken by events. The Pyongyang summit of June 2000 between the leaders of North and South, the visit of Secretary of State Albright to Pyongyang, and the invitation for the President to visit, had transformed the climate. Peace was about to break out and if Bush had decided 'to pick up where Clinton had left off' it would have.

And that was the rub. All new administrations, and not merely American ones, seek to distinguish themselves from their predecessors. However, the Bush administration took this further than most and its policy was soon labelled the ABC (Anything But Clinton) policy. The Bush administration did not pay much attention to Asia. The ideologues in it, the neocons, were from the outset focussed on the Middle East and this focus became a fixation for the administration as a whole after 9/11. Asia, and the Korean peninsula, was a sideshow.

That being so, it is might be considered curious that the administration did not let events take their course and where there were problems, seek to resolve them expeditiously so it could concentrate on the major challenge. Events in Northeast Asia were moving towards defusing of tension and in the direction of normal economic and diplomatic interactions. The two major fissures, between North and South Korea and between North Korea and Japan were closing over and, if not interrupted, would heal.

Therein perhaps lay the problem. Asia might be a sideshow but it was still of vital, and growing, importance to the United States. The rise of China was, and continues to be, a major concern and the United States does not know how to cope with that. But one underlying strategy is the necessity of keeping Japan and (South)Korea outside China's orbit and aligned to the United States. North Korea, or more precisely a North Korea which is seen as hostile and threatening, is a key part of that. A North–South rapprochement might be acceptable because it would be assumed that it would primarily be on the South's terms. By that reckoning, if the South came to 'own' the North that would be fine because the United States effectively 'owned' South Korea. A counter-argument would be that this ownership of South Korea was primarily a soft-power one, that could not be enforced if the security environment changed. In other words, without a hostile North the South would be less tractable to US pressure. A unified Korea might turn out to be far too independent for America's liking.

Be that as it may, it was a Tokyo–Pyongyang rapprochement that offered the greatest, and most immediate, danger. It was, we have argued, the Kim–Koizumi summit of 2002 which triggered the present crisis.

However, the foundations had already been laid. The new administration had early made known both its antipathy towards North Korea, and towards Kim Jong Il personally, and its unwillingness to pick up where Clinton had left off and push forward bilateral negotiations. The 'Axis of Evil' speech and the fingering of North Korea as a target in the Nuclear Posture Review were all manifestations of this antipathy, but they were probably not part of a considered strategy. It was said that the Bush administration had an attitude towards North Korea, but not a policy.[66] This is in contrast to Iraq where there was a policy, or at least well-laid plans amongst the neocons to bring about an invasion and to remodel the Middle East. US policy towards Korean events under the first Bush administration was reactive, but the reactions were informed by extreme hostility towards the DPRK, verging on the irrational. After all, despite all the hyperbole, North Korea has never threatened the United States except in retaliation for attack, nor in reality can it threaten. On the contrary, its over-riding policy objectives have been to stop the United States threatening it and to move to normalisation of relations and perhaps some form of friendship. There are two major reasons behind the US hostility. One is the need to have a bogey in Northeast Asia. The other is to have rogue states as a justification for Missile Defense.

Nevertheless, whatever the underlying reasons for the hostility it still must be articulated through some sort of policy and strategy. The core of the US Korea strategy under Powell was a refusal to enter into meaningful bilateral negotiations with the DPRK.

There are probably three reasons for this. Firstly, Clinton had engaged in bilateral negotiations. Secondly, bilateral negotiations would accord the DPRK a legitimacy as a sovereign, independent state. The imperial vision, despite the anti-imperialist rhetoric, has always been part of American foreign policy with its underlying assumptions of manifest destiny and exceptionalism. However, imperial hubris grew markedly under George W. Bush. Thirdly, and tying the two other reasons together, is the belief of Powell and Armitage that they could achieve more, and pay less, using what they termed the 'multilateral approach'.

The multilateral approach, or Powell's' policy of pressure as we might better call it, was based on the premise that US pressure on the regional powers (South Korea, Japan, China and Russia) would bring about them applying pressure on the DPRK to comply with US demands. According to this strategy little inducement or compensation would be given to Pyongyang, and what was given would be provided by the others, not the United States. In this they were actually following the precedent set by Clinton, whereby the bulk of the KEDO (Korean Peninsula Energy Development Organization) bill would be met by South Korea and Japan.

The pressure strategy had a lot going for it. For each of the four the relationship with the United States was of huge importance. Similarly, the DPRK needed good relations with each of the four in different ways, and so might be seen to be susceptible to pressure. However there were limits and Washington, presumably out of arrogance, asked more than anyone would deliver.

This was especially true of China and South Korea who were in a position to apply the most pressure on North Korea but baulked at going anywhere near as far America wanted. Japan, for its own internal reasons, has been the most obliging of the four.

China, for instance, would sacrifice the interest of its 'traditional ally' the DPRK if needs be, to keep its relationship with the United States on an even keel. However, it would not sacrifice its own interests just to satisfy the Americans. And yet there is a feeling amongst Americans that it is quite natural and proper for other countries to subordinate their interests to those of the United States. Call it American solipsism, or imperial hubris, but there is a definite assumption that what is good for America is good for the world. For example, Dan Blumenthal, writing in the *Washington Post*, was at a loss to explain why China was acting like a 'strategic competitor'. Did they not realise that they should be advancing 'common Sino–American interests?'[67]

For Blumenthal, 'common Sino–American interests' included, rather bizarrely, Taiwan, an issue over which the positions of the two sides are clearly different (China wants reunification and reserves the sovereign right of force, the US want to preserve the de facto independence of Taiwan but does not want Taipei to declare formal independence because that would force Beijing to act).[68] In respect of Korea, Blumenthal declared that

> The spirit of obstructionism rules even in the case of North Korea. By any rational measure, the elimination of Kim Jong Il's nuclear arsenal should be a shared Sino–US. interest. Instead, Beijing acts as if the United States and North Korea are equally to blame for the standoff.[69]

What Blumenthal can't come to grips with is that while Washington and Beijing might both want a non-nuclear North Korea, their reasons are different, and their strategies for achieving it are at variance. He complains that 'On North Korea, Beijing earns plaudits in Washington even as it refuses to put any real pressure on Pyongyang.' His remedy which, as we will see in a moment, mirrors Eberstadt's proposed treatment of South Korea, is to get tough on China 'with the same iconoclastic spirit that guides its foreign policy elsewhere in the world'.[70]

No country can flout US demands directly, but the only member of the four which has really complied with US requests for pressure on North Korea has been Japan and that, as we have seen, is to a large degree for domestic reasons.

If Powell's policy of multilateral pressure was designed to force the DPRK to disarm then it has clearly failed. With the departure of Powell, and Armitage, the second Bush administration has the opportunity of reassessing its Korea policy. The incoming Secretary of State, Condoleezza Rice, has broadly three options:

1　Continuation of the Powell policy
2　Multiple regime change
3　Negotiations on the basis of accepting the DPRK.

1　Continuation of the Powell Policy

Option 1 might at first sight be out of the running since it seems to have failed. But has it? That depends on what is to be achieved. Consider this succinct, and accurate, description from the *Guardian*:

> The current nuclear stand-off started in October 2002 when US officials returned from a trip to Pyongyang claiming a senior North Korean diplomat, Kang Sok Ju, had admitted the existence of a covert uranium programme.
>
> North Korea denied this and the South Korean government expressed doubts about the US's interpretation of events.
>
> But the US claims were enough to disrupt a year of otherwise surprisingly good relations between Pyongyang and its neighbours. They also killed the 'Agreed Framework' – the nuclear freeze put in place by the Clinton administration and condemned by neo-conservatives in the Bush administration.[71]

The Agreed Framework has been killed off, with the blame passed to North Korea. More importantly, 'surprisingly good relations between Pyongyang and its neighbours' have been disrupted, and in the case of Japan they are currently very bad, with Tokyo threatening to cut off food aid and impose sanctions.[72] The remilitarisation of Japan is proceeding at a good pace.[73] The rogue state needed to bolster the US divide and rule strategy in East Asia, and to provide a justification for Missile Defense is alive and well. Japan's relations with China are deteriorating and she is sidestepping constraints of the 'Peace Constitution' to participate more fully, and profitably, in Missile Defense.[74] All this without a single US casualty.

On the debit side, some might consider, is the increasing likelihood that Pyongyang will develop, and demonstrate, a nuclear deterrent. However, hawks may be comfortable with this. It increases the perceived threat of the rogue state without actually posing any real danger to the United States. It would probably complete the re-militarisation of Japan, with the legal constraints of the constitution being removed, and there would be a strong possibility of Japan developing and deploying nuclear weapons. Again, the hawks may not be worried about this, considering that Japan would always remain subservient to the United States. Moreover, this would fuel an arms race in East Asia, especially between China and Japan. This would blunt China's rapid economic growth, and hence its challenge to US hegemony, while providing lucrative business in Japan for US defence industries. All this without a single US casualty.

There would be, it is true, flak on the domestic front, with liberals and Democrats who would argue that the Bush administration has let a nuclear threat develop and that the United States is less safe than it was. This would be an irritant but, given the nature of the American political system, only a minor one, until the next presidential election at least, and then only if there were a stronger challenger than Kerry. In the meantime, the administration would point to the Six-Party talks and say, 'What else can we do?'

2   Multiple Regime Change

Option 2 tries to answer that question with a bold plan of multiple regime change. The most informed and articulate advocate of this strategy is Nicholas Eberstadt of the American Enterprise Institute who published an essay 'Tear down this tyranny' on 29 November 2004.[75] This is the neocon prescription and has been enthusiastically circulated by William Kristol who published the essay in the *Weekly Standard* (which he edits) and then, as chairman of the Project for the New American Century sent a 'memorandum' to an undisclosed number of 'opinion leaders' drawing their attention to the article and suggesting that 'Eberstadt's clear headed and practical advice provides a good action agenda for an incoming secretary of state and a new policy team.'[76]

Eberstadt is refreshingly forthright and muscular, though short on specifics in what is but a brief article. He is basically arguing for multiple regime change. Negotiations with Pyongyang are a waste of time and anyway the declared aim should be regime change; 'Unless and until we have a better class of dictator running North Korea, we will be faced with an ongoing and indeed growing North Korean nuclear crisis.'[77] To bring this about there needs to be regime change in the State Department, Powell and team are not up to the challenge. His essay was written before Condoleezza Rice was nominated but presumably he will be happier with her. He advocates being tough with China – 'Washington has been far too complacent about China's unprincipled ambiguity' – although he doesn't suggest how. However, the main part of the essay is the third regime change, that in Seoul.

Eberstadt recognises that Roh Moo-hyun's government is a major constraint on using American power, from air strikes to interdiction of sea routes. They are a 'pro-appeasement crowd', and he argues that

> U.S. policy on the North Korean crisis suffered a setback, and a serious one, with the December 2002 South Korean presidential election, thanks to which a coterie of New Left-style academics and activists assumed great influence over their government's security policies.[78]

The result is that 'For all intents and purposes, South Korea is now a runaway ally', and this must be changed: 'America should be speaking over their heads directly to the Korean people, building and nurturing the coalitions in South Korean domestic politics that will ultimately bring a prodigal ally back into the fold.'[79]

This sounds relatively innocuous and is, indeed, what America has been trying to do for a long time. For instance, Washington made no secret of its preference for the conservative candidate Lee Hoi-chang in the buildup to the 2002 presidential election (and an attempt to push the vote his way might have been one of the motivations behind unleashing the crisis that October).[80] It was not so much that America's words fell on deaf ears, but rather that because of anti-Americanism, the endorsement was counter-productive. Not here would the lavish disbursement of money and marketing expertise produce a 'pro-American' government the way it did in Serbia,

Georgia and Belarus.[81] The conservatives in South Korea are too rich, and too experienced by now in 'democratic politics' for that to have much effect. Moreover, the South Korean political system is modelled on the American one, with a directly elected president not dependent on votes in the national assembly. In a parliamentary system governments can lose office before their tenure is up, but President Roh will be in office until his successor takes over, on 25 February 2008.

Will he last out? In 2003 the conservatives mounted a legislative coup and impeached President Roh. This, as we saw in Chapter 4, blew up in their faces. The Uri party won sweeping gains in the election and the supreme court overturned the impeachment. This suggests that if Roh and his supporters are to be removed from office before 2007 more forceful measures would be needed.

Eberstadt does not explicitly advocate a military coup in Seoul, but that is the logical outcome of his argument. Let us assume that option 2, with or without him, entails exerting enough pressure on China (by whatever means) to impose sanctions and withdraw support from Pyongyang, and rearranging the government in Seoul (by whatever means) so that it also imposes sanctions, withdraws aid and allows the US to bomb North Korea. This course is fraught with peril for the United States (let alone the hapless inhabitants of the region). It would probably lead to an upsurge in anti-Americanism in South Korea, China and beyond. It would probably unleash retaliation by North Korea, with massive casualties and destruction. At the least, a collapse in the North might propel a flood of refugees into China and into South Korea, causing immense social and economic problems. Resistance in the North and anti-American demonstrations-cum-riots in the South might embroil the United States in another Iraq.

Even if American power prevails and the Korean peninsula can be pacified under a friendly government in Seoul, what then? A Pandora's box of uncertainties. The economy would be seriously damaged and perhaps crippled. The government would be increasingly authoritarian and repressive as it grappled with the huge problems facing it. Alternatively, as some suggest, China might inherit the North and the US would not get it after all.[82]

On top of all this, with North Korea gone, what happens to Missile Defense? Perhaps Iran or Pakistan are placed at the top of the league of rogue states, but it would still make a dent in the justification. More important, what would happen to US strategy in East Asia? Without the bogeyman in Pyongyang the US might well find keeping Japan and Korea under control, and distanced from China, increasingly difficult.

Option 2 would seem to offer much danger and little potential benefit. Like the invasion of Iraq it would demonstrate the enormity of American power, but it would show its limitations. However, some variant of it cannot be ruled out.

3   Negotiations on the Basis of Accepting the DPRK

Option 3 would entail a commitment to real negotiations, somewhat on the lines of those that led to the Agreed Framework, but this time in a multilateral context. There are a number of recipes for negotiation but two particularly authoritative ones were published in the aftermath of the 2004 US election.

The first is the proposal by the International Crisis Group, *North Korea: Where Next for the Nuclear Talks?*, released on 15 November 2004. Since it was widely presumed before the election that Powell would leave after it, this report was clearly aimed at his successor. The International Crisis Group likes to think of itself as 'middle of the road' and its composition both high-powered and mainstream. The current chief executive is Gareth Evans, former Australian foreign minister and its North East Asia Project Director is Peter Beck, a well-regarded Koreanist who is Director of Research & Academic Affairs of the Korea Economic Institute in Washington. Its advisory board includes Chris Patten, George Soros and Stephen Solarz. If the Church of England was the Tory Party at prayer, this is mainstream international capitalism deep in thought.

We need not concern ourselves here with details, though in actual negotiations they would be of crucial importance. It is unlikely that the opening negotiations proposal would be acceptable to Pyongyang as it stands; it asks too much and offers too little. But perhaps the important question is whether the *principle* of negotiation would be acceptable to Washington, and that is what seems to be behind the ICG report. Its previous report, *North Korea: A Phased Negotiation Strategy* was endorsed by Jack Pritchard, and it is likely that this one would also be approved.[83] We can see the ICG proposals as coming from those who were critical of the Powell/Bush policy (Pritchard, it will be recalled, was Powell's North Korea officer before he resigned in protest) from a rather conservative standpoint. Peter Beck, for his part, published an essay with the uncompromising title *The Bush Administration's Failed North Korea Policy* in April 2004.[84]

The other proposal is *Ending the North Korean Nuclear Crisis* by the Task Force on US Korea policy, chaired by Selig Harrison.[85] This offers a rather stronger, and better prescription, because Harrison is more empathetic; he actually goes to Pyongyang and talks with officials. The task force brings together a wide range of US expertise on Korea, from the historian Bruce Cumings to the former State Department official Jack Pritchard and includes former ambassador, and current chairman of the Korea Society Donald P. Gregg, Peter Hayes of the Nautilus Institute, the journalist Dan Oberdorfer, Ken Quinones, Leon Sigal, David Steinberg and Joel Wit.

Like the ICG proposal, and in contradistinction to the Powell approach, the task force suggests a series of steps, and this is in line with both the Agreed Framework and consistent with DPRK demands for 'simultaneous actions'.[86] However, the proposal focusses too much on the plutonium issue and not enough on locating an over-arching framework for the resolution of the US–DPRK confrontation. Nevertheless, the task force does tackle the HEU problem more forcefully than the ICG. It specifically says that the early stages of negotiations should leave the uranium issue out and only confront it 'in the final stages of the process after greater trust has been developed through step-by-step mutual concessions'.[87]

The HEU issue will remain an awkward issue and a legacy of the Armitage policy. If it exists, the DPRK will find it difficult to admit to it, partly for reasons of face but also because the distributed nature of such a programme would open the possibility that the Americans would never be satisfied that they had discovered it all. Pyongyang fears it would give the US the excuse to 'scour the country' to give it military information for an invasion, as in Iraq.[88] Such a situation would also give the US an excuse, if needed, never to comply with its side of a bargain. If it does not exist, or is just a civilian programme, then Washington will find it difficult to walk away from the allegations. The best solution would be to do as the task force suggests, push it to the back of the process by which time it might be solvable.

Both proposals concentrate too much on what they think is imperative to remove danger to America, rather than seeking a win-win solution. In reality the danger to the United States is very slight compared to the danger to the DPRK. It would be wiser, if the US is going to negotiate, to do so in a spirit of generosity. If, instead of offering the minimal rewards it thinks it can get away with in exchange for Korean concessions, it actually came forward with genuine and positive proposals for rehabilitating the DPRK economy this would both achieve more in negotiations and also make compliance more likely. Thus instead of just lifting sanctions it could offer assistance and support to increase North Korean exports. It should be stressed that the United States, in concert with its allies, principally Japan, has the power, at relatively little financial cost and at no danger to itself, to bring about over a fairly short period of time an economic transformation in North Korea. It is likely that such a transformation, involving as it would, greatly increased linkages with the outside world, would bring about social and political change, as it has in China. Moreover, if peace and a degree of prosperity got under way, it might be possible to edge the HEU issue out of the way, with both sides saving face.

However, little financial cost is only part of the story because such a transformation would have serious implications for America's imperial posture, from Missile Defense to its position in Asia, and that might well scupper the idea.

On the other hand, the path to peace would improve Washington's relations with Beijing and with Seoul. It would also lessen the chances of Japanese re militarisation and nuclearisation. The US might well find a resurgent 'normal' Japan a tiger too difficult to ride.

Negotiations would also offer Condoleezza Rice the opportunity of differentiating herself from her predecessor.

The ICG claims that

> Talks with North Korea are never easy. There is some scepticism that Pyongyang will ever accept a deal, however objectively reasonable. The only way to find out once and for all is to offer it one that at least all five other parties see as such. And that will require more being put on the table than has been the case so far.[89]

In reality, talks are only inordinately difficult if the United States chooses to make them so. North Koreans resist being bullied but they respond to genuine negotiations.[90] The American hand is so much stronger that if they want resolution they can have it. Compared with the situation in the Middle East, that on the Korean peninsula can relatively easily be negotiated and resolved.

WHITHER CONDOLEEZZA RICE?

With a second administration and a new team in the State Department, the United States is in a position to reassess its Korea policy. Rice will have to choose between the three options outlined above. At this stage it is unclear which one she will opt for. Each has advantages and disadvantages.

What is clear is that, as former ROK Unification Minister Lim Dong-won has pointed out, criticising American intransigence, 'The U.S. holds the key to resolution.'[91] Which door of the three options will it try, and which way will it turn the key?

Appendix I   Economic Statistics

Table A1.1   GNP, per capita GNP and growth, North and South Korea, 1946–90

1 Year	2 NK won m	3 US$m official	4 US$m trade	5 pc GNP US$ official	5 pc GNP US$ trade	6 Growth %	7 GNP US$m	8 pcGNP US$	9 Growth %
		North Korea						South Korea	
1946	511.9	426.6	232.7	46	25	–	na	na	na
1949	1121.0	934.2	509.5	97	53	–	na	na	na
1953	855.4	712.8	388.8	84	46	–	1353	67	–
1956	1610.4	1499.5	732.0	160	78	31.8	1450	66	–1.4
1960	4209.7	3508.0	1913.5	325	177	7.4	1948	79	1.1
1961	4763.4	3969.5	2165.2	357	195	13.1	2103	82	5.6
1962	5290.9	4409.1	2404.9	386	211	11.0	2315	87	2.2
1963	5790.3	4825.3	2632.0	411	225	9.4	2718	100	9.1
1964	6369.3	5307.8	2895.1	440	240	9.9	2876	103	9.6
1965	6603.2	5502.6	3001.5	454	248	3.6	3006	105	5.8
1966	6986.0	5821.7	3175.5	468	255	5.8	3671	125	12.7
1967	7391.2	6159.3	2876.0	482	225	5.8	4274	142	6.6
1968	7819.9	6516.6	3042.8	496	232	5.8	5226	169	11.3
1969	8263.4	6894.6	3219.2	510	239	5.8	6625	210	13.8
1970	10838.2	9031.8	4217.2	650	304	31.0	8105	252	7.6
1971	12572.3	11326.4	5327.2	794	374	15.9	9456	288	9.1
1972	14583.9	13201.6	6179.6	901	422	16.0	10632	318	5.3
1973	17354.8	15634.9	6353.7	1040	489	18.9	13446	395	14.0
1974	20339.8	21187.3	8618.6	1374	559	17.1	18701	540	8.5
1975	24407.9	25424.9	11906.3	1603	751	20.0	20795	590	6.8
1976	27092.7	28221.5	12601.3	1735	775	10.9	28550	797	13.4
1977	26009.0	27092.7	12097.2	1624	725	–4.0	36629	1008	10.7
1978	30430.5	32720.9	16360.5	1912	956	16.9	51341	1392	11.0
1979	34995.0	41660.8	19550.3	2374	1114	14.9	61361	1640	7.0
1980	35590.0	41383.7	20935.3	2295	1161	1.7	60327	1589	–4.8
1981	36479.7	39651.8	20610.0	2147	1116	2.5	66238	1734	5.9
1982	40930.2	42196.1	19306.7	2229	1020	12.2	71300	1824	7.2
1983	45923.7	45023.3	21065.9	2346	1042	12.2	79500	2002	12.6
1984	47163.7	39303.0	19984.6	2002	1018	2.7	87000	2158	9.3
1985	48437.1	45268.3	19933.0	2220	978	2.7	89695	2194	7.0
1986	49454.3	48484.6	22176.8	2324	1063	2.1	102789	2505	12.9
1987	51086.3	54347.1	23872.1	2544	1117	3.3	128921	3110	13.0
1988	52618.8	55977.5	25056.6	2558	1145	3.0	172776	4127	12.4
1989	54197.4	55873.6	25808.3	2481	1146	3.0	211200	4994	6.8
1990	55443.9	57158.6	26401.8	2233	1031	2.3	237900	5569	9.0

Source: Hwang, Eui Gak. *The Korean Economies: a Comparison of North and South*. New York: Oxford University Press, 1993, Table 3.11, pp. 120–1. Hwang uses two sets of exchange rates to convert estimates of North Korean GNP/per capita GNP into US$. For his discussion of this see Hwang, pp. 119–23.

Appendix II   Armed Forces, Military Expenditure and Exports

The US currently spends $3 billion a year in direct costs of its military presence in South Korea, and is planning an $11 billion increase over three years. The ROK Defense Ministry has requested an $18.6 billion budget for 2004, up 28.3 per cent.[1] By contrast, in October 2002, at the time of the Kelly visit, the DPRK announced that it was planning to reduce troop numbers by 500,000 bringing them down to the ROK's 700,000.[2] There was a report in a Seoul newspaper in November 2002 that the DPRK planned to cut troop numbers by 10 per cent in order to release labour into industry.[3] Then in May 2003 it was announced that the DPRK was cutting the length of mandatory military service by three years.[4]

Table A2.1   World military spending, 2001–02

Country	1	2	3	4
		2001		2002
	US$bn	%	US$bn	%
USA	281.4	36	382.2	45
Russia	43.9	6	65	8
France	40	5	29.5	4
Japan	38.5	5	42.6	5
UK	37	5	38.4	5
Germany	32.4	4	24.9	3
China	27	3	47	6
Saudi Arabia	26.6	3	21.3	3
Italy	24.7	3	19.4	2
Brazil	14.1	2	10.5	1
India	12.9	2	15.6	2
South Korea	10.2	1	14.1	2
Israel	9.1	1	9.4	1
Turkey	8.9	1	5.8	1
Spain	8	1	8.4	1
World total	772	100	841.8	100
North Korea	na	na	1.4	0.2
Iraq	na	na	1.4	0.2

Sources and notes:

Columns 1, 2:

Stockholm International Peace Research Institute. *The Fifteen Major Spenders in 2001, 1998–2001.* Stockholm: SIPRI, 2003. Available from http://projects.sipri.se/milex/mex_major_spenders.html (accessed 24 February 2003)

Figures are constant 1998 prices and exchange rates.

Figure for Russia is based on purchasing power parity exchange calculation.
SIPRI notes: If the market exchange rate is used for Russia, its military expenditure in 2001 amounts to $12.7 billion at constant (1998) prices and exchange rates.
Column 3:
Hellman, Christopher. *World Military Spending 2002*. Available from www.cdi.org/budget/2004/world-military-spending.cfm (accessed 24 February 2003)
Russia, China, Brazil, Iraq – data for 2001
The original table gives a figure of $399.1bn for the United States, that being from the annual budget request for fiscal year 2004. It notes that this is $16.9bn 'above current levels'. I have subtracted this from the request amount to give a time period comparable to the other countries.
Column 4:
My calculation.

Table A2.2   Comparative military expenditure, US, Japan and the Koreas, 1988–2001

(a) Constant 1998 US$, millions

Year	USA	Japan	South Korea	Sub-total	North Korea
1988	404,136		7,194	411,330	1,756
1989	399,719	33,379	7,413	440,511	1,845
1990	382,266	34,353	7,530	424,149	1,961
1991	335,473	35,141	7,768	378,382	2,030
1992	354,507	35,989	8,220	398,716	2,083
1993	335,940	36,384	8,597	380,921	2,133
1994	316,776	36,554	8,849	362,179	2,190
1995	298,376	36,920	9,309	344,605	..
1996	282,231	37,664	9,811	329,706	..
1997	280,785	37,845	10,048	328,678	..
1998	274,278	37,748	9,700	321,726	1,327
1999	275,057	37,819	9,437	322,313	1,327
2000	285,679	38,080	10,016	333,775	1,364
2001	281,426	38,468	10,201	330,095	1,409

(b) North Korea as percentage

Year	US	Japan	South Korea	US, JP, SK	
1988	0.4		24.4	0.4	100.0
1989	0.5	5.5	24.9	0.4	100.0
1990	0.5	5.7	26.0	0.5	100.0
1991	0.6	5.8	26.1	0.5	100.0
1992	0.6	5.8	25.3	0.5	100.0
1993	0.6	5.9	24.8	0.6	100.0
1994	0.7	6.0	24.7	0.6	100.0
		No NK data available 1995–97			
1998	0.5	3.5	13.7	0.4	100.0
1999	0.5	3.5	14.1	0.4	100.0
2000	0.5	3.6	13.6	0.4	100.0
2001	0.5	3.7	13.8	0.4	100.0

Notes:

Figures for North Korea 1988–94 are described as estimates.

No data are shown for North Korea, 1995–97.

Japan and South Korea are converted at market exchange rates.

North Korea is converted at PPP rate which gives a higher figure than market rate conversion

Data is for calendar years.

Source: Stockholm International Peace Research Institute. *Military Expenditure Database 2004*. Stockholm: SIPRI, 2004. Available from http://web.sipri.org/contents/milap/milex/mex_data_index. html (accessed 11 October 2004)

Table A2.3   The world's top 15 individual arms exporters, 1997–99

Rank		1999			1997–99	
	Country	$bn	% of US	Country	$bn	% of US
1	US	33.0	100.0	US	91.5	100.0
2	UK	5.2	15.8	UK	15.7	17.2
3	Russia	3.1	9.4	France	15.7	17.2
4	France	2.9	8.8	Russia	7.9	8.6
5	Germany	1.9	5.8	Germany	4.5	4.9
6	Sweden	0.7	2.1	Sweden	2.9	3.2
7	Israel	0.6	1.8	China	2	2.2
8	Australia	0.6	1.8	Canada	1.6	1.7
9	Canada	0.6	1.8	Israel	1.6	1.7
10	Ukraine	0.6	1.8	Ukraine	1.5	1.6
11	Italy	0.4	1.2	Italy	1.3	1.4
12	China	0.3	0.9	Australia	1.1	1.2
13	Belarus	0.3	0.9	Netherlands	1.1	1.2
14	Bulgaria	0.2	0.6	Belarus	0.9	1.0
15	North Korea	0.1	0.3	Spain	0.8	0.9

Note:

The calculation of percentage of US level is mine.

Source: *World Military Expenditures and Arms Transfers, Volume 28*. Washington, DC: US State Department, 2003.

Appendix III   Documentary Sources

This is a selection of links to some key documents. The links were active on 30 June 2003. Where possible I have given two sources for the same document in case of discrepancies between texts, and to lessen the chance of dead links. I have not been able to locate a web source for the DPRK–China Treaty of Friendship, Cooperation and Mutual Assistance of 11 July 1961, which is still in force and affords the DPRK some protection in the case of attack.[1]

DPRK

Foreign Policy Statements

Letter from FM Paek to UN Security Council
28 June 2003
www.kcna.co.jp/item/2003/200306/news06/30.htm#10

Statement of DPRK Government on its withdrawal from NPT
10 January 2003
www.kcna.co.jp/item/2003/200301/news01/11.htm#1

Economics and Foreign Investment

Foreign trade and investment laws
KOTRA
http://crm.kotra.or.kr/main/info/nk/eng/law/law.php3
People's Korea
www.korea-np.co.jp/pk/economy/category13.htm

Basic Law of Sinuiju Special Administrative Region
www.korea-np.co.jp/pk/184th_issue/2002092803.htm

Rajin-Sonbong Economic and Trade Zone
www.tumenprogramme.org/tumen/region/rason

JAPAN

DPRK–Japan Pyongyang Declaration

17 September 2002
People's Korea
www.korea-np.co.jp/pk/184th_issue/2002091801.htm
Kimsoft
www.kimsoft.com/2002/dprk-jp.htm

ROK

Documents on Inter-Korean Relations

ROK Ministry of Unification
www.unikorea.go.kr/en/interkorean/interkorean.php?page_code=ue0304&ucd
=eng0204

Joint Declaration of 15 June 2000 (Pyongyang Summit)

People's Korea
www.korea-np.co.jp/pk/142th_issue/2000061501.htm
ROK Ministry of Unification
www.unikorea.go.kr/en/interkorean/interkorean.php?mode=view&page_co
de=ue0304&ucd=eng0204&ewn_num=52&cur_page=4

Basic Agreement of 1991/92

The agreement was signed 13 December 1991 but came into force 19 February
1992. The DPRK dates it as 1991 and the ROK as 1992.
People's Korea
www.korea-np.co.jp/pk/011th_issue/97100101.htm
Ministry of Unification
www.unikorea.go.kr/en/interkorean/interkorean.php?mode=view&page_co
de=ue0304&ucd=eng0204&ewn_num=30&cur_page=6

Joint Declaration on the Denuclearisation of the Korean Peninsula

20 January 1992
www.unikorea.go.kr/en/interkorean/interkorean.php?mode=view&page_co
de=ue0304&ucd=eng0204&ewn_num=29&cur_page=6

The July 4 South–North Joint Communiqué

4 July 1972
Ministry of Unification www.unikorea.go.kr/en/interkorean/interkorean.
php?mode=view&page_code=ue0304&ucd=eng0204&ewn_num=69&cur_
page=6

RUSSIA

DPRK–Russia Joint Declaration
20 July 2000
www.korea-np.co.jp/pk/143th_issue/2000072101.htm

USA

Agreed Framework between the USA and the DPRK

People's Korea
www.korea-np.co.jp/pk/011th_issue/971001genevaagreemet.htm

KEDO

www.kedo.org/pdfs/AgreedFramework.pdf

Appendix IV A Timeline of Nuclear and Missile Issues and Activities

This chronology does not claim to be exhaustive or comprehensive but it does attempt to capture the main events that enable us to understand the confrontation between the United States and the DPRK over nuclear and missile issues. In particular, and in contrast to other chronologies, it puts North Korean events within the context of global developments and especially US nuclear and missile activities.

1945

6 August	US drops first atomic bomb on Hiroshima, 140,000 civilians dead, *Hibakusha* (survivors) more than 300,000
9 August	Second bomb dropped on Nagasaki; 70,000 civilians dead
15 August	Japan surrenders; liberation of Korea

1946

1 July	US A-bomb tests at Bikini

1947

October	US A-bomb stockpile reaches 56; 150 is immediate target

1949

29 August	Soviet Union detonates first A-bomb

1950

	A-bomb arsenal: US: 298; USSR: 5

1951

April	US Joint Chiefs of Staff agree on contingency plan for atomic attack on Chinese forces in Manchuria

1952

1 November	US explodes first hydrogen bomb, 700 times more powerful than Hiroshima bomb

1953

February	US embarks on development of intercontinental ballistic missiles (ICBM)

1954

1 March	US H-bomb test at Bikini; massive radiation which affects Japanese fishing boat 100 miles away

1955

22 November	Soviet Union tests H-bomb
	US nuclear arsenal reaches 2,422

1957

15 May	British H-bomb test at Christmas Island
4 October	Soviet Union launches Sputnik, world's first artificial satellite

1958

	US develops Polaris, submarine-based ballistic missile
3 February	US exhibits nuclear artillery and missiles at base in South Korea

1959

US deploys ICBM (Atlas); works on anti-ballistic missile (ABM) systems

1960

February   France tests A-bomb

1962

22 October   Cuban missile crisis

1963

8 August   Limited Test Ban Treaty

1964

October   China tests first A-bomb at Lop Nor

1966

August–   US report argues against use of tactical nuclear weapons in
September   Vietnam because political effects would 'be uniformly bad and could be catastrophic'

22 October   China tests first guided missile

28 December   China tests first thermonuclear device

1968

Nuclear Non-Proliferation Treaty (NPT)

1969

20 July   US Apollo Moon landing

1970

Treaty of Almelo, under which Britain, Germany and the Netherlands agree to develop centrifuges to enrich uranium jointly, ensuring for their nuclear power industry a fuel source independent of the United States

1972

May   Strategic Arms Limitation Treaty 1 (SALT 1) between US and USSR

1974

India tests first A-bomb

16 September   DPRK joins International Atomic Energy Agency (IAEA)

Worried by South Korea's nuclear weapons programme Kim Il Sung asks for Chinese assistance. US subsequently forces Park Chung-hee officially to cease weapons programme, but experiments continue in secret

1975

Following fall of Saigon US threatens DPRK with nuclear weapons; brings nuclear-capable F-111s and announces Team Spirit '76

30 May   Reported that US has at least 1,000 nuclear weapons and 54 nuclear-capable aircraft deployed in South Korea

1977

12 July   Jimmy Carter decides on development of Neutron bomb

1978

March   Secret US report on vulnerability of North Korean forces to tactical nuclear weapons

April   ROK's first nuclear power plant comes into operation

1979

June	SALT 2
22 September	Suspected South African nuclear test

1982

April–May	South Korean scientists at Korea Atomic Energy Research Institute conduct secret experiments on reprocessing plutonium

1983

23 March	Ronald Reagan's 'Strategic Defense Initiative' ('Star Wars'), predecessor of Missile Defense, seeks to give US a shield against ballistic attack, or retaliation

1985

12 December	DPRK signs NPT, but does not complete a safeguards agreement with the International Atomic Energy Agency (IAEA) because of US nuclear weapons in South Korea

1986

26 April	Chernobyl nuclear power plant disaster

1987

	DPRK starts 5mw reactor, which in theory can produce enough plutonium each year for one nuclear weapon
28 Apr	CIA report stresses energy as prime reason for North Korea's nuclear efforts. The possibility of ability to produce weapons-grade plutonium is mentioned but not emphasised

1991

17 January	Hundreds of cruise missiles launched from surface ships, submarines and B-52s during Gulf War. US also uses depleted uranium. Unknown number of Iraqi casualties
July	Strategic Arms Reduction Treaty (START) aims to cut US warheads by 15 per cent, Soviet by 25 per cent
27 September	President George H. Bush announces worldwide withdrawal of US tactical nuclear weapons
18 December	President Roh Tae-woo announces that there are no nuclear weapons in South Korea (but US does not withdraw them until following July)

1992

10 January	North Korea signs International Atomic Energy Safeguards Agreement
20 January	North–South Joint Declaration on Denuclearisation of the Korean Peninsula forbids uranium enrichment
30 January	DPRK and IAEA sign the nuclear safeguard accord in Vienna
6 March	US imposes sanctions on DPRK companies for missile exports
11 May	IAEA Director Hans Blix visits DPRK to tour research facilities at Yongbyon
2 July	US announces withdrawal of nuclear weapons from South Korea

31 August	A team of IAEA officials led by Wily Theis, a section chief in the Safeguards Department, arrives for the third ad hoc inspections
September	IAEA inspectors discover discrepancies in DPRK's 'initial report'

1993

9 February	The IAEA demands special inspections of two sites that are believed to store nuclear waste. North Korea refuses the IAEA's request
March	South Africa reveals manufacturing and dismantling of six nuclear bombs
12 March	Amid demands for special inspections, North Korea announces its intention to withdraw from the NPT in three months
11 June	Following talks with the United States, in which assurances are given on the threat and use of force, including nuclear weapons, North Korea suspends its decision to pull out of the NPT and agrees to the full and impartial application of IAEA safeguards (withdrawal reactivated 10 January 2003)
19 July	Second round of talks; DPRK ready to negotiate IAEA inspections of its nuclear facilities, suggestions that US will replace the graphite nuclear reactors with light-water reactors (LWRs), which are proliferation-resistant
December	US nuclear information released; 1,051 nuclear tests, including 204 secret underground tests (under 20kt), radiation experiments on living persons, 600 persons, 800 times
late 1993	US intelligence agencies estimate that North Korea has separated about 12 kilograms of plutonium, enough for at least one or two nuclear weapons

1994

January	CIA estimates that North Korea may have produced one or two nuclear weapons
1 March	IAEA inspectors arrive in North Korea for the first inspections since 1993
19 May	The IAEA confirms that North Korea has begun removing spent fuel from its 5-mw nuclear research reactor even though international monitors were not present
13 June	North Korea announces its withdrawal from the IAEA
15 June	Jimmy Carter negotiates a deal in which Pyongyang confirms its willingness to 'freeze' its nuclear weapons program. By broadcasting on CCN from Pyongyang forces Clinton administration to accept in principle
9 July	Kim Il Sung dies
21 October	Agreed Framework signed in Geneva
28 November	The IAEA announces that DPRK has complied with its obligations to freeze reactors

1995

2 September	French atomic tests in South Pacific (Mururoa)
December	US nuclear stockpile 9,000 – 7,000 in US, 480 in Europe, 1,500 on submarines

1996

January	North Korea agrees in principle to a meeting on missile exports but demands easing of economic sanctions first
21–22 April	US–DPRK missile talks in Berlin. US wants DPRK to adhere to the Missile Technology Control Regime (MTCR), which controls sales of ballistic missile systems (but not cruise and other missiles); Korea demands compensation for lost sales
24 May	US imposes sanctions on North Korea and Iran for missile technology-related transfers
8 July	International Court of Justice gives advisory opinion that use, or threat, of nuclear weapons is illegal
29 July	Final Chinese test at Lop Nor; total of 42 tests since 1990, and world total at 1,452
10 September	Comprehensive Test Ban Treaty signed by US, Russia, UK and 96 non-nuclear weapon states
16 October	After detecting North Korean preparations for a test of its medium-range Nodong missile, the United States deploys a reconnaissance ship and aircraft to Japan
8 November	State Department confirms that the missile test has been cancelled

1997

11–13 June	The second round of US–North Korean missile talks takes place in New York, with US negotiators pressing North Korea not to deploy the Nodong missile and to end sales of Scud missiles and their components. The parties reach no agreement
6 August	US imposes new sanctions on DPRK companies for unspecified missile exports
21 August	US deploys improved nuclear warheads useable by B-2 and F-16 aircraft

1998

17 April	US imposes sanctions on North Korea and Pakistan in response to Pyongyang's transfer of missile technology and components to Pakistan's Khan Research Laboratory
6 May	At a meeting on NPT, China reiterates its policy on Negative Security Assurances: 'Since the very first day when China came into possession of nuclear weapons, China has solemnly declared that at no time and under no circumstances will it be the first to use nuclear weapons. China has also undertaken unconditionally not to use or threaten to use nuclear weapons against non-nuclear-weapon states or nuclear-weapon-free zones. China is the only nuclear-weapon state in the world that has made and abided by such commitments'
28 May	Pakistan tests nuclear weapons
16 June	KCNA reports that Pyongyang will only end its missile technology exports if it is suitably compensated for financial losses.
15 July	Rumsfeld commission concludes that the United States may have 'little or no warning' before facing a long-range ballistic missile threat from 'rogue states', such as North Korea and Iran. Set foundation for Missile Defense

20 August	Following bombings at US embassies in Kenya and Tanzania, US launches cruise missiles at targets in Afghanistan and Sudan. Pharmaceutical factory destroyed in Sudan on grounds it was producing nerve gas; this is later found to be untrue
31 August	North Korea launches a three-stage Taepodong-1 rocket with a range of 1,500–2,000 kilometres that flies over Japanese territory. Pyongyang announces that the rocket successfully placed a small satellite into orbit, a claim contested by US Space Command
1 October	The third round of US–North Korean missile talks makes little progress. US wants Pyongyang to terminate its missile programs in exchange for relief from economic sanctions, but North Korea wants compensation, arguing that the lifting of sanctions is promised by Agreed Framework
12 November	President Bill Clinton appoints former Secretary of Defense William Perry to serve as North Korea policy coordinator
4–11 December	US and DPRK hold talks to address US concerns about a suspected underground nuclear facility at Kumchangri. Pyongyang reportedly accepts in principle the idea of a US inspection, but no agreement on compensation
16–19 December	US and UK bombing campaign against Iraq for obstructing weapons inspectors whom the Iraqis had accused of spying. The UN later acknowledged that inspectors had been passing information on to US intelligence service. Unknown number of casualities

1999

2 February	CIA Director George Tenet testifies before the Senate Armed Services Committee that, with some technical improvements, North Korea would be able to use the Taepodong-1 to deliver small payloads to parts of Alaska and Hawaii. Tenet also says that Pyongyang's Taepodong-2, if it had a third stage like the Taepodong-1, would be able to deliver large payloads to the continental United States, albeit with poor accuracy
29–31 March	Fourth round of US–DPRK missile talks; no agreement but meetings to continue
March	Working group chaired by Richard Armitage, and including Paul Wolfowitz published 'A comprehensive approach to North Korea', a critique of Clinton policy and a blueprint for a Republican administration. Armitage and Wolfowitz subsequently assume leading roles in State and Defense Department respectively
25 April	US establishes the Trilateral Coordination and Oversight Group (TCOG) with Japan and South Korea to institutionalise close consultation and policy coordination in dealing with North Korea. Subsequent events show that US has limited success in controlling the North Korea policy of its 'allies'
20–24 May	After agreeing to give food aid, a US inspection team visits the North Korean suspected nuclear site in Kumchangri and

	finds no evidence of nuclear activity or violation of the Agreed Framework
25–28 May	Perry visits DPRK, meets with senior North Korean political, diplomatic and military officials but not Kim Jong Il. Perry delivers a letter from President Clinton. US reportedly makes demands beyond the scope of the Agreed Framework
7–12 September	During talks in Berlin, North Korea agrees to a moratorium on testing any long-range missiles for the duration of talks with the United States. The United States agrees to a partial lifting of economic sanctions on North Korea. The two parties agree to continue high-level discussions. (Sanctions are not actually lifted until June 2000 after the Pyongyang summit)
9 September	A US National Intelligence Estimate reports that North Korea will 'most likely' develop an ICBM capable of delivering a 200kg warhead to the US mainland by 2015
15 September	North Korean policy coordinator Perry submits his review of US policy toward North Korea to President Clinton and Congress
12 October	Unclassified version of Perry report issued. Perry argues, in effect, that DPRK will not collapse and that step-by-step negotiations on the lines of the Agreed Framework must continue
13 October	US Senate refuses to ratify CTBT
3 November	Republican Representative Benjamin Gilman releases report claiming that DPRK has an enriched uranium programme and that 'North Korea's efforts to acquire uranium technologies, that is, a second path to nuclear weapons, and their efforts to weaponize their nuclear material do not violate the 1994 Agreed Framework. That is because the Clinton Administration did not succeed in negotiating a deal with North Korea that would ban such efforts. It is inexplicable and inexcusable'
19 November	US–DPRK talks in Berlin on bilateral relations and preparations for a North Korean high-level visit to the United States.
15 December	Five years after signing of Agreed Framework, and well behind schedule, KEDO officials sign a turnkey contract with the Korea Electric Power Corporation to begin construction on the two LWRs in Kumho, North Korea
2000	
4 January	Italy and DPRK establish diplomatic relations, marking beginning of new DPRK offensive, supported this time by Seoul, to expand relations with the West
January–February	South Korean scientists at Korea Atomic Energy Research Institute carried out secret work on enriching uranium, in violation of North–South Joint Declaration on Denuclearisation of the Korean Peninsula and NPT
9–10 February	Russia–DPRK Treaty of Friendship, Good Neighbourliness and Cooperation
6 April	US imposes sanctions on DPRK firm for missile exports to Iran

10 April	ROK and DPRK simultaneously announce June summit
25–27 May	Second US inspection of Kumchangri, still no evidence of nuclear activity
15 June	Pyongyang summit between Kim Jong Il and Kim Dae-jung
19 June	US relaxes sanctions on North Korea, allowing a 'wide range' of trade in commercial and consumer goods, easing restrictions on investment, and eliminating prohibitions on direct personal and commercial financial transactions, but sanctions related to terrorism and missile proliferation remain in place and effect is slight. The next day, North Korea reaffirms its moratorium on missile tests
12 July	Fifth round of US–DPRK missile talks are held in Kuala Lumpur. US rejects Korean demand for $1 billion compensation for halting exports but says it will move towards 'economic normalisation' in return for addressing US concerns
19 July	During a meeting with Russian President Vladimir Putin, Kim Jong Il reportedly promises to end his country's missile programme in exchange for assistance with satellite launches; this is later said to have been said in jest
28 July	DPRK invited to join ASEAN Regional Forum (ARF). DPRK Foreign Minister Paek Nam Sun meets US Secretary of State Madeleine Albright in Bangkok
27 September	US–North Korean talks resume in New York on nuclear issues, missiles, and terrorism. The two countries issue a joint statement on terrorism, but North Korea remains on the State Department's terrorism list thus automatically imposing sanctions and debarring it from membership of international financial institutions
9–12 October	Kim Jong Il's second-in-command, Vice Marshal Jo Myong Rok, visits Washington as a special envoy. He delivers a letter to President Clinton and meets with the Secretaries of State and Defense
12 October	US, DPRK issue a joint statement noting that resolution of the missile issue would 'make an essential contribution to fundamentally improved relations' and reiterating the two countries' commitment to implementation of the Agreed Framework. The statement also says that Albright will visit North Korea in the near future to prepare for a possible visit by President Clinton
24 October	Secretary Albright concludes a two-day visit to Pyongyang to meet with Kim Jong Il. During the visit, Kim says that North Korea would not further test the Taepodong-1 missile. In addition to discussing Pyongyang's indigenous missile programme, the talks cover North Korean missile technology exports, nuclear transparency, the normalisation of relations, and a possible trip by President Clinton to Pyongyang
1–3 November	Despite the Albright visit, a seventh round of missile talks in Kuala Lumpur between Pyongyang and Washington ends without an agreement

12 December	US Supreme Court awards election to George W. Bush
28 December	President Clinton announces that he will not travel to North Korea before the end of his term, citing 'insufficient time to complete the work at hand'

2001

1 January	US imposes sanctions on North Korean company for exports to Iran
6 March	At a joint press briefing with the Swedish foreign minister, Secretary of State Colin Powell says that the administration 'plan[s] to engage with North Korea to pick up where President Clinton left off. Some promising elements were left on the table and we will be examining those elements'
7 March	Kim Dae-jung has summit with Bush, but is embarrassingly rebuffed in attempts to persuade him to endorse 'Sunshine policy'. Later, John Kerry accused Bush of having 'pulled the rug out from under Kim Dae-jung'.
15 March	KCNA statement attacks US for impeding North–South dialogue and for its new 'hostile' policies. It says Pyongyang is 'fully prepared for both dialogue and war' but calls on Washington to 'honestly implement the DPRK–US Agreed Framework'.
3 May	At a press conference in Pyongyang, a European Union delegation headed by Swedish Prime Minister Göran Persson reports that Kim Jong Il pledged that he will extend Pyongyang's moratorium on missile testing until 2003 and that Kim was 'committed' to a second inter-Korean summit
6 June	US North Korea policy review completed. President Bush declares, 'I have directed my national security team to undertake serious discussions with North Korea', but commentator Leon Sigal notes that the review 'reneged' on past US commitments and reinterpreted agreements with the North unilaterally
13 June	US special envoy Jack Pritchard meets in New York with the DPRK representative to the UN, Yi Hyong Chol, to make arrangements for bilateral talks
26 June	US imposes renewed sanctions on North Korean company for unspecified missile-related sales to Iran
6 July	US Deputy Secretary of State Richard Armitage confirms that DPRK tested a rocket engine late June but admitted this did not violate moratorium on rocket launches
12 July	US Defense Secretary Rumsfeld suggests that US will withdraw from ABM treaty
4 August	At summit meeting with Vladimir Putin, Kim Jong Il reiterates that moratorium on rocket testing will continue until 2003
9 September	9/11 attack on World Trade Center in New York and on the Pentagon by Islamic militants who have hijacked US planes with knives
12 September	DPRK Foreign Ministry condemns attacks, saying 'The very regretful and tragic incident reminds it once again of the

gravity of terrorism. As a UN member the DPRK is opposed to all forms of terrorism and whatever support to it and this stance will remain unchanged.' South Korean report that Pyongyang sent secret cable to Washington that it regretted the attacks and had nothing to do with them. Message also sent via Swedish government

7 October   US invades Afghanistan; US and Britain launch 50 cruise missiles. It also makes use of 'daisy-cutter' bombs, inflicting large casualties though no count is made

October   Anthrax attacks in US; later disclosed that material came from US labs

12 November   DPRK's UN representative Ri Hyong Chol signs the two major anti-terror treaties: the 1999 International Convention for the Suppression of the Financing of Terrorism and the 1979 International Convention Against the Taking of Hostages

13 December   President Bush announces that US is withdrawing from Anti-Ballistic Missile (ABM) Treaty, becoming 'the first nation since World War II to withdraw from a major international security agreement'

14 December   Congress approves funding for Missile Defense

pre-Christmas   Donald Rumsfeld, moving towards the invasion of Iraq, calls DPRK 'terrorist regime – teetering on the verge of collapse' and boasts that US can fight two wars at once

25 December   Reports that DPRK has told Swedish leader of EU delegation that it was ready to sign five further anti-terrorism agreements: (1) the 1997 International Convention for the Suppression of Terrorist Bombings; (2) the 1980 Convention on the Physical Protection of Nuclear Material; (3) the 1988 Convention for the Suppression of Unlawful Acts against the Safety of Maritime Navigation; (4) the 1988 Protocol for the Suppression of Unlawful Acts against the Safety of Fixed Platforms Located on the Continental Shelf; and (5) the 1991 Convention on the Marking of Plastic Explosives for the Purpose of Detection

2002

9 January   US Department of Defense releases sanitised abstract of Nuclear Posture Review

29 January   In annual State of the Union speech President Bush labels North Korea, Iraq and Iran as an 'Axis of Evil, aiming to threaten the peace of the world'

5 February   Secretary of State Powell at a Senate hearing claims that the administration will talk with North Korea 'any time, any place, or anywhere without any preconditions'. However, the extended agenda, including conventional arms and missiles, indicates that they do not regard themselves bound by Clinton's Agreed Framework

9 March   Leaked details of Nuclear Posture Review published in *Los Angeles Times*; sets new targets and weapons for striking targets in Iraq, Iran, North Korea, Syria and Libya; stresses need to develop earth-penetrating nuclear weapons to destroy

	heavily fortified underground bunkers. It argues that US may need to resume nuclear testing
13 March	Angry KCNA commentary on the Nuclear Posture Review states that 'the US is openly threatening the DPRK with nuclear weapons [and this] proves once again how just it was when it exerted tremendous efforts to increase its capacity for self-defence'
19 March	CIA Director Tenet admits that DPRK plutonium programme remains frozen, as required by Agreed Framework
1 April	President Bush states that he that he will not certify North Korea's compliance with the Agreed Framework. However, he waives US law so that US funding of KEDO can continue, stopping short of a US breach of the AF
6 May	John Bolton, Undersecretary of State for Arms Control, and a noted hawk, accused both Iraq and North Korea of having 'covert nuclear programs, in violation of the Nuclear Non-Proliferation Treaty'
29 June	Clash in West Sea over crab fishing. South Korean naval vessel rams northern one, which opens fire, sinking the southern vessel
2 July	US cancels a delegation to DRPK, citing Korean failure to respond about the date of the meeting, and the 29 June North–South naval clash
31 July	Powell briefly meets DPRK Foreign Minister Paek Nam Sum at ASEAN Regional Forum meeting in Brunei
7 August	KEDO holds a ceremony at Kumho to mark the to mark the pouring of the concrete foundation for the first LWR, now years behind schedule. Jack Pritchard, the US representative to KEDO and State Department special envoy for negotiations with North Korea, attends the ceremony, the highest US official to visit DPRK since Albright
16 August	US imposes fresh sanctions on North Korea for missile technology to Yemen, even though the latter is now counted as a US 'ally in the war on terror'
27 August	Japanese Prime Minister Junichiro Koizumi reveals to Richard Armitage, who is visiting Tokyo, that he will be having a summit with Kim Jong Il in September. Until now, preparations have been kept secret from the Americans
29 August	John Bolton at a speech in Seoul threatens that US will withdraw from AF if DPRK does not allow 'inspection of its past nuclear activities', i.e. activities outside of the agreement. He also reject Korean calls for compensation for the delay in providing LWRS. He claims "North Korea is capable of producing and delivering warheads using a wide variety of chemical agents and has a minimum of 2,500 tons of lethal chemicals'
30 August	Editorial in Seoul's *Korea Times* comments that Bolton's speech 'makes us doubt [US] intention to reopen talks with North Korea'. It complained that US was derailing North–South

dialogue and said, 'If reports are true that the government asked Bolton to refrain from making remarks that might undermine the budding detente on the peninsula, he displayed inconsideration for a blood-tied ally'

20 September   Bush unveils new 'National Security Strategy of the US'. Claims right to use 'pre-emptive strikes' against possible enemies, and that US is above law; 'We will take the actions necessary to ensure that our efforts to meet our global security commitments and protect Americans are not impaired by the potential for investigations, inquiry, or prosecution by the International Criminal Court (ICC), whose jurisdiction does not extend to Americans and which we do not accept'

17 September   Koizumi and Kim Jong Il meet in Pyongyang. Kim admits abductions, Koizumi apologises for Japanese colonialism. Both agree to press ahead on normalisation. US scholar Pollack notes that the 'DPRK had opened the door to a new relationship with America's most important Asian ally'

3–5 October   James Kelly, Assistant Secretary of State for East Asian and Pacific affairs, visits North Korea. It is reported that he 'reiterates US concerns about North Korea's nuclear and missile programs, export of missile components, conventional force posture, human rights violations, and humanitarian situation'. He is not empowered to negotiate, merely to state US demands.

16 October   State Department says Kelly charged Pyongyang with having a clandestine uranium enrichment programme and that, 'North Korean officials [Kang Sok Ju] acknowledged that they have such a program'

25 October   Lengthy DPRK Foreign Ministry statement, 'Conclusion of non-aggression treaty between DPRK and US called for' outlines position. Claims, inter alia, that Kelly was told that 'DPRK was entitled to possess not only nuclear weapon but any type of weapon more powerful than that so as to defend its sovereignty and right to existence from the ever-growing nuclear threat by the US'. However, it also implicitly denies HEU programme; 'Producing no evidence, he asserted that the DPRK has been actively engaged in the enriched uranium program in pursuit of possessing nuclear weapons in violation of the DPRK–US agreed framework'

early
November   Veteran US journalist Don Oberdorfer meets Kang Sok Ju in Pyongyang. Kang reiterates there was no admission of a HEU programme, and refers him to 25 October statement

6 November   South Korean press reports that if KEDO follows Washington requests and stops heavy fuel oil shipments, which account for 30 per cent of North Korea's energy this will end the Agreed Framework

14 November   ROK Unification Minister Jeong Se-hyun reported as saying Kelly 'might have misunderstood' North Korean counterpart Kang Sok Ju

	KEDO agrees to US request
14 November	South Korean press reports that Kelly claim that DPRK 'admitted storing bio-weapons'. Armitage later admits they misunderstood that the Koreans were talking metaphorically
18 November	BBC reports North Korean nuclear 'admission' in doubt
	Last shipment of heavy fuel oil reaches North Korea
29 November	IAEA criticises DPRK statement that it is entitled to have nuclear weapons and calls for clarification about 'reported information that the DPRK has a programme to enrich uranium for nuclear weapons'
9 December	US uses Spanish forces to intercept DPRK ship carrying missiles to Yemen. Forced to let ship on its way after strong protests from Yemeni government. Admits that it had no legal right to seize ship
12 December	DPRK government says that because of the cessation of heavy fuel oil agreed under the AF it will immediately 'resume the operation and construction of nuclear facilities to generate electricity'. However, it adds, 'Whether the DPRK re-freezes its nuclear facilities or not entirely depends on the attitude of the US'
14 December	DPRK writes to IAEA saying that 'The US has completely broken the DPRK–US Agreed Framework by giving up unilaterally its HFO supply obligation after systematically violating the Agreed Framework.' It argues that the freezing of the facilities was done under the AF, not in any agreement with IAEA, who should now remove their cameras
31 December	IAEA inspectors leave DPRK .
2003	
6 January	IAEA reiterates call for DPRK to 'give up any nuclear weapons program expeditiously and in a verifiable manner'
10 January	DPRK announces that it is reactivating its withdrawal from NPT because IAEA is a tool of US. However, it adds, 'Though we pull out of the NPT, we have no intention to produce nuclear weapons and our nuclear activities at this stage will be confined only to peaceful purposes such as the production of electricity'
18 January	DPRK Foreign Ministry bureau director O Song Chol claims Kelly 'framed-up' admission and that DPRK had expressly denied having an HEU programme
24 January	US TV reports plans to launch 600–800 cruise missiles against Iraq in the first two days of war. 'There will not be a safe place in Baghdad', said one Pentagon official
28 January	Japan reveals that 206kg of plutonium unaccounted for over 25 years
12 February	IAEA Board declares 'that the DPRK is in further non-compliance with its obligations under its Safeguards Agreement with the Agency'. Sends issue to UN Security Council

27 February	IAEA deplores that DPRK has 'restarted its nuclear reactor at Nyongbyong' [Yongbyon]
19 March	US and allies invade Iraq
10 April	UN Security Council expresses its 'concern' about the DPRK restarting
23 March	US imposes sanctions on DPRK companies for exports to Khan Research Laboratories in Pakistan
23–25 April	Three-Party talks held in Beijing as China effects a compromise between US demand for multilateral talks and DPRK demand for bilateral ones
25 April	*New York Times* reports that US officials say that North Koreans at Beijing talks privately said they had a nuclear arsenal
27 April	In CNN interview on Iraq and DPRK, IAEA Director General Mohamed ElBaradei calls for intrusive inspections 'to make sure that we will not be cheated once more in North Korea'
28 April	State Department spokesman Boucher claims that DPRK told US delegation it possessed nuclear weapons
30 April	KCNA in commentary on Beijing talks says that US demand that 'DPRK should scrap its nuclear program before dialogue' and 'verifiable inspection' is unacceptable. It calls on US to drop policy of hostility and notes that 'The Iraqi war proved that inspection is a prelude to a war'
2 May	President Bush lands on aircraft carrier to proclaim 'Mission Accomplished' and that Iraq is conquered. His pilot is subsequently killed in Iraq
12 May	Lengthy KCNA statement entitled 'US to blame for derailing process of denuclearisation on Korean Peninsula' outlines history of US and ROK nuclear weapon activities over the years, including large-scale military exercises
14 May	US Senate approves development of 'bunker-busters' and other nuclear devices
22 May	ElBaradei, in an essay entitled 'No nuclear blackmail' in the *Wall Street Journal*, calls for intrusive inspections because 'as now seems apparent – [DPRK] continued its clandestine pursuit of nuclear weapons'
3 June	Republican Representative Curt Weldon returns from trip to Pyongyang with ten-point peace plan. Claims this received enthusiastically in Pyongyang. The plan appears to have been rejected by Washington
4 June	Bolton, in testimony to House of Representatives committee says 'We continue to insist that North Korea must terminate its nuclear weapons program completely, verifiably, and irreversibly. And there will be no inducements to get them to do so.' CVID, 'complete, verifiable, irreversible dismantlement' of nuclear programmes before any concessions to Pyongyang becomes US mantra
9 June	KCNA reports 'The DPRK will build up a powerful physical deterrent force capable of neutralising any sophisticated and

	nuclear weapons with less spending unless the US gives up its hostile policy toward the DPRK'
20 June	Reports that US officials had privately told Japanese that DPRK possesses several small nuclear warheads for ballistic missiles
12 July	KCNA, in commenting on Powell's remarks that US insists on DPRK dismantlement of nuclear programme before dialogue, otherwise that would be 'rewarding bad behaviour', reiterates that it is building a nuclear deterrent for self-defence not for bargaining
21 July	US press reveals Pentagon plan 5030, an operations plan for military harassment of the DPRK just short of war
22 July	US again rejects non-aggression pledge
13 August	Secretary Powell is quoted as saying, 'We won't do non-aggression pacts or treaties, things of that nature'
25 August	Jack Pritchard, senior State Department official for North Korea resigns in protest at administration policy
27–29 August	First round of Six-Party talks end in acrimony. US wants CVID as first step, DPRK wants simultaneous steps to resolve issues. DPRK again denies it has an enriched uranium programme, but US insist that it has
2 September	China's senior envoy warns US policy is the biggest obstacle to progress
13 September	DPRK condemns PSI exercise 'Pacific Protector' as being 'aimed to intercept and seize DPRK-flagged ships in high seas'
17 September	Pyongyang marks anniversary of Kim–Koizumi summit with calls for Japan to honour 'Pyongyang Declaration'
18 September	US announces new sanctions on DPRK on grounds of alleged 'human trafficking'
19 September	IAEA General Conference urges 'the DPRK to completely dismantle any nuclear weapons programme in a prompt, transparent, verifiable and irreversible manner'
22 September	DPRK denounces US Missile Defense upgrade in ROK
23 September	US announces it has deployed new unmanned spy planes in the ROK as part of a $11 billion increase in spending
2 October	Pyongyang announces it has 'successfully finished the reprocessing of some 8,000 spent fuel rods' from the Yongbyon reactor
23 October	President Bush, on tour of Asia and Australia, says 'We're all willing to sign some sort of document, not a treaty, that says "we won't attack you", but he (DPRK leader Kim Jong-Il) needs to abandon his nuclear program, and do so in a verifiable way'
26 October	KCNA condemns White House veto of another trip by Representative Curt Weldon, already agreed by DPRK. Weldon was to visit Yongbyon reactor and KCNA asks, 'We wonder if the administration is not getting nervous about the possibility of the state of our nuclear activity being confirmed by the delegation'

27 October	DPRK Foreign Ministry says they are studying Bush's proposal but reiterates that simultaneous, confidence-building measures are the key to resolving the issues
4 November	ROK tries to keep KEDO reactor project suspended rather than cancelled
18 November	Rumsfeld on visit to Seoul brands DPRK as 'evil' for spending money on defence while people go hungry, and says US may use nuclear weapons in a conflict
21 November	KEDO suspends the Agreed Framework LWR project for further year
2 December	DPRK again calls for compensation for US failure to supply LWRs as pledged in Agreed Framework
18 December	ROK President Roh Moo-hyun says his government will not remain idle if the US tries to resolve the DPRK nuclear crisis 'with fists'
19 December	Libya, in deal with Britain and US apparently for lifting of sanctions and normalisation of relations, announces it is renouncing WMD programmes. Trumpeted as victory in Washington and London, and an example for North Korea, it later transpires that Libya's WMD intentions and capabilities have been 'sexed-up'
24 December	State Department announces that Joseph DeTrani has been appointed 'special envoy for negotiations with the DPRK'
28 December	ElBaradei visits Libya and decides it was far from producing nuclear weapons, nor had any enriched uranium been discovered by IAEA inspectors
2004	
6 January	Unofficial US delegation, Stanford Professor John Lewis, Los Alamos nuclear scientist Sigfried Hecker and former State Department official Jack Pritchard visit DPRK and are taken to Yongbyon
7 January	US press reports reveal that China does not believe US allegations that DPRK has enriched uranium weapons programme
15 January	Jack Pritchard, in discussion at Brookings Institution in Washington, says 'that China is skeptical of the United States approach on certain key points. It has publicly called on Washington to make concessions. It reportedly no longer accepts US claims about North Korea's highly enriched uranium program to create fissile material. And China has welcome North Korea's proposal to freeze its plutonium program, and it sees this as a good step, a good first step, one that the United States should welcome, not spurn'
21 January	John Lewis in interview with *Cincinnati Enquirer* says that the North Korean transcript of the meeting (in October between Kelly and Kang) quoted Kang as saying, 'We are entitled to have a nuclear program.' Lewis says that, in the Korean language, there is 'a small difference between to have and entitled to have'

21 January	Siegfried Hecker, in testimony to Senate Foreign Relations Committee says North Korean were adamant that they had no HEU programme. He also says that he is not convinced that 'Pyongyang can build a plutonium-based nuclear device'
21 January	Jack Pritchard, in op-ed in *New York Times*, criticises Bush administration for not negotiating with Pyongyang over the past year because it 'has relied on intelligence that dismissed North Korean claims that it restarted its nuclear program at Yongbyon with the express purpose of re-processing previously sealed and monitored spent fuel to extract plutonium to make a "nuclear deterrent"'
26 January	KCNA condemns news that US administration has research institutes to recommence work on small nuclear weapons
29 January	US expert Jon Wolfsthal commenting on China's reported scepticism of US allegations on HEU, notes, 'Now, quietly, South Korean officials are beginning to express the same doubts. Echoes of these doubts are being heard in Japan'
31 January	Pakistani scientist A. Q. Khan, known as the father of Pakistan's bomb, 'confesses' to passing uranium enrichment technology to North Korea, Iran and Libya
4 February	Official worries that the Khan affair 'may jeopardize the $3 billion US economic and military package promised by President George W. Bush in 2003 and may even result in the re-imposition of sanctions'
6 February	*New York Times* reports that US is 'irked' that 'China has refused to accept the US contention that North Korea is developing nuclear weapons based on highly enriched uranium'
11 February	Bush outlines fresh controls on trade in nuclear fuel on grounds that it may lead to weapons
12 February	ElBaradei, writing in *New York Times*, admits 'We must abandon the unworkable notion that it is morally reprehensible for some countries to pursue weapons of mass destruction yet morally acceptable for others to rely on them for security – and indeed to continue to refine their capacities and postulate plans for their use'
21 February	KCNA says *New York Times* story 'that a Pakistani nuclear expert visited the DPRK more than 10 times at the end of the 1990s to help it in the technology of developing nuclear weapons based on enriched uranium' is 'misinformation'. It adds, 'The story about the "enriched uranium program" much touted by the US is nothing but a whopping lie. The US ultra-neo-conservatives fabricated it after having a confab for more than 10 days in the wake of US presidential envoy Kelly's Pyongyang visit in October 2002'
25–28 February	Second round of Six-Party talks in Beijing. DPRK again denies HEU programme. Reports that US now wants to veto civilian nuclear programme.
4 March	*Washington Post* reveals that a 'curt directive' from the White House scuttled a Chinese-drafted joint statement at the end

	of the Six-Party talks because it contained a reference to DPRK complaints about the US 'hostile policy'
12 March	President Roh Moo-hyun impeached by National Assembly on trivial technicality; popularity soars
21 March	Pyongyang condemns impeachment of Roh, saying it has 'disturbed inter-Korean relations'
15 April	Reacting to impeachment, elections in South Korea bring in left-leaning assembly that puts 'the South Korean president in a stronger position than ever to adopt a more independent line towards Washington and a more conciliatory stance towards Pyongyang'
20 April	North Korean newspaper hails South Korean election, saying that with it 'victory of democratic patriotic forces' has 'dealt a heavy blow to the flunkeyist treacherous forces following the lead of outside forces and the separatist forces seeking confrontation'
28 April	*Washington Post* reports that US intelligence now estimates that DPRK has at least eight weapons and notes that 'the leap in Pyongyang's nuclear capabilities during President Bush's tenure could leave the administration vulnerable to charges that it has mishandled the North Korea crisis'
4 May	South Korean report about DPRK beginning work on deploying IRBMs with 3,000–4,000 km range, sufficient to reach 'vicinity of Hawaii'. Claimed that this is behind 'hastened development' of Missile Defense
13 May	South Korean newspaper *Donga Ilbo* reports on Rumsfeld's recent testimony to Senate Appropriations Defense Subcommittee on necessity to continue research on nuclear bunker busters
12–14 May	Working Group meeting of Six-Party talks. DPRK claims 'At the meeting the DPRK side clarified its will to maintain the general goal of the denuclearisation of the Korean peninsula and to freeze its nuclear facilities as the first-phase action and displayed utmost flexibility from a sincere stand to settle the issue at any cost. 'The DPRK's proposal of "reward for freeze" commanded support and sympathy from the majority of the participants in the meeting for its justice and fairness'
14 May	South Korean Constitutional Court overturns Roh's impeachment. *The Economist* notes that Roh's 'young, anti-establishment supporters share this antipathy towards the United States, and would rather accommodate North Korea than stand up to it'
29 May	Pyongyang claims that article in *New York Times* on 22 May alleging that it had sold uranium hexafluoride to Libya is a fabrication
1 June	Iran denies it has ever 'had nuclear relations with North Korea'
21 June	ElBaradei has meeting with Powell on Iran, Libya and North Korea

23–26 June	Third round of Six-Party talks. Some slight signs of progress
28 June	DPRK Foreign Ministry commends US side for not mentioning CVID and for promising to give serious consideration to DPRK proposal of 'reward for freeze', but concludes no substantial change in US position. It says issue can still be resolved 'If the US seriously studies the DPRK proposal "reward for freeze", drops its unreasonable assertion about an enriched uranium program and the like, commits itself to renounce its hostile policy toward the DPRK ... '. It adds, 'The DPRK will closely follow the US future attitude, pushing forward as planned the work to increase its capability for self-defence to cope with the threat of aggression from outside forces'
15 July	James Kelly, in lengthy prepared statement to Senate Foreign Relations Committee gives detailed description of US policy. Whilst there is some mention of 'corresponding measures' he reiterates that DPRK must dismantle nuclear programmes before US concessions, which are considerably less that those under the Agreed Framework. He insist that the 'HEU program', which the DPRK denies, must be included
21 July	KCNA condemns US moves to set up Missile Defense facilities in Central Europe
16 August	ElBaradei, in a statement to IAEA Board of Governors focusses on the 1992 declaration but makes no mention of alleged HEU programme
23 August	South Korea admits to IAEA that it had conducted experiments to produce enriched uranium in 2000, thus violating the North–South Joint Denuclearisation Declaration and the NPT. It also conducted experiments on plutonium separation in 1982
8 Sep	DPRK diplomat at UN, Han Sung Ryol, complains that US has a double standard, condoning ROK's uranium programme while condemning DPRK's 'non-existent' programme. He warns of a nuclear arms race in Northeast Asia.
11 September	DPRK says that there are 'strong suspicions that the disclosed [ROK nuclear] experiments might be conducted on the instructions of the United States as they were military in nature'
12 September	South Korea denies that it has a nuclear weapons programme
12 September	South Korean reports that North has conducted a nuclear test on 9 September. Subsequently admitted that it was a combination of blasting for a hydroelectric dam and a natural cloud formation some 90km away. US, which had withheld information from Seoul, confirmed North's explanation. Suspicions that story was 'sexed-up' to divert attention from SK nuclear revelations
13 September	ElBaradei, in a statement to IAEA Board of Governors, says, 'It is a matter of serious concern that the conversion and enrichment of uranium and the separation of plutonium were not reported to the Agency as required by the ROK

	safeguards agreement.' On DPRK he notes 'The Agency has never been allowed by the DPRK to verify the completeness and correctness of the DPRK's initial 1992 declaration'
20 September	ElBaradei says that 40 countries with peaceful nuclear programmes could retool them for weapons
22 September	North Korean defector Hwang Jang-yop tells South Korean National Assembly that North has been able to conduct underground nuclear tests since 1993. No such tests have been reported
22 September	Iran says that it will press ahead with producing uranium fuel for nuclear energy despite US objections and threats
23 September	Brazil continues to deny IAEA access to its enriched uranium program
23 September	South Korean reports that North may be about to test a missile. No test takes place. Suspicions that story was 'sexed-up' to divert attention from SK nuclear revelations
2 November	George W. Bush re-elected President of the United States
10 November	Task Force on US Korea Policy publishes *Ending the North Korean Nuclear Crisis*, its recommendations for the US negotiating position. Crucially this suggests leaving the HEU issue until trust has been built up
15 November	International Crisis Group publishes 'North Korea: where next for the nuclear talks?', its recommendations for the US negotiating position.
December	Article by Selig Harrison to be published in January/February 2005 issue of *Foreign Affairs* released. Harrison argues that no credible evidence to support HEU allegation has been produced

SOURCES

This timeline has been compiled from the following chronologies, supplemented by newspaper and journal reports, and US Congressional hearings.

Arms Control Organization. *Chronology of US–North Korean Nuclear and Missile Diplomacy*, June 2003.

Nautilus Institute. *DPRK timeline*. Available from www.nautilus.org/archives/DPRKbriefingbook/dprktimeline.html (last entry 19 April 2004)

Tokyo Physicians for Elimination of Nuclear Weapons. *Chronological Table of Nuclear Weapons*, 2003.

UCLA Asia Institute. *North Korean Nuclear Challenge – a Brief Chronology*, 7 March 2003.

Wampler, Robert A. (ed.). *North Korea and Nuclear Weapons: the Declassified US Record*. National Security Archive Electronic Briefing Book No. 87, 25 April 2003.

Notes

INTRODUCTION

1. 'North Korea has bigger harvest, but millions still need food aid'. World Food Programme press release, 23 November 2004.
2. 'DPRK hails end of "Arduous March"'. *People's Korea*, October 2000.
3. Hong, Jung-wook. 'Ultimate US goal is NK regime change'. *Korea Herald*, 24 February 2005.
4. US State Department. *Background Note: North Korea*, August 2004. Available from www.state.gov/r/pa/ei/bgn/2792.htm (accessed 14 December 2004)
5. Gilman, Benjamin A. 'Gilman releases North Korea Report'. Press release, 3 November 1999.
6. 'J. Kelly failed to produce "evidence" in Pyongyang; framed up admission story. Interview with DPRK FM Director O Song Chol.' *People's Korea*, 19 January 2003.
7. Harrison, Selig S. 'Did North Korea cheat?' *Foreign Affairs,* January/February 2005.
8. Pollack, Jonathan D. 'The United States, North Korea, and the end of the Agreed Framework'. *Naval War College Review*, Vol. LVI, No. 3, 2003.
9. Harrison, 'Did North Korea cheat?'
10. Le Leu, Seth. *North Korea – An Enigma and an Opportunity*, Salvation Army, 19 November 2004.
11. Willoughby, Robert. 'Friendship glows amid flickering lights'. *Guardian Weekly*, 10–16 April 2003.
12. Zellweger, Kathi. '45th visit to the DPRK (17 to 28 February 2004)'. *Caritas*, 21 July 2004.
13. Worthington, Jim. *An American in Rajin*, July 2001. Available from www.vuw.ac.nz/~caplabtb/dprk/Worthington.htm (accessed 15 December 2004)
14. Hecker, Siegfried S. *Visit to the Yongbyon Nuclear Scientific Research Center in North Korea*. Washington, DC: Senate Committee on Foreign Relations, 2004.
15. Sigal, Leon V. 'North Korea's tactics'. Nautilus Policy Forum, 15 February 2005.
16. 'Pyongyangites welcome S. Korean defector'. KCNA (Korean Central News Agency), 23 February 2005.
17. Na, Jeong-ju. 'NK defectors seeking to move to US'. *Korea Times*, 17 November 2004.
18. Park, Song-wu. 'Poverty forces over 50% of NK defections'. *Korea Times*, 5 December 2004.
19. 'Aiding North Korean defectors becomes a business'. *JoongAng Ilbo*, 22 November 2004.

1 THE ROOTS OF MODERN KOREA

1. 'Blasphemy against Tangun under fire'. KCNA, 15 December 2001.
2. Yoo, Dong-ho. 'Park viewed to be next GNP leader'. *Korea Times*, 22 February 2004. Choe had the nickname of 'Choetler' because of alleged similarities between his political style and that of Adolph Hitler.
3. 'Pyongyang eager to get Koguryo Tomb Murals registered as world heritage'. *People's Korea*, 12 May 1999; Lee,Yong-sung. 'Koguryo Tombs may become world heritage'. *Korea Times*, 18 January 2004.
4. 'Data-wise overseas Korean society'. *People's Korea*, 27 October 1999.
5. *Omniglot Guide to Writing Systems: Korean*. Omniglot.com, 2004. Available from www.omniglot.com/writing/korean.htm (accessed 2004)
6. Kim, Hyun-chul. 'Two Koreas break ground in Gaeseong'. *Korea Herald*, 30 June 2003. 'Gaesong' is the new official southern spelling of Kaesong.
7. Demick, Barbara. 'Korea or Corea? debate is historical, political'. *Seattle Times*, 17 September 2003.
8. Fairbank, John K., Edwin O. Reischauer and Albert M. Craig. *East Asia, the Modern Transformation*. London: Allen & Unwin, 1965, p. 72.
9. Brooke, James. 'Courtship of Beijing and Seoul: a new twist for an old bond'. *New York Times*, 26 February 2004.
10. 'Korea's China play'. *Business Week*, 29 March 2004.
11. Baker, Don. 'Looking for God in the streets of Seoul: the resurgence of religion in 20th century Korea'. *Harvard Asia Quarterly*, Vol. 5, No. 4, 2001.
12. Ibid.
13. Personal observation in July 2001.
14. Cho, M. A. 'First Russian orthodox church to be established in North Korea'. *KOTRA*, 11 June 2003.
15. 'President Kim Dae Jung gives banquet'. *People's Korea*, 15 June 2000.
16. Cumings, Bruce. *Korea's Place in the Sun: a Modern History*. New York: W. W. Norton, 1997.
17. Madsen, Wayne. 'Moon shadow: the Rev, Bush & North Korea'. *Counterpunch*, 14 January 2003.
18. 'Pyonghwa builds NK auto plant'. *Financial Times*, 7 April 2002.
19. Belke, Thomas J. *Juche: a Christian Study of North Korea's State Religion*. Bartlesville, OK: Living Sacrifice Book Company, 1999.
20. Art, Robert J. and Patrick M. Cronin (eds). *The United States and Coercive Diplomacy*. Washington, DC: United States Institute of Peace, 2003.
21. Fairbank et al., *East Asia*, p. 312.
22. '"Iron Silkroad" to connect Korean Peninsula and Europe envisaged'. *Yonhap News*, 16 June 2000.
23. 'Treaty of Annexation of Korea by Japan'. USC-UCLA Joint East Asian Studies Center, *East Asian Studies Documents*, 22 August 1910.
24. Na, Jeong-ju. '"Comfort Women" to mark 600th Wednesday rally'. *Korea Times*, 16 March 2004.
25. 'Japan's brazen-faced distortion of history'. KCNA, 18 March 2004.
26. Soh, Ji-young. 'Comfort Women's frustrating struggle continues'. *Korea Times*, 17 March 2004.

27. Park, Song-wu. 'Japan collaborators face probe'. *Korea Times*, 2 March 2004.
28. Ryu, Jin. 'Speaker faces charges of dad working for colonial Japan'. *Korea Times*, 15 March 2004.
29. Lee, Wha Rang. 'War of liberation continues: South Korea is still a Japanese colony. The sons and daughters of pro-Japanese traitors rule South Korea'. *Kimsoft*, March 2004.
30. 'Japanese PM visits "Yasukuni Shrine"; DPRK warns against Japan's trend toward militarism'. *People's Korea*, 17 January 2004.
31. Lee, Young-jong. 'North silent on new GNP head'. *JoongAng Ilbo*, 25 March 2004.
32. Yoon, Won-sup. 'GNP young turks propose active support for NK'. *Korea Times*, 1 March 2004.
33. Fairbank et al., *East Asia*, p.763.
34. Ibid., p. 763.
35. 'Rightwing' and 'pro-US' are not the same and we may find a growth in rightwing nationalism in Korea.
36. Captured by the Soviets in 1945 he was subsequently handed over to the Chinese and, in another act of Confucian pragmatism, finished his life as a gardener in Beijing, an example of the magnanimity of the new government. His ghosted autobiography was subsequently made into a famous film by Bernardo Bertolucci in 1987.
37. Fairbank et al., *East Asia*. p. 792.
38. Cumings, *Korea's Place in the Sun*, p. 160.
39. Ibid., p.187.
40. Ibid., p. 187. Rusk later went on to become Secretary of State 1961–69, and an architect of the US–Vietnam War.
41. Showa Emperor Hirohito, 'Emperor Hirohito, accepting the Potsdam Declaration, radio broadcast'. Federal Communications Commission, 14 August 1945.
42. Cumings, *Korea's Place in the Sun*,. p. 199.

2 YEARS OF STRUGGLE, YEARS OF HOPE

1. Hoare, James, and Susan Pares. *Conflict in Korea: an Encyclopedia*. Santa Barbara, CA: ABC-CLIO, 1999.
2. Cumings, Bruce. *Korea's Place in the Sun: a Modern History*. New York: W. W. Norton, 1997, p. 204.
3. Ibid., p. 303.
4. Choe, Sang-Hun. 'Last communist rebel dies in South Korea'. Associated Press, 2 April 2004.
5. Rang, Lee Wha. 'The Mt Kuwoi partisans'. *Korea Web Weekly*, 5 February 2004.
6. This was more important to the DPRK because it gave it a virtual embassy in the United States.
7. Acheson, Dean. *Present at the Creation: My Years at the State Department*. New York: W. W. Norton, 1969, pp. 355–8.
8. The term 'military-industrial complex' was popularised by Dwight Eisenhower in his valedictory speech. Eisenhower, Dwight D. 'Farewell

Address to the Nation (17 January 1961)'. Available from www. eisenhower.archives.gov/farewell.htm (accessed 24 February 2003)

9. Planning for a postwar occupation of Korea started within six months of Pearl Harbor; Cumings, Bruce. *North Korea: Another Country*. New York: New Press, 2003, p. 122.

10. Schaller, Michael. 'The Korean war: the economic and strategic impact on Japan, 1950–1953'. In William Stueck (ed.) *The Korean War in World History*. Lexington, KY: University of Kentucky Press, 2004; Halevi, Joseph. 'US militarism and imperialism and the Japanese "Miracle"'. *Monthly Review*, Vol. 53, No. 4, 2001.

11. Cumings, Bruce and Kathryn Weathersby. 'Bruce Cumings and Kathryn Weathersby: an exchange on Korean War origins'. Cold War International History Project, Bulletin 6–7, 11 July 1995.

12. Stone, I. F. *The Secret History of the Korean War*. New York: Monthly Review Press, 1952.

13. See in particular his dispute with Kathryn Weathersby; Cumings and Weathersby, 'Bruce Cumings and Kathryn Weathersby'.

14. Cumings, *Korea's Place in the Sun*. p. 252.

15. 'Gen. Shin detained over embezzlement'. *Korea Times*, 9 May 2004.

16. Norris, Robert S., Hans M. Kristensen and Joshua Handler. 'North Korea's nuclear program 2003'. *Bulletin of the Atomic Scientists*, Vol. 59, No. 2, 2003, pp. 74–7.

17. Staines, Reuben. 'US trained for strikes on NK'. *Korea Times*, 7 November 2004.

18. Kwon, Soon-Taek. 'Research on nuclear weapons to destroy bunker is necessary'. *Donga Ilbo*, 13 May 2004.

19. 'Large-scale US–South Korea landing exercise in S. Korea'. KCNA, 28 March 2004.

20. Yoo, Yong-won. 'North fires surface to ship missile'. *Chosun Ilbo*, 26 February 2003.

21. Glantz, James. 'This tme it's real: an antimissile system takes shape'. *New York Times*, 4 May 2004.

22. Woollacott, Martin. 'How America's right bears the longest grudge'. *Guardian*, 27 February 2004.

23. 'The truth comes out: ulterior motive at work in '50s, '60s'. *Asahi Shimbun*, 19 May 2004.

24. Oberdorfer, Don. *The Two Koreas: a Contemporary History*, second edition. New York: Basic Books, 2001, p. 32.

25. Kim was subsequently tried and executed. It is said that Chun Doo-hwan thought he was a US CIA agent. There are currently moves afoot in ROK to honour him officially for his 'contribution to democracy'. 'Honors to Kim Jae-kyu'. *Korea Herald*, 19 May 2004.

26. Oh, John Kie-chiang. 'The Kwangju Uprising'. *Korea Times*, 17 May 2001.

27. Park, Song-wu. 'GNP leader may visit NK as special envoy'. *Korea Times*, 30 April 2004.

28. 'How the South views its brother from another planet'. International Crisis Group, 2004.

29. Gregg, Donald P. 'Angst and opportunities on the Korean Peninsula'. *Korea Society Quarterly*, Vol. 4, No. 1, 2004.

30. Kang, Seok-jae. 'Report says 10,000 spies sent to North'. *Korea Herald*, 31 October 2000.

31. Chi, Minnie. 'Preview of "Silmido": blowback on the Korean Peninsula'. *Asia Media*, 2004; Lee, Chul-hee. 'Film recalls bloody rebellion'. *JoongAng Ilbo*, 19 January 2004; MacIntyre, Donald. 'Korea's dirty dozen'. *Time Asia*, Vol. 159, No. 19, 2002.

32. *Joint Statement of North and South*, 4 July 1972. Available from http://210.145.168.243/pk/011th_issue/97100103.htm (accessed 2004)

33. Smith, Craig. Roots of Pakistan atomic scandal traced to Europe'. *New York Times*, 19 February 2004.

34. Pollack, Jonathan D. 'The United States, North Korea, and the end of the Agreed Framework'. *Naval War College Review*, Vol. LVI, No. 3, 2003.

35. Ryu, Jin. 'N. Korea did not deny HEU program: officials'. *Korea Times*, 2004.

36. Hoare and Pares, *Conflict in Korea*, p. 236.

37. Relations were restored on 8 May 2000.

38. Park, Song-wu. 'Politicians to head for May 18 Cemetery in Kwangju'. *Korea Times*, 17 May 2004.

39. 'Chun, Roh, others sentenced in S. Korean "trial of century"'. *CNN Interactive*, 26 August 1996.

40. 'Happy in Insein'. *JoongAng Ilbo*, 9 October 2003.

41. Taylor, Walter A. 'Korea: one place where things go right for U.S.'. *US News & World Report*, 2 April 1984.

42. Hoare and Pares, *Conflict in Korea*, p. 237.

43. Pike, John. *US Forces Korea – Exercises*. GlobalSecurity.org, 2003. Available from www.globalsecurity.org/military/ops/ex-usfk.htm (accessed 21 May 2004)

44. Larson, Eric V., Norman D. Levin, Seonhae Baik and Bogdan Savych. *Ambivalent Allies? A Study of South Korean Attitudes Toward the US*. Santa Monica, CA: Rand Corporation, 2004, p. 17.

45. Mansourov, Alexandre. 'North Korea goes nuclear, Washington readies for war, South Korea holds key'. Nautilus Institute Policy Forum, 9 December 2002.

46. *Nuclear Non-Proliferation Treaty*. International Atomic Energy Agency, 1968. Available from www.iaea.org/Publications/Documents/Infcircs/Others/infcirc140.pdf (accessed 2003)

47. *Statement by the Chinese Delegation on the Issue of Negative Security Assurances*. Preparatory Committee for the 2000 Review Conference of the Parties to the Treaty on the Non-Proliferation of Nuclear Weapons, second session, 1998. Available from www.basicint.org/nuclear/NPT/1998prepcom/98NSA-chinese.htm (accessed 23 May 2004)

48. *US Nuclear Policy: 'Negative Security Assurances'*. Arms Control Association, 2002. Available from www.armscontrol.org/factsheets/negsec.asp (accessed 23 May 2004)

49. Ibid.

50. Soh, Ji-young. 'Court orders disclosure of files on KAL bombing'. *Korea Times*, 3 February 2004.
51. *Patterns of Global Terrorism 2003*. Washington, DC: US State Department, 2004.
52. 'China, South Korea exchange greetings on anniversary of forging ties'. *People's Daily*, 24 August 2002.
53. Sanger, David E. and William J. Broad. 'South Koreans say secret work refined uranium'. *New York Times*, 3 September 2004.
54. Harrison, Selig S. *Korean Endgame: a Strategy for Reunification and US Disengagement*. Princeton, NJ: Princeton University Press, 2002.
55. *Hecker Testimony Transcript*. Washington, DC: Senate Committee on Foreign Relations, 2004.
56. 'Intelligence service calls nukes primitive at best'. *JoongAng Ilbo*, 16 February 2005.
57. 'NK's Taepodong missiles could be operational by 2015: LaPorte'. *Korea Times*, 10 March 2005.
58. *Opening Statement at Hearing on the North Korean Nuclear Calculus: Beyond the Six Power Talks*. Washington, DC: Senate Committee on Foreign Relations, 2004.
59. 'John Kerry on national security'. *Guardian,* 28 May 2004.
60. Pollack, 'The United States, North Korea'.
61. Harrison, *Korean Endgame*. Harrison was instrumental in arranging the Carter visit.
62. Oberdorfer, *The Two Koreas*, p. 113.
63. Ri, Tae Sun. 'North–South talks in 1990s'. *Tongil Pyongron via People's Korea*, 30 March 1999.

3   CREATION OF THE AGREED FRAMEWORK

1. Weisman, Steven R. and David E. Sanger. 'US to tie North Korea aid to dismantling of weapons'. *International Herald Tribune*, 20 February 2004.
2. Allison, Graham. '94 deal with North Korea holds lessons for today'. *New York Times*, 20 July 2004.
3. Oberdorfer, Don. *The Two Koreas: a Contemporary History*, second edition. New York: Basic Books, 2001, pp. 288–9.
4. Staines, Reuben. 'US trained for strikes on NK'. *Korea Times*, 7 November 2004.
5. Shin, Hye-Jin. *Economic Significance of North Korea's Designation as a Terrorism-Supporting Nation by the US: An Obstacle to North Korea–US Trade Expansion*. Washington, DC: KOTRA, 2001.
6. Pritchard, Charles 'Jack'. 'Statement before the Senate Foreign Relations Committee hearing on North Korea', 15 July 2004.
7. Sigal, Leon V. 'North Korea is no Iraq: Pyongyang's negotiating strategy'. *Arms Control Today,* December 2002.
8. Rumsfeld, Donald. *Commission to Assess the Ballistic Missile Threat to the United States*. Washington, DC, 1998.
9. Ibid.; *Iran Missile Update 2004*. Wisconsin Project On Nuclear Arms Control, March–April 2004. Available from www.wisconsinproject. org/countries/iran/missile2004.htm (accessed 16 December 2004)

10. *Worldwide Ballistic Missile Inventories.* Arms Control Association, May 2002. Available from www.armscontrol.org/factsheets/missiles.asp (accessed 3 August 2004)

11. 'North Korean scientists on DPRK artificial satellite technology'. *People's Korea*, 11 September 1998.

12. When the DPRK test-launched a shore-to-ship missile in Febarury 2003 Japan was given advance warning. Yoo, Yong-won. 'North fires surface to ship missile'. *Chosun Ilbo*, 26 February 2003.

13. Reiss, Mitchell B. 'Negotiating with North Korea: lessons learned (and relearned?)'. Nautilus Institute Policy Forum, 30 January 2003.

14. Armitage, Richard L. 'A comprehensive approach to North Korea'. National Defense University, Institute for Strategic Studies, *Strategic Forum*, No. 159, 1999.

15. Pritchard, Charles 'Jack'. 'What I saw in North Korea'. *New York Times*, 21 January 2004.

16. Perry, William J. *Review of United States Policy Toward North Korea: Findings and Recommendations, Unclassified Report by Dr William J. Perry, US North Korea Policy Coordinator and Special Advisor to the President and the Secretary of State 1999.* Washington, DC: US Department of State, 1999.

17. Wit, Joel S., Daniel B. Poneman and Robert L. Gallucci. *Going Critical: the First North Korean Nuclear Crisis.* Washington, DC: Brookings Institution Press, 2004.

18. Gilman, Benjamin A. 'Gilman releases North Korea report'. Press release, 3 November 1999.

19. Moon, Chung-in and David I. Steinberg (eds) *Kim Dae-jung Government and Sunshine Policy: Promises and Challenges.* Seoul: Yonsei University Press, 1999.

20. Oberdorfer, *The Two Koreas*, p. 279.

21. Jagan, Larry. 'Kim Dae-jung: a political profile'. BBC, 13 June 2000.

22. Kim, Dae-jung. *Address by President Kim Dae-jung of the Republic of Korea at the School of Oriental and African Studies London University.* London [s.n.], 1998.

23. Kim, Dae-jung. *Inaugural Address*, 25 February 1998.

24. *Address by President Kim Dae-jung of the Republic of Korea, Lessons of German Reunification and the Korean Peninsula.* Presented at the Free University of Berlin, 9 March 2000.

25. Oberdorfer, *The Two Koreas*, p. 273.

26. Ibid., p. 324.

27. Seo, Soo-min. 'Ex-unification minister slams US policy toward North Korea'. *Korea Times*, 28 January 2004.

28. 'Sunshine policy still valid: Kim Dae-jung'. *Nihon Keizai Shinbum*, 26 March 2004.

29. Brooke, James. 'Koreans look to China: seeing a market and a monster'. *New York Times*, 10 February 2004.

30. For Kim Jong Il's comments on Kim Dae-jung, see ibid.

31. *Kim Dae-jung – Biography.* Nobel e-Museum, 2002. Available from www. nobel.se/peace/laureates/2000/dae-jung-bio.html (accessed 2003)

32. Oberdorfer, *The Two Koreas*, p. 135.

33. Ranard, Donald A. 'Kim Dae Jung's close call: a tale of three dissidents'. *Washington Post*, 23 February 2003. Ranard claims that it was Ambassador Habib and his father acting at kilter with Kissinger's policy that secured Kim's rescue.

34. Yun, Philip W. 'Facing the Bogeyman: a Korean American diplomat recounts his trips to North Korea'. *Korea Society Quarterly*, Vol. 4, No. 1, 2004. pp. 6–14.

35. Perry, *Review of United States Policy Toward North Korea*.

36. 'South Korean media heads interview Kim Jong Il'. *Chosun Ilbo* via Kimsoft, 12 August 2000.

37. '10 years of DPRK with Songun policy'. *People's Korea,* 17 July 2004.

38. Shim, Jae-yun. 'NK to reduce armed forces by 500,000'. *Korea Times*, 15 October 2002.

39. Zellweger, Kathi. 'Caritas and the North Korean crisis', *Korea Society Quarterly*, Vol. 4, No. 1, 2004.

40. 'NK death tolls "exaggerated"'. *Korea Times*, 21 March 2004.

41. Natsios, Andrew S. *Statement at Senate hearings on life in North Korea.* US Senate, Subcommittee on East Asian and Pacific Affairs, 5 June 2003.

42. Smith, Hazel *Overcoming Humanitarian Dilemmas in the DPRK (North Korea)*. Washington, DC: United States Institute of Peace, July 2002.

43. 'There nothing news in Kim Dae Jung's "Berlin Declaration"': Pyongyang–Seoul urged to show positive changes in action (sic)'. *People's Korea*, 24 March 2000.

44. Na, Jeong-ju. 'Independent counsel for "Cash-for-Summit"'. *Korea Times*, 16 March 2003.

45. 'Roh urges efforts to open pilot complex in NK' *Yonhap* via KOTRA, 31 July 2004.

46. Kim, Dae-jung. 'Welcoming remarks by President Kim Dae-jung of the Republic of Korea at a dinner he hosted in Pyongyang'. Korean Information Service, 14 June 2000.

47. 'S. Korean naval warships commit military provocation'. KCNA, 15 November 2000; Sah, Dong-seok. 'Seoul denies sending boats into NK waters'. *Korea Times*, 15 November 2000.

48. Reyes, Alejandro. 'A big song and dance', *AsiaWeek*, Vol. 26, No. 31, 2000.

49. Adam, Werner. 'Pants off to North Korea'. *Frankfurter Allgemeine Zeitung*, 6 September 2000.

50. 'US censured for its brigandish act'. KCNA, 5 September 2000.

51. 'US declares end of hostility to DPRK'. *People's Korea*, 14 October 2000.

52. Perlez, Jane. 'Albright receives a spectacular welcome to North Korea'. *New York Times*, 24 October 2000.

4   CRISIS REIGNITED

1. Hong, Jung-wook. 'Ultimate US goal is NK regime change'. *Korea Herald*, 24 February 2005.

2. Rusling, M. 'Japan tests North Korea sanctions waters'. *Asia Times Online*, 3 March 2005.

3. Cody, Edward. 'China protests US–Japan accord'. *Washington Post*, 21 February 2005; Park, Shin-hong. 'Minister's visit to Japan canceled due to disputes'. *JoongAng Ilbo*, 5 March 2005.

4. Editorial. 'George W. Bush victory'. *Korea Times*, 8 November 2000.

5. White, Michael. 'Britain prepares for a cooling of the "special relationship"'. *Guardian*, 8 November 2000.

6. 'President Kim hopes to meet US President-elect soon'. *Korea Times*, 8 November 2000.

7. Sohn, Suk-joo. 'Opposition irked by Powell's breach of protocol'. *Korea Times*, 9 March 2001.

8. Friedman, Thomas L. 'Macho on North Korea'. *New York Times*, 9 March 2001.

9. Bush, George W. *Statement by the President* [on North Korea Policy Review]. Washington, DC: White House, 2001.

10. Abramowitz, Morton I. , James T. Laney and Robert A. Manning. *Testing North Korea: the Next Stage in US and ROK policy*. Washington, DC: Council on Foreign Relations, 2001.

11. Sigal, Leon V. 'North Korea is no Iraq: Pyongyang's negotiating strategy'. *Arms Control Today*, December 2002.

12. 'Kim Jong Il stresses economic renovation with new thinking'. *People's Korea*, 25 January 2001.

13. 'Kim tours tech firms in Shanghai'. *AsiaTimes Online*, 18 January 2001.

14. 'DPRK–Russia Moscow Declaration'. *People's Korea*, 7 August 2001.

15. 'US in great panic'. KCNA, 12 September 2001.

16. 'DPRK stance towards terrorist attacks on U.S'. KCNA, 12 September 2001.

17. Oh, Young-jin. 'Has Pyongyang missed golden opportunity?' *Korea Times*, 18 September 2001.

18. 'DPRK signs anti-terror conventions'. *People's Korea*, 13 December 2001; 'DPRK ready to join 5 more anti-terror pacts'. *People's Korea*, 25 December 2001.

19. Oh, Young-jin and Key-young Son. 'NK sent US private cable on anti-terrorism'. *Korea Times*, 23 September 2001.

20. Ramesh, Randeep. 'The two faces of Rumsfeld'. *Guardian*, 9 May 2003.

21. 'US sees more arms ties between Pakistan and Korea'. *New York Times*, 14 March 2004.

22. *Special Briefing on the Nuclear Posture Review*. Washington, DC: Department of Defense, 2002.

23. Bleek, Philipp C. 'Nuclear posture review leaks: outlines targets, contingencies'. *Arms Control Today*, April 2002.

24. *Nuclear Posture Review* [excerpts by GlobalSecurity.org]. Washington, DC: Department of Defense, 2002.

25. Ibid., p. 16.

26. 'KCNA on US reckless nuclear war scenario'. KCNA, 13 March 2002.

27. 'US view of DPRK and Agreed Framework'. *Napsnet Daily Report*, 19 March 2002.

28. 'DPRK non-certification', *Napsnet Daily Briefing*, 20 March 2002.

29. Bush, George W. *State of the Union Address 2002*. Presented at the White House, 29 January 2002. Washington, DC: White House.
30. Parry, Nat. 'Bush and the end of reason'. *ConsortiumNews*, 17 June 2003.
31. Sigal, 'North Korea is no Iraq'.
32. Monbiot, George. 'Our lies led us into war'. *Guardian*, 20 July 2004. Monbiot is focussing on the British media, but his argument is extendable across the Atlantic.
33. Wolfsthal, Jon B. 'Crying wolf on Iraqi WMD costs US credibility on North Korea'. *Christian Science Monitor*, 29 January 2004.
34. Significantly, perhaps, he cut his teeth on ways to preserve monopolies of power early in his career, 'after law school, he established a relationship with Senator Jesse Helms, the North Carolina Republican, and he worked on a campaign that sought to counter a voter registration drive on behalf of blacks and organized labor. Marquis, Christopher. 'Absent from the Korea talks: Bush's hard-liner'. *New York Times*, 2 September 2003 (editor's note appended 12 September).
35. Sigal, 'North Korea is no Iraq'.
36. See, for instance, Article 51, Chapter VII of the Charter of the United Nations.
37. 'Top EU delegation visits DPRK'. *People's Korea*, 12 May 2001.
38. 'EU to set up diplomatic ties with DPRK'. *People's Korea*, 26 May 2001.
39. Editorial, 'Now, ball is in US court'. *Korea Times*, 4 May 2001.
40. Perlez, Jane. 'Fatherly advice to the President on North Korea'. *New York Times*, 10 June 2001.
41. Shorrock, Tim. 'Carlyle's tentacles embrace Asia'. *AsiaTimes Online*, 20 March 2002.
42. 'Pyongyang stresses developed ties with EU; 1st anniv. of DPRK visit by top-level del. marked'. *People's Korea*, 11 May 2002.
43. 'Japanese Prime Minister Koizumi to visit Pyongyang to meet DPRK leader Kim Jong Il'. *People's Korea*, 4 September 2002.
44. Pollack, Jonathan D. 'The United States, North Korea, and the end of the Agreed Framework'. *Naval War College Review*, Vol. LVI, No. 3, 2003.
45. 'Koizumi aides clash over N. Korea policy for Bush talks', *Kyodo*, 27 May 2003.
46. For a selection of articles see *Special Report: Koizumi Visits North Korea*. Asia Source, 2002. Available from www.asiasource.org/news/at_mp_ 02.cfm?newsid=86610 (accessed 13 August 2004)
47. Clark, Gregory. 'Abduction issue – rightwing's political football'. *Japan Times*, 27 February 2004.
48. Pollack, 'The United States, North Korea'.
49. Ibid.
50. *James A. Kelly Biography*. Washington, DC: US State Department, 22 May 2001.
51. Boucher, Richard. *North Korean Nuclear Program*. Washington, DC: US State Department, 16 October 2002.
52. Pollack, 'The United States, North Korea'.

53. Hersh, Seymour M. 'The cold test: what the administration knew about Pakistan and the North Korean nuclear program'. *New Yorker*, 27 January 2003.

54. 'Re-imposition of sanctions feared: US aid may be jeopardized – official'. *Dawn*, 5 February 2004.

55. Sanger, David E. 'US sees more arms ties between Pakistan and Korea', *New York Times*, 14 March 2004.

56. Ibid.

57. 'Remarkably, North Korea's efforts to acquire uranium technologies, that is, a second path to nuclear weapons, and their efforts to weaponize their nuclear material do not violate the 1994 Agreed Framework.' Gilman, Benjamin A. 'Gilman releases North Korea report'. Press release, 3 November 1999.

58. 'S. Korea says North's nuclear accusation "absolutely untrue"'. *Yonhap*, 12 September 2004.

59. Oh, Young-jin. 'Cultural differences often stump US diplomats in handling NK'. *Korea Times*, 14 November 2002.

60. Pritchard, Charles 'Jack'. *The North Korea Deadlock: a Report from the Region*. Presented at the Brookings Institution, Washington, DC, 15 January 2004.

61. Steinberg, James (moderator), Richard Buss, Jae Ho Chung, Ivo Daalder, Don Oberdorfer and Michael O'Hanlon. 'Challenge for the Bush administration: dealing with a nuclear North Korea (transcript)'. *Brookings Institution Forum*, 14 January 2003.

62. 'US says N.Korea atomic program more advanced'. *New York Times*, 14 February 2004.

63. Oh, 'Cultural differences'.

64. Editorial. 'Kahn's nuclear confession'. *Korea Herald*, 10 February 2004.

65. Katagiri, Noriyuki. 'North Korea's nuclear programme: analyzing "confessional diplomacy"'. *CDI.org*, 28 October 2002; French, Howard W. 'North Korea's confession: why?' *New York Times*, 21 October 2002.

66. *Briefing on Democratic People's Republic of Korea*. London: Campaign for Nuclear Disarmament, July 2003.

67. 'N Korean nuclear "admission" in doubt'. BBC Asia Pacific, 18 November 2002.

68. 'Conclusion of non-aggression treaty between DPRK and US called for'. KCNA, 25 October 2002.

69. 'J. Kelly failed to produce "evidence" in Pyongyang: framed up admission story. Interview with DPRK FM Director O Song Chol'. *People's Korea*, 19 January 2003.

70. Goodby, James E. 'Negotiating with a nation that's really gone nuclear'. *Washington Post*, 15 February 2004.

71. Goodman, A. 'Official: Spain perplexed by Scud decision'. CNN, 11 December 2002.

72. Woollacott, Martin. 'At least Korea is united over one thing – anger at the US'. *Guardian*, 20 December 2002.

73. 'Perle quits Pentagon advisory board'. *New York Times*, 26 February 2004.
74. Kelley, Matt. 'Pentagon: N. Korea not mobilizing army'. *Kansas City Star*, 31 January 2003.
75. 'Japan's insincerity makes DPRK reconsider moratorium on missile launch: FM spokesman'. *People's Korea*, 30 November 2002.
76. 'Statement of DPRK government on its withdrawal from NPT'. KCNA, 10 January 2003.
77. Auster, Bruce B., Kevin Whitelaw and Thomas Omestad. 'Upping the ante for Kim Jong Il; Pentagon Plan 5030, a new blueprint for facing down North Korea'. *US News and World Report, Nation & World*, 21 July 2003.
78. 'DPRK to put spurs to increasing its nuclear deterrent force for self-defence'. KCNA, 18 June 2003.
79. 'War criminal should be judged'. KCNA, 10 June 2003.
80. 'KCNA refutes US smear campaign'. KCNA, 10 June 2003.
81. 'KCNA on DPRK's nuclear deterrent force'. KCNA, 9 June 2003.
82. Pritchard, Charles 'Jack'. 'What I saw in North Korea'. *New York Times*, 21 January 2004.
83. Seo, Soo-min. 'North Korea may complete uranium program in 1–2 years'. *Korea Times*, 26 January 2004.
84. Hecker, Siegfried S. *Visit to the Yongbyon Nuclear Scientific Research Center in North Korea*. Washington, DC: Senate Committee on Foreign Relations, 2004.
85. Kessler, Glenn. 'More N. Korean bombs likely, US official says'. *Washington Post*, 16 July 2004.
86. Hecker, *Visit to the Yongbyon Nuclear Scientific Research Center*.
87. Schifferes, Steve. 'US splits deepen over North Korea'. *BBC News World edition*, 18 June 2003.
88. 'Spokesman for DPRK foreign ministry on prospect of six-party talks'. KCNA, 16 August 2004.
89. Shim, Jae-yun. 'US seeks North Korea's surrender'. *Korea Times*, 16 February 2004.
90. 'Article 9 hindering US ties, bid for UNSC seat: Armitage'. *Japan Times*, 23 July 2004.
91. Eum, Tae-min and Myo-ja Ser. 'Park's 1970s nuclear arms program revealed'. *JoongAng Ilbo*, 2 August 2004.
92. Cossa, Ralph A. 'North Korea: searching for A. Q. Kim'. *Korea Times*, 12 July 2004.
93. 'Richard L. Armitage: US won't relent on North Korean nuke issue'. *Asahi Shimbun*, 7 February 2004.
94. 'Rumsfeld clears Musharraf of nuclear trafficking'. *New York Times*, 28 March 2004.
95. Kessler, Glenn. 'Chinese not convinced of North Korean uranium effort'. *Washington Post*, 7 January 2004; Wolfsthal, 'Crying wolf on Iraqi WMD'; 'China irks US in stand on North Korean weapons'. *New York Times*, 6 February 2004.

96. 'Inter-Korean summit looms'. *Korea Times*, 8 August 2004; 'Koreas may hold summit next month, ex-lawmaker says'. *Korea Herald*, 13 August 2004.
97. Choi, Hoon, and Seong-jae Min. 'Roh: 6-way talks, then summit'. *JoongAng Ilbo*, 4 December 2004.

INTRODUCTION TO PART II

1. Eberstadt, Nicholas. 'What surprise? The nuclear core of North Korea's strategy'. *Washington Post*, 1 March 2005.

5   THE HUMAN RIGHTS RECORD

1. Beaumont, Peter. 'PM admits graves claim "untrue"'. *Observer*, 18 July 2004.
2. On Iraq – Fisk, Robert. 'This looming war isn't about chemical warheads or human rights: it's about oil'. *Independent*, 18 January 2003; On Sudan – Laughland, John. 'The mask of altruism disguising a colonial war'. *Guardian*, 2 August 2004.
3. Nye, Joseph S. 'The decline of America's soft power'. *Foreign Affairs*, May/June 2004.
4. Kessler, Glenn. 'State Dept. study cites torture of prisoners'. *Washington Post*, 1 March 2005.
5. Ibid.
6. Jehl, D. and D. Johnston. 'Rule change lets C.I.A. freely send suspects abroad to jails'. *New York Times*, 6 March 2005.
7. Cody, Edward. 'China, others criticize US report on rights; double standard at State Dept. alleged'. *Washington Post*, 4 March 2005.
8. 'Full text of human rights record of the US in 2004'. *People's Daily*, 3 March 2005.
9. 'US termed world's biggest human rights abuser'. KCNA, 30 March 2004.
10. 'Foreign Ministry spokesman refutes U.S. report on human rights'. KCNA, 6 March 2005.
11. Pilger, John. 'Calling the humanitarian bombers to account'. *CounterPunch*, 11–12 December 2004.
12. Shanker, Thom and Gary Schmitt. 'Pentagon weighs use of deception in a broad arena'. *New York Times*, 13 December 2004.
13. Yu Tae-jun is also spelt Yu Tae-chun.
14. 'Former North Korean was "publicly executed"'. *Human Rights Without Frontiers* website, 28 February 2003.
15. Foster-Carter, Aidan. 'They shoot people, don't they?'. *Asia Times Online*, 22 March 2001.
16. Seo, Soo-min. 'Video footage shows defector alive in NK'. *Korea Times*, 31 August 2001.
17. 'Defector pardoned by NK leader, mother says'. *Korea Times*, 15 February 2002.

18. Ser, Myo-ja. 'Twice he fled North: now jail awaits'. *JoongAng Ilbo*, 24 May 2003.
19. Kang, Seok-jae. 'Report says 10,000 spies sent to North'. *Korea Herald*, 31 October 2000.
20. Breen, Michael. 'So, we spied on North Korea after all'. *Korea Times*, 5 October 2000.
21. *Facts and Figures on the Death Penalty.* Amnesty International, 17 December 2004. Available from http://web.amnesty.org/pages/deathpenalty-facts-eng (accessed 19 December 2004)
22. 'Singapore's execution rate decried'. *Arizona Daily Star*, 15 January 2004.
23. Huggler, Justin. 'Axis of execution: American justice ranked alongside world's most repressive regimes'. *Independent*, 7 April 2004.
24. Frenkiel, Olenka. Within prison walls'. BBC, 30 January 2004.
25. Barnett, Antony. 'Revealed: the gas chamber horror of North Korea's gulag'. *Observer*, 1 February 2004.
26. Borger, Julian. 'US intelligence fears Iran duped hawks into Iraq war'. *Guardian*, 25 May 2004.
27. 'Britain voices concerns over NK human rights violation reports'. *Yonhap*, 17 February 2004.
28. 'DPRK and the BBC'S evidence'. *Financial Times*, 15 February 2004.
29. 'Lawmakers slam leniency on NK abuses'. *Korea Herald*, 18 February 2004.
30. Koehler, Joseph. '"Camp 22" document a fake?'. *The Marmot's Hole*, 3 February 2004.
31. Soh, Ji-young'NK used prisoners to test chemical weapons'. *Korea Times*, 12 February 2004.
32. Croddy, Eric. 'Vinalon, the DPRK, and chemical weapons precursors'. *Center for Nonproliferation Studies Issue Brief*, 4 February 2003.
33. Frenkiel, 'Within prison walls'.
34. 'China should not deport refugee'. *Korea Times*, 11 February 2004.
35. 'Defector returned to N Korea'. *BBC World*, 31 March 2004.
36. 'Truth behind false report about "Experiment of Chem. Weapons on Human Bodies" in DPRK disclosed'. KCNA, 30 March 2004. This was also described in a slightly different way in *People's Korea* on 10 April: Kang, Byong Sop and Song Hak Kang. 'We make false documents of showing chemical weapons testing on prisoners'. *People's Korea*, 10 April 2004.
37. Kang and Kang, 'We make false documents'.
38. 'Defector "faked" gas chamber documents'. *Age*, 1 April 2004.
39. Frenkiel, 'Within prison walls'.
40. Williams, Peter and David Wallace. *Unit 731: the Japanese Army's Secret of Secrets.* London: Hodder & Stoughton, 1989.
41. 'Police probe Porton Down deaths'. BBC, 18 October 1999; Evans, Rob and Sandra Laville. 'Porton Down unlawfully killed airman in sarin tests'. *Guardian*, 16 November 2004.
42. Sweeney, Fionnuala. 'International correspondents – Olenka Frankiel'. CNN, 8 February 2004.
43. Ibid.

44. Staines, Reuben. 'Seoul won't address NK human testing'. *Korea Times*, 3 August 2004.
45. Staines, Reuben. 'Seoul pressed to address claims of human experiments in NK'. *Korea Times*, 2 August 2004.
46. Staines, 'Seoul won't address NK human testing'.
47. For instance, Fic, Victor. 'North Korea human rights crisis'. *Korean Web Weekly*, 2004; *North Korean Human Rights Act of 2004*. Washington, DC: House of Representatives of the United States, 2004; McCormack, Gavan. 'Gulags on both sides of the DMZ'. ABC Radio National *Book Talk*, 1 March 2003; Lee, Brian. 'US harshly condemns North for rights abuse'. *JoongAng Ilbo*, 2 March 2005.
48. Hawk, David. *The Hidden Gulag: Exposing North Korea's Prison Camps Prisoners' Testimonies and Satellite Photographs*. Washington, DC: US Committee for Human Right in North Korea, 1 November 2003.
49. Woodward, Bob. *Bush at War*. New York: Simon & Schuster, 2002.
50. *Summary of Concerns for 1999*. London: Amnesty International, 1 February 1999.
51. Khan, Irene. *Open Letter to Newly Elected Members of the 17th National Assembly: a Historic Opportunity to Consolidate Human Rights Gains*. London: Amnesty International, 2 July 2004.
52. *Summary of Concerns for 1999*.
53. Suh, Sung. *Unbroken Spirits: Nineteen Years in South Korea's Gulag*. New York: Rowman and Littlefield, 2001.
54. McCormack, 'Gulags on both sides of the DMZ'.
55. Ibid.
56. 'The truth comes out: ulterior motive at work in '50s, '60s'. *Asahi Shimbun*, 19 May 2004.
57. McCormack, 'Gulags on both sides of the DMZ'.
58. Ibid.
59. Vallot, Daniel. 'Political reform eludes South Korea'. *Le Monde Diplomatique* (English version), November 1999, p. 12.
60. Kim, Rahn. 'Foreign democracy fighters to pay tribute to Koreans'. *Korea Times*, 8 September 2004.
61. Kim, Hyeon-gyeong and In-sung Chun. 'Song Du-yul is freed after court of appeals overturns treason case'. *JoongAng Ilbo*, 22 July 2004.
62. Lee, Jin-woo. 'Professor Song leaves for Germany'. *Korea Times*, 5 August 2004.
63. Na, Jeong-ju. 'MBC program creates stir over Song'. *Korea Times*, 14 July 2004.
64. 'Song Du-yul's release'. *Korea Times*, 22 July 2004.
65. Khan, Irene. *Open Letter to Acting President Goh Kun – Continued Use of the Draconian National Security Law: Amnesty International's Concerns about Professor Song Du-Yul's Case*. London: Amnesty International, 1 April 2004.
66. Baker, Don. 'Looking for God in the streets of Seoul: the resurgence of religion in 20th century Korea'. *Harvard Asia Quarterly*, Vol. 5, No. 4, 2001.
67. Ostling, Richard N. 'Papal nod to a Christian boom: Protestants and Catholics are thriving in the "hermit kingdom"'. *Time*, Vol. 123, 1984, p. 54.

68. Weingartner, Erich. 'A chronicle of the dialogue between Christians in North and South Korea'. *Mennonite Central Committee Peace Office Newsletter*, Vol. 30, No. 3, 2000.

69. Barnett, 'Revealed: the gas chamber horror'.

70. Borrie, Don. 'Reflections on a visit to the Democratic Peoples' Republic of Korea, 9-19 April, 2004'. In *Study Leave Report to the Presbyterian Church of Aoteroa/New Zealand*. Wellington: Study Leave Report to the Presbyterian Church of Aoteroa/New Zealand, 2004.

71. Ibid.

72. Zellweger, Kathi. '45th visit to the DPRK (17 to 28 February 2004)'. *Caritas*, 21 July 2004.

73. Cho, M. A. 'First Russian orthodox church to be established in North Korea'. KOTRA, 11 June 2003.

74. 'Russian provincial government of Primorskii Krai donates US$10,000 for the construction of a Russian [Orthodox church in Pyongyang]'. ITAR-TASS via KOTRA, 18 August 2004.

75. Belke, Thomas J. *Juche: a Christian Study of North Korea's State Religion.* Bartlesville, OK: Living Sacrifice Book Company, 1999, p. xiv.

76. Namkung, K A. *The Bush Administration's North Korea Policy and the Opening of the American Mind.* Presented at the Korean Forum Foundation, Los Angeles, 15 May 2002.

77. 'N. Korea wants illuminated church crosses removed'. *New York Times*, 23 August 2004.

78. Borrie, 'Reflections on a visit'.

79. MacLaren, D. 'Caritas celebrates 10 years of activity in the DPRK'. Caritas press statement, 8 March 2005.

80. 'US: no normal relations with N. Korea'. *New York Times*, 15 July 2004.

81. At the time of writing, in August 2004, neither had passed through Senate.

82. 'The Korean civil society statement on human rights'. *The Korean Civil Society Statement* (by email), April 2004.

83. Park, Song-wu. 'Uri Party assails US human rights bill'. *Korea Times*, 25 July 2004.

84. 'SK lawmakers decry NK human rights act'. *Ohmynews*, 21 August 2004.

85. Lunch hosted by Wellington Regional Chamber of Commerce and Korea–NZ Business Council, Wellington, 27 August 2004.

86. Smith, Hazel. 'Brownback bill will not solve North Korea's problems'. *Jane's Intelligence Review*, February 2004, pp. 42–5.

87. 'North Korea has bigger harvest, but millions still need food aid'. World Food Programme press release, 23 November 2004.

88. *North Korea Human Rights Act of 2004.*

89. 'UNEP launches first report on the State of the Environment in the DPR Korea'. United Nations Environment Programme press release, 27 August 2004.

90. 'North Korea has bigger harvest'.

91. Arie, Sophie, and Jason Burke. 'Who cares?' *Observer*, 15 August 2004.

92. 'Electricity shortage acute in Korea'. KCNA, 30 January 2003.
93. Roberts, Les, Riyadh Lafta, Richard Garfield, Jamal Khudhairi and Gilbert Burnham. 'Mortality before and after the 2003 invasion of Iraq: cluster sample survey'. *Lancet*, 29 October 2004.
94. Lee, C. H. 'NK makes all-out effort to solve food shortage problem'. KOTRA, 20 February 2003.
95. 'Seoul, Washington in talks over Kaesong Industrial Complex'. *Yonhap* via KOTRA, 6 August 2004.
96. Jung, Sung-ki. 'N. Korea–China trade volume soars 40.5%'. *Korea Times*, 17 November 2004.
97. Cortright, David. 'A hard look at Iraq sanctions'. *Nation*, 3 December 2001.
98. Vick, Karl. 'Children pay cost of Iraq's chaos'. *Washington Post*, 21 November 2004.
99. 'WFP survey shows high prevalence of food insecurity in Iraq'. World Food Programme news release, 28 September 2004.
100. 'North Korea has bigger harvest'.
101. Vick, 'Children pay cost'.
102. *Annual Performance Report for 2003*. Rome: World Food Programme, 2004, Annex VII.B.
103. Krugman, Paul. 'The martial plan'. *New York Times*, 21 February 2003.
104. As of November 2004 RK had spent $1.23 billion on KEDO, followed by Japan with $406 and the US with $406 million; Staines, Reuben. 'Freeze on NK reactor project extended'. *Korea Times*, 26 November 2004.
105. 'Humanitarian aid of $462 million provided to NK under Kim DJ'. *Chosun Ilbo*, 12 February 2003.
106. 'Sunshine policy still valid: Kim Dae-jung'. *Nihon Keizai Shinbum*, 26 March 2004.
107. *MSF in North Korea*. Médicins sans Frontières Available from www.msf.org/countries/index.cfm?indexid=22D113E8-BEC7-11D4-852200902789187E (accessed 17 June 2003)
108. 'DPRK will accept humanitarian offer'. KCNA, 5 October 1998.
109. Terry, Fiona. 'Feeding the dictator'. *Guardian*, 6 August 2001.
110. Woollacott, Martin. 'Humanitarians must avoid becoming tools of power'. *Guardian*, 2 April 2004.
111. Hyder, Masood. 'In North Korea, first, save lives'. *Washington Post*, 4 January 2004.
112. Ibid.
113. *Report on the DPRK Nutrition Assessment 2002*. Pyongyang: Central Bureau of Statistics, DPRK, 2002.
114. Ibid.
115. Ibid.
116. Ibid.
117. Vick, 'Children pay cost'.
118. Smith, Hazel. 'Improving intelligence on North Korea'. *Jane's Intelligence Review*, April 2004, pp. 48–51.

119. 'Rice aid eyed if North responds'. *Asahi Shimbun*, 18 May 2004; 'Tokyo to cut off food aid, plans sanctions on North'. *JoongAng Ilbo*, 11 December 2004.

120. *Foreign Operations, Export Financing, and Related Programs Appropriations Act*. Washington, DC: US Senate, 2004.

121. Zellweger, Kathi. 'Caritas and the North Korean crisis'. *Korea Society Quarterly*, Vol. 4, No. 1, 2004.

122. Ibid.

123. Le Leu, Seth. *North Korea – An Enigma and an Opportunity*. Salvation Army, 19 November 2004. Available from www.salvationarmy.org/ihq/www_sa.nsf/vw-news/CA5C57C922E0173F80256F5100464D2B?open document (accessed 7 December 2004)

124. Ibid.

125. See especially the publications and websites of the WFP and FAO. A convenient portal is ReliefWeb which links the UN agencies: www.reliefweb.int/w/rwb.nsf

126. *Consolidated Inter-Agency Appeal 2003, DPRK*. New York: United Nations, 2003.

127. 'German doctor plans anti-N. Korean protest ahead of 6-party talks'. *Yonhap*, 13 February 2004.

128. Vollertsen, Norbert. 'South Korea's spoilers'. *Wall Street Journal*, 22 August 2003.

129. Kim, Dae-jung. *Address by President Kim Dae-jung of the Republic of Korea, Lessons of German Reunification and the Korean Peninsula*. Presented at the Free University of Berlin, 9 March 2000.

130. Vollertsen, 'South Korea's spoilers'.

131. Na, Jeong-ju. 'NK defectors seeking to move to US'. *Korea Times*, 17 November 2004.

132. Staines, Reuben. 'China repatriates 70 defectors to NK'. *Korea Times*, 9 November 2004.

133. Brooke, James. 'China fears once and future kingdom'. *New York Times*, 25 August 2004; Staines, Reuben. 'History dispute over Koguryo deepens: China's disintegration fears drive diplomatic friction'. *Korea Times*, 6 August 2004.

134. Kim, Rahn. 'China aims to expand territory by distorting history'. *Korea Times*, 18 August 2004.

135. 'NK hits China for laying claim on Koguryo kingdom'. *Korea Times*, 27 August 2004.

136. 'Aiding North Korean defectors becomes a business'. *JoongAng Ilbo*, 22 November 2004.

137. Lee, Hyo-sik. 'Inter-Korean income gap widens to 15.5 times'. *Korea Times*, 9 December 2004.

138. 'Aiding North Korean defectors'.

139. Ser, Myo-ja. 'US explains North Korean refugee policy'. *JoongAng Ilbo*, 18 November 2004.

140. Park, Song-wu and Reuben Staines. 'US court rejects NK defector's asylum bid'. *Korea Times*, 24 November 2004.

141. '3 of 4 defectors here on welfare, data say'. *JoongAng Ilbo*, 3 October 2004.

142. 'Mongolia under pressure to serve as haven for refugees'. *New York Times*, 21 November 2004.
143. Na, 'NK defectors seeking to move to US'.
144. Park and Staines, 'US court rejects NK defector's asylum bid'.
145. Park, Song-wu. 'Poverty forces over 50% of NK defections'. *Korea Times*, 5 December 2004.
146. Korean Peace Network. Letter of appeal to the American public [advertisment]'. *New York Times*, 27 October 2004.
147. 'US special forces "inside Iran"'. BBC, 17 January 2005.
148. Choe, Sang-Hun. 'Last communist rebel dies in South Korea'. Associated Press, 2 April 2004.
149. Roberts et al., 'Mortality before and after the 2003 invasion of Iraq'; Vick, 'Children pay cost of Iraq's chaos'.
150. 'Conservatives' protest'. *JoongAng Ilbo*, 4 October 2004.
151. Yuh, Ji-yeon. 'North Korean refugees'. Personal communication with the author, 29 November 2004.
152. Ibid.

6   DRUGS AND GENERALS

1. Engel, Matthew. 'Drugs and forgery "sustain North Korean economy"'. *Guardian*, 20 January 2003.
2. Spaeth, Anthony. 'To fund his lifestyle-and his nukes-Kim Jong Il helms a vast criminal network'. *Time*, 9 June 2003.
3. Nartker, Mike. 'North Korea: Pyongyang funds WMD programs by selling drugs, counterfeit currency'. *Global Security Newswire*, 16 May 2003.
4. Miller, Judith and William J. Broad. 'US analysts link Iraq labs to germ arms'. *New York Times*, 21 May 2003.
5. Beaumont, Peter and Antony Barnett. 'Blow to Blair over "mobile labs"'. *Observer*, 8 June 2003.
6. The Editors. 'The *Times* and Iraq'. *New York Times*, 26 May 2004.
7. 'Seoul, Washington in talks over Kaesong Industrial Complex'. *Yonhap* via KOTRA, 6 August 2004.
8. Gilman, Benjamin A. *North Korea Advisory Group Report to the Speaker US House of Representatives*. Washington, DC: North Korea Advisory Group, 1999.
9. *International Narcotics Control Strategy Report 2003*. Washington, DC: US State Department, 2004.
10. Engel, 'Drugs and forgery'.
11. Wortzel, Larry M. 'North Korea's connection to international trade in drugs, counterfeiting, and arms'. Senate Governmental Affairs Subcommittee on Financial Management, Budget, and International Security, 20 May 2003.
12. Kim, Ki-tae. 'Australia tough on NK's illegal trafficking'. *Korea Times*, 20 June 2003.
13. 'Australia to spend up to $450m on cruise missiles'. *Sydney Morning Herald*, 26 August 2004.

14. Wortzel, 'North Korea's connection', p. 6.
15. Former North Korean high-level government official. 'Testimony'. Senate Governmental Affairs Subcommittee on Financial Management, Budget, and International Security, 20 May 2003.
16. Foster-Carter, Aidan. 'Beware defective tales of defectors'. *Asia Times online*, 23 May 2003.
17. Veteran Intelligence Professionals for Sanity. 'Intelligence fiasco'. *Dissentvoice.org*, 2 May 2003.
18. Lee, Jung-min. '2 defectors' appearance in US was news to Seoul'. *JoongAng Ilbo*, 4 June 2003.
19. Gittelsohn, John. 'Defections and doubts'. *OCRegister.com*, 8 June 2003. Lee refers to Lee Bok-koo, the alias of one of the defectors who testified.
20. Seoul and Washington are also wrangling over top defector Hwang Jang-yop whom the Americans want to be allowed to come to Washington to testify. South Korea, knowing the uses to which he will be put, is resisting. 'Washington ups ante in defector's travel'. *JoongAng Ilbo*, 19 June 2003.
21. Spaeth, 'To fund his lifestyle'.
22. Nartker, 'North Korea'.
23. *International Narcotics Control Strategy Report 2003*.
24. Kim, 'Australia tough'.
25. Gittelsohn, John. 'Defections and doubts'. *OCRegister.com*, 8 June 2003.
26. *International Narcotics Control Strategy Report 2003*.
27. 'Gangster behind heroin ship, court told'. MSNNine.Com, 19 November 2003; Carbonell, Rachel. 'Pong Su crew to sue'. Australian Broadcasting Commission, 5 March 2004.
28. Simpson, Cam. 'N. Korea drug-trade charges in question'. *Chicago Tribune*, 10 March 2004.
29. Ibid.
30. Jolley, Mary Ann. 'North Korea – Pong Su'. Australian Broadcasting Commission, 27 July 2004.
31. McCoy, Alfred and David Barsamian (interviewer). 'The CIA and the politics of narcotics'. *Prevailing Winds Research*, 17 February 1990.
32. Smith, David. 'Britain's war on drugs is naive, says US'. *Guardian*, 1 August 2004.
33. Stillwater, Jane. '"American" Afghanistan's three major crops: opium, human organs and children'. *Baltimore Chronicle*, 27 August 2004.
34. *Terrorism in the United States 1999*. Washington, DC: Federal Bureau of Investigation, 2000.
35. Gilfeather, Paul. 'Fallujah napalmed'. *Sunday Mirror*, 24 November 2004.
36. Cumings, Bruce. *Korea's Place in the Sun: a Modern History*. New York: W. W. Norton, 1997, p. 145.
37. Ibid., p. 197.
38. Park, Myung-lim. 'The internalization of the Cold War in Korea'. *International Journal of Korean History*, Vol. 2, 2001.
39. Ibid.

40. Kang, Seok-jae. 'Report says 10,000 spies sent to North'. *Korea Herald*, 31 October 2000.

41. Shanker, Thom. 'In Iraq, US learned how to scare top North Korean'. *New York Times*, 11 May 2003.

42. Lee, Chul-hee. 'Film recalls bloody rebellion'. *JoongAng Ilbo*, 19 January 2004; MacIntyre, Donald. 'Korea's dirty dozen'. *Time Asia*, 20 May 2002.

43. 'Honors to Kim Jae-kyu'. *Korea Herald*, 19 May 2004.

44. Oberdorfer, Don. *The Two Koreas: a Contemporary History*, second edition. New York: Basic Books, 2001, p. 114.

45. 'South Korean media heads interview Kim Jong Il'. *Chosun Ilbo via Kimsoft,* 12 August 2000. Park Jung Hee is the Northern spelling of Park Chung-hee

46. Johnson, Marguerite. 'No words for the bitterness: a nation in mourning points a finger at its northern neighbor'. *Time*, 24 October 1983.

47. *Wicked Creatures of the Global Village: a Fanatic Terrorist Junta*. Seoul: Liberal Review Press, 1983.

48. *Kim Dae-jung – Biography*. Nobel e-Museum, 2002. Available from www.nobel.se/peace/laureates/2000/dae-jung-bio.html (accessed 2003)

49. Clark, Gregory. 'Label that foils compromise'. *Japan Times, 2002.*

50. 'Tears and anger: Flt. 858 recalled'. *JoongAng Ilbo*, 30 November 2004.

51. Park, Song-wu. 'KAL bombing constant source of dispute'. *Korea Times*, 11 July 2004.

52. Park, Song-wu. 'Anti-spy agency to reinvestigate suspicious cases'. *Korea Times*, 26 August 2004.

53. *North Korea on the Terrorism List*. Washington, DC: Congressional Research Service, 2004.

54. *Patterns of Global Terrorism 2003*. Washington, DC: US State Department, 2004.

55. Ibid.

56. MacKinnon, Rebecca. 'Interview with Selig Harrison'. *North Korea Zone*, 4 May 2004.

57. Roberts, Les, Riyadh Lafta, Richard Garfield, Jamal Khudhairi and Gilbert Burnham. 'Mortality before and after the 2003 invasion of Iraq: cluster sample survey'. *Lancet*, 29 October 2004.

58. Struck, Doug. 'US focuses on N. Korea's hidden arms'. *Washington Post*, 23 June 2003.

59. Kwon, Soon-Taek. 'Research on nuclear weapons to destroy bunker is necessary'. *Donga Ilbo*, 13 May 2004.

60. '"He has learnt from the past year": responses to George Bush's non-proliferation programme'. *Guardian*, 17 February 2004.

61. MacAskill, Ewen. 'Minister's mission to North Korea'. *Guardian*, 10 September 2004.

62. Agrawal, Brahm Swaroop. 'Korean nuclear controversy'. *Korea Times*, 2 June 2004.

63. Norton-Taylor, Richard. 'Nuclear weapons treaty may be illegal'. *Guardian*, 27 July 2004; Kim, Myong-chol. *US, UK Are in Material Breach of Nuclear Non-Proliferation Treaty that Bans Transfer of Nuclear Hardware, Software to any Recipient*. Center for Korean-American Peace,

2004. Available from http://cfkap.com/commentary/072804US_UK_ violateNPT.html (accessed 21 December 2004)

64. *World Military Expenditures and Arms Transfers.* Washington, DC: US State Department, 2003. See also Appendix II.

65. *ECN Site Lines: Porton Down.* Environmental Change Network. Available from www.ecn.ac.uk/ecnnews/ecnnews9/ecnews93.htm (accessed 7 December 2004)

66. Gilman, *North Korea Advisory Group Report.*

67. *Chemical and Biological Weapons Site – North Korea.* Center for Defense Information, 16 November 2000. Available from www.cdi.org/issues/ cbw/NorthKorea.html (accessed 7 December 2004)

68. *Chemical and Biological Weapons Site – North Korea.* Center for Defense Information, 16 November 2000. Available from www.cdi.org/issues/ cbw/NorthKorea.html (accessed 7 December 2004)

69. Ibid.

70. Shim, Jae-yun. 'US warns of collapse of 1994 Nuke Accord'. *Korea Times,* 29 August 2002.

71. Chipman, John. 'North Korea's weapons programmes: a net assessment'. International Institute for Strategic Studies, press release, 21 January 2004.

72. Endicott, Stephen and Edward Hagerman. *The United States and Biological Warfare.* Bloomington and Indianapolis, IN: Indiana University Press, 1998.

73. Wald, Matthew L. 'CIA denies being source of anthrax'. *Los Angeles Times,* 17 December 2001.

74. Wolf, John S. 'Iraq update and other nonproliferation issues'. *State Department Briefing,* 7 February 2003.

75. Appendix II, Table A2.3.

76. 'Possible sale of Patriot PAC-3 to South Korea, Netherlands'. US Department of Defense release, 9 November 1999.

77. Seong, Chaiki. 'A decade of economic crisis in North Korea: impacts on the military'. *Korea Institute for Defense Analyses Papers,* Vol. 3, 2003.

78. Perkins, Alvin A. *US Policy towards North Korea with respect to Ballistic Missiles.* Carlisle, PA: US Army War College, 10 April 2001.

79. *Worldwide Ballistic Missile Inventories.* Arms Control Association, May 2002. Available from www.armscontrol.org/factsheets/missiles.asp (accessed 3 August 2004)

80. Boese, Wade. 'GAO says feds lax in countering cruise missile, UAV threats'. *Arms Control Today,* April 2004.

81. Perkins, *US Policy towards North Korea.*

82. Ibid.

83. Cotton, James. 'North Korea's nuclear and missile proliferation and regional security'. *Australian Parliamentary Library Current Issues,* Vol. 1999–2000, No. 1, 1999.

84. *Strong at Home, Respected in the World: the 2004 Democratic National Platform for America.* Democratic Platform Committee, 27 July 2004.

85. Harrison, Selig S. 'Inside North Korea: leaders open to ending nuclear crisis'. *Financial Times,* 4 May 2004. The official DPRK Foreign Ministry response to Cheney's remarks was inchoate, and a sad contrast to

Harrison's lucid report; 'DPRK foreign ministry spokesman blasts Cheney's anti-DPRK remarks'. KCNA, 18 April 2004.

86. Rumsfeld, Donald. *Commission to Assess the Ballistic Missile Threat to the United States*. Washington, DC, 1998.

87. Myrah, John M. 'The proliferation of ballistic missiles: what should we do to stop it?'. *Commission to Assess the Ballistic Missile Threat to the United States; Appendix III: Unclassified Working Papers*, 15 July 1998.

88. Ibid.

89. Harrison, Selig S. 'Missile capabilities in Northeast Asia: Japan, South Korea and North Korea'. *Commission to Assess the Ballistic Missile Threat to the United States; Appendix III: Unclassified Working Papers*, 15 July 1998.

90. Ignatius, David. 'Weapons we can't afford'. *Washington Post*, 12 October 2004.

91. Rumsfeld, *Commission*.

92. 'KCNA on first artificial satellite of DPRK'. *People's Korea*, 8 September 1998.

93. Samore, Gary. 'US–DPRK missile negotiations'. *Nonproliferation Review*, Vol. 9, No. 2, 2002.

94. 'Japan's insincerity makes DPRK reconsider moratorium on missile launch: FM spokesman'. *People's Korea*, 30 November 2002.

95. *Nodong Launch Facility*. Federation of American Scientists, 25 March 2000. Available from www.fas.org/nuke/guide/dprk/facility/nodong.htm (accessed 6 December 2004)

96. Evans, Michael. 'Spy pictures show Korea's empty threat'. *Times*, 12 January 2000.

97. Kim, Min-seok and Myo-ja Ser. 'North reported to be preparing missile launch'. *JoongAng Ilbo*, 23 September 2004.

98. Harrison, 'Inside North Korea'.

99. 'NK's Taepodong missiles could be operational by 2015: LaPorte'. *Korea Times*, 10 March 2005.

100. Eberstadt, Nicholas and Judith Bannister. *The Population of North Korea*. Berkeley, CA: Institute of East Asian Studies, University of California at Berkeley, 1992, pp. xii–xiv.

101. Hersh, Seymour M. 'The cold test: what the administration knew about Pakistan and the North Korean nuclear program'. *The New Yorker*, 27 January 2003.

102. Beal, Tim. 'Journey to a far away place: personal observations of a visit to North Korea'. *New Zealand Journal of East Asian Studies*, Vol. VI, No. 1, 1998, pp. 105–19.

103. Cumings, *Korea's Place in the Sun*, pp. 270, 286–8.

104. Oberdorfer, *The Two Koreas*, p. 101.

105. Ibid., p. 103.

106. Kim, Min-seok and Byung-gun Chae. 'Defense gurus downplay risk of North's guns'. *JoongAng Ilbo*, 5 October 2004.

107. Yoo, Dong-ho. 'US to cut 12,500 troops by 2008'. *Korea Times*, 10 October 2004.

108. 'Dispute over N. Korea military briefly halts Assembly audit'. *Korea Herald*, 6 October 2004.

109. Ibid.
110. Hwang, Dong Jong. *The ROK National Defense Improvement: Goals and Directions for the Next Decade*. Seoul: Korea Institute for Defense Analysis, 2004.
111. Stockholm International Peace Research Institute. *Military Expenditure Database 2004*. Stockholm: SIPRI, 2004. Available from http://web.sipri. org/contents/milap/milex/mex_data_index.html (accessed 11 October 2004)
112. Ser, Myo-ja. 'Russian tanks to face off along demilitarized zone'. *JoongAng Ilbo*, 9 March 2004.
113. Campbell, Kurt, Derek Mitchell and Carola McGiffert. *Conventional Arms Control on the Korean Peninsula*. Washington, DC: Center for Strategic and International Studies, 2002.
114. MacIntyre, Donald. 'Kim's war machine'. *Time Asia*, 24 February 2003.
115. Harrison, Selig S. *Korean Endgame: a Strategy for Reunification and US Disengagement*. Princeton, NJ: Princeton University Press, 2002.
116. Yoo, Dong-ho. 'US may launch surgical strikes on NK'. *Korea Times*, 5 October 2004.
117. Lee, Brian. 'US envoy sees no chance of raid on North'. *JoongAng Ilbo*, 7 October 2004.
118. 'South Korea's arms buildup under fire'. KCNA, 5 October 2004.
119. Lee, Young-jong. 'Plan to cope with fall of North divulged'. *JoongAng Ilbo*, 4 October 2004.
120. Oberdorfer, *The Two Koreas*, p. 35.
121. Ibid., p. 118.
122. Ibid., pp. 122–5.
123. Krauthammer, Charles. 'A better defense'. *Washington Post*, 20 August 2004.
124. Harrison, *Korean Endgame*, p. xxiv.
125. Yoo, Dong-ho. 'Parties caught again in secret ammunition leakage'. *Korea Times*, 11 October 2004.
126. Eisenhower, Dwight D. 'Farewell Address to the Nation (17 January 1961)'. Available from www.eisenhower.archives.gov/farewell.htm (accessed 24 February 2003)
127. 'False military report'. *Korea Times*, 18 July 2004. See also Ryu, Jin. 'Military to be probed for coverup of NK radio messages'. *Korea Times*, 16 July 2004; Ryu, Jin. 'Navy covered up hotline failure, says Defense Chief'. *Korea Times, 25 July 2004.
128. For recent DPRK statements on the Songun policy see '10 years of DPRK with Songun policy'. *People's Korea,* 17 July 2004; 'Rodong Sinmun on unique idea and theory in socio-class relations'. KCNA, 13 August 2004. For a standard Western perspective see Aidan Foster-Carter, 'North Korea: guns or butter?' Nautilus Institute Policy Forum, 6 April 2004.
129. Lee, Brian. 'Defense to cost 99 trillion won through 2008'. *JoongAng Ilbo*, 19 November 2004; Yoon, Won-sup. 'More self-reliant defense posture envisioned'. *Korea Times*, 18 November 2004.
130. Hwang, J. J. 'USFK unveils plan for forces buildup'. *Korea Herald*, 2 June 2003.

131. Choi, Hoon. 'Roh sees little threat in future on peninsula'. *JoongAng Ilbo*, 16 November 2004.
132. Lee, Young-jong and Ser Myo-ja. 'Pyeongyang regime is stable, says top aide on North Korea'. *JoongAng Ilbo*, 2004.

7   THE NUCLEAR CONFRONTATION

1. *IAEA In Focus*. International Atomic Energy Authority, 2004. Available from www.iaea.org/NewsCenter/Focus/index.html (accessed 8 October 2004)
2. Oberdorfer, Don. *The Two Koreas: a Contemporary History*, second edition. New York: Basic Books, 2001, pp. 268–78.
3. Wit, Joel S., Daniel B. Poneman and Robert L Gallucci. '"Lessons learned: the road ahead" from going critical: the first North Korean nuclear crisis'. Nautilus Institute Policy Forum, 24 June 2004.
4. Wit, Joel S., Daniel B. Poneman and Robert L. Gallucci. *Going Critical: the First North Korean Nuclear Crisis*. Washington, DC: Brookings Institution Press, 2004, p. 43.
5. Not without some Parthian shots. On Cheney he said, 'Yes, the rumors that Cheney is alive are somewhat exaggerated. It's Mark Twain in reverse.' He also commented, 'I think maybe we foreigners should have the right to vote in your next election, since we are so dependent on you.' Solomon, Deborah. 'What weapons? Questions for Hans Blix'. *New York Times*, 28 March 2004
6. Williams, Ian. 'Boutros-Ghali bites back (a review of *Unvanquished: A US–UN Saga* by Boutros Boutros-Ghali)'. *Nation*, 14 June 1999.
7. 'IAEA chief in South Korea for nuclear talks'. *New York Times*, 3 October 2004.
8. Lee, Brian. 'Nuclear agency chief goes easy on Seoul'. *JoongAng Ilbo*, 6 October 2004.
9. Ryu, Jin. 'ElBaradei discounts Seoul's nuclear lab test'. *Korea Times*, 6 October 2004.
10. 'IAEA chief says world getting Impatient with N. Korea'. *New York Times*, 6 October 2004.
11. Linzer, Dafna. 'IAEA leader's phone tapped: US pores over transcripts to try to oust nuclear chief'. *Washington Post*, 12 December 2004.
12. Shah, Anup. 'Militarization of outer space'. GlobalIssues.org, 27 June 2004; *US Militarization of Space*. Western States Legal Foundation, 15 September 2004. Available from www.wslfweb.org/space/spacedocs.htm (accessed 4 October 2004)
13. 'UN nuke inspectors: no access in Brazil'. *New York Times*, 23 September 2004.
14. *Energy, Electricity and Nuclear Power Estimates for the Period up to 2030*. Vienna: International Atomic Energy Agency, 2003.
15. 'US wrong approach to nuclear issue refuted'. KCNA, 27 July 2004.
16. Harrison, Selig S. 'Gas and geopolitics in Northeast Asia: pipelines, regional stability and the Korean nuclear crisis'. *World Policy Journal*, Vol. XIX, No. 4, 2003.

17. Pollack, Jonathan D. 'The United States, North Korea, and the end of the Agreed Framework'. *Naval War College Review*, Vol. LVI, No. 3, 2003.

18. Ryu, Jin. 'N. Korea did not deny HEU program: officials'. *Korea Times*, 15 August 2004.

19. Smith, Craig. Roots of Pakistan atomic scandal traced to Europe'. *New York Times*, 19 February 2004.

20. Norris, Robert S., Hans M. Kristensen and Joshua Handler. 'North Korea's nuclear program 2003'. *Bulletin of the Atomic Scientists*, Vol. 59, No. 2, 2003, pp. 74–7.

21. *A 10-Year Projection of Possible Events of Nuclear Proliferation Concern*. Washington, DC: Directorate of Intelligence, 1983.

22. Directorate of Intelligence. *North Korea's Nuclear Efforts*. Langley, VA: Central Intelligence Agency, 1987.

23. Pollack, 'The United States, North Korea'.

24. For instance, Kessler, Glenn. 'N. Korea nuclear estimate to rise'. *Washington Post*, 28 April 2004.

25. Bush, George W., John F. Kerry and Jim Lehrer (moderator). 'First presidential debate (transcript)'. *Washington Post,* 30 September 2004.

26. Editorial. 'The choice on North Korea'. *Washington Post*, 4 October 2004.

27. 'Reports on N. Korea nukes may lack proof'. *New York Times*, 1 October 2004.

28. 'In theory', because reports have emerged that they were there until at least 1998. Staines, Reuben. 'US trained for strikes on NK'. *Korea Times*, 7 November 2004.

29. 'Statement of DPRK government on its withdrawal from NPT'. KCNA, 10 January 2003.

30. Choe, Su Hon. 'Statement by H.E. Mr. Choe Su Hon Head of the Delegation of the Democratic People's Republic of Korea at the General Debate of the Fifty-ninth Session of the United Nations General Assembly'. In *DPRK Delegation to the United Nations*. New York: DPRK Delegation to the United Nations, 2004.

31. Pritchard, Charles 'Jack'. *The North Korea Deadlock: a Report from the Region*. Presented at the Brookings Institution, Washington, DC, 15 January 2004.

32. Ibid.

33. Hersh, Seymour M. 'The cold test: what the administration knew about Pakistan and the North Korean nuclear program'. *New Yorker,* 27 January 2003.

34. 'J. Kelly failed to produce "evidence" in Pyongyang: framed up admission story. Interview with DPRK FM Director O Song Chol'. *People's Korea*, 19 January 2003.

35. Oberdorfer, *The Two Koreas*, p. 277.

36. Wolfsthal, Jon B. 'Crying wolf on Iraqi WMD costs US credibility on North Korea'. *Christian Science Monitor*, 29 January 2004.

37. 'China irks US in stand on North Korean weapons'. *New York Times*, 6 February 2004.

38. Harrison, Selig S. 'Did North Korea cheat?' *Foreign Affairs*, January/February 2005.
39. Ereli, Adam. 'Daily press briefing'. Washington, DC: State Department, 10 December 2004.
40. Bright, Martin. 'Guantanamo has "failed to prevent terror attacks"'. *Observer*, 3 October 2004.
41. Barstow, David, William J. Broad and Jeff Gerth. 'How the White House embraced disputed arms intelligence'. *New York Times*, 3 October 2004.
42. Staines, Reuben. 'Seoul rejects claims of intelligence breakdown'. *Korea Times*, 2004.
43. Dixon, Norm. 'Libya disposes of phantom arsenal to curry Washington's favor'. *NewStandard*, 19 January 2004.
44. Sigal, Leon V. 'North Korea is no Iraq: Pyongyang's negotiating strategy'. *Arms Control Today*, December 2002.
45. Pollack, 'The United States, North Korea'.
46. Harrison, 'Did North Korea cheat?'
47. Harrison, Selig S. 'Inside North Korea: leaders open to ending nuclear crisis'. *Financial Times*, 4 May 2004; Harrison, Selig S. 'Riding a tiger in North Korea'. *Newsweek International*, 17 May 2004; Harrison, Selig S. 'The North Korean conundrum'. *Nation*, 7 June 2004.
48. 'SK lawmakers decry NK human rights act'. *Ohmynews*, 21 August 2004.
49. Kessler, Glenn. 'Bush signals patience on North Korea is waning'. *Washington Post*, 4 March 2004.
50. Kessler, Glenn. 'Impact from the shadows'. *Washington Post*, 5 October 2004.
51. 'N. Korea vows will never dismantle its nuclear arms'. Reuters via *New York Times*, 18 September 2004.
52. Williams, 'Boutros-Ghali bites back'.
53. Baker, James. 'Cable to Secretary Cheney'. US Department of State, 18 November 1991.

8 ON THE PRECIPICE

1. ROK is China's fourth largest export market (4.8 per cent) and third largest import source (9.7 per cent).
2. Zhebin, Alexander. *Russia's Efforts for Reconciliation and Peace in Korea*. Presented at the 2nd World Congress of Korean Studies, Pyongyang, 2004.
3. 'China–US secret agreement on Iraq and North Korea'. *Kimsoft Web Weekly*, 3 February 2003.
4. Shim, Jae-yun. 'Seoul, Moscow hail summit as success'. *Korea Times*, 22 September 2004.
5. Zhebin, *Russia's Efforts for Reconciliation*.
6. You, Chul-jong. 'Lack of 6-party progress invites war, Russian says'. *JoongAng Ilbo*, 1 March 2004.

7. It has been suggested that Washington rejected Losyukov's efforts to mediate. Blagov, Sergei. 'Russia's lost Korean opportunity'. *Asia Times*, 25 June 2003.

8. Teather, David and Jonathan Watts. 'End of an era as firm that brought us the PC sells out to Chinese pretender for $1.75bn'. *Guardian*, 9 December 2004.

9. 'Year of epochal significance in DPRK–China friendship'. KCNA, 6 December 2004.

10. Suvendrini, Kakuchi. 'Tokyo feels the heat as inter-Korean ties warm'. *Asia Times Online*, 7 June 2000.

11. The *People's Daily* noted that it was the first time in 48 years that the Japanese coastguard had used such force. 'Japanese destroyer sinks fishing ship over international water'. *People's Daily*, 21 December 2001.

12. 'Koizumi to visit Pyongyang Sept. 17'. *Japan Times*, 31 August 2002.

13. DPRK–Japan Pyongyang Declaration.

14. 'First DPRK–Japan summit makes breakthrough in changing long-hostility into normalcy'. *People's Korea*, 28 September 2002.

15. Nam, Woo-suk. 'Anticipated economic effects of normalized NK–Japan relations'. KOTRA, 9 September 2002.

16. Pollack, Jonathan D. 'The United States, North Korea, and the end of the Agreed Framework'. *Naval War College Review*, Vol. LVI, No. 3, 2003.

17. 'Pyongyang urges Tokyo to sincerely implement Pyongyang Declaration'. KCNA, 17 September 2003.

18. Johnston, Eric. 'Kin of kidnapped fret lack of focus on Pyongyang in Upper House poll'. *Japan Times*, 2 July 2004.

19. 'DPRK and Japan hold talks on abducted Japanese citizens'. *People's Korea*, 27 November 2004.

20. 'North Korea caught in lie on Megumi remains'. *Asahi Shimbun*, 9 December 2004.

21. Hellman, Christopher. *World Military Spending 2002*. Available from www.cdi.org/budget/2004/world-military-spending.cfm (accessed 24 February 2003)

22. Berkofsky, Axel. 'Japan: hawks coming out of the woodwork'. *Asia Times Online*, 26 February 2003.

23. 'Article 9 hindering US ties, bid for UNSC seat: Armitage'. *Japan Times*, 23 July 2004.

24. Erikson, Marc. 'Japan could 'go nuclear' in months'. *Asia Times Online*, 14 January 2003.

25. Roh, Moo-hyun. *Toward an Era of Peace and Prosperity* (inaugural speech). Seoul, 2003.

26. Bank of Korea. *Gross Domestic Product of North Korea in 2002*. KOTRA, 11 June 2003.

27. Smith, Dan Col. 'Truth in spending'. *Foreign Policy in Focus*, October 2003.

28. Noland, Marcus. *Avoiding the Apocalypse: the Future of the Two Koreas*. Washington, DC: Institute for International Economics, 2000.

29. Sohn, Hong-keun. 'Negotiation of substance'. *Korea Times*, 10 February 2003.
30. 'Off the hook'. *The Economist*, 14 May 2004.
31. Lee, Young-jong. 'North silent on new GNP head'. *JoongAng Ilbo*, 25 March 2004.
32. Faiola, Anthony. 'As tensions subside between two Koreas, US strives to adjust: thaw strains South's alliance with Washington'. *Washington Post*, 25 July 2004.
33. Jung, Sung-ki. '"Fahrenheit 9/11" heats up anti-dispatch move'. *Korea Times*, 19 July 2004.
34. Oh, Young-hwan and Jie-ho Choi. 'New US policy on North took lots of work'. *JoongAng Ilbo*, 12 July 2004.
35. Ryu, Jin. 'Navy covered up hotline failure, says Defense Chief'. *Korea Times*, 25 July 2004.
36. Sanger, David E. 'Kerry says Bush has ignored North Korean threat'. *New York Times*, 13 September 2004.
37. Choi, Hoon and Seong-jae Min. 'Bush, Roh said to agree on how to handle North'. *JoongAng Ilbo*, 22 November 2004.
38. Ibid.
39. Choi, Hoon and Seong-jae Min. 'Roh seeks allies beyond the US'. *JoongAng Ilbo*, 8 December 2004.
40. Ryu, Jin. 'President Roh wins support over NK nukes through summits'. *Korea Times*, 7 December 2004.
41. Choi, Hoon and Seong-jae Min. 'Roh: 6-way talks, then summit'. *JoongAng Ilbo*, 4 December 2004.
42. Choi, Hoon and Young-jong Lee. 'Roh says North Korea will not collapse'. *JoongAng Ilbo*, 2004.
43. Choi, Hoon and Seong-jae Min. 'Roh, in Paris, is even more outspoken on North Korea'. *JoongAng Ilbo*, 7 December 2004.
44. Ryu, Jin. 'Roh rejects calls for "regime change" in North Korea'. *Korea Times*, 2004.
45. Choi and Min, 'Roh seeks allies beyond the US.'
46. Oh, Young-hwan and Yong-su Jeong. 'Korea, US trade barbs on Iraq-North link'. *JoongAng Ilbo*, 4 December 2004.
47. Choi and Min, 'Roh: 6-way talks, then summit'.
48. Staines, Reuben and Song-wu Park. 'South Korea isolated in opposing NK regime change: US expert'. *Korea Times*, 7 December 2004.
49. Ser, Myo-ja and Shin-hong Park. 'Publisher to become envoy to US'. *JoongAng Ilbo*, 18 December 2004.
50. Ryu, Jin. 'December surprise: Hong to be US ambassador'. *Korea Times*, 17 December 2004.
51. Sigal, Leon V. *Disarming Strangers: Nuclear Diplomacy with North Korea*, edited by Jack L. Snyder and Richard H. Ullman. Princeton, NJ: Princeton University Press, 1998.
52. 'DPRK proposes conclusion of non-aggression treaty to US'. *People's Korea*, 25 October 2002.
53. Lipson, Michael. 'The reincarnation of COCOM: explaining post-Cold War export controls'. *Nonproliferation Review*, Vol. 6, No. 2, 1999.

54. Koizumi's reneging on the Pyongyang Declaration would appear to substantiate this.
55. 'Pyongyang ready to consider Washington's offer of written security assurance'. DPRK Foreign Ministry statement, 25 October 2003.
56. Ibid.
57. Ibid.
58. 'DPRK foreign ministry spokesman on six-party talks'. KCNA, 28 June 2004.
59. 'Kerry: nuclear terrorism is gravest threat to US'. *New York Times*, 1 June 2004.
60. Kessler, Glenn. 'North Korean UN envoy visits Capitol Hill'. *Washington Post*, 21 July 2004.
61. Ser, Myo-ja and Young-jong Lee. 'North envoy sees no hope in US vote'. *JoongAng Ilbo*, 6 November 2004.
62. 'Spokesman for DPRK FM on prospect of resumption of six-party talks'. KCNA, 13 November 2004.
63. Armitage, Richard L. 'A comprehensive approach to North Korea'. National Defense University, Institute for Strategic Studies, *Strategic Forum*, No. 159, 1999.
64. Samore, Gary. 'US–DPRK missile negotiations'. *Nonproliferation Review*, Vol. 9, No. 2, 2002.
65. Ibid.
66. Reiss, Mitchell B. 'Negotiating with North Korea: lessons learned (and relearned?)'. Nautilus Institute Policy Forum, 30 January 2003.
67. Blumenthal, Dan. 'Unhelpful China'. *Washington Post*, 6 December 2004.
68. He is writing out of ideology, not ignorance because he is described as 'a resident fellow in Asian studies at the American Enterprise Institute, was until recently the senior country director for China and Taiwan in the Office of the Secretary of Defense'.
69. Blumenthal, 'Unhelpful China'.
70. Ibid.
71. Watts, Jonathan. 'Experts rebel over US stance on N Korea'. *Guardian*, 11 December 2004.
72. 'Tokyo to cut off food aid, plans sanctions on North'. *JoongAng Ilbo*, 11 December 2004.
73. Faiola, Anthony. 'Exercise displays Japan's ambitions'. *Washington Post*, 7 November 2004; Faiola, Anthony and Sachiko Sakamaki. 'Japan extends Iraq mission up to a year'. *Washington Post*, 10 December 2004.
74. Brooke, James. 'Japan shifts threat focus to N. Korea and China'. *New York Times*, 11 December 2004; 'Japan eases arms export ban for new missile shield'. *New York Times*, 10 December 2004.
75. Eberstadt, Nicholas. 'Tear down this tyranny'. *Weekly Standard*, 29 November 2004.
76. Kristol, William. *Toward Regime Change in North Korea*. Project for the New American Century, 22 November 2004.
77. Eberstadt, 'Tear down this tyranny'.
78. Ibid.
79. Ibid.

80. 'US welcome of Lee Hoi-chang raises Seoul's eyebrows'. *Korea Times*, 25 January 2002.
81. Traynor, Ian. 'US campaign behind the turmoil in Kiev'. *Guardian*, 26 November 2004.
82. Yoon, Won-sup. 'Lee fears pro-China regime in NK'. *Korea Times*, 10 November 2004.
83. Pritchard, Charles 'Jack'. 'The new US administration and the North Korean nuclear issue strategy for solving the North Korean nuclear crisis and the future of six-party talks: US policy for 2005'. *2004 Sejong-SAIS Workshop*, 11 November 2004.
84. Beck, Peter M. *The Bush Administration's Failed North Korea Policy*. Friends Committee on National Legislation website, 14 April 2004.
85. Harrison, Selig S. (chairman). *Ending the North Korean Nuclear Crisis*. Task Force on US Korea Policy, 10 November 2004.
86. 'DPRK foreign ministry spokesman on six-party talks'.
87. Harrison, *Ending the North Korean Nuclear Crisis*.
88. 'DPRK FM spokesman refutes US story about "transfer of N-technology" to DPRK'. KCNA, 10 February 2004.
89. 'North Korea: where next for the nuclear talks?' In *Asia Report*, No. 87. Seoul/Brussels: International Crisis Group, 2004.
90. Sigal, *Disarming Strangers*; Sigal, Leon V. 'North Korea is no Iraq: Pyongyang's negotiating strategy'. *Arms Control Today*, December 2002.
91. Seo, Soo-min. 'Ex-unification minister slams US policy toward North Korea'. *Korea Times*, 28 January 2004.

APPENDIX II   ARMED FORCES, MILITARY EXPENDITURE AND EXPORTS

1. 'Defense Ministry requests huge funds for new arms'. *Korea Herald*, 12 June 2003.
2. Shim, Jae-yun. 'NK to reduce armed forces by 500,000'. *Korea Times*, 15 October 2002.
3. Kim, Min-seok and Young-jong Lee. 'Seoul official says North to cut its forces by 10%'. *JoongAng Ilbo*, 6 November 2002.
4. 'DPRK reduces mandatory military service by 3 years'. *Korea Herald*, 28 May 2003.

APPENDIX III   DOCUMENTARY SOURCES

1. Article 2 states, 'The two signatory nations guarantee to adopt immediately all necessary measures to oppose any country or coalition of countries that might attack either nation.' Harrison, Selig S. *Korean Endgame: a Strategy for Reunification and US Disengagement*. Princeton, NJ: Princeton University Press, 2002, p. 322.

Bibliography

'3 of 4 defectors here on welfare, data say'. *JoongAng Ilbo*, 3 October 2004.

'10 years of DPRK with Songun policy'. *People's Korea*, 17 July 2004.

A 10-Year Projection of Possible Events of Nuclear Proliferation Concern. Washington, DC: Directorate of Intelligence, 1983.

Abramowitz, Morton I. , James T. Laney and Robert A. Manning. *Testing North Korea: the Next Stage in US and ROK policy*. Washington, DC: Council on Foreign Relations, 2001.

Acheson, Dean. *Present at the Creation: My Years at the State Department*. New York: W. W. Norton, 1969.

Adam, Werner. 'Pants off to North Korea'. *Frankfurter Allgemeine Zeitung*, 6 September 2000.

Agrawal, Brahm Swaroop. 'Korean nuclear controversy'. *Korea Times*, 2 June 2004.

'Aiding North Korean defectors becomes a business'. *JoongAng Ilbo*, 22 November 2004.

Allison, Graham. '94 deal with North Korea holds lessons for today'. *New York Times*, 20 July 2004.

Annual Performance Report for 2003. Rome: World Food Programme, 2004.

Arie, Sophie, and Jason Burke. 'Who cares?'. *Observer*, 15 August 2004.

Armitage, Richard L. 'A comprehensive approach to North Korea'. National Defense University, Institute for Strategic Studies, *Strategic Forum*, No. 159, 1999.

Arms Control Organization. *Chronology of US–North Korean Nuclear and Missile Diplomacy*. June 2003.

Art, Robert J. and Patrick M. Cronin (eds). *The United States and Coercive Diplomacy*. Washington, DC: United States Institute of Peace, 2003.

'Article 9 hindering US ties, bid for UNSC seat: Armitage'. *Japan Times*, 23 July 2004.

Auster, Bruce B., Kevin Whitelaw and Thomas Omestad. 'Upping the ante for Kim Jong Il; Pentagon Plan 5030, a new blueprint for facing down North Korea'. *US News and World Report, Nation & World*, 21 July 2003.

'Australia to spend up to $450m on cruise missiles'. *Sydney Morning Herald*, 26 August 2004.

Baker, Don. 'Looking for God in the streets of Seoul: the resurgence of religion in 20th century Korea'. *Harvard Asia Quarterly*, Vol. 5, No. 4, 2001.

Baker, James. 'Cable to Secretary Cheney'. US Department of State, 18 November 1991.

Bank of Korea. *Gross Domestic Product of North Korea in 2002*. KOTRA, 11 June 2003.

Barnett, Antony. 'Revealed: the gas chamber horror of North Korea's gulag'. *Observer*, 1 February 2004.

Barstow, David, William J. Broad and Jeff Gerth. 'How the White House embraced disputed arms intelligence'. *New York Times*, 3 October 2004.

Beal, Tim. 'Journey to a far away place: personal observations of a visit to North Korea'. *New Zealand Journal of East Asian Studies*, Vol. VI, No. 1, 1998, pp. 105–19.

Beaumont, Peter. 'PM admits graves claim "untrue"'. *Observer*, 18 July 2004.

Beaumont, Peter and Antony Barnett. 'Blow to Blair over "mobile labs"'. *Observer*, 8 June 2003.

Beck, Peter M. *The Bush Administration's Failed North Korea Policy*. Friends Committee on National Legislation website, 14 April 2004.

Belke, Thomas J. *Juche: a Christian Study of North Korea's State Religion*. Bartlesville, OK: Living Sacrifice Book Company, 1999.

Berkofsky, Axel. 'Japan: hawks coming out of the woodwork'. *Asia Times Online*, 26 February 2003.

Blagov, Sergei. 'Russia's lost Korean opportunity'. *Asia Times*, 25 June 2003.

'Blasphemy against Tangun under fire'. KCNA, 15 December 2001.

Bleek, Philipp C. 'Nuclear posture review leaks: outlines targets, contingencies'. *Arms Control Today*, April 2002.

Blumenthal, Dan. 'Unhelpful China'. *Washington Post*, 6 December 2004.

Boese, Wade. 'GAO says feds lax in countering cruise missile, UAV threats'. *Arms Control Today*, April 2004.

Borger, Julian. 'US intelligence fears Iran duped hawks into Iraq war'. *Guardian*, 25 May 2004.

Borrie, Don. 'Reflections on a visit to the Democratic Peoples' Republic of Korea, 9-19 April, 2004'. In *Study Leave Report to the Presbyterian Church of Aoteroa/New Zealand*. Wellington: Study Leave Report to the Presbyterian Church of Aoteroa/New Zealand, 2004.

Boucher, Richard. *North Korean Nuclear Program*. Washington, DC: US State Department, 16 October 2002.

Breen, Michael. 'So, we spied on North Korea after all'. *Korea Times*, 5 October 2000.

Briefing on Democratic People's Republic of Korea. London: Campaign for Nuclear Disarmament, July 2003.

Bright, Martin. 'Guantanamo has "failed to prevent terror attacks"'. *Observer*, 3 October 2004.

'Britain voices concerns over NK human rights violation reports'. *Yonhap*, 17 February 2004.

Brooke, James. 'China fears once and future kingdom'. *New York Times*, 25 August 2004.

——. 'Courtship of Beijing and Seoul: a new twist for an old bond'. *New York Times*, 26 February 2004.

——. 'Japan shifts threat focus to N. Korea and China'. *New York Times*, 11 December 2004.

——. 'Koreans look to China: seeing a market and a monster'. *New York Times*, 10 February 2004.

——. 'Mongolia under pressure to serve as haven for refugees'. *New York Times*, 21 November 2004.

Bush, George W., John F. Kerry and Jim Lehrer. 'First presidential debate (transcript)'. *Washington Post*, 30 September 2004.

Bush, George W. State of the Union Address 2002. Presented at the White House, 29 January 2002. Washington, DC: White House.

——. Statement by the President [on North Korea Policy Review]. Washington, DC: White House, 2001.

Campbell, Kurt, Derek Mitchell and Carola McGiffert. *Conventional Arms Control on the Korean Peninsula*. Washington, DC: Center for Strategic and International Studies, 2002.

Carbonell, Rachel. 'Pong Su crew to sue'. Australian Broadcasting Commission, 5 March 2004.

Chemical and Biological Weapons Site – North Korea. Center for Defense Information, 16 November 2000. Available from www.cdi.org/issues/cbw/NorthKorea.html (accessed 7 December 2004)

Chi, Minnie. 'Preview of "Silmido": blowback on the Korean Peninsula'. *Asia Media*, 2004.

'China irks US in stand on North Korean weapons'. *New York Times*, 6 February 2004.

'China should not deport refugee'. *Korea Times*, 11 February 2004.

'China, South Korea exchange greetings on anniversary of forging ties'. *People's Daily*, 24 August 2002.

'China–US secret agreement on Iraq and North Korea'. *Kimsoft Web Weekly*, 3 February 2003.

Chipman, John. 'North Korea's weapons programmes: a net assessment'. International Institute for Strategic Studies, press release, 21 January 2004.

Cho, M. A. 'First Russian orthodox church to be established in North Korea'. KOTRA, 11 June 2003.

Cho, M. A. 'North Korea's 2003 foreign trade (abstract)'. KOTRA, 13 August 2004.

Choe, Sang-Hun. 'Last communist rebel dies in South Korea'. Associated Press, 2 April 2004.

Choe, Su Hon. 'Statement by H.E. Mr. Choe Su Hon Head of the Delegation of the Democratic People's Republic of Korea at the General Debate of the Fifty-ninth Session of the United Nations General Assembly'. In *DPRK Delegation to the United Nations*. New York: DPRK Delegation to the United Nations, 2004.

Choi, Hoon. 'Roh sees little threat in future on peninsula'. *JoongAng Ilbo*, 16 November 2004.

Choi, Hoon and Young-jong Lee. 'Roh says North Korea will not collapse'. *JoongAng Ilbo*, 2004.

Choi, Hoon and Seong-jae Min. 'Bush, Roh said to agree on how to handle North'. *JoongAng Ilbo*, 22 November 2004.

——. 'Roh seeks allies beyond the US'. *JoongAng Ilbo*, 8 December 2004.

——. 'Roh, in Paris, is even more outspoken on North Korea'. *JoongAng Ilbo*, 7 December 2004.

——. 'Roh: 6-way talks, then summit'. *JoongAng Ilbo*, 4 December 2004.

'Chun, Roh, others sentenced in S. Korean "trial of century"'. *CNN Interactive*, 26 August 1996.

Clark, Gregory. 'Abduction issue – rightwing's political football'. *Japan Times*, 27 February 2004.

——. 'Label that foils compromise'. *Japan Times*, 2002.

Cody, Edward. 'China, others criticize US report on rights; double standard at State Dept. alleged'. *Washington Post*, 4 March 2005.

Cody, Edward. 'China protests US–Japan accord'. *Washington Post*, 21 February 2005.

'Conclusion of non-aggression treaty between DPRK and US called for'. KCNA, 25 October 2002.

'Conservatives' protest'. *JoongAng Ilbo*, 4 October 2004.

Consolidated Inter-Agency Appeal 2003, DPRK. New York: United Nations, 2003.

Cortright, David. 'A hard look at Iraq sanctions'. *Nation*, 3 December 2001.

Cossa, Ralph A. 'North Korea: searching for A. Q. Kim'. *Korea Times*, 12 July 2004.

Cotton, James. 'North Korea's nuclear and missile proliferation and regional security'. *Australian Parliamentary Library Current Issues*, Vol. 1999–2000, No. 1, 1999.

Croddy, Eric. 'Vinalon, the DPRK, and chemical weapons precursors'. *Center for Nonproliferation Studies Issue Brief*, 4 February 2003.

Cumings, Bruce. *Korea's Place in the Sun: a Modern History*. New York: W. W. Norton, 1997.

———. *North Korea: Another Country*. New York: New Press, 2003.

Cumings, Bruce and Kathryn Weathersby. 'Bruce Cumings and Kathryn Weathersby: an exchange on Korean War origins'. Cold War International History Project, Bulletin 6–7, 11 July 1995.

'Data-wise overseas Korean society'. *People's Korea*, 27 October 1999.

'Defector "faked" gas chamber documents'. *Age*, 1 April 2004.

'Defector pardoned by NK leader, mother says'. *Korea Times*, 15 February 2002.

'Defector returned to N Korea'. *BBC World*, 31 March 2004.

'Defense Ministry requests huge funds for new arms'. *Korea Herald*, 12 June 2003.

Demick, Barbara. 'Korea or Corea? debate is historical, political'. *Seattle Times*, 17 September 2003.

Directorate of Intelligence. *North Korea's Nuclear Efforts*. Langley, VA: Central Intelligence Agency, 1987.

'Dispute over N. Korea military briefly halts Assembly audit'. *Korea Herald*, 6 October 2004.

Dixon, Norm. 'Libya disposes of phantom arsenal to curry Washington's favor'. *NewStandard*, 19 January 2004.

'DPRK and Japan hold talks on abducted Japanese citizens'. *People's Korea*, 27 November 2004.

'DPRK and the BBC'S evidence'. *Financial Times*, 15 February 2004.

'DPRK FM spokesman refutes US story about "transfer of N-technology" to DPRK'. KCNA, 10 February 2004.

'DPRK foreign ministry spokesman blasts Cheney's anti-DPRK remarks'. KCNA, 18 April 2004.

'DPRK foreign ministry spokesman on six-party talks'. KCNA, 28 June 2004.

'DPRK hails end of "Arduous March"'. *People's Korea*, October 2000.

'DPRK non-certification'. *Napsnet Daily Briefing*, 20 March 2002.

'DPRK proposes conclusion of non-aggression treaty to US'. *People's Korea*, 25 October 2002.

'DPRK ready to join 5 more anti-terror pacts'. *People's Korea*, 25 December 2001.

'DPRK reduces mandatory military service by 3 years'. *Korea Herald*, 28 May 2003.

'DPRK signs anti-terror conventions'. *People's Korea*, 13 December 2001.

'DPRK stance towards terrorist attacks on U.S'. KCNA, 12 September 2001.

'DPRK to put spurs to increasing its nuclear deterrent force for self-defence'. KCNA, 18 June 2003.

'DPRK will accept humanitarian offer'. KCNA, 5 October 1998.

'DPRK–Russia Moscow Declaration'. *People's Korea*, 7 August 2001.

Eberstadt, Nicholas. 'Tear down this tyranny'. *Weekly Standard*, 29 November 2004.

Eberstadt, Nicholas. 'What surprise? The nuclear core of North Korea's strategy'. *Washington Post*, 1 March 2005.

Eberstadt, Nicholas and Judith Bannister. *The Population of North Korea*. Berkeley, CA: Institute of East Asian Studies, University of California at Berkeley, 1992.

ECN Site Lines: Porton Down. Environmental Change Network. Available from www.ecn.ac.uk/ecnnews/ecnnews9/ecnews93.htm (accessed 7 December 2004)

Editorial. 'George W. Bush victory'. *Korea Times*, 8 November 2000.

Editorial. 'The choice on North Korea'. *Washington Post*, 4 October 2004.

——. 'Kahn's nuclear confession'. *Korea Herald*, 10 February 2004.

——. 'Now, ball is in US court'. *Korea Times*, 4 May 2001.

Eisenhower, Dwight D. 'Farewell Address to the Nation (17 January 1961)'. Available from www.eisenhower.archives.gov/farewell.htm (accessed 24 February 2003)

'Electricity shortage acute in Korea'. KCNA, 30 January 2003.

Endicott, Stephen and Edward Hagerman. *The United States and Biological Warfare*, Bloomington and Indianapolis: Indiana University Press, 1998.

Energy, Electricity and Nuclear Power Estimates for the Period up to 2030. Vienna: International Atomic Energy Agency, 2003.

Engel, Matthew. 'Drugs and forgery "sustain North Korean economy"'. *Guardian*, 20 January 2003.

Ereli, Adam. 'Daily press briefing'. Washington, DC: State Department, 10 December 2004.

Erikson, Marc. 'Japan could "go nuclear" in months'. *Asia Times Online*, 14 January 2003.

'EU to set up diplomatic ties with DPRK'. *People's Korea*, 26 May 2001.

Eum, Tae-min and Myo-ja Ser. 'Park's 1970s nuclear arms program revealed'. *JoongAng Ilbo*, 2 August 2004.

Evans, Michael. 'Spy pictures show Korea's empty threat'. *Times*, 12 January 2000.

Evans, Rob and Sandra Laville. 'Porton Down unlawfully killed airman in sarin tests'. *Guardian*, 16 November 2004.

Facts and Figures on the Death Penalty. Amnesty International, 17 December 2004. Available from http://web.amnesty.org/pages/deathpenalty-facts-eng (accessed 19 December 2004)

Faiola, Anthony. 'As tensions subside between two Koreas, US strives to adjust: thaw strains South's alliance with Washington'. *Washington Post*, 25 July 2004.

——. 'Exercise displays Japan's ambitions'. *Washington Post*, 7 November 2004.

Faiola, Anthony and Sachiko Sakamaki. 'Japan extends Iraq mission up to a year'. *Washington Post*, 10 December 2004.

Fairbank, John K., Edwin O. Reischauer and Albert M. Craig. *East Asia, the Modern Transformation.* London: Allen & Unwin, 1965.

'False military report'. *Korea Times*, 18 July 2004.

Fic, Victor. 'North Korean human rights crisis'. *Korean Web Weekly*, 2004.

'First DPRK–Japan summit makes breakthrough in changing long-hostility into normalcy'. *People's Korea*, 28 September 2002.

Fisk, Robert. 'This looming war isn't about chemical warheads or human rights: it's about oil'. *Independent*, 18 January 2003.

Foreign Operations, Export Financing, and Related Programs Appropriations Act. Washington, DC: US Senate, 2004.

'Foreign Ministry spokesman refutes U.S. report on human rights'. KCNA, 6 March 2005.

Former North Korean high-level government official. 'Testimony'. Senate Governmental Affairs Subcommittee on Financial Management, Budget, and International Security, 20 May 2003.

'Former North Korean was "publicly executed"'. *Human Rights Without Frontiers* website, 28 February 2003.

Foster-Carter, Aidan. 'Beware defective tales of defectors'. *Asia Times online*, 23 May 2003.

——. 'North Korea: guns or butter?' Nautilus Institute Policy Forum, 6 April 2004.

——. 'They shoot people, don't they?' *Asia Times Online*, 22 March 2001.

French, Howard W. 'North Korea's confession: why?' *New York Times*, 21 October 2002.

Frenkiel, Olenka. 'Within prison walls'. BBC, 30 January 2004.

Friedman, Thomas L. 'Macho on North Korea'. *New York Times*, 9 March 2001.

'Full text of human rights record of the US in 2004'. *People's Daily*, 3 March 2005.

'Gangster behind heroin ship, court told'. *MSNNine.Com*, 19 November 2003.

'Gen. Shin detained over embezzlement'. *Korea Times*, 9 May 2004.

'German doctor plans anti-N. Korean protest ahead of 6-party talks'. *Yonhap*, 13 February 2004.

Gilfeather, Paul. 'Fallujah napalmed'. *Sunday Mirror*, 24 November 2004.

Gilman, Benjamin A. 'Gilman releases North Korea report'. Press release, 3 November 1999.

——. *North Korea Advisory Group Report to the Speaker US House of Representatives.* Washington, DC: North Korea Advisory Group, 1999.

Gittelsohn, John. 'Defections and doubts'. *OCRegister.com*, 8 June 2003.

Glantz, James. 'This tme it's real: an antimissile system takes shape'. *New York Times*, 4 May 2004.

Goodby, James E. 'Negotiating with a nation that's really gone nuclear'. *Washington Post*, 15 February 2004.

Goodman, A. 'Official: Spain perplexed by Scud decision'. CNN, 11 December 2002.

Gregg, Donald P. 'Angst and opportunities on the Korean Peninsula'. *Korea Society Quarterly*, Vol. 4, No. 1, 2004.

Halevi, Joseph. 'US militarism and imperialism and the Japanese "Miracle"'. *Monthly Review*, Vol. 53, No. 4, 2001.

'Happy in Insein'. *JoongAng Ilbo*, 9 October 2003.

Harrison, Selig S. 'Did North Korea cheat?'. *Foreign Affairs*, January/February 2005.

——. (chairman). *Ending the North Korean Nuclear Crisis*. Task Force on US Korea Policy, 10 November 2004.

——. 'Gas and geopolitics in Northeast Asia: pipelines, regional stability and the Korean nuclear crisis'. *World Policy Journal*, Vol. XIX, No. 4, 2003.

——. 'Inside North Korea: leaders open to ending nuclear crisis'. *Financial Times*, 4 May 2004.

——. *Korean Endgame: a Strategy for Reunification and US Disengagement*. Princeton, NJ: Princeton University Press, 2002.

——. 'Missile capabilities in Northeast Asia: Japan, South Korea and North Korea'. *Commission to Assess the Ballistic Missile Threat to the United States; Appendix III: Unclassified Working Papers*, 15 July 1998.

——. 'Riding a tiger in North Korea'. *Newsweek International*, 17 May 2004.

——. 'The North Korean conundrum'. *Nation*, 7 June 2004.

Hawk, David. *The Hidden Gulag: Exposing North Korea's Prison Camps Prisoners' Testimonies and Satellite Photographs*. Washington, DC: US Committee for Human Right in North Korea, 1 November 2003.

'"He has learnt from the past year": responses to George Bush's non-proliferation programme'. *Guardian*, 17 February 2004.

Hecker, Siegfried S. *Visit to the Yongbyon Nuclear Scientific Research Center in North Korea*. Washington, DC: Senate Committee on Foreign Relations, 2004.

Hecker Testimony Transcript. Washington, DC: Senate Committee on Foreign Relations, 2004.

Hellman, Christopher. *World Military Spending 2002*. Available from www.cdi.org/budget/2004/world-military-spending.cfm (accessed 24 February 2003)

Hersh, Seymour M. 'The cold test: what the administration knew about Pakistan and the North Korean nuclear program'. *New Yorker*, 27 January 2003.

Hirohito, Showa Emperor. 'Emperor Hirohito, accepting the Potsdam Declaration, radio broadcast'. Federal Communications Commission, 14 August 1945.

Hoare, James, and Susan Pares. *Conflict in Korea: an Encyclopedia*. Santa Barbara, CA: ABC-CLIO, 1999.

Hong, Jung-wook. 'Ultimate US goal is NK regime change'. *Korea Herald*, 24 February 2005.

'Honors to Kim Jae-kyu'. *Korea Herald*, 19 May 2004.

'How the South views its brother from another planet'. International Crisis Group, 2004.

Huggler, Justin. 'Axis of execution: American justice ranked alongside world's most repressive regimes'. *Independent*, 7 April 2004.

'Humanitarian aid of $462 million provided to NK under Kim DJ'. *Chosun Ilbo*, 12 February 2003.

Hwang, Dong Jong. *The ROK National Defense Improvement: Goals and Directions for the Next Decade*. Seoul: Korea Institute for Defense Analysis, 2004.

Hwang, Eui Gak. *The Korean Economies: a Comparison of North and South*. New York: Oxford University Press, 1993.

Hwang, J. J. 'USFK unveils plan for forces buildup'. *Korea Herald*, 2 June 2003.

Hyder, Masood. 'In North Korea, first, save lives'. *Washington Post*, 4 January 2004.

'IAEA chief in South Korea for nuclear talks'. *New York Times*, 3 October 2004.

'IAEA chief says world getting Impatient with N. Korea'. *New York Times*, 6 October 2004.

IAEA In Focus. International Atomic Energy Authority, 2004. Available from www.iaea.org/NewsCenter/Focus/index.html (accessed 8 October 2004)

Ignatius, David. 'Weapons we can't afford'. *Washington Post*, 12 October 2004.

'Intelligence service calls nukes primitive at best'. *JoongAng Ilbo*, 16 February 2005.

'Inter-Korean summit looms'. *Korea Times*, 8 August 2004.

International Narcotics Control Strategy Report 2003. Washington, DC: US State Department, 2004.

Iran Missile Update 2004. Wisconsin Project On Nuclear Arms Control, March–April 2004. Available from www.wisconsinproject.org/countries/iran/missile2004.htm (accessed 16 December 2004)

'"Iron Silkroad" to connect Korean Peninsula and Europe envisaged'. *Yonhap News*, 16 June 2000.

'J. Kelly failed to produce "evidence" in Pyongyang: framed up admission story'. Interview with DPRK FM Director O Song Chol'. *People's Korea*, 19 January 2003.

Jagan, Larry. 'Kim Dae-jung: a political profile'. BBC, 13 June 2000.

James A. Kelly Biography. Washington, DC: US State Department, 22 May 2001.

'Japan eases arms export ban for new missile shield'. *New York Times*, 10 December 2004.

'Japanese destroyer sinks fishing ship over international water'. *People's Daily*, 21 December 2001.

'Japanese PM visits "Yasukuni Shrine"; DPRK warns against Japan's trend toward militarism'. *People's Korea*, 17 January 2004.

'Japanese Prime Minister Koizumi to visit Pyongyang to meet DPRK leader Kim Jong Il'. *People's Korea*, 4 September 2002.

'Japan's brazen-faced distortion of history'. KCNA, 18 March 2004.

'Japan's insincerity makes DPRK reconsider moratorium on missile launch: FM spokesman'. *People's Korea*, 30 November 2002.

Jehl, D. and D. Johnston. 'Rule change lets C.I.A. freely send suspects abroad to jails'. *New York Times*, 6 March 2005.

'John Kerry on national security'. *Guardian*, 28 May 2004.

Johnson, Marguerite. 'No words for the bitterness: a nation in mourning points a finger at its northern neighbor'. *Time*, 24 October 1983.

Johnston, Eric. 'Kin of kidnapped fret lack of focus on Pyongyang in Upper House poll'. *Japan Times*, 2 July 2004.

Joint Statement of North and South, 4 July 1972. Available from http://210.145.168.243/pk/011th_issue/97100103.htm (accessed 2004)

Jolley, Mary Ann. 'North Korea – Pong Su'. Australian Broadcasting Commission, 27 July 2004.

Jung, Sung-ki. '"Fahrenheit 9/11" heats up anti-dispatch move'. *Korea Times*, 19 July 2004.

——. 'N. Korea–China trade volume soars 40.5%'. *Korea Times*, 17 November 2004.

Kang, Byong Sop and Song Hak Kang. 'We make false documents of showing chemical weapons testing on prisoners'. *People's Korea*, 10 April 2004.

Kang, Seok-jae. 'Report says 10,000 spies sent to North'. *Korea Herald*, 31 October 2000.

Katagiri, Noriyuki. 'North Korea's nuclear programme: analyzing "confessional diplomacy"'. *CDI.org*, 28 October 2002.

'KCNA on DPRK's nuclear deterrent force'. KCNA, 9 June 2003.

'KCNA on first artificial satellite of DPRK'. *People's Korea*, 8 September 1998.

'KCNA on US reckless nuclear war scenario'. KCNA, 13 March 2002.

'KCNA refutes US smear campaign'. KCNA, 10 June 2003.

Kelley, Matt. 'Pentagon: N. Korea not mobilizing army'. *Kansas City Star*, 31 January 2003.

'Kerry: nuclear terrorism is gravest threat to US'. *New York Times*, 1 June 2004.

Kessler, Glenn. 'Bush signals patience on North Korea is waning'. *Washington Post*, 4 March 2004.

——. 'Chinese not convinced of North Korean uranium effort'. *Washington Post*, 7 January 2004.

——. 'Impact from the shadows'. *Washington Post*, 5 October 2004.

——. 'More N. Korean bombs likely, US official says'. *Washington Post*, 16 July 2004.

——. 'N. Korea nuclear estimate to rise'. *Washington Post*, 28 April 2004.

——. 'North Korean UN envoy visits Capitol Hill'. *Washington Post*, 21 July 2004.

——. 'State Dept. study cites torture of prisoners'. *Washington Post*, 1 March 2005.

Khan, Irene. *Open Letter to Acting President Goh Kun – Continued Use of the Draconian National Security Law: Amnesty International's Concerns about Professor Song Du-Yul's Case*. London: Amnesty International, 1 April 2004.

——. *Open Letter to Newly Elected Members of the 17th National Assembly: a Historic Opportunity to Consolidate Human Rights Gains*. London: Amnesty International, 2 July 2004.

Kim, Dae-jung. *Address by President Kim Dae-jung of the Republic of Korea at the School of Oriental and African Studies London University*. London [s.n.], 1998.

——. *Address by President Kim Dae-jung of the Republic of Korea, Lessons of German Reunification and the Korean Peninsula*. Presented at the Free University of Berlin, 9 March 2000.

——. *Inaugural Address*, 25 February 1998.

——. 'Welcoming remarks by President Kim Dae-jung of the Republic of Korea at a dinner he hosted in Pyongyang'. Korean Information Service, 14 June 2000.

Kim Dae-jung – Biography. Nobel e-Museum, 2002. Available from www.nobel.se/peace/laureates/2000/dae-jung-bio.html (accessed 2003)

Kim, Hyeon-gyeong and In-sung Chun. 'Song Du-yul is freed after court of appeals overturns treason case'. *JoongAng Ilbo*, 22 July 2004.

Kim, Hyun-chul. 'Two Koreas break ground in Gaeseong'. *Korea Herald*, 30 June 2003.

'Kim Jong Il stresses economic renovation with new thinking'. *People's Korea*, 25 January 2001.

Kim, Ki-tae. 'Australia tough on NK's illegal trafficking'. *Korea Times*, 20 June 2003.

Kim, Min-seok and Byung-gun Chae. 'Defense gurus downplay risk of North's guns'. *JoongAng Ilbo*, 5 October 2004.

Kim, Min-seok and Young-jong Lee. 'Seoul official says North to cut its forces by 10%'. *JoongAng Ilbo*, 6 November 2002.

Kim, Min-seok and Myo-ja Ser. 'North reported to be preparing missile launch'. *JoongAng Ilbo*, 23 September 2004.

Kim, Myong-chol. *US, UK Are in Material Breach of Nuclear Non-Proliferation Treaty that Bans Transfer of Nuclear Hardware, Software to any Recipient*. Center for Korean-American Peace, 2004. Available from http://cfkap.com/commentary/072804US_UK_violateNPT.html (accessed 21 December 2004)

Kim, Rahn. 'China aims to expand territory by distorting history'. *Korea Times*, 18 August 2004.

——. 'Foreign democracy fighters to pay tribute to Koreans'. *Korea Times*, 8 September 2004.

'Kim tours tech firms in Shanghai'. *AsiaTimes Online*, 18 January 2001.

Koehler, Joseph. '"Camp 22" document a fake?' *The Marmot's Hole*, 3 February 2004.

'Koizumi aides clash over N. Korea policy for Bush talks'. *Kyodo*, 27 May 2003.

'Koizumi to visit Pyongyang Sept. 17'. *Japan Times*, 31 August 2002.

Korean Peace Network. 'Letter of appeal to the American public [advertisment]'. *New York Times*, 27 October 2004.

'Korea's China play'. *Business Week*, 29 March 2004.

'Koreas may hold summit next month, ex-lawmaker says'. *Korea Herald*, 13 August 2004.

Krauthammer, Charles. 'A better defense'. *Washington Post*, 20 August 2004.

Kristol, William. *Toward Regime Change in North Korea*. Project for the New American Century, 22 November 2004.

Krugman, Paul. 'The martial plan'. *New York Times*, 21 February 2003.

Kwon, Soon-Taek. 'Research on nuclear weapons to destroy bunker is necessary'. *Donga Ilbo*, 13 May 2004.

'Large-scale US–South Korea landing exercise in S. Korea'. KCNA, 28 March 2004.

Larson, Eric V., Norman D. Levin, Seonhae Baik and Bogdan Savych. *Ambivalent Allies? A Study of South Korean Attitudes Toward the US* Santa Monica, CA: Rand Corporation, 2004.

Laughland, John. 'The mask of altruism disguising a colonial war'. *Guardian*, 2 August 2004.

'Lawmakers slam leniency on NK abuses'. *Korea Herald*, 18 February 2004.

Le Leu, Seth. *North Korea – An Enigma and an Opportunity*. Salvation Army, 19 November 2004. Available from www.salvationarmy.org/ihq/www_sa.nsf/vw-news/CA5C57C922E0173F80256F5100464D2B?opendocument (accessed 7 December 2004)

Lee, Brian. 'Defense to cost 99 trillion won through 2008'. *JoongAng Ilbo*, 19 November 2004.

——. 'Nuclear agency chief goes easy on Seoul'. *JoongAng Ilbo*, 6 October 2004.

——. 'US envoy sees no chance of raid on North'. *JoongAng Ilbo*, 7 October 2004.

Lee, Brian. 'US harshly condemns North for rights abuse'. *JoongAng Ilbo*, 2 March 2005.

Lee, C. H. 'NK makes all-out effort to solve food shortage problem'. KOTRA, 20 February 2003.

Lee, Chul-hee. 'Film recalls bloody rebellion'. *JoongAng Ilbo*, 19 January 2004.

Lee, Hyo-sik. 'Inter-Korean income gap widens to 15.5 times'. *Korea Times*, 9 December 2004.

Lee, Jin-woo. 'Professor Song leaves for Germany'. *Korea Times*, 5 August 2004.

Lee, Jung-min. '2 defectors' appearance in US was news to Seoul'. *JoongAng Ilbo*, 4 June 2003.

Lee, Wha Rang. 'War of liberation continues: South Korea is still a Japanese colony. The sons and daughters of pro-Japanese traitors rule South Korea'. *Kimsoft*, March 2004.

Lee, Yong-sung. 'Koguryo Tombs may become world heritage'. *Korea Times*, 18 January 2004.

Lee, Young-jong. 'North silent on new GNP head'. *JoongAng Ilbo*, 25 March 2004.

——. 'Plan to cope with fall of North divulged'. *JoongAng Ilbo*, 4 October 2004.

Lee, Young-jong and Ser Myo-ja. 'Pyeongyang regime is stable, says top aide on North Korea'. *JoongAng Ilbo*, 2004.

Linzer, Dafna. 'IAEA leader's phone tapped: US pores over transcripts to try to oust nuclear chief'. *Washington Post*, 12 December 2004.

Lipson, Michael. 'The reincarnation of COCOM: explaining post-Cold War export controls'. *Nonproliferation Review*, Vol. 6, No. 2, 1999.

Long-term trends – world exports, production, GDP, from 1950. World Trade Organization, 2003. Available from www.wto.org/english/res_e/statis_e/its2002_e/section2_e/ii01.xls (visited 20 May 2003)

MacAskill, Ewen. 'Minister's mission to North Korea'. *Guardian*, 10 September 2004.

MacIntyre, Donald. 'Kim's war machine'. *Time Asia*, 24 February 2003.

——. 'Korea's dirty dozen'. *Time Asia*, 20 May 2002.

MacKinnon, Rebecca. 'Interview with Selig Harrison'. *North Korea Zone*, 4 May 2004.

MacLaren, D. 'Caritas celebrates 10 years of activity in the DPRK'. Caritas press statement, 8 March 2005.

Madsen, Wayne. 'Moon shadow: the Rev, Bush & North Korea'. *Counterpunch*, 14 January 2003.

Mansourov, Alexandre. 'North Korea goes nuclear, Washington readies for war, South Korea holds key'. Nautilus Institute Policy Forum, 9 December 2002.

Marquis, Christopher. 'Absent from the Korea talks: Bush's hard-liner'. *New York Times*, 2 September 2003.

McCormack, Gavan. 'Gulags on both sides of the DMZ'. ABC Radio National *Book Talk*, 1 March 2003.

McCoy, Alfred and David Barsamian (interviewer). 'The CIA and the politics of narcotics'. *Prevailing Winds Research*, 17 February 1990.

Miller, Judith and William J. Broad. 'US analysts link Iraq labs to germ arms'. *New York Times*, 21 May 2003.

Monbiot, George. 'Our lies led us into war'. *Guardian*, 20 July 2004.

Moon, Chung-in and David I. Steinberg (eds) *Kim Dae-jung Government and Sunshine Policy: Promises and Challenges.* Seoul: Yonsei University Press, 1999.

MSF in North Korea. Médicins sans Frontières. Available from www.msf.org/countries/index.cfm?indexid=22D113E8-BEC7-11D4-852200902789187E (accessed 17 June 2003)

Myrah, John M. 'The proliferation of ballistic missiles: what should we do to stop it?' *Commission to Assess the Ballistic Missile Threat to the United States; Appendix III: Unclassified Working Papers*, 15 July 1998.

'N Korean nuclear "admission" in doubt'. BBC Asia Pacific, 18 November 2002.

'N. Korea vows will never dismantle its nuclear arms'. Reuters via *New York Times*, 18 September 2004.

'N. Korea wants illuminated church crosses removed'. *New York Times*, 23 August 2004.

Na, Jeong-ju. '"Comfort Women" to mark 600th Wednesday rally'. *Korea Times*, 16 March 2004.

——. 'Independent counsel for "Cash-for-Summit"'. *Korea Times*, 16 March 2003.

——. 'MBC program creates stir over Song'. *Korea Times*, 14 July 2004.

——. 'NK defectors seeking to move to US'. *Korea Times*, 17 November 2004.

Nam, Woo-suk. 'Anticipated economic effects of normalized NK–Japan relations'. KOTRA, 9 September 2002.

Namkung, K A. *The Bush Administration's North Korea Policy and the Opening of the American Mind*. Presented at the Korean Forum Foundation, Los Angeles, 15 May 2002.

Nartker, Mike. 'North Korea: Pyongyang funds WMD programs by selling drugs, counterfeit currency'. *Global Security Newswire*, 16 May 2003.

Natsios, Andrew S. *Statement at Senate hearings on life in North Korea*. US Senate, Subcommittee on East Asian and Pacific Affairs, 5 June 2003.

Nautilus Institute. *DPRK timeline*. Available from www.nautilus.org/archives/DPRKbriefingbook/dprktimeline.html (last entry 19 April 2004)

'NK death tolls "exaggerated"'. *Korea Times*, 21 March 2004.

'NK hits China for laying claim on Koguryo kingdom'. *Korea Times*, 27 August 2004.

'NK's Taepodong missiles could be operational by 2015: LaPorte'. *Korea Times*, 10 March 2005.

Nodong Launch Facility. Federation of American Scientists, 25 March 2000. Available from www.fas.org/nuke/guide/dprk/facility/nodong.htm (accessed 6 December 2004)

Noland, Marcus. *Avoiding the Apocalypse: the Future of the Two Koreas*. Washington, DC: Institute for International Economics, 2000.

Norris, Robert S., Hans M. Kristensen and Joshua Handler. 'North Korea's nuclear program 2003'. *Bulletin of the Atomic Scientists*, Vol. 59, No. 2, 2003, pp. 74–7.

'North Korea caught in lie on Megumi remains'. *Asahi Shimbun*, 9 December 2004.

'North Korea has bigger harvest, but millions still need food aid'. World Food Programme press release, 23 November 2004.

North Korea on the Terrorism List. Washington, DC: Congressional Research Service, 2004.

'North Korea: where next for the nuclear talks?' In *Asia Report,* No. 87. Seoul/Brussels: International Crisis Group, 2004.

North Korean Chemical and Biological Weapons Threats Elaborated. Henry L. Stimpson Center, 2000. Available from www.stimson.org/cbw/?sn=cb20020113258 (accessed 7 December 2004)

North Korea Human Rights Act of 2004. Washington, DC: House of Representatives of the United States, 2004.

'North Korean scientists on DPRK artificial satellite technology'. *People's Korea*, 11 September 1998.

Norton-Taylor, Richard. 'Nuclear weapons treaty may be illegal'. *Guardian*, 27 July 2004.

Nuclear Non-Proliferation Treaty. International Atomic Energy Agency, 1968. Available from www.iaea.org/Publications/Documents/Infcircs/Others/infcirc140.pdf (accessed 2003)

Nuclear Posture Review [excerpts by GlobalSecurity.org]. Washington, DC: Department of Defense, 2002.

Nye, Joseph S. 'The decline of America's soft power'. *Foreign Affairs*, May/June 2004.

Oberdorfer, Don. *The Two Koreas: a Contemporary History*, second edition. New York: Basic Books, 2001.

'Off the hook'. *Economist*, 14 May 2004.

Oh, John Kie-chiang. 'The Kwangju Uprising'. *Korea Times*, 17 May 2001.

Oh, Young-hwan and Jie-ho Choi. 'New US policy on North took lots of work'. *JoongAng Ilbo*, 12 July 2004.

Oh, Young-hwan and Yong-su Jeong. 'Korea, US trade barbs on Iraq-North link'. *JoongAng Ilbo*, 4 December 2004.

Oh, Young-jin. 'Cultural differences often stump US diplomats in handling NK'. *Korea Times*, 14 November 2002.

——. 'Has Pyongyang missed golden opportunity?' *Korea Times*, 18 September 2001.

Oh, Young-jin and Key-young Son. 'NK sent US private cable on anti-terrorism'. *Korea Times*, 23 September 2001.

Omniglot Guide to Writing Systems: Korean. Omniglot.com, 2004. Available from www.omniglot.com/writing/korean.htm (accessed 2004)

Opening Statement at Hearing on the North Korean Nuclear Calculus: Beyond the Six Power Talks. Washington, DC: Senate Committee on Foreign Relations, 2004.

Ostling, Richard N. 'Papal nod to a Christian boom: Protestants and Catholics are thriving in the "hermit kingdom"'. *Time*, Vol. 123, 1984, p. 54.

Park, Myung-lim. 'The internalization of the Cold War in Korea'. *International Journal of Korean History*, Vol. 2, 2001.

Park, Shin-hong. 'Minister's visit to Japan canceled due to disputes'. *JoongAng Ilbo*, 5 March 2005.

Park, Song-wu. 'Anti-spy agency to reinvestigate suspicious cases'. *Korea Times*, 26 August 2004.

——. 'GNP leader may visit NK as special envoy'. *Korea Times*, 30 April 2004.

——. 'Japan collaborators face probe'. *Korea Times*, 2 March 2004.

——. 'KAL bombing constant source of dispute'. *Korea Times*, 11 July 2004.

——. 'Politicians to head for May 18 Cemetery in Kwangju'. *Korea Times*, 17 May 2004.

——. 'Poverty forces over 50% of NK defections'. *Korea Times*, 5 December 2004.

——. 'Uri Party assails US human rights bill'. *Korea Times*, 25 July 2004.

Park, Song-wu and Reuben Staines. 'US court rejects NK defector's asylum bid'. *Korea Times*, 24 November 2004.

Parry, Nat. 'Bush and the end of reason'. *ConsortiumNews*, 17 June 2003.

Patterns of Global Terrorism 2003. Washington, DC: US State Department, 2004.

Perkins, Alvin A. *US Policy towards North Korea with respect to Ballistic Missiles*. Carlisle, PA: US Army War College, 10 April 2001.

'Perle quits Pentagon advisory board'. *New York Times*, 26 February 2004.

Perlez, Jane. 'Albright receives a spectacular welcome to North Korea'. *New York Times*, 24 October 2000.

——. 'Fatherly advice to the President on North Korea'. *New York Times*, 10 June 2001.

Perry, William J. *Review of United States Policy Toward North Korea: Findings and Recommendations, Unclassified Report by Dr William J. Perry, US North Korea Policy Coordinator and Special Advisor to the President and the Secretary of State 1999*. Washington, DC: US Department of State, 1999.

Pike, John. 'Korea crisis – blockade'. *Global Security*, 26 August 2003.

——. *US Forces Korea – Exercises*. GlobalSecurity.org, 2003. Available from www.globalsecurity.org/military/ops/ex-usfk.htm (accessed 21 May 2004)

Pilger, John. 'Calling the humanitarian bombers to account'. *CounterPunch*, 11–12 December 2004.

'Police probe Porton Down deaths'. BBC, 18 October 1999.

Pollack, Jonathan D. 'The United States, North Korea, and the end of the Agreed Framework'. *Naval War College Review*, Vol. LVI, No. 3, 2003.

'Possible sale of Patriot PAC-3 to South Korea, Netherlands'. US Department of Defense release, 9 November 1999.

'President Kim Dae Jung gives banquet'. *People's Korea*, 15 June 2000.

'President Kim hopes to meet US President-elect soon'. *Korea Times*, 8 November 2000.

Pritchard, Charles 'Jack'. 'The new US administration and the North Korean nuclear issue strategy for solving the North Korean nuclear crisis and the future of six-party talks: US policy for 2005'. *2004 Sejong-SAIS Workshop*, 11 November 2004.

——. *The North Korea Deadlock: a Report from the Region*. Presented at the Brookings Institution, Washington, DC, 15 January 2004.

——. 'Statement before the Senate Foreign Relations Committee Hearing on North Korea'. 15 July 2004.

——. 'What I saw in North Korea'. *New York Times*, 21 January 2004.

'Pyonghwa builds NK auto plant'. *Financial Times*, 7 April 2002.

'Pyongyang eager to get Koguryo Tomb Murals registered as world heritage'. *People's Korea*, 12 May 1999.

'Pyongyang ready to consider Washington's offer of written security assurance'. DPRK Foreign Ministry statement, 25 October 2003.

'Pyongyang stresses developed ties with EU; 1st anniv. of DPRK visit by top-level del. marked'. *People's Korea*, 11 May 2002.

'Pyongyang urges Tokyo to sincerely implement Pyongyang Declaration'. KCNA, 17 September 2003.

'Pyongyangites welcome S. Korean defector'. KCNA, 23 February 2005.

Ramesh, Randeep. 'The two faces of Rumsfeld'. *Guardian*, 9 May 2003.

Ranard, Donald A. 'Kim Dae Jung's close call: a tale of three dissidents'. *Washington Post*, 23 February 2003.

Rang, Lee Wha. 'The Mt Kuwoi partisans'. *Korea Web Weekly*, 5 February 2004.

'Re-imposition of sanctions feared: US aid may be jeopardized – official'. *Dawn*, 5 February 2004.

Reiss, Mitchell B. 'Negotiating with North Korea: lessons learned (and relearned?)'. Nautilus Institute Policy Forum, 30 January 2003.

Report on the DPRK Nutrition Assessment 2002. Pyongyang: Central Bureau of Statistics, DPRK, 2002.

'Reports on N. Korea nukes may lack proof'. *New York Times*, 1 October 2004.

Reyes, Alejandro. 'A big song and dance', *AsiaWeek*, Vol. 26, No. 31, 2000.

Ri, Tae Sun. 'North–South talks in 1990s'. *Tongil Pyongron via People's Korea*, 30 March 1999.

'Rice aid eyed if North responds'. *Asahi Shimbun*, 18 May 2004.

'Richard L. Armitage: US won't relent on North Korean nuke issue'. *Asahi Shimbun*, 7 February 2004.

Roberts, Les, Riyadh Lafta, Richard Garfield, Jamal Khudhairi and Gilbert Burnham. 'Mortality before and after the 2003 invasion of Iraq: cluster sample survey'. *Lancet*, 29 October 2004.

'Rodong Sinmun on unique idea and theory in socio-class relations'. KCNA, 13 August 2004.

Roh, Moo-hyun. *Toward an Era of Peace and Prosperity* (inaugural speech). Seoul, 2003.

'Roh urges efforts to open pilot complex in NK' *Yonhap* via KOTRA, 31 July 2004.

'Rumsfeld clears Musharraf of nuclear trafficking'. *New York Times*, 28 March 2004.

Rumsfeld, Donald. *Commission to Assess the Ballistic Missile Threat to the United States*. Washington, DC, 1998.

Rusling, M. 'Japan tests North Korea sanctions waters'. *Asia Times Online*, 3 March 2005.

'Russian provincial government of Primorskii Krai donates US$10,000 for the construction of a Russian [Orthodox church in Pyongyang]'. ITAR-TASS via KOTRA, 18 August 2004.

Ryu, Jin. 'December surprise: Hong to be US ambassador'. *Korea Times*, 17 December 2004.

——. 'ElBaradei discounts Seoul's nuclear lab test'. *Korea Times*, 6 October 2004.

——. 'Military to be probed for coverup of NK radio messages'. *Korea Times*, 16 July 2004.

——. 'N. Korea did not deny HEU program: officials'. *Korea Times*, 15 August 2004.

——. 'Navy covered up hotline failure, says Defense Chief'. *Korea Times*, 25 July 2004.

——. 'President Roh wins support over NK nukes through summits'. *Korea Times*, 7 December 2004.

——. 'Roh rejects calls for "regime change" in North Korea'. *Korea Times*, 2004.

——. 'Speaker faces charges of dad working for colonial Japan'. *Korea Times*, 15 March 2004.

'S. Korea says North's nuclear accusation "absolutely untrue"'. *Yonhap*, 12 September 2004.

'S. Korean naval warships commit military provocation'. KCNA, 15 November 2000.

Sah, Dong-seok. 'Seoul denies sending boats into NK waters'. *Korea Times*, 15 November 2000.

Samore, Gary. 'US–DPRK missile negotiations'. *Nonproliferation Review*, Vol. 9, No. 2, 2002.

Sanger, David E. 'Kerry says Bush has ignored North Korean threat'. *New York Times*, 13 September 2004.

——. 'US sees more arms ties between Pakistan and Korea'. *New York Times*, 14 March 2004.

Sanger, David E. and William J. Broad. 'South Koreans say secret work refined uranium'. *New York Times*, 3 September 2004.

Schaller, Michael. 'The Korean war: the economic and strategic impact on Japan, 1950–1953'. In William Stueck (ed.) *The Korean War in World History*. Lexington, KY: University of Kentucky Press, 2004.

Schifferes, Steve. 'US splits deepen over North Korea'. *BBC News World edition*, 18 June 2003.

Seo, Soo-min. 'Ex-unification minister slams US policy toward North Korea'. *Korea Times*, 28 January 2004.

——. 'North Korea may complete uranium program in 1-2 years'. *Korea Times*, 26 January 2004.

——. 'Video footage shows defector alive in NK'. *Korea Times*, 31 August 2001.

Seong, Chaiki. 'A decade of economic crisis in North Korea: impacts on the military'. *Korea Institute for Defense Analyses Papers*, Vol. 3, 2003.

'Seoul, Washington in talks over Kaesong Industrial Complex'. *Yonhap* via KOTRA, 6 August 2004.

Ser, Myo-ja. 'Russian tanks to face off along demilitarized zone'. *JoongAng Ilbo*, 9 March 2004.

——. 'Twice he fled North: now jail awaits'. *JoongAng Ilbo*, 24 May 2003.

——. 'US explains North Korean refugee policy'. *JoongAng Ilbo*, 18 November 2004.

Ser, Myo-ja and Young-jong Lee. 'North envoy sees no hope in US vote'. *JoongAng Ilbo*, 6 November 2004.

Ser, Myo-ja and Shin-hong Park. 'Publisher to become envoy to US'. *JoongAng Ilbo*, 18 December 2004.

Shah, Anup. 'Militarization of outer space'. *GlobalIssues.org*, 27 June 2004.

Shanker, Thom. 'In Iraq, US learned how to scare top North Korean'. *New York Times*, 11 May 2003.

Shanker, Thom and Gary Schmitt. 'Pentagon weighs use of deception in a broad arena'. *New York Times*, 13 December 2004.

Shim, Jae-yun. 'NK to reduce armed forces by 500,000'. *Korea Times*, 15 October 2002.

——. 'Seoul, Moscow hail summit as success'. *Korea Times*, 22 September 2004.

——. 'US seeks North Korea's surrender'. *Korea Times*, 16 February 2004.

——. 'US warns of collapse of 1994 Nuke Accord'. *Korea Times*, 29 August 2002.

Shin, Hye-Jin. *Economic Significance of North Korea's Designation as a Terrorism-Supporting Nation by the US: An Obstacle to North Korea–US Trade Expansion*. Washington, DC: KOTRA, 2001.

Shorrock, Tim. 'Carlyle's tentacles embrace Asia'. *AsiaTimes Online*, 20 March 2002.

Sigal, Leon V. *Disarming Strangers: Nuclear Diplomacy with North Korea*, edited by Jack L. Snyder and Richard H. Ullman. Princeton, NJ: Princeton University Press, 1998.

——. 'North Korea is no Iraq: Pyongyang's negotiating strategy'. *Arms Control Today*, December 2002.

——. 'North Korea's tactics'. Nautilus Policy Forum, 15 February 2005.

Simpson, Cam. 'N. Korea drug-trade charges in question'. *Chicago Tribune*, 10 March 2004.

'Singapore's execution rate decried'. *Arizona Daily Star*, 15 January 2004.

'SK lawmakers decry NK human rights act'. *Ohmynews*, 21 August 2004.

Smith, Craig. Roots of Pakistan atomic scandal traced to Europe'. *New York Times*, 19 February 2004.

Smith, Dan Col. 'Truth in spending'. *Foreign Policy in Focus*, October 2003.

Smith, David. 'Britain's war on drugs is naive, says US'. *Guardian*, 1 August 2004.

Smith, Hazel. 'Brownback bill will not solve North Korea's problems'. *Jane's Intelligence Review*, February 2004, pp. 42–5.

——. 'Improving intelligence on North Korea'. *Jane's Intelligence Review*, April 2004, pp. 48–51.

——. *Overcoming Humanitarian Dilemmas in the DPRK (North Korea)*. Washington, DC: United States Institute of Peace, July 2002.

Soh, Ji-young. 'Comfort Women's frustrating struggle continues'. *Korea Times*, 17 March 2004.

——. 'Court orders disclosure of files on KAL bombing'. *Korea Times*, 3 February 2004.

——. 'NK used prisoners to test chemical weapons'. *Korea Times*, 12 February 2004.

Sohn, Hong-keun. 'Negotiation of substance'. *Korea Times*, 10 February 2003.

Sohn, Suk-joo. 'Opposition irked by Powell's breach of protocol'. *Korea Times*, 9 March 2001.

Solomon, Deborah. 'What weapons? Questions for Hans Blix'. *New York Times*, 28 March 2004.

'Song Du-yul's release'. *Korea Times*, 22 July 2004.

'South Korean media heads interview Kim Jong Il'. *Chosun Ilbo via Kimsoft*, 12 August 2000.

'South Korea's arms buildup under fire'. KCNA, 5 October 2004.

Spaeth, Anthony. 'To fund his lifestyle-and his nukes-Kim Jong Il helms a vast criminal network'. *Time*, 9 June 2003.

Special Briefing on the Nuclear Posture Review. Washington, DC: Department of Defense, 2002.

Special Report: Koizumi Visits North Korea. Asia Source, 2002. Available from www.asiasource.org/news/at_mp_02.cfm?newsid=86610 (accessed 13 August 2004)

'Spokesman for DPRK FM on prospect of resumption of six-party talks'. KCNA, 13 November 2004.

'Spokesman for DPRK foreign ministry on prospect of six-party talks'. KCNA, 16 August 2004.

Staines, Reuben. 'China repatriates 70 defectors to NK'. *Korea Times*, 9 November 2004.

——. 'Freeze on NK reactor project extended'. *Korea Times*, 26 November 2004.

——. 'History dispute over Koguryo deepens: China's disintegration fears drive diplomatic friction'. *Korea Times*, 6 August 2004.

——. 'Seoul pressed to address claims of human experiments in NK'. *Korea Times*, 2 August 2004.

——. 'Seoul rejects claims of intelligence breakdown'. *Korea Times*, 2004.

——. 'Seoul won't address NK human testing'. *Korea Times*, 3 August 2004.

——. 'US trained for strikes on NK'. *Korea Times*, 7 November 2004.

Staines, Reuben and Song-wu Park. 'South Korea isolated in opposing NK regime change: US expert'. *Korea Times*, 7 December 2004.

Statement by the Chinese Delegation on the Issue of Negative Security Assurances. Preparatory Committee for the 2000 Review Conference of the Parties to the Treaty on the Non-Proliferation of Nuclear Weapons, second session, 1998. Available from www.basicint.org/nuclear/NPT/1998prepcom/98NSA-chinese.htm (accessed 23 May 2004)

'Statement of DPRK government on its withdrawal from NPT'. KCNA, 10 January 2003.

Steinberg, James (moderator), Richard Buss, Jae Ho Chung, Ivo Daalder, Don Oberdorfer and Michael O'Hanlon. 'Challenge for the Bush administration: dealing with a nuclear North Korea (transcript)'. *Brookings Institution Forum*, 14 January 2003.

Stillwater, Jane. '"American" Afghanistan's three major crops: opium, human organs and children'. *Baltimore Chronicle*, 27 August 2004.

Stockholm International Peace Research Institute. *Military Expenditure Database 2004.* Stockholm: SIPRI, 2004. Available from http://web.sipri.org/contents/milap/milex/mex_data_index.html (accessed 11 October 2004)

Stockholm International Peace Research Institute. *The Fifteen Major Spenders in 2001, 1998–2001.* Stockholm: SIPRI, 2003. Available from http://projects.sipri.se/milex/mex_major_spenders.html (accessed 24 February 2003)

Stone, I. F. *The Secret History of the Korean War.* New York: Monthly Review Press, 1952.

Strong at Home, Respected in the World: the 2004 Democratic National Platform for America. Democratic Platform Committee, 27 July 2004.

Struck, Doug. 'US focuses on N. Korea's hidden arms'. *Washington Post*, 23 June 2003.

Suh, Sung. *Unbroken Spirits: Nineteen Years in South Korea's Gulag.* New York: Rowman and Littlefield, 2001.

Summary of Concerns for 1999. London: Amnesty International, 1 February 1999.

'Sunshine policy still valid: Kim Dae-jung'. *Nihon Keizai Shinbum*, 26 March 2004.

Suvendrini, Kakuchi. 'Tokyo feels the heat as inter-Korean ties warm'. *Asia Times Online*, 7 June 2000.

Sweeney, Fionnuala. 'International correspondents – Olenka Frankiel'. CNN, 8 February 2004.

Taylor, Walter A. 'Korea: one place where things go right for U.S'. *US News & World Report*, 2 April 1984.

'Tears and anger: Flt. 858 recalled'. *JoongAng Ilbo*, 30 November 2004.

Teather, David and Jonathan Watts. 'End of an era as firm that brought us the PC sells out to Chinese pretender for $1.75bn'. *Guardian*, 9 December 2004.

Terrorism in the United States 1999. Washington, DC: Federal Bureau of Investigation, 2000.

Terry, Fiona. 'Feeding the dictator'. *Guardian*, 6 August 2001.

The Editors. 'The *Times* and Iraq'. *New York Times*, 26 May 2004.

'The Korean civil society statement on human rights'. *The Korean Civil Society Statement* (by email), April 2004.

'The truth comes out: ulterior motive at work in '50s, '60s'. *Asahi Shimbun*, 19 May 2004.

'There nothing news in Kim Dae Jung's "Berlin Declaration": Pyongyang–Seoul urged to show positive changes in action (sic)'. *People's Korea*, 24 March 2000.

Tokyo Physicians for Elimination of Nuclear Weapons. *Chronological Table of Nuclear Weapons.* 2003.

'Tokyo to cut off food aid, plans sanctions on North'. *JoongAng Ilbo*, 11 December 2004.

'Top EU delegation visits DPRK'. *People's Korea*, 12 May 2001.

Traynor, Ian. 'US campaign behind the turmoil in Kiev'. *Guardian*, 26 November 2004.

'Treaty of Annexation of Korea by Japan'. USC-UCLA Joint East Asian Studies Center, *East Asian Studies Documents*, 22 August 1910.

'Truth behind false report about "Experiment of Chem. Weapons on Human Bodies" in DPRK disclosed'. KCNA, 30 March 2004.

UCLA Asia Institute. *North Korean Nuclear Challenge – a Brief Chronology.* 7 March 2003.

'UN nuke inspectors: no access in Brazil'. *New York Times*, 23 September 2004.

'UNEP launches first report on the State of the Environment in the DPR Korea'. United Nations Environment Programme press release, 27 August 2004.

'US censured for its brigandish act'. KCNA, 5 September 2000.

'US declares end of hostility to DPRK'. *People's Korea*, 14 October 2000.

'US in great panic'. KCNA, 12 September 2001.

US Militarization of Space. Western States Legal Foundation, 15 September 2004. Available from www.wslfweb.org/space/spacedocs.htm (accessed 4 October 2004)

'US: no normal relations with N. Korea'. *New York Times*, 15 July 2004.

US Nuclear Policy: 'Negative Security Assurances'. Arms Control Association, 2002. Available from www.armscontrol.org/factsheets/negsec.asp (accessed 23 May 2004)

'US says N.Korea atomic program more advanced'. *New York Times*, 14 February 2004.

'US special forces "inside Iran"'. BBC, 17 January 2005.

US State Department. *Background Note: North Korea*, August 2004. Available from www.state.gov/r/pa/ei/bgn/2792.htm (accessed 14 December 2004)

'US termed world's biggest human rights abuser'. KCNA, 30 March 2004.

'US view of DPRK and Agreed Framework'. *Napsnet Daily Report*, 19 March 2002.

'US welcome of Lee Hoi-chang raises Seoul's eyebrows'. *Korea Times*, 25 January 2002.

'US wrong approach to nuclear issue refuted'. KCNA, 27 July 2004.

Vallot, Daniel. 'Political reform eludes South Korea'. *Le Monde Diplomatique* (English version), November 1999.

Veteran Intelligence Professionals for Sanity. 'Intelligence fiasco'. *Dissentvoice. org*, 2 May 2003.

Vick, Karl. 'Children pay cost of Iraq's chaos'. *Washington Post*, 21 November 2004.

Vollertsen, Norbert. 'South Korea's spoilers'. *Wall Street Journal*, 22 August 2003.

Wald, Matthew L. 'CIA denies being source of anthrax'. *Los Angeles Times*, 17 December 2001.

Walmsley, Roy. *World Prison Population List*, fourth edition. London: Home Office, 2003.

Wampler, Robert A. (ed.). *North Korea and Nuclear Weapons: the Declassified US Record*. National Security Archive Electronic Briefing Book No. 87, 25 April 2003.

'War criminal should be judged'. KCNA, 10 June 2003.

'Washington ups ante in defector's travel'. *JoongAng Ilbo*, 19 June 2003.

Watts, Jonathan. 'Experts rebel over US stance on N Korea'. *Guardian*, 11 December 2004.

Weingartner, Erich. 'A chronicle of the dialogue between Christians in North and South Korea'. *Mennonite Central Committee Peace Office Newsletter*, Vol. 30, No. 3, 2000.

Weisman, Steven R. and David E. Sanger. 'US to tie North Korea aid to dismantling of weapons'. *International Herald Tribune*, 20 February 2004.

'WFP survey shows high prevalence of food insecurity in Iraq'. World Food Programme news release, 28 September 2004.

White, Michael. 'Britain prepares for a cooling of the "special relationship"'. *Guardian*, 8 November 2000.

Wicked Creatures of the Global Village: a Fanatic Terrorist Junta. Seoul: Liberal Review Press, 1983.

Williams, Ian. 'Boutros-Ghali bites back (a review of *Unvanquished: A US–UN Saga* by Boutros Boutros-Ghali)'. *Nation*, 14 June 1999.

Williams, Peter and David Wallace. *Unit 731: the Japanese Army's Secret of Secrets*. London: Hodder & Stoughton, 1989.

Willoughby, Robert. 'Friendship glows amid flickering lights'. *Guardian Weekly*, 10–16 April 2003.

Wit, Joel S., Daniel B. Poneman and Robert L Gallucci. '"Lessons learned: the road ahead" from going critical: the first North Korean nuclear crisis'. Nautilus Institute Policy Forum, 24 June 2004.

Wit, Joel S., Daniel B. Poneman and Robert L. Gallucci. *Going Critical: the First North Korean Nuclear Crisis*. Washington, DC: Brookings Institution Press, 2004.

Wolf, John S. 'Iraq update and other nonproliferation issues'. *State Department Briefing*, 7 February 2003.

Wolfsthal, Jon B. 'Crying wolf on Iraqi WMD costs US credibility on North Korea'. *Christian Science Monitor*, 29 January 2004.

Woodward, Bob. *Bush at War*. New York: Simon & Schuster, 2002.

Woollacott, Martin. 'At least Korea is united over one thing – anger at the US'. *Guardian*, 20 December 2002.

——. 'How America's right bears the longest grudge'. *Guardian*, 27 February 2004.

——. 'Humanitarians must avoid becoming tools of power'. *Guardian*, 2 April 2004.

World Military Expenditures and Arms Transfers. Washington, DC: US State Department, 2003.

Worldwide Ballistic Missile Inventories. Arms Control Association, May 2002. Available from www.armscontrol.org/factsheets/missiles.asp (accessed 3 August 2004)

Worthington, Jim. *An American in Rajin*, July 2001. Available from www.vuw. ac.nz/~caplabtb/dprk/Worthington.htm (accessed 15 December 2004)

Wortzel, Larry M. 'North Korea's connection to international trade in drugs, counterfeiting, and arms'. Senate Governmental Affairs Subcommittee on Financial Management, Budget, and International Security, 20 May 2003.

'Year of epochal significance in DPRK–China friendship'. KCNA, 6 December 2004.

Yoo, Dong-ho. 'Park viewed to be next GNP leader'. *Korea Times*, 22 February 2004.

——. 'Parties caught again in secret ammunition leakage'. *Korea Times*, 11 October 2004.

——. 'US may launch surgical strikes on NK'. *Korea Times*, 5 October 2004.

——. 'US to cut 12,500 troops by 2008'. *Korea Times*, 10 October 2004.

Yoo, Yong-won. 'North fires surface to ship missile'. *Chosun Ilbo*, 26 February 2003.

Yoon, Won-sup. 'GNP young turks propose active support for NK'. *Korea Times*, 1 March 2004.

——. 'Lee fears pro-China regime in NK'. *Korea Times*, 10 November 2004.

——. 'More self-reliant defense posture envisioned'. *Korea Times*, 18 November 2004.

You, Chul-jong. 'Lack of 6-party progress invites war, Russian says'. *JoongAng Ilbo*, 1 March 2004.

Younge, Gary. '30% of black men in US will go to jail'. *Guardian*, 18 August 2003.

Yuh, Ji-Yeon. 'North Korean refugees'. Personal communication with the author, 29 November 2004.

Yun, Philip W. 'Facing the Bogeyman: a Korean American diplomat recounts his trips to North Korea'. *Korea Society Quarterly*, Vol. 4, No. 1, 2004. pp. 6–14.

Zellweger, Kathi. '45th visit to the DPRK (17 to 28 February 2004)'. *Caritas*, 21 July 2004.

——. '46th visit to the DPRK (1 to 15 June 2004)'. *Caritas*, 21 July 2004.

——. 'Caritas and the North Korean crisis'. *Korea Society Quarterly*, Vol. 4, No. 1, 2004.

Zhebin, Alexander. *Russia's Efforts for Reconciliation and Peace in Korea*. Presented at the 2nd World Congress of Korean Studies, Pyongyang, 2004.

Index

Compiled by Elaine N. Hall

Note: Entries under the names of countries have been minimised. Users should search under specific topics.